www.brookscole.com

www.brookscole.com is the World Wide Web site for Thomson Brooks/Cole and is your direct source to dozens of online resources.

At *www.brookscole.com* you can find out about supplements, demonstration software, and student resources. You can also send email to many of our authors and preview new publications and exciting new technologies.

www.brookscole.com
Changing the way the world learns®

Cultural Competence, Practice Stages, and Client Systems

A Case Study Approach

Doman Lum

California State University, Sacramento

THOMSON

BROOKS/COLE

Australia • Canada • Mexico • Singapore • Spain
United Kingdom • United States

Executive Editor: *Lisa Gebo*
Assistant Editor: *Alma Dea Michelena*
Editorial Assistant: *Sheila Walsh*
Marketing Manager: *Caroline Concilla*
Marketing Assistant: *Mary Ho*
Project Manager, Editorial Production: *Emily Smith*
Print/Media Buyer: *Lisa Claudeanos*

Permissions Editor: *Stephanie Lee*
Production Service: *Mary Deeg, Buuji, Inc.*
Copy Editor: *Robin Gold*
Compositor: *Buuji, Inc.*
Cover Designer: *Roger Knox*
Cover Image: *Roger Knox*
Text and Cover Printer: *Malloy Incorporated*

Printed in the United States of America
1 2 3 4 5 6 7 08 07 06 05 04

For more information about our products, contact us at:
Thomson Learning Academic Resource Center
1-800-423-0563

For permission to use material from this text or product, submit a request online at
http://www.thomsonrights.com.

Any additional questions about permissions can be submitted by email to
thomsonrights@thomson.com.

Library of Congress Control Number: 2004101176

ISBN 0-534-63198-3

Thomson Brooks/Cole
10 Davis Drive
Belmont, CA 94002
USA

Asia
Thomson Learning
5 Shenton Way #01-01
UIC Building
Singapore 068808

Australia/New Zealand
Thomson Learning
102 Dodds Street
Southbank, Victoria 3006
Australia

Canada
Nelson
1120 Birchmount Road
Toronto, Ontario M1K 5G4
Canada

Europe/Middle East/Africa
Thomson Learning
High Holborn House
50/51 Bedford Row
London WC1R 4LR
United Kingdom

Latin America
Thomson Learning
Seneca, 53
Colonia Polanco
11560 Mexico D.F.
Mexico

Spain/Portugal
Paraninfo
Calle Magallanes, 25
28015 Madrid, Spain

To the faculty, staff, and students of California State University, Sacramento, Division of Social Work who have been an integral part of my professional academic career for thirty years;

To the board of directors and the Commission on Accreditation of the Council on Social Work Education for the past experiences on those two bodies; and

To my wife, Joyce, and children: Lori and her husband, Noel; Jonathan; Amy; and Matthew Lum

Contents

CHAPTER 4

Social Work Practice with Latino Americans   88
by Claudia L. Moreno and Marietta Guido

CHAPTER 5

Social Work Practice with Asian Americans   112
by Paula T. Tanemura Morelli

CHAPTER 6

Social Work Practice with Multiracial/Multiethnic Clients   146
by Rowena Fong

CHAPTER 7

Social Work Practice with Women of Color   173
by Valli Kalei Kanuha

CHAPTER 10

Social Work Practice with Persons with Disabilities   287
by Ruth I. Freedman

CHAPTER 11

Social Work Practice with Older Adults of Color   320
by Blanca M. Ramos, Lani Jones, and Ronald Toseland

Preface

This book on cultural competence, practice stages, client intersectional systems, and case studies brings new and traditional themes together. In the past, social work practice has been concerned about working with a client through the beginning, the middle, and the end, which have been termed *stages of helping*. The case study has been the paramount teaching tool for social work practice where the life experiences of a client (individual, family, group, community, organization) are shared to illumine the person and the problem situational environment. Recently, cultural competence has entered the cultural diversity helping scene and has challenged the helping professions to identify and strengthen abilities and capabilities of working with cultural and ethnic persons who have multiple and diverse identities. This text seeks to integrate these themes in a single cover.

Cultural Competence, Practice Stages, and Client Systems: A Case Study Approach is actually the third book in a trilogy of literary works that are closely related and connected to a single theme. Little did I know that in my 30-year career in social work education from 1974 to 2004, I would be fortunate enough to write three interrelated books. I want to thank Lisa Gebo, social work editor of Thomson Brooks/Cole, for suggesting this third book and observing that this would form a trilogy.

In the mid 1980s, after teaching for 10 years, I began to write a text on practicing with ethnic minorities called *Social Work Practice and People of Color: A Process-Stage Approach*. The first edition was published in 1986 under Claire Verduin, who was the social work editor for Brooks/Cole at that time. Brooks/Cole was the only publisher then who was willing to accept my manuscript in this area. To my surprise, this book caught fire and went through five printings. The second edition appeared in 1992, followed by the third edition in 1996, the fourth edition in 2000, and the fifth edition in 2004. It has sustained an amazing run in the classroom as a text.

About 1997, as a result of leading a workshop on cultural competence at the annual program meeting of the Council on Social Work Education in Chicago, I began to write a textbook on cultural competence entitled *Culturally Competent Practice: A Framework for Growth and Action.* It was published in 1999 just as the social work academic and practitioner diversity community began to talk about the importance of cultural competence as a standard for the social work profession. The cultural competence movement has been in high gear since the latter half of the 1990s in academic, professional, and governmental settings. In 2003, the second edition, *Culturally Competent Practice: A Framework for Understanding Diverse Groups and Justice Issues,* was expanded to include contributors on diverse groups and social and economic justice issues.

Just as the discussion about revising the fifth edition of *Social Work Practice and People of Color* was taking place, Lisa Gebo suggested the need for a practice casebook on cultural competence and practice stages that would bridge the people of color process stage text and the culturally competent practice volume.

The last of this trilogy comes at a time when I have retired as professor of social work at California State University, Sacramento. It is a wonderful cap to my professional academic writing career. Because our university has a faculty early retirement program that will allow me to continue to teach part-time, I will be able to contribute in the classroom, continue my writing, and enjoy time with my family.

ABOUT THE BOOK

This book brings together a number of outstanding social work educators who are experts in various practice areas. I serve as the editor of this text and wrote the introductory chapter on Cultural Competence, Practice Stages, Client Intersectional Systems, and Case Studies, which introduces a number of themes. I also wrote the Epilogue, which reviews the major emphases and points to the future concerning these interrelated themes.

I am indeed privileged to introduce the following contributors:

- *Maria Yellow Horse Brave Heart* and *Josephine Chase* of the Takini Network, Rapid City, South Dakota. Chapter Two: Social Work Practice with First Nations Peoples
- *Teresa Jones,* associate professor of social work, Michigan State University. Chapter Three: Social Work Practice with African Americans
- *Claudia Moreno,* assistant professor of social work, Rutgers University, and *Marietta Guido,* geriatric social worker for the Visiting Nurse Service of New York. Chapter Four: Social Work Practice with Latino Americans

- *Paula Tanemura Morelli,* associate professor of social work, University of Hawaii, Manoa. Chapter Five: Social Work Practice with Asian Americans
- *Rowena Fong,* professor of social work, University of Texas at Austin. Chapter Six: Social Work Practice with Multiracial/Multiethnic Clients
- *Valli Kalei Kanuha,* associate professor of social work, University of Hawaii, Manoa. Chapter Seven: Social Work Practice with Women of Color
- *Nancy Nystrom,* assistant professor of social work, Michigan State University, East Lansing. Chapter Eight: Social Work Practice with Lesbian, Gay, Bisexual, and Transgender People
- *Uma Segal,* professor of social work, University of Missouri–St. Louis. Chapter Nine: Social Work Practice with Immigrants and Refugees
- *Ruth Freedman,* associate dean for academic affairs (social work) and associate professor of social work, Boston University. Chapter Ten: Social Work Practice with Persons with Disabilities
- *Blanca Ramos, Lani Jones,* and *Ronald Toseland* of the State University of New York, Albany. Chapter Eleven: Social Work Practice with Older Adults of Color

The chapters were written from a common agreed-upon outline, which brings consistency and coherence to the text. These fourteen contributors have opened new doors to our learning about these diverse population groups from the perspectives of cultural competence and working in a number of the helping stages.

ACKNOWLEDGMENTS

I want to thank Christine T. Lowery, who has written the foreword to this text. Dr. Lowery is an associate professor of social work at the University of Wisconsin–Milwaukee and was the keynote speaker for the 2001 Cultural Competency in Child Welfare: Substance Abuse and Family Violence conference held at the University of Texas at Austin. She has spent a sabbatical year (2002–2003) studying sociocultural change and aging in the seven villages of the Laguna Pueblo tribe in a small village, Paguate, New Mexico. Her thoughts in this foreword reflect the refreshment and insights that she has experienced and learned as she has investigated and uncovered the cultural experiences and meanings of her extended family and relatives in a rural setting.

I also want to acknowledge the former dean, Jesse McClure, who recruited me to the social work faculty of California State University, Sacramento, nearly 30 years ago. He asked me to come to a program that was in transition and to a community that was opening up and growing to maturity. We settled in Sacramento, raised and educated our children here, worked and made our contributions to the university and the city, and formed lasting friendships and loyalty to this area.

Special thanks goes to Lisa Gebo, human services and social work executive editor, of Thomson Brooks/Cole for her sensitivity to issues, compassion for people and authors, leadership in publishing, and her vision of the social work professional needs. She has guided me for two decades and without her, academic teaching and writing would be less of a joy and satisfaction. I am warmed by her friendly concern and gentle direction.

I want to thank the manuscript reviewers for their wise and helpful suggestions as this manuscript took shape. Behind a good manuscript are a group of good reviewers, and I want to acknowledge them: Ruth Bounous, Our Lady of the Lake University; Rita Takahashi, San Francisco State University; David Woody, III, University of Texas at Arlington; Roger Delgado, California State University, Los Angeles; Robyn Lugar, Indiana State University; Margaret Elbow, Texas Tech University.

I am also indebted to the Thomson Brooks/Cole publishing staff who have worked with me on a number of book projects and have offered their skills and creativity to the writing and publishing process: Alma Dea Michelena, Assistant Editor; Sheila Walsh, Editorial Assistant; Caroline Concilla, Marketing Manager; Mary Ho, Marketing Assistant; Emily Smith, Project Manager, Editorial Production; Lisa Claudeanos, Print/Media Buyer; and Stephanie Lee, Permissions Editor. Also Robin Gold for her copyediting skills and Mary Deeg and the production staff at Buuji, Inc.

Above all, as I depart the full-time social work education teaching scene and join the ranks of those colleagues in my program and in other social work education institutions across the country who are now professors emeritus and emerita, I want to say that it has been a long, fulfilling, and satisfying experience teaching, writing, advising, and researching. I would not trade any other career and have no regrets. My thanks goes to my family who have made my life truly a blessing: my wife, Joyce, who is a first-grade teacher at Mary Tsukamoto Elementary School, Elk Grove, California, and soon ready for her retirement; my daughter, Lori, who works for the Pfizer Pharmaceutical Company, and her husband, Noel; my son, Jonathan, who is an occupational therapist at the University of Southern California–Los Angeles County Medical Center; my daughter, Amy, who recently finished her Master of Business Administration degree at San Francisco State University; and my son, Matthew, who is working for the Jet Propulsion Laboratory, Pasadena, California.

Doman Lum, Ph.D., Th.D.
Professor Emeritus of Social Work
California State University, Sacramento

Contributors

Maria Yellow Horse Brave Heart   Dr. Brave Heart is a Hunkpapa/Oglala Lakota and a member of the Wapaha Ska (White Lance—a Wounded Knee survivor and cousin of Sitting Bull) *tiospaye* (extended kinship network). She is the president, director, and co-founder of the Takini Network, Inc., and resides in Denver, Colorado. She is also associate research professor of social work for the University of Denver, Graduate School of Social Work. Dr. Brave Heart specializes in trauma work for indigenous communities, is the author of more than 16 journal articles and book chapters, and has delivered more than 60 presentations and workshops on historical trauma and unresolved grief among the Natives—the culmination of more than 24 years of work on the phenomenon of intergenerational transfer of indigenous traumatic history. She is the lead editor/author of the forthcoming book, *Historical Trauma within the American Experience: Roots, Effects, and Healing* (Haworth Press) and is a member of the International Society for Traumatic Stress Studies.

Josephine Chase   Ms. Chase is Mandan Hidatsa/Hunkpapa Lakota/ Yanktonai Dakota. She is the vice president and associate director and a founding member of the Takini Network, Inc., Rapid City, South Dakota. Ms. Chase received her MSW from the University of Denver, is a Ph.D. candidate at Smith College, North Hampton, Massachusetts, and has extensive experience in the child welfare and mental health arenas. She is former site supervisor, Fort Berthold Reservation Casey Family Program. Ms. Chase has developed a Native American Kinship Care Model for providing services to children in out-of-home placement with relatives. She currently provides workshops and training and is involved with the development of a parenting and training curricula in historical trauma.

Rowena Fong   Dr. Fong is professor of social work at the University of Texas at Austin School of Social Work. She has an edited book on *Culturally Competent Practice with Immigrant and Refugee Children and Families* (Guilford Press, 2004) and has co-authored a book with Dr. Sharlene Furuto on *Culturally Competent Practice: Skills, Interventions, and Evaluations* (Allyn & Bacon, 2001). Dr. Fong's research and publications are on children and families, child welfare, culturally competent practice, and intercountry adoptions in the People's Republic of China. She is also the mother of two biracial young adults, one living in Hawaii, the other in California.

Ruth I. Freedman   Dr. Freedman is Associate Dean for Academic Affairs and associate professor of social work at Boston University School of Social Work. She is a fellow of the American Association on Mental Retardation and previously served as a mental health research fellow at the Kennedy School of Government, Harvard University. Her research and publications center on individuals with disabilities and their families, particularly regarding aging, family caregiving and family supports, self-determination, health care decision-making, and research ethics. Dr. Freedman recently served as principal investigator of a multiyear external evaluation of services provided to persons with mental retardation and their families, funded by the Massachusetts Department of Mental Retardation.

Marietta Guido   Ms. Guido graduated from Columbia University School of Social Work in 1997 and works as a geriatric social worker for the Visiting Nurse Service of New York (VNS Choice). Currently she is completing training as a psychoanalyst at the Institute for Contemporary Psychotherapy in New York and is also in private practice.

Lani V. Jones   Dr. Jones is assistant professor of social work in the School of Social Welfare at the University at Albany, State University of New York. Her research interest is in the area of evidenced practice with a focus on psychosocial competence, group work, and positive mental health outcomes with families and their children in urban communities.

Teresa C. Jones   Dr. Jones was associate professor of social work at Michigan State University School of Social Work and the director of the school's Kinship Care Project and Kinship Care Resource Center. She received her MSW and Ph.D. in social welfare from the University of Washington, where she completed her dissertation on the experiences of African American adoptive families. Dr. Jones has worked as a practitioner in the fields of substance abuse and child welfare, primarily with African American families and single mothers, and as a trainer and consultant to social service agencies. Her current research interests include the roles and outcomes of kinship care in African American families.

Valli Kalei Kanuha Dr. Kanuha is assistant professor of social work at the University of Hawaii at Manoa School of Social Work. Dr. Kanuha has worked as an activist, clinician, and consultant with community agencies, domestic violence programs, and HIV/AIDS organizations in the continental United States and Hawaii for 30 years. Her research and professional interests include violence against women of color; feminist theory; lesbian, gay, and transgender issues; and multicultural practice. Dr. Kanuha teaches social work practice with individuals, families, and groups.

Doman Lum Dr. Lum is professor emeritus of social work at California State University, Sacramento, Division of Social Work. His books include *Social Work Practice and People of Color: A Process-Stage Approach, Culturally Competent Practice: A Framework for Understanding Diverse Groups and Justice Issues, Social Work and Health Care Policy,* and *Responding to Suicidal Crisis.* He has written chapters and articles on Asian Americans, spiritual diversity, cultural and ethnic diversity, cultural competence, programs and service delivery systems, the older person, cultural values, suicide and the church, Japanese suicide, health care system, health maintenance organizations, the mental health of children, lay counseling, the church and alcoholic prevention, and Christian conversion. Dr. Lum is a consulting editor for the *Journal of Ethnic and Cultural Diversity in Social Work* and *Arete.* He has served on the board of directors and the Commission on Accreditation for the Council on Social Work Education; and received the Distinguished Recent Contributions in Social Work Education award from the Council on Social Work Education in 2000, and a lifetime achievement award from the Asian/Pacific Islander Social Work Educators Association of the Council on Social Work Education in 2004.

Paula T. Tanemura Morelli Dr. Morelli is associate professor of social work at the University of Hawaii at Manoa School of Social Work She is a third-generation Filipino–Japanese American who was born in Chicago and raised on the islands of Molokai and Oahu, state of Hawai'i. Dr. Morelli received her MSW from the University of Southern California in 1968 and her Ph.D. in social welfare from the University of Washington in 1996. Her social work practice has focused on children and families in the juvenile justice system, protective services, psychiatric facilities, and private practice in California and Hawai'i. Her principal research interests are in social work practices, interventions, and training that contribute to the well-being of Asian and Pacific Islanders.

Claudia L. Moreno Dr. Moreno is assistant professor of social work at Rutgers University and is a research fellow for the Center for Intervention and Prevention Research for HIV and Drug Abuse at Columbia University School of Social Work. She was formerly on the social work faculty of Columbia University where she was the school coordinator for Human Behavior in the Social Environment (HBSE) curriculum. Dr. Moreno has published in the areas of developmental disabilities, HIV/AIDS, and Latina women.

Nancy M. Nystrom   Dr. Nystrom was assistant professor of social work at Michigan State University School of Social Work and has taught aging policy, community organizing, social work policy, and social work practice classes. Dr. Nystrom was a recipient of a NIMH fellowship for her studies of social services to gay men and lesbians. She is an intern for Old Lesbians Organizing for Change, an activist group that advocates for the old. She is the founder of the Cluster Housing Collective in the state of Washington, an experimental housing development for women. She is a member of the National Gay and Lesbian Task Force Policy Institute, American Society on Aging, and the National Organization of Gay and Lesbian Scientists. Dr. Nystrom currently is involved in organizing older lesbians, forming active support groups to enable successful aging.

Blanca M. Ramos   Dr. Ramos is assistant professor of social work and holds a joint appointment in the Department of Latin American and Caribbean Studies at the University at Albany, State University of New York. She teaches courses on social work direct practice, diversity, immigrant families, and research in Latino communities. Her scholarly interests focus on cross-cultural social work with a particular emphasis on elderly Latinos. She is a licensed social worker and has extensive experience as a practitioner and community organizer with diverse populations. Dr. Ramos is the current first vice president of the National Association of Social Workers and a member of the Institute for the Advancement of Social Work Research.

Uma A. Segal   Dr. Segal is professor of social work and director of the baccalaureate social work program at the University of Missouri–St. Louis. She also holds research fellow positions in the Center for International Studies and the Public Policy Research Center and provides program evaluation for the International Institute of Metropolitan St. Louis, a major refugee resettlement agency. Her major research interest areas are immigrants and refugee concerns, Asian American acculturation, and cross-national issues in family violence. She serves on a task force on new immigrants with the nonprofit organization, FOCUS St. Louis, that engages citizens in creating a cooperative region and is a board member of the St. Louis chapter of the Alzheimer's Association. Her cross-national research has been funded by the Japan Society for the Promotion of Science, the Social Science Research Council, and the American Institute of Indian Studies.

Ronald W. Toseland   Dr. Toseland is professor of social work and director of the Institute of Gerontology at the School of Social Welfare, the University at Albany, State University of New York, and a licensed clinical social worker practicing part-time at the Consultation Center. He serves on a number of editorial boards, including *Gerontological Social Work, Social Work with Groups,* and *Small Group Research.* He has published 5 books and more than 80 articles and book chapters, many of which have focused on clinical practice with the frail elderly and their family caregivers.

Foreword

Students in my cultural diversity course read the story of the Hollow Water healing circles recounted by Rupert Ross (1996). The Ojibwe women of Hollow Water have worked to heal themselves from substance abuse and sexual abuse, so that they can, in turn, show others how they might do the same. The women understand themselves in light of their historical oppression, and they can recognize the oppressor within (Friere, 1994). They have worked to liberate one another through their shared pain and healing stories over a long period of time.

In this telling of his own metamorphosis, Ross (1996) writes of an encounter with an Inuit woman in Yellowknife. While watching and listening to Ross talk about the justice system and the events around a particular crime, the woman shared with him a story about her grandfather and his explanation of the waves in Hudson Bay. Ross admits his interpretation may not be accurate, but he shares nonetheless.

> The first waves are those joined with the building winds, not yet forceful, but waves that would gain strength as the weather changed.
>
> The second waves were those left by a weather system, now waning, but with winds still present.
>
> The third waves were those maintained by ocean currents, "winding around the points and over the shoals, for they would present their own forces against the waves from the winds" (p. 73).
>
> The fourth waves were those shaped by the Gulf Stream.
>
> The fifth waves were those moved by the rotation of the earth.

One's safety amidst the waves on any given day is based on knowledge, experience, and prayer. One needs to understand, not only the forces, but the living confluence of the forces, to predict potential interactions, and thus, the potential working environment.

Global communication and economic forces push and pull us together in cultures and subcultures, some new and some not yet formed; cultures and oppressions, yet unknown. We must understand the nature of our sociopolitical environment, born of change; in-process with no end; and yet with history and patterns we can study and predict. Most importantly, we must understand how these forces in a changing landscape shape and challenge our connectedness and obligations as humans, one to one another.

Doman Lum says this will be his final work. It is useful work that influences the next waves of his life. He shares this particular work, primarily with women of color, and leaves a substantial current. From this point, who will continue to enter the flow and influence the work of cultural diversity, history of oppression, and social work? And what form will this emergence take?

Christine Lowery (Laguna-Hopi), Ph.D.
University of Wisconsin–Milwaukee

Friere, P. et al. (1994). *Pedagogy of the oppressed* (rev. ed.). New York: Continuum.
Ross, R. (1996). *Returning to the teachings: Exploring aboriginal justice.* Canada: Penguin Books Canada.

Cultural Competence, Practice Stages, Client Intersectional Systems, and Case Studies

We are at an interesting crossroad where it is crucial to connect culturally competent social work and the practice stages of beginning, middle, and end with specific diverse groups. The history of the cultural competence movement can be traced back to the work of Terry L. Cross, a First Nations Peoples social worker, who taught a social work course that included cultural competence material and later edited a meso organizational text entitled *Towards a Culturally Competent System of Care* (Cross, Bazron, Dennis & Isaacs, 1989). Cultural competence and social work evolved with a culturally competent practice model consisting of cultural awareness, knowledge acquisition, skill development, and inductive learning (Lum, 1999). Next, the model delineated assessment, intervention, and evaluation skills for individuals, families, communities, and organizations with African Americans, Latino Americans, Asian and Pacific Islander Americans, and First Nations Peoples (Fong & Furuto, 2001). Then the National Association of Social Workers (2001) issued the *NASW Standards for Cultural Competence in Social Work Practice,* 10 standards that offered guidelines, goals, and objectives of cultural competence for social workers. This was the first time a national professional practitioner body emphasized the need for cultural competence in its membership. The cultural competence movement further grew by addressing the social context of diversity, racism, sexism, homophobia, discrimination, and oppression and including ethnic, gender, and sexual orientation groups and social and economic justice concerns (Lum, 2003). However, I believe that cultural competence ought to be tied to a solid foundation of how to move a client through the helping stages of beginning, middle, and end. The authors of this text seek to connect these two themes: culturally competent social work and practice stages.

Traditional and standard social work practice focused on practice stages with clients with techniques and guidelines for planned change phases of process (Sheafor & Horejsi, 2003), target groups and phases (Shulman, 1999), or skills and practice phases (Hepworth, Rooney & Larsen, 2002). Moreover, the 2002 Council on Social Work Education's 2002 *Educational Policy and Accreditation Standards* emphasized applying knowledge and skills to work with individuals, families, groups, organizations, and communities; engaging clients; and using skills in empirically based interventions. Yet, often in standard practice stage texts, minimal attention is given to ethnic and cultural clients. We want to address these themes and to connect cultural competence, practice stages, and various target groups in the following chapters of this book.

In addition to these connections, social work has historically been taught and learned through the life story of the client. Social workers who assisted clients were historically called social caseworkers because each client represented a unique case history of events, significant others, and experiences. Thus, we have included a series of case studies to illustrate how cultural competence and practice stages come together in integrative and practical ways in working with actual people.

Social work practice has an applied social science foundation, which bases practice principles on the social case study. Beginning with Mary E. Richmond's emphasis on social evidence and a thorough investigation of the client, the family, relatives, and outside sources such as medical, school, employment, documentary, and neighborhood aspects, social work has taught from and relied on the social case study as the basis for understanding the client.

This book brings together these four themes (cultural competence, practice stages, client intersectional systems, and case studies) into an integrated model (see Figure 1.1, The Cultural Competence, Practice Stages, Client Intersectional Systems, and Case Studies Model). This chapter explains each component in detail, updating the reader to the trends, particularly in cultural competence. Next, we have asked several social work educator/practitioner contributors to focus on ethnic diversity and gender, sexual orientation, and transitional diverse groups. Using a common outline, contributors address demographics, historical oppression and survival values, culturally competent knowledge and skills, and particular practice stage skills and offer an integrative case study that draws the reader into the material as a participant. Finally, cultural competence, practice stages, client intersectional systems, and case study themes are summarized in the last chapter.

The contributors particularly have been asked to relate the subject of their chapters to case study integration exercises on contact, problem identification, and assessment skills, intervention, and termination skills. They have been encouraged to select a case study that illustrates an integrative micro, meso,

Figure 1.1 | Cultural Competence, Practice Stages, Client Intersectional Systems, and Case Studies Model

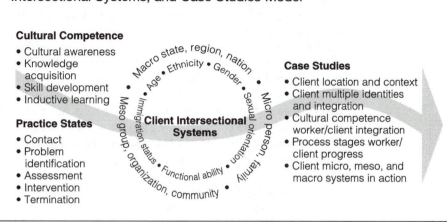

Cultural Competence
- Cultural awareness
- Knowledge acquisition
- Skill development
- Inductive learning

Practice States
- Contact
- Problem identification
- Assessment
- Intervention
- Termination

Macro state, region, nation • Age • Ethnicity • Gender • Sexual orientation • Micro person, family • Functional ability • Immigration status • Meso group, organization, community

Client Intersectional Systems

Case Studies
- Client location and context
- Client multiple identities and integration
- Cultural competence worker/client integration
- Process stages worker/ client progress
- Client micro, meso, and macro systems in action

and macro intervention approach. The client may be an individual, a family, a group, or a community or a combination of various elements. Contributors have also been asked to discuss the client location and context (e.g., geographic and psychological location, setting, social environmental factors related to the client), client multiple identities and integration (e.g. ethnic, gender, sexual orientation, socioeconomic, and age identities and how these multiple factors are integrated into understanding who the client is), and cultural competence worker-client integration (e.g., how the cultural understanding and fit between the worker and the client affect the relationship). As they structured the case study exercises for student learning in the classroom, the contributors were also asked to describe the process stages worker-client progress (the goals of the worker and the client in the process stages of contact, problem identification, assessment, intervention, and termination) and the client micro, meso, and macro systems in action (changes occurring in the individual, family, group, community, institutions and organizations and planning, policy, and administrative systems affecting the client).

In the following pages, you shall see how successfully we were able to meet these learning expectations as clearly and relevantly as possible.

THE CULTURAL COMPETENCE, PRACTICE STAGES, CLIENT INTERSECTIONAL SYSTEMS, AND CASE STUDIES MODEL

The Cultural Competence, Practice Stages, Client Intersectional Systems, and Case Studies Model is based on a systems theory approach. System theory focuses on the interrelationships of various subsystems and the transactions between inputs, throughputs, and outputs. These dynamics characterize an open system that flows like a river.

Our model suggests that the essential elements of cultural competence and practice stages are inputs that the social worker introduces in the helping relationship and that these two elements address and affect the various multidimensions of the client systems. This assumption underlies the mutuality of worker and client relations and interactions. The resulting throughput is how a social worker interacts and addresses the unique client intersectional multidimensional systems. The case study output or product integrates previous cultural competent skills, practice growth stages, and client intersectional diverse systems and is a coming together as a functional or unified whole of a person who has been interacting with a social worker.

Cultural competence is the mastery of a particular set of knowledge, skills, policies, and programs used by the social worker that address the cultural needs of individuals, families, groups, and communities. Cultural competence consists of at least four spheres of cultural awareness (self and other), knowledge acquisition (diverse groups), skill development (effective practice), and inductive learning (continuous investigation). The contributors will address these aspects of culturally competent practice in detail as they cover each diverse group. On the one hand, cultural competence must be focused on detailing the many facets of the client intersectional systems, uncovering and identifying various ways to deal effectively with various group configurations. On the other hand, cultural competence must also incorporate competence knowledge and skills in the practice stages of contact or engagement/relationship building, problem identification or problem reframing, psychosocial assessment, micro-meso-macro intervention, and termination of the client.

Practice stages connote the fact that the client moves through beginning, middle, and ending phases as the worker engages the client in a change strategy that affects the person and the problem situation. The *beginning phase* consists of contact where engagement and relationship building occur; the *middle phase* involves the assessment of the biopsychosocial and the cultural-gender-spiritual dimensions and the change influence of intervention strategies; and the *ending phase* centers on termination and follow-up strategies. In this text, we review historical and current models of practice to understand where social work practice came from and where it is heading. Practice stages are then applied in subsequent chapters to various client groups to make the point that there may be unique configurations of how knowledge and skills are shaped.

At the center of the model is *client intersectional systems*. We use the term *intersectional,* to denote multiple group identities that are interconnected and interrelated. The client is an intersectional system consisting of multiple levels of identities or entities. Among them are ethnicity, gender, sexual orientation, functional ability, and immigration status. These configurations may be understood on the micro (person and family), meso (group, organization, and community), and macro (state, regional, and national) levels. These intersectional identities hold many combinations that accurately depict who the client is.

For example, the client may be a 60-year-old (age) African American (ethnicity) lesbian (sexual orientation) woman (gender) who has been paralyzed on her right side by a recent stroke (functional ability) and who immigrated from South Africa (immigration status) when she was 40 years old. We may discuss this client as an individual and in relationship with her family. We may also want to focus on African American lesbian women in general and elderly and disabled in particular. We may be concerned about which social organizations are available for this client or whether there is an African American lesbian women support group and caring community that readily accepts newcomers. We may want to know the social, medical, and economic needs of elderly African American lesbian women on the state, regional, and national levels for advocacy and lobbying groups who will address their needs for provider health care legislation or policy program directions.

In short, our model has a number of entities that can be used to carve out the identifying client intersectional system that compose the particular person that you are understanding and dealing with. The social worker uses cultural competence and practice stages to affect the client in the helping process.

Finally, *case studies* are the output of the interaction between the client and the social worker. Cultural competence and practice stages of helping play a crucial input role in the interaction with various client intersectional systems and the end product, the case study that brings all the entities together. Much understanding of the case study centers on client location and context. That is, where the client is from the past and present perspectives and what the social context or setting is that may color the tone of the worker-client relationship? What are the multiple identities of the client and how are these entities integrated in the client, creating a unique person, family, or community? To what extent are the worker and client aware of cultural competence in the relationship or topics of culturally significant conversation and to what extent is cultural competence integrated in their work with each other?

In the actual case study, what practice stages progress guideposts can the worker and the client point to as positive signs? What client micro, meso, and macro systems are in concert action with each other and meshing so that there is movement and change? The contributors of the subsequent chapters present case studies with exercises to guide readers toward an integrative understanding of how to work with a client and how the client can function as a whole person in a positive outcome. The contributors employ various culturally competent skills, explain the various practice stages of beginning, middle, and end with client intersectional systems, and integrate these entities in a case study that has positive results.

The major components of this model interconnect with, interrelate to each other, and move us toward the completion of the case study from a cultural competence, practice stage, and client intersectional system approach. In the following sections, we will explain each component of the model in detail.

CULTURAL COMPETENCE

The Meaning of Cultural Competence

Cultural competence has been defined as knowledge, skills, behaviors, attitudes, and policies (Substance Abuse and Mental Health Services Administration, 1997), academic and interpersonal skills (Orlandi, 1992), personal characteristics of the individual (LaFromboise, Coleman, & Gerton, 1993), knowledge, skills, and value bases (Manoleas, 1994), practitioner, agency, and community levels (Miley, O'Melia & DuBois, 2001), a system of care (Cross et al., 1989), cultural awareness, knowledge acquisition, skill development, and inductive learning (Lum, 1999), and professional competence standards (National Association of Social Workers, 2001).

Underlying these culturally competent characteristics are basic social patterns, among which are an understanding of values and social class. *Cultural values* may include such collective values as family interdependence and obligation, harmony with nature and spirituality, and ethnic group identity. As a complement, *social work values* have a high regard for persons and for individual rights and freedom such as the dignity and uniqueness of the individual, self-determination of the client, and accessibility of resources. To be culturally competent means to honor and respect the cultural collective values and to temper individual values within the larger context. I (Lum, 2004) discuss multicultural family values (e.g., maintenance of ethnic identification and solidarity, extended family and kinship network, and vertical hierarchy of authority), multicultural religious and spiritual values, and multicultural identity values (e.g., harmony, affiliation, nurturance, appreciation, and pleasure and suffering).

Cultural competence also discerns the implications of *social class*. Rather than discussing social class and the culture of poverty that tend to be a deficit model, the term, *ethclass* (Gordon, 1978), recognizes the existence of ethnic and social stratification in society. Access to life-sustaining and life-enhancing resources differs according to ethnic groups in general and to members of an ethnic group in particular. The majority members of a society may deny minority members of an ethnic group despite their socioeconomic status because of racial and ethnic barriers. As a result, there is a sense of individual, family, and community powerlessness that is expressed as systemic oppression and control of resources and privilege by a dominant group in power over oppressed groups who internalize powerlessness as low social status, low self-esteem, and devalued individuals. Part of the culturally competent rebuilding process is to work with *ethclass issues* by empowering people to gain political and social power and to institute strategies that will redistribute resources (Lum, 2004). We believe that cultural competence has an effect on people's lives and want to introduce you to two new culturally competent paradigms that may help us in the social worker–client relationship.

A recent conceptualization of cultural competence (Cultural Competence Online, 1999–2001) configures this term in a creative way. It features a number of areas: delivery of services, organizational diversity, developmental and family-oriented care, skills and practices, and quality improvement. In specific, cultural competence is defined in these categories:

Delivery of services: The willingness and ability of a system to value the importance of culture in the delivery of services to all segments of the population.

Organizational diversity: The use of a systems perspective that values differences and is responsive to diversity at all levels of an organization, that is, policy, governance, administrative, workforce, provider, and consumer/client.

Developmental and family-oriented care: The promotion of quality services to underserved, racial/ethnic groups through the valuing of differences and integration of cultural attitudes, beliefs, and practices into relevant diagnostic and treatment methods, and throughout the system to support the delivery of culturally relevant competent care.

Skills and practices: The development and continued promotion of skills and practices important in practice, cross-cultural interactions, and system practices among providers and staff to ensure that services are delivered in a culturally competent manner.

Quality improvement: The development of skills through training, use of self-assessment tools for providers and systems, implementation of objectives to ensure that governance, administrative policies, practices, and clinical skills and practices are responsive to the culture and diversity of the population served, which is a process of continuous quality improvement. (See Cultural Competence Online, 1999–2001 www.culturalcompetence2.com)

We can also understand cultural competence as a five-stage continuum that constitutes a system:

- Understanding one's own cultural background
- Acknowledging the client's different culture, value systems, beliefs, and behaviors
- Recognizing that cultural difference is not synonymous with cultural inferiority
- Learning about the client's culture
- Adapting optimal service delivery to an acceptable cultural framework

(See http://www.aafp.org/fpm/20001000/58cult.html)

As one can tell from the categories and continuum, cultural competence includes micro concerns about the client and family, meso concerns about organizations and communities, and macro concerns about service delivery systems. Cultural competence is a subject theme that thoroughly pervades our whole system of care as we endeavor to become culturally competent with others and ourselves.

The Scope of Cultural Competence

Cultural competence has grown in many directions. Cultural competence has emerged as a distinct concept that has *systemic meaning and application.* Benjamin (2001) points out that cultural competence differs from cultural sensitivity and cultural awareness. *Cultural sensitivity* is the knowledge that cultural differences and similarities exist between groups but there is no assignment of values (e.g., better or worse, right or wrong) to these cultural differences. *Cultural awareness* is the development of understanding of another group that usually involves internal changes of attitudes and values and qualities of openness and flexibility to others. However, *cultural competence* moves beyond cultural sensitivity and awareness and integrates and transforms knowledge about individuals and groups into specific standards, policies, practices, and attitudes to be used in appropriate cultural settings to operate effectively in different cultural contexts. In this sense, the scope of *cultural competence changes the operations of practitioners, providers, and social service organizations.*

Cultural competence has been further identified as a *strengths model* where it is important to know and understand diverse groups by *culturally-based strengths, resources, and assets.* The trend is away from focusing on the deficits of diverse groups such as cultural myths, negative attributes, old and new stereotypes, and general fears. Instead, the move is toward cultural strengths. Accordingly, human service professional education, cross-cultural curriculum, and service bureaucracies are improving cultural competence training. This is imperative given that many are prone to focus on pathology as a problem in culturally diverse communities. As Switzer points out, "Coupled with the segregation of American society (de facto or de jure) many cultural and racial myths and fears have become widespread. Many Americans have been influenced by cultural and racial stereotypes, deficit based curriculum, and otherwise misleading theories, not just the bigots. If agencies and professional organizations do not provide strengths based training as an alternative, creating culturally competent systems of care may again be difficult. Accountability measures need to be developed regarding the training necessary to serve a multicultural community" (1998, p. 5). She further stresses the importance of building accountability measures that promote cross-cultural knowledge in staff training and development. She recommends, "Training and development must prepare staff to: be aware of the diverse cultural groups in a service area, comprehend and utilize culturally competent approaches, understand why cultural competence is important for all customers, and work in concert with the clients support system" (1998, p. 6). Moreover, there are only a few culturally diverse professionals, consumers, and advocates active in planning, policy, and decision-making meetings to help design services for diverse communities. Part of this planning process is to know the ecological conditions in designing services and programs such as life expectancy, socioeconomic situation, housing patterns, crime rates, infant and adult disability rates, and national origins and languages. Service utilization rates and outcomes, client functioning patterns, and satisfaction rates with services are important to find out about the cultural groups served by the agency program. Using this information will help empower individuals and communities, which are part of the strengths perspective.

Cultural competence has identified a number of *agency values* conducive to creating a culturally competent system of care. The Child and Adolescent Service System Program of the Georgetown University Child Development

Center has developed a list of 12 values that are essential for *creating and maintaining an organizational culture that subscribes to cultural competence:*

- Respect the unique, culturally defined needs of diverse client populations
- Acknowledge culture as a prevailing factor in shaping client behaviors and values as well as human and health service organizations and institutions
- Understand when values of diverse cultural groups are in conflict with mainstream or organizational values
- Believe that diversity within cultures is important as diversity between cultures
- Acknowledge and accept that cultural differences exist and have an impact on how services are delivered and received
- View natural systems (e.g. family, community, places of worship, natural healers) as primary support resources
- Recognize that an understanding of individual, family, and community can differ from culture to culture and within cultural subgroups
- Start with the family as the primary and preferred point of intervention in a culture
- Respect the family as indispensable to understanding the individual
- Respect cultural preferences which value *process* rather than product and *harmony* or *balance* in one's life rather than achievement
- Recognize that people of color tend to be bicultural, which creates a set of behavioral issues
- Advocate for culturally competent services

Understanding these values (Switzer, 1998, pp. 6–7) is crucial for the developing staff and program accountability because they are essential in *the operationalization of cultural competence on the organizational level.*

Cultural competence also is a *bridge to manage diversity across practice.* In this sense, cultural competence is a universal theme that transcends the ethnic box. Fong (2002) points out that diversity must be seen as the multiple identities or characteristics of people such as race, ethnicity, gender, sexual orientation, physical abilities, religion, geographic location, and age. The goals for social workers are to build competencies and manage diversity across practice in assessment and intervention skills. Fong offers a three-step model of recognition, prioritization, and operationalization:

- Recognize the validity of the client's diverse identities and identify the important identities according to the client
- Prioritize the combinations of multiple identities that dominate the client's attitudes and behaviors, asking the client what these variables mean to him or her and which are most important
- Operationalize these combinations into the assessment and intervention process so that they play a role or affect the client and his or her problem

Building competencies so that they affect assessment and intervention skills are important when working with any client. It depends on how the client and the worker configure the important diversity characteristics or variables and apply them in the helping process.

The Applications of Cultural Competence

Cultural competence as an organizing theme has been applied in a number of social service settings. Cultural competence can be traced to organizations on the federal, professional, state, and local levels. The group Communities Can! observes, "Federal agencies have defined cultural competence within the context of government programs and the duties assigned to them. Some states have legislation around cultural and linguistic competency. Local service agencies have developed definitions of cultural competence with specific guidelines for its application in the delivery of services" (2001, p. 1). One can readily see that cultural competence is an organizing framework that is integrated in the fabric of health and human services. A directory of cultural competence resources lists organizations that address cultural competence, provides information on cultural competence, and offers cultural competence training programs and conferences (see Cultural Competence Resources, www.air-dc.org /cecp/cultural/resources.htm)

On the federal level, the U.S. Department of Health and Human Services, Office of Minority Health has taken the leadership and has developed national standards for culturally and linguistically appropriate services (CLAS) in health care. This is a major effort to introduce cultural competence in health care (U.S. Department of Health and Human Services, 2001). The Department of Health and Human Services recognizes the significant increases in ethnic and foreign-born populations and their impacts on health service delivery.

The 14 CLAS standards in health care are important to understand because they mark a milestone in the effort to incorporate uniform criteria on cultural competence across the United States for health care organizations:

- **Standard 1.** Health care organizations should ensure that patients/consumers receive from all staff members effective, understandable, and respectful care that is provided in a manner compatible with their cultural health beliefs and practices and preferred language.
- **Standard 2.** Health care organizations should implement strategies to recruit, retain, and promote at all levels of the organization a diverse staff and leadership that are representative of the demographic characteristics of the service area.
- **Standard 3.** Health care organizations should ensure that staff at all levels and across all disciplines receive ongoing education and training in culturally and linguistically appropriate service delivery.
- **Standard 4.** Health care organizations must offer and provide language assistance services, including bilingual staff and interpreter services, at no cost to each patient/consumer with limited English proficiency at all points of contact, in a timely manner during all hours of operation.
- **Standard 5.** Health care organizations must provide to patients/consumers in their preferred language both verbal offers and written notices informing them of their right to receive language assistance services.
- **Standard 6.** Health care organizations must assure the competence of language assistance provided to limited English proficient patients/consumers

by interpreters and bilingual staff. Family and friends should not be used to provide interpretation services (except on request by the patient/consumer).

- **Standard 7.** Health care organizations must make available easily understood patient-related materials and post signage in the languages of the commonly encountered groups and/or groups represented in the service area.
- **Standard 8.** Health care organizations should develop, implement, and promote a written strategic plan that outlines clear goals, policies, operational plans, and management accountability/oversight mechanisms to provide culturally and linguistically appropriate services.
- **Standard 9.** Health care organizations should conduct initial and ongoing organizational self-assessments of CLAS-related activities and are encouraged to integrate cultural and linguistic competence-related measures into their internal audits, performance improvement programs, patient satisfaction assessment, and outcome-based evaluations.
- **Standard 10.** Health care organizations should ensure that data on the individual patient's/consumer's race, ethnicity, and spoken and written language are collected in health records, integrated into the organization's management information systems, and periodically updated.
- **Standard 11.** Health care organizations should maintain a current demographic, cultural, and epidemiological profile of the community as well as a needs assessment to accurately plan for and implement services that respond to the cultural and linguistic characteristics of the service area.
- **Standard 12.** Health care organizations should develop participatory, collaborative partnerships with communities and utilize a variety of formal and informal mechanisms to facilitate community and patient/consumer involvement in designing and implementing CLAS-related activities.
- **Standard 13.** Health care organizations should ensure that conflict and grievance resolution processes are culturally and linguistically sensitive and capable of identifying, preventing, and resolving cross-cultural conflicts or complaints by patients/consumers.
- **Standard 14.** Health care organizations are encouraged to regularly make available to the public information about their progress and successful innovations in implementing the CLAS standards and to provide public notice in their communities about the availability of this information. (U.S. Department of Health and Human Services, 2001)

CLAS mandates are current federal requirements for all recipients of federal funds and are used by policymakers, accreditation and credentialing agencies, purchasers, patients, advocates, educators, and the health care community in general.

On the professional level, social work has adopted the most comprehensive statement on cultural competence of any profession in the helping disciplines. The National Association of Social Workers (NASW) disseminated the 2001 *Standards for Cultural Competence in Social Work Practice,* which address 10 areas:

- **Standard 1. Ethics and Values:** Social workers shall function in accordance with the values, ethics, and standards of the profession, recognizing how personal and professional values may conflict with or accommodate the needs of diverse clients.
- **Standard 2. Self-Awareness:** Social workers shall develop an understanding of their own personal and cultural values and beliefs as a first step in appreciating the importance of multicultural identities in the lives of people.
- **Standard 3. Cross-Cultural Knowledge:** Social workers shall have and continue to develop specialized knowledge and understanding about the history, traditions, values, family systems, and artistic expression of major client groups served.
- **Standard 4. Cross-Cultural Skills:** Social workers shall use appropriate methodological approaches, skills, and techniques that reflect the workers' understanding of the role of culture in the helping process.
- **Standard 5. Service Delivery:** Social workers shall be knowledgeable about and skillful in the use of services available in the community and broader society and be able to make appropriate referrals for their diverse clients.
- **Standard 6. Empowerment and Advocacy:** Social workers shall be aware of the effect of social policies and programs on diverse client populations, advocating for and with clients whenever appropriate.
- **Standard 7. Diverse Workforce:** Social workers shall support and advocate for recruitment, admissions and hiring, and retention efforts in social work programs and agencies that ensure diversity within the profession.
- **Standard 8. Professional Education:** Social workers shall advocate for and participate in educational and training programs that help advance cultural competence within the profession.
- **Standard 9. Language Diversity:** Social workers shall seek to provide and advocate for the provision of information, referrals, and services in the language appropriate to the client, which may include the use of interpreters.
- **Standard 10. Cross-Cultural Leadership:** Social workers shall be able to communicate information about diverse client groups to other professionals.

There are some similarities between the CLAS and NASW standards, notably in the areas of training and education and language. However, much is expected from social workers who must integrate cultural competence into ethics and values, self-awareness, and knowledge and skills. I hope this book will help meet some of these concerns.

Turning from the practitioner and agency dimensions of cultural competence to the state level, there was a 2001–2002 planning taskforce in California (Cultural Competency Legislative Hearing Planning, 2001) to identify cultural competency issues related to the unmet capacity of California social service institutions to service culturally diverse communities. The California legislature is working with the State Department of Health and Human Services to address four areas: organizational cultural competence, recruitment, retention, and training. Organizational cultural competence requires focusing on the institutionalization of cultural competence through

1.1 | Application Exercise

NASW, in its Standards for Cultural Competence in Social Work Practice, is the only helping profession to develop national professional criteria in cultural competence. I have developed this assessment instrument to rate your level of cultural competence as a learning tool.

These standards reflect your own and your agency's participation in cultural competence as a social work practitioner. If you are a social work student and have a field placement or visualize a field experience including developing cultural competent skills, this instrument will help you to measure your involvement.

Your score on the assessment instrument is determined by counting the numbers you have circled and adding them together (see scoring information at the end of the instrument). There are four possible levels. You are expected to score in the Level 1 or 2 range unless you have had a strong multicultural life and work experience or extensive course work in ethnic studies.

You will score the instrument yourself and need not disclose the results to anyone else. However, your instructor may wish to use this experience as a learning tool in the classroom.

The NASW Standards for Cultural Competence in Social Work Practice

(This assessment instrument was written by Doman Lum, PhD; all rights reserved.)

Introduction

This instrument operationalizes the NASW Cultural Competence Standards in terms of measuring your cultural competence according to ten areas. Strict confidentiality is observed regarding the results of this self-assessment.

Rate yourself on your level of competence on a scale of 1–4: 1 = Unlikely, 2 = Not very likely, 3 = Likely, and 4 = Definitely. Circle the appropriate number.

Standard 1. Ethics and Values: *Social workers shall function in accordance with the values, ethnics, and standards of the profession, recognizing how personal and professional values may conflict with or accommodate the needs of diverse clients.*

1. I am sensitive to the cultural and ethnic diversity of a client when I am in a helping relationship.

Circle one:	Unlikely	Not very likely	Likely	Definitely
	1	2	3	4

2. I endeavor to learn about the cultural traditions and norms and the cultural background of my client.

Circle one:	Unlikely	Not very likely	Likely	Definitely
	1	2	3	4

3. I make input into the planning of cultural sensitive social services program delivery in my agency.

Circle one:	Unlikely	Not very likely	Likely	Definitely
	1	2	3	4

(continued)

1.1 | Application Exercise *continued*

4. I recognize the cultural strengths of the client.

   Circle one: Unlikely   Not very likely   Likely   Definitely
                      1   2   3   4

5. I endeavor to work through cultural value conflict dilemmas with my client.

   Circle one: Unlikely   Not very likely   Likely   Definitely
                      1   2   3   4

Standard 2. Self-Awareness: *Social workers shall develop an understanding of their own personal and cultural values and beliefs as a first step in appreciating the importance of multicultural identities in the lives of people.*

6. I have examined my own cultural backgrounds and identities.

   Circle one: Unlikely   Not very likely   Likely   Definitely
                      1   2   3   4

7. I am culturally aware of my own heritage as well as those of others.

   Circle one: Unlikely   Not very likely   Likely   Definitely
                      1   2   3   4

8. I am moving from cultural awareness through cultural sensitivity to cultural competence.

   Circle one: Unlikely   Not very likely   Likely   Definitely
                      1   2   3   4

Standard 3. Cross-Cultural Knowledge: *Social workers shall have and continue to develop specialized knowledge and understanding about the history, traditions, values, family systems, and artistic expression of major client groups served.*

9. I am expanding my knowledge about culture, behavior, language, social service policy impacts, resources, and power relationships, particularly providers and client groups.

   Circle one: Unlikely   Not very likely   Likely   Definitely
                      1   2   3   4

10. I am knowledgeable about social, cultural, and political systems in the United States.

   Circle one: Unlikely   Not very likely   Likely   Definitely
                      1   2   3   4

11. I understand the limitations and strengths of current and relevant theories and principles concerning client cultural groups.

   Circle one: Unlikely   Not very likely   Likely   Definitely
                      1   2   3   4

Standard 4. Cross-Cultural Skills: *Social workers shall use appropriate method-ological approaches, skills, and techniques that reflect the workers' understanding of the role of culture in the helping process.*

12. I maintain acceptance and openness to differences among people.

Circle one: Unlikely   Not very likely   Likely   Definitely
                    1   2   3   4

13. I understand the role of language in the client's culture.

Circle one: Unlikely   Not very likely   Likely   Definitely
                    1   2   3   4

14. I assess cultural norms and behaviors as strengths rather than problematic or symptomatic behaviors.

Circle one: Unlikely   Not very likely   Likely   Definitely
                    1   2   3   4

15. I practice advocacy and empowerment skills.

Circle one: Unlikely   Not very likely   Likely   Definitely
                    1   2   3   4

Standard 5. Service Delivery: *Social workers shall be knowledgeable about and skillful in the use of services available in the community and broader society and be able to make appropriate referrals for their diverse clients.*

16. My agency recruits multiethnic staff and includes cultural competence job requirements.

Circle one: Unlikely   Not very likely   Likely   Definitely
                    1   2   3   4

17. My agency reviews demographic trends to determine interpretation and trans-lation services needed.

Circle one: Unlikely   Not very likely   Likely   Definitely
                    1   2   3   4

18. My agency has program décor and design which reflect the cultural heritage of clients.

Circle one: Unlikely   Not very likely   Likely   Definitely
                    1   2   3   4

19. My agency has developed culturally competent performance measures.

Circle one: Unlikely   Not very likely   Likely   Definitely
                    1   2   3   4

Standard 6. Empowerment and Advocacy: *Social workers shall be aware of the effect of social policies and programs on diverse client populations, advocating for and with clients whenever appropriate.*

20. I practice empowerment which involves consciousness-raising, the develop-ment of personal power, and skills for social change.

Circle one: Unlikely   Not very likely   Likely   Definitely
                    1   2   3   4

(continued)

1.1 | Application Exercise *continued*

21. I practice advocacy which involves a client's understanding of what it means to advocate based on respectful collaboration and mutually agreed-on goals for change.

    Circle one: Unlikely   Not very likely   Likely   Definitely
                      1   2   3   4

Standard 7. Diverse Workforce: *Social workers shall support and advocate for recruitment, admissions and hiring, and retention efforts in social work programs and agencies that ensure diversity within the profession.*

22. My agency recruits and retains a diverse cadre of social workers who have some indigenous sense of cultural competence.

    Circle one: Unlikely   Not very likely   Likely   Definitely
                      1   2   3   4

23. My agency makes efforts to increase culturally competent skills of the staff.

    Circle one: Unlikely   Not very likely   Likely   Definitely
                      1   2   3   4

Standard 8. Professional Education: *Social workers shall advocate for and participate in educational and training programs that help advance cultural competence within the profession.*

24. There are continuing education courses offered in culturally competent practice.

    Circle one: Unlikely   Not very likely   Likely   Definitely
                      1   2   3   4

25. It is important to provide culturally sensitive supervision and field instruction.

    Circle one: Unlikely   Not very likely   Likely   Definitely
                      1   2   3   4

Standard 9. Language Diversity: *Social workers shall seek to provide and advocate for the provision of information, referrals, and services in the language appropriate to the client, which may include the use of interpreters.*

---

the participation of managers and administrators in ongoing training, the development of an open organizational environment, and the involvement of consumers in the community based on population-based assessment. Recruitment of bilingual/bicultural students into social services calls for early identification, application and funding support, a culturally competent environment and curricula, and streamlined hiring. Retention means ongoing cultural competence training for managers, supervisors, and administrators and the mentoring and promotion of bilingual and bicultural human service professionals. Training requires university curricula on cultural competence knowledge and skills, competencies for human service state agencies, and a

26. Agencies should provide services and information in appropriate languages for limited English speaking clients.

    Circle one: Unlikely   Not very likely   Likely   Definitely
                        1   2   3   4

27. Language interpreters and translators should be trained in the ethics and linguistic of interpreting social services in an effective and confidential manner.

    Circle one: Unlikely   Not very likely   Likely   Definitely
                        1   2   3   4

Standard 10. Cross-Cultural Leadership: *Social workers shall be able to communicate information about diverse client groups to other professionals.*

28. I practice empowering diverse client populations.

    Circle one: Unlikely   Not very likely   Likely   Definitely
                        1   2   3   4

29. I endeavor to disseminate information about diverse client groups

    Circle one: Unlikely   Not very likely   Likely   Definitely
                        1   2   3   4

30. I advocate for fair and equitable treatment of diverse clients at the interpersonal and institutional levels.

    Circle one: Unlikely   Not very likely   Likely   Definitely
                        1   2   3   4

Please count your score on the 30 self-assessment items and rate your level of cultural competence. Circle the appropriate level and write your raw score in one of the following levels:

    Level 1: Unlikely (scores 30–46)

    Level 2: Not very likely (scores 47–60)

    Level 3: Likely (scores 61–90)

    Level 4: Definitely (scores 91–120)

clearinghouse to exchange information on cultural competent models and program practice. The intent of this planning effort is to provide taskforce focus groups to draft legislative proposals to affect state agencies and programs through legislation and funding.

On the county level, there has been an interface between county and state mental health department units on the development of cultural competent services. San Joaquin County Department of Mental Health Services developed a cultural competency plan in conjunction with the California State Department of Mental Health. This plan involved developing a planning structure, a committee format, facilitator leadership, the effect of time constraints on the quality of the plan, cultural sensitivity of the plan participants, and the evaluation of the plan itself.

The draft of the Cultural Competency Plan that was submitted by San Joaquin County Mental Health Services in May 1997 contained five sections: Section 1: Cultural Competency as a Developmental Process, Section 2: Administration and Policy, Section 3: Consumer and Family Services, Section 4: Human Resources, and Section 5: Research and Evaluation. Central to the plan were the following: (1) the consumer and family services goals of involvement in the development and delivery of culturally competent services in the preferred languages of consumers with culture-specific specialty services and prevention services supportive of different cultures; and (2) the recruitment of professionals with bilingual proficiency, staff training in cultural sensitivity and competence, and the support and retention of staff to delivery culturally competent services. The mental health director, program chief, and senior administrative staff as well as representatives from state advisory committees worked to develop culturally competent standards, guidelines, and outcome measures. (For details of the planning process of this particular effort, see Ford, 1999).

At the grass-roots level, there are examples of various cultural competence efforts shared in *Cultural Competence: A Journey* (2002). Across the United States, through the efforts of the Bureau of Primary Health Care, part of the Health Resources and Services Administration, Department of Health and Human Services, significant breakthroughs for cultural competence are occurring:

- At the Sunset Park Family Health Center Network in south Brooklyn, New York, facilities were redesigned for low-income Asian patients: Chinese lettering, Feng Shui interior design, gold and yellow fish for good luck in the fish tank. An Islamic prayer room for Muslim patients was added, and the Caribbean-American Family Health Center was opened in the Flatbush section of Brooklyn.
- The Red Tail Training and Health Center of Minneapolis sponsored by the Indian Health Board of Minnesota offers healing ceremonies, vision quests, herbal remedies, and visits to a sweat lodge as part of the medical services. Likewise, Papa Ola Lokahi, the umbrella organization for five health care systems in Hawaii, uses native healers and refers patients to a lomi-lomi specialist for massage, a ho'oponopono practitioner for dispute resolution, or an expert in herbal medicine.
- At the International District Community Health Services in Seattle, nontraditional practices such as on-site acupuncture and herbal medicine and treatment for posttraumatic stress disorder were incorporated as part of the program.
- The Everglades Health Center of the Community Health Centers of South Dade County, Florida, has signs in Spanish, English, and Creole Haitian and multilingual brochures and educational material. It also offers literacy programs, health education audiocasettes, and mini soap opera radio programs to reach farm workers regarding HIV prevention.

| 1.2 | **Application Exercise** |

1. In small groups, discuss the various definitions, standards, and program expressions of cultural competence. Which ones do you like? Why did you make these choices?
2. How would you explain the meaning of cultural competence in your own words to someone who is unfamiliar with this program?

- La Clinica de la Raza in the Fruitvale neighborhood of Oakland, California, offers a dance class with salsa music for exercise and recreation and launched a sting operation with the local authorities to stop local stores from selling cigarettes to minors as part of an anti-smoking campaign for health education.

Among the public health and cultural competence connections are that providers can obtain more specific and complete information to make appropriate diagnoses, develop treatment plans that are followed by the patient and supported by the family, reduce delays in seeking care, improve the use of health services, enhance communication and clinical interaction between the patient, and increase the compatibility between Western and traditional cultural health practices.

All in all, cultural competence has made major strives in the lives of people through multilevel efforts and is part of the education, planning, and service delivery structure.

In the following section, we turn to a discussion of practice stages, recognizing that we need to connect cultural competence to practice stages so that culturally competent knowledge and skills are integrated in the beginning, middle, and end of the helping process.

PRACTICE STAGES

The Practice Process Stages of Helping

The practice process stages of helping are fundamental social work themes. The concept, *process,* refers to the interaction between the worker and the client and other clients such as family or group member (Shulman, 1999), the evolutionary change in the relationship between the client and the worker; and the process of challenge and growth in the helping stages. I (Lum, 2004) discuss *practice process stages* as the logical step-by-step sequence of client and worker movement in the helping process, which are traditionally described as beginning, middle, and end. In this culturally diverse practice framework, the process stages are contact and problem identification (beginning), assessment and intervention (middle), and termination (end).

Practice Process Helping Models

Mary Richmond's Social Diagnosis Process Model   In her book, *Social Diagnosis,* written in 1917 while she was director of the Charity Organization Department for the Russell Sage Foundation of New York City, Mary E. Richmond (1964) sets forth a process diagnosis model that forms the basis for social casework. Richmond starts with the collection of social evidence coming from the relationship of the social worker with the client, the client's family, and sources of insight outside the family group. For Richmond, evidence is based on diagnosis or social investigation that relied on witnesses, fact, and real, testimonial, and circumstantial evidence. Inferences based on facts are made according to reason and hypothesis. According to Richmond, processes lead to diagnosis; hence our understanding of Richmond's model as a diagnosis process perspective.

The process starts with the first interview with the client, early contacts with the client's immediate family, further insight and resources outside the family, and the careful weighing of these separate items of evidence and their interpretation. Key to the interviewing is the family with a focus on the family as a whole, the husband and father, the wife and mother, the children, and other relatives. Furthermore, outside sources for uncovering information include social agencies and churches, doctors and health agencies, former and present neighborhoods, relatives, former and present employers, schools, friends, and public records. Richmond's emphasis is on obtaining a comprehensive understanding of the client in a scientific and objective approach. She compares and interprets the material gathered, observing individual differences and the wider self or the connection of various social relationship situations.

Richmond's work is a pioneering task of providing social work and social workers with a methodological procedural text on how to work with a client. She states her intention: "We should welcome, therefore, the evident desire of social workers to abandon claims to respect based upon good intentions alone; we should meet halfway their earnest endeavors to subject the processes of their task to critical analysis; and should encourage them to measure their work by the best standards supplied by experience-standards which, imperfect now, are being advanced to a point where they can be called professional" (p. 25). Richmond started social work by evolving a practice process procedure of gathering and interpreting social evidence so that a social worker would know how to work with a client with a thorough background of information available. Throughout the century of social work, Mary E. Richmond's emphasis on practice process starting with social evidence and leading to social diagnosis has been improved by successive generations of social work thinkers.

Hepworth, Rooney, and Larsen's Helping Process Model   Hepworth, Rooney, and Larsen (2002) have explained the helping process in three phases. Phase I, exploration, engagement, assessment, and planning, teaches students the following tasks:

- Explore clients' problems by eliciting comprehensive data about the person(s), the problem, and the environment, including factors influencing the referral for contact
- Establish rapport and enhance motivation
- Formulate multidimensional assessment (systems playing a significant role in the difficulties, relevant resources to be tapped or developed)
- Negotiate goals to be accomplished in remedying or alleviating the problem and formulate a contract
- Make referrals

Phase II, implementation and goal attainment, translates plans into actions, dissecting goals into tasks that identify strategies (general and specific) to be employed. Interventions are designed to accomplish goals and tasks and are related to the problems and consequent goals. During this phase, there is self-efficacy or the belief that one can accomplish tasks or perform behaviors associated with specific goals: monitoring progress and evaluating the effectiveness of change strategies and interventions, guiding clients toward goal attainment, keeping abreast of clients' reactions to progress, and concentrating on goal attainment and evaluation; individual, family, group, and organizational barriers to goal accomplishment; relational reactions that could impair the effectiveness of the working relationship; development of client self-awareness; and the conscious use of self to facilitate growth and accomplishment.

Finally, Phase III, termination, includes assessing satisfactory goal attainment and planning termination; effecting successful termination; and planning for the maintenance of change, continued growth, and the evaluation of the results of the helping process.

The Hepworth, Rooney, and Larsen model provides theory content, case examples, and helpful application exercises with an emphasis on task-centered outcome effectiveness in an individual, family, and group context.

Shulman's Interactional Helping Process Model   Shulman (1999) offers an interactional model that is based on working with individuals, families, and groups in four phases: preliminary, beginning and contracting, work, and endings and transitions. He is influenced by Schwartz (1977) in constructing a triangular model of the worker, clients, and agency-family-peers and the interaction between these three systems. At the core of the interactional theory is the helping process that involves the skill of the worker, a positive working relationship and the outcomes of practice with interaction going on between these three entities.

Shulman is concerned about the developing workers' skills for helping clients to manage their feelings and problems and has delineated 22 specific skills. Feelings management includes reaching inside of silences, putting the client's feelings into words, displaying understanding of the client's feelings, and sharing the worker's feelings. Problem management involves clarifying the worker's purpose and role, reaching for client feedback, partializing client concerns, and supporting clients in taboo areas. Skills are set in four phases:

preliminary or the period before the first encounter with the client; beginning or the first sessions, which include the development of a working contract and relationship; middle or the period where the work is done; and ending and transition where the relationship is brought to an end and transitions are made to new experiences. The model is extended to address individuals, families, groups, and community and system work, using the same theme patterns for consistency.

Sheafor and Horejsi's Techniques and Guidelines Change Process Model

Sheafor and Horejsi (2003) base their change process model on the dynamic state of constant change and on planned change where intervention is a deliberate action that alters a situation or interferes with an expected course of events. Change involves actors in planned change such as the change agent system, client system, target system, and action system; the situation as an arena of change; and individual, family and group, organizational, and community change. The change process occurs in phases or stages: intake and engagement, data collection and assessment, planning and contracting, intervention and monitoring, and termination and evaluation.

Phase I, intake and engagement, involves such pre-intake considerations such as understanding a history of prior efforts to secure assistance, setting for the first meeting, behavior of other employees, agency's physical features, and the worker's preparation for the first meeting; engagement (relationship building, energy and hopefulness, and sound judgment to reduce client fear and anger and to build confidence); formal intake (understanding why the client is seeking help, referral, and role induction, which prepares the client for using the social worker as a helper).

Phase II, data collection and assessment, focuses on individualizing the client and the problem situation, gathering essential and relevant information, thinking through the facts and arriving at tentative conclusions, attending to client strengths as the source of hopefulness, sorting out value choices and preferences, drawing from multidimensional sources, drawing working hypotheses, and clarifying the client and target systems.

Phase III, planning and contracting, involves a plan of action that bridges assessment and intervention (goals and objectives), contracting (clarification of roles and responsibilities of the worker and client), and Phase IV, intervention and monitoring, depends on the role of the worker and the function of the agency, evaluation of the success of the intervention, and stabilizing the desired change as the ongoing functioning of the client. Phase V, evaluation and termination, addresses how and when the termination occurred and how to deal with unexpected termination as well as evaluating the effectiveness of services, staff performance, and review of the change process.

The Application of Process Stages to Client Groups

The preceding process models help us understand how process stages are integrated with skills, target groups, and client-worker interaction. The task of cultural competence is to apply cultural competence areas (e.g., cultural

> ### 1.3 | Application Exercise
>
> 1. Given the preceding practice process models, what practice process stages would you use in working with a client?
> 2. How would you begin to incorporate the cultural competence skill: *Start with the family as the primary and preferred point of intervention* with a client who has cultural concerns? (From the culturally competent values list of the Child and Adolescent Service System Program of the Georgetown University Child Development Center). (See Switzer, 1998)

awareness, knowledge acquisition, skill development, inductive learning) and cultural competencies (skill level statements related to culturally diverse individuals, groups, and communities) to the practice stages of the helping process. In the social work cultural competence literature, Fong and Furuto (2001) combine assessment, intervention, and evaluation skills and ethnic groups, individuals, families, communities, and organizations, and I (Lum, 2003) integrate a cultural competence framework into cultural and ethnic diversity, gender, and sexual orientation groups.

The objective of this text is to move culturally competent social work practice toward the integration of practice skills; ethnic, gender, sexual orientation, and transitional diverse groups; case studies; and practice process stages. The contributors specifically address practice process stages and cultural competence skills related to their diverse group. Relating these four entities in cultural competence will make a major contribution to culturally diverse social work practice.

Cultural competence and practice stages are major systems inputs that interact with the multiple dimensions of the client intersectional systems. In the following section, we focus on the major components of the client.

CLIENT INTERSECTIONAL SYSTEMS

Categories and Combinations

The concept of diversity moves the field of culturally competent practice beyond one dimension (e.g., ethnicity) toward a multidimensional understanding of a person. We now speak about multiple or multidimensional identities. This theme came from the concept of intersectionality that was introduced by Collins (1990) who wrote about the intersecting oppressions of race, class, and gender experienced by black women. Crenshaw (1991) applied intersectionality to women of color in general, and later Collins (2000, p. 18) related intersectionality to oppression on the macro level: "Intersectionality refers to particular forms of intersecting oppression, for example, intersections of race and gender, or of sexuality and nation. Intersectional paradigms remind us that oppression cannot be reduced to one fundamental type, and that oppression works together in producing injustice." Spencer, Lewis, and Gutierrez (2000) further applied intersectionality to a broad spectrum of multiple group memberships and identities.

Next, Schriver (2001) wrote about "diversity within diversity," "multiple diversities," and "interrelatedness and interconnectedness of human beings." Then I (Lum, 2003) categorized intersectionality and multiple identities by external intersections (age/life span, ethnicity, language, gender, social class, disability, size, personal appearance, and others) and internal intersections (culture, sexual orientation, education, career, family background, partnership status, residency, faith and religion, and others). Thus, intersectionality has evolved into an inclusive term that allows us to understand the essence of who a person is.

Emerging Multiple Identities

The client intersectional systems recognize the multiple identities of a person and help us understand the multidimensional diversity of a person. Our text model has two circular subsystems composing the client intersectional systems. One might think of the two circles as two flywheels that hold multiple combinations. One flywheel contains age, ethnicity, gender, sexual orientation, functional ability, and immigration status as major categories. Even within each category, diversity-within-diversity qualities can make further distinctions. For example, the client may be a multiracial ethnic person whose mother was Filipino-Chinese and whose father was Irish, German, and American Indian from an ethnic viewpoint. Other variables have yet to be joined together. The other flywheel contains the system levels: micro (person, family), meso (group, organization, community), and macro (state, region, nation). One can understand how all three systems interrelate to the client by how the individual relates to his or her family, which is part of a group and community and how the concerns of the client are connected to local, state, regional, and national issues and programs. Thus, using these client intersectional systems categories may provide us an understanding of how we may connect the emerging multiple identities of a person.

In the following chapters, our contributors have been asked to focus on the multiple identities of the client, which may reveal meaningful combinations of a particular client intersectional system. We hope that this will provide a deeper understanding of the variety of client intersectional systems related to multidimensional levels.

Finally, there is an end product or output where the case study integrates the effects of cultural competence, practice stages, and client intersectional systems toward the positive wholeness of the person. We now turn to the section on case studies, which is a primary teaching/learning tool of social work practice.

1.4	Application Exercise

1. Explain your own unique multiple identities (your age, ethnicity, gender, sexual orientation, functional ability, and immigration status) that are important to understanding who you are.
2. How do you further identify yourself as a member of a family, organizations, and community (local, state, regional, and national) so that a person can understand how you are connected to larger groups?

CASE STUDIES

Case Study Method, Design, and Analysis

Social work has traditionally used the case study as its primary instrument for gathering information. Early social workers helping individuals and families were called social caseworkers and prepared detail studies of the psychosocial situation. The life aspects of people are interesting material for assessing the problem and formulating an intervention plan. The case study method of learning also is used in the field of business administration to uncover organizational issues. Harvard University Graduate School of Business structures its curriculum learning around the case study method.

Part of this text incorporates cases of individuals, families, and communities that illustrate the diverse groups. It is therefore important for us to discuss the case method, design, and analysis so we can grasp the significance of the case study. Case study research originated in Europe, predominantly in France, and was used in the United States by the University of Chicago Department of Sociology during the early 1900s until 1935. Several of the early sociologists from the Chicago school, notably E. Franklin Frazier, made pioneering contributions in social work education. Chicago became the case study laboratory to study various ethnic immigrant groups and social conditions such as poverty and unemployment.

The case study method paid special attention to completeness in observation, reconstruction, and analysis of cases. It also incorporated the views of subjects under study. Qualitative research, single-subject design, postmodernism, and grounded theory are current renaissance trends, which are linked to the case study. The case study approach satisfies the three tenets of the qualitative method: describing, understanding, and explaining. There is an attempt to collect a number of cases in a multiple case study and to replicate cases. Tellis (1997) identifies three types of case studies: exploratory, explanatory, and descriptive. Exploratory case studies are preliminary investigations of field subjects based on pilot projects providing learning. Explanatory case studies deal with causal factors that are knowledge-driven, problem-solving, or social interaction efforts. Descriptive cases start with a theory orientation and a comparison of patterns.

Among the features of the case study approach are the following:

- A holistic understanding of cultural system of actions or sets of inter-related activities involving the subjects in a social situation
- Unit of analysis related to a system of action rather than to an individual or a group of individuals
- A multiperspective analysis of the interaction of various actors
- Research methodology that addresses the study's primary question (what questions which are open-ended), a stated purpose in the form of a proposition, issue oriented units of analysis, sources of evidence (interviews, direct observation, participant-observation, documents, archival records), and data analysis (categorize the data into groups, examining relationships such as similarities and differences, use of theoretical propositions as units of organization, development of a case description)

Client Location and Context

The case study component of our model starts with the concept of client location and context. *Client location* means the particular position or place of the client. From a cultural perspective, we may discuss one's position in the collective family hierarchy or one's place in geographic proximity to a natural support system such as the extended family. By the same token, the client could be quite isolated and distant from these cultural structures. *Client context* refers to the client's surrounding settings that create how a situation, background, or environment may affect a person. I (Lum, 2004, p. 276) write about the contextual perspective, which includes and yet goes beyond the person and the environment: "We may speak about *person-centered context,* which helps us to understand the various *intrapersonal* and *interpersonal* contexts regarding what happens to and with the individual, or we may choose to concentrate on *environmental-centered context,* which focuses on how the surrounding settings affect the person." The client context is where this interplay and exchange occurs between the person and the environment.

In their book, *Pathways to Power: Readings in Contextual Social Work Practice,* Kemp, Whittaker, and Tracy talk about the relationship between empowerment, environment, and context:

> In empowering practice, this expanded understanding of the environment translates into conscious efforts to bring critical appraisal of everyday environments more fully into the work that social workers do, including analysis of the power relations embedded in clients' everyday environments and careful attention to environmental resources and strengths, as well as to environmental barriers and constraints. Although we emphasize the social and structural aspects of environmental contexts, our framework is sensitive also to the meanings that environments have for the people who live in them, to the many and detailed ways that people make places for themselves in the world, and to human agency, ingenuity, and persistence in even the most devastating and toxic of environments. Our focus, in other words, is on person-environment transactions and negotiations in all their richness and variability. (2002, p. 27)

Thus, case study integration delineates the specific environmental scope of client location and context as an essential part of the case study.

Client Multiple Identities and Integration

Our discussion of client multiple identities points out the need to integrate the many dimensions of client identity in our case study integration. Van Soest and Garcia (2003) discuss the complex interaction of multiple social identities through the following three characteristics:

- The complex interaction of racism with the systemic dynamics of oppression based on other identities such as gender, ethnicity, class, sexual orientation, ability, and religion
- The historical and ongoing oppression and privilege that different social identity groups experience in our society
- The intersection and complex interaction of multiple social identities and a continuum of harm and privilege that these identities confer

At times, multiple identities should be seen against the backdrop of racism, oppression, and privilege where certain aspects of one's identity are tested. Yet, at the same time, the richness of understanding of the complexity and variety of many multiple identity characteristics takes us to a new and higher level of understanding about how a unique person is configured or put together. There is a need for more discussion and investigation of the nature of multiple identities.

Cultural Competence Worker-Client Integration

Cultural competence worker-client integration addresses the worker's understanding of the client's cultural dimensions by imparting cultural awareness of self and others, knowledge theory understanding, skill development application, and inductive learning about the client. Likewise, to the extent the client has become more culturally aware of self and others, understood aspects of cultural knowledge, applied cultural coping skills, and participated in inductive learning all affect cultural competence. Okayama, Furuto, and Edmondson remind us, "Social workers who learn about themselves and ethnic groups on the general and advanced levels can apply this knowledge to develop culturally competent skills on the micro, meso, and macro levels. This knowledge, along with the aforementioned attitudes and following skills, complete the components necessary for culturally competent practice" (2001, p. 94). Furthermore, they say, "What may be most important is for social workers to maintain culturally component attitudes as we continue to attain new knowledge and skills while building new relationships. Awareness, the valuing of all cultures, and a willingness to make changes are underlying attitudes that support everything that can be taught or learned" (2001, p. 97). How cultural competence affects the worker and the client in their helping and cultural interaction relationship is the major point. As the worker understands and communicates cultural competence, the client should gain a respect for understanding and using cultural competencies as tools for learning and functioning.

Process Stages Worker-Client Progress

Process stages worker-client progress is concerned about the extent to which the client progresses through the beginning, middle, and end stages of the helping process and the degree to which the client has learned and used culturally competent skills as a member of a diverse group from the case study perspective. Fong blends these various components together into a process mosaic when she states,

> The task of multicultural social work practice remains to deepen the interracial, interblending of cultures found within a single ethnic group. For example, interracial marriages, international adoptions, and foster care situations allow clients to experience multiracial/multicultural experiences. In these experiences, social workers need to be prepared in assessments and interventions to deal with the multi-ethnic identities and differing environments of clients. The knowledge of cultural competency that has been advocated in the past has focused on thinking and learning factual and descriptive knowledge about the client, with attributes presented as tangential to the functioning of the person or community. The value and belief systems that comprise traditions and cultural norms need to be presented as central to the ethnic client's functioning. New paradigms and models need to be created to instill the practice of adopting the client's values as the norms. (2001, pp. 4–5)

If the worker and the client are able to implement these practice themes in the change process, these are signs of process progress.

Client Micro, Meso, and Macro Systems in Action

Client systems in action presupposes that we can no longer understand the micro individual, family apart from the meso group, community, organization and the macro state, region, nation levels. Micro, meso, and macro systems interrelate and interconnect with each other. Where is the starting point? Is it with the individual and family? In some cultures where the family is of significant importance, the micro family system is the unit of focus or change (Fong, 1994). Thus, when describing the case study client system, one should focus on the micro family and then interconnect the other system levels. In other instances, working from the macro state and national levels to affect legislative and policy program change is the way to affect communities and organizations. The meso community change systems can also be the entry point. Furuto, Nicolas, Kim, and Fiaui discuss three aspects of community change: "*Community-based* is having staff hired from the community, and the program is located in the community it serves. *Community-driven* means that people from that community are involved in making key decisions about the structure and content of the program, such as 'who, what, where and how.' *Culturally competent* is having staff with a deep understanding of the people and place, an understanding reflected in program content, policies, procedures, and the living character of the program" (2001, p. 329). Identifying the starting point in the client cohort micro, meso, and macro systems continuum and explaining how the other systems' component responses help to understand that once we determine a system level as an entry point, we must connect the other systems so that there is interaction.

In the following chapters, we shall see various case study configurations of how cultural competence comes together in meaningful ways in the lives of individuals, families, and communities as they interact with organizations on the local, state, regional, and national levels.

CONCLUSION

We have laid a basic foundation for connecting the client, cultural competence, practice stages, and case study integration into a working model. Each component has been explained and interrelated to other parts. In subsequent chapters, contributors have been asked to write chapters on various diverse groups, starting with background demographics, history of oppression, and survival values; moving to cultural competent knowledge and skills; explaining practice process skills stages; and involving case study integration exercises. We hope that the reader will readily see how the model can be applied to the various ethnic, gender, sexual orientation, and transitional diversity groups.

References

Benjamin, M. (2001). How does cultural competency differ from cultural sensitivity/awareness? http://www.air.org/cecp/cultural /Q_howdifferent.htm

Bureau of Primary Health Care (2002). *Cultural Competence: A Journey.* http://bphc.hrsa.gov

Collins, P. H. (1990). *Black feminist thought: Knowledge, consciousness, and the politics of empowerment.* New York and London: Routledge.

Collins, P. H. (2000). *Black feminist thought: Knowledge, consciousness, and the politics of empowerment.* New York and London: Routledge.

Communities Can! (2001). Cultural competence. www.gucdc .georgetown.edu /com mcan5.html

Crenshaw, K. W. (1991). Mapping the margins: Intersectionality, identity politics, and violence against women of color. *Stanford Law Review 43(6),* 1241–1299.

Cross, T. L., Bazron, B. J., Dennis, K. W., & Isaacs, M. R. (1989). *Towards a culturally competent system of care.* Washington, DC: Georgetown University Child Development Center.

Cultural competence online. (1999–2001). What is cultural competence? www.culturalcompetence2.com/

Cultural competency legislative hearing planning. (2001). Discussion key points. Elihu M. State Building, Oakland, CA.

Fong, R. (1994). Family preservation: Making it work for Asians. *Child Welfare, 73,* 331–341.

Fong, R. (2001). Culturally competent social work practice: Past and present. In R. Fong & S. B. C. L. Furuto (Eds.), *Culturally competent practice: Skills, interventions, and evaluations* (pp. 1–9). Boston: Allyn & Bacon.

Fong, R. (2002). Building competencies to manage diversity across practice.

Council on Social Work Education Faculty Development Institute, Annual Program Meeting, Nashville, TN, February 2002.

Fong, R. & Furuto, S. B. C. L. (2001). *Culturally competent practice: Skills, intervention, and evaluations.* Boston: Allyn & Bacon.

Ford, M. M. (1999). *Developing cultural competency: A case study.* An unpublished Master of Social Work thesis, California State University, Sacramento.

Furuto, S. B. C. L., San Nicholas, R. J., Kim, G. E, & Fiaui, L. M. (2001). Interventions with Kanaka Maoli, Chamorro, and Samoan communities. In R. Fong & S. B. C. L. Furuto (Eds.), *Culturally competent practice: Skills, interventions, and evaluations* (pp. 327–342). Boston: Allyn & Bacon.

Gordon, M. M. (1978). *Human nature, class, and ethnicity.* New York: Oxford University Press.

Hepworth, D. H., Rooney, R. H., & Larsen, J. A. (2002). *Direct social work practice: Theory and skills.* Pacific Grove, CA: Brooks/Cole.

Kemp, S. P., Whittaker, J. K., & Tracy, E. M. (2002). Contextual social work practice. In M. O'Melia & K. K. Miley (Eds.), *Pathways to power: Readings in contextual social work practice* (pp. 15–34). Boston: Allyn & Bacon.

LaFromboise, T., Coleman, H. L. K., & Gerton, J. (1993). Psychological impact of biculturalism: Evidence and theory. *Psychological Bulletin, 114,* 395–412.

Lum, D. (1999). *Culturally competent practice: A framework for growth and action.* Pacific Grove, CA: Brooks/Cole.

Lum, D. (2003). *Culturally competent practice: A framework for understanding diverse groups and justice issues.* Pacific Grove, CA: Brooks/Cole–Thomson Learning.

Lum, D. (2004). *Social work practice & people of color: A process-stage approach.* Belmont, CA: Brooks/Cole–Thomson Learning.

Manoleas, P. (1994). An outcome approach to assessing the cultural competence of MSW students. *Journal of Multicultural Social Work, 3,* 43–57.

Miley, K. K., O'Melia, M., & DuBois, B. (2001). *Generalist social work practice: An empowering approach.* Boston: Allyn & Bacon.

National Association of Social Workers Standards for Cultural Competence in Social Work Practice (2001). www.naswdc.org/pubs/standards/cultural.htm

Okayama, C. M., Furuto, S. B. C. L., & Edmondson, J. (2001) Components of cultural competence: Attitudes, knowledge, and skills. In R. Fong & S. B. C. L. Furuto (Eds.), *Culturally competent practice: Skills, interventions, and evaluations* (pp. 89–100). Boston: Allyn & Bacon.

Orlandi, M. A. (1992). The challenge of evaluating community-based prevention programs: A cross-cultural perspective. In M. A. Orlandi, R. Weston, & L. G. Epstein (Eds.), *Cultural competence for evaluators: A guide for alcohol and other drug abuse prevention practitioners working with ethnic/racial communities* (pp. 1–22). Rockville, MD: U.S. Department of Health and Human Services, Office for Substance Abuse Prevention.

Richmond, M. E. (1964). *Social diagnosis.* New York: Russell Sage Foundation.

Schriver, J. M. (2001). *Human behavior and the social environment: Shifting paradigms in essential knowledge for social work practice.* Boston: Allyn & Bacon.

Schwartz, W. (1977). Social group work: The interactionist approach. In *Encyclopedia of social work,* Vol. II. New York: National Association of Social Workers.

Sheafor, B. W., & Horejsi, C. R. (2003). *Techniques and guidelines for social work practice.* Boston: Allyn & Bacon.

Shulman, L. (1999). *The skills of helping individuals, families, groups, and communities.* Itasca, IL: F. E. Peacock.

Spencer, M., Lewis, E., & Gutierrez, L. (2000). Multicultural perspectives on direct practice in social work. In P. Allen-Meares & C. Garvin (Eds.), *The handbook of social work direct practice* (pp. 131–149). Thousand Oaks, CA: Sage.

Substance Abuse and Mental Health Services Administration (1997). *Cultural competence guidelines in managed care mental health services for Asian and Pacific Islander populations.* The Asian and Pacific Islander American Task Force. The Western Interstate Commission for Higher Education Mental Health Program.

Switzer, M. E. (1998). Cultural competence in service programs. www.mswitzer.org/sem98/papers/mason.html

Tellis, W. (1997). Application of a case study methodology. http:www.nova.edu/ssss/QR/QR3-3/tellis2.html

U.S. Department of Health and Human Services, Office of Minority Health. (2001). National Standards for Culturally and Linguistically Appropriate Services in Health Care. Executive Summary. Prepared by IQ Solutions, Inc. Rockville, MD 20852.

Van Soest, D. & Garcia, B. (2003). *Diversity education for social justice: Mastering teaching skills.* Alexandria, VA: Council on Social Work Education.

Social Work Practice with First Nations Peoples

Maria Yellow Horse Brave Heart and Josephine Chase

First Nations or Native Peoples, also referred to as American Indians and Alaska Natives as well as Natives, are a diverse collective of indigenous nations. In this chapter, we describe some of the diversity, demographics, and cultures of First Nations, particularly Lakota and Northern Plains culture, as one Native example. We also focus on common cultural traits and representative experiences of First Nations that may be generalizable to most First Nations Peoples. Further, we suggest culturally competent practice skills, grounded in clinical social work practice, including assessment and intervention with First Nations. Native experience of genocide and oppression across generations is emphasized, particularly for the Lakota (Teton Sioux). Our rationale for this emphasis is our identities and experiences as Lakota women and our immersion and competence in our own culture. We feel that we can therefore offer the reader a unique and informed perspective that will enhance the reader's learning. We include a case study with exercises focused on assessment, intervention, and termination skill development. We conclude with recommendations.

THE DEMOGRAPHICS OF FIRST NATIONS PEOPLES

Native people of North America consist of diverse tribal groups; at present 500 different tribes have federally recognized tribe status, which denotes those tribes who treated with the United States Government and, as such, retain the right to self-governance and are viewed as nations within the nation. Each tribe has a specific language, individual customs, and beliefs; yet similarities of values and culture do exist. Just as tribes differ, individual Natives differ in preference of self-identification. Commonly used terms of identification are *American Indian* and *Native American,* which are often used interchangeably; a more recent identification is that of *Indigenous* or *First Nations.* For the purpose of this chapter, we use the terms *First Nations* and *Natives* or *Native Peoples;* on a more sensitive note, it is preferable to use the specific name of the individual's tribal name rather than *Native American, American Indian,* or *First Nations.*

Since the first European contact, the numbers of Native tribes and people in the United States have been diminished by war and disease by as much as 95% (Stiffarm & Lane, 1992). Today, Natives live in a variety of geographic settings ranging from rural reservations in the Dakotas to large urban centers such as Chicago or New York. The focus of this chapter will be to enhance sensitivity to tribal cultural differences while attending to unique cultural and familial nuances.

Many Natives either do not speak their tribal languages or are not fluent in them because of forced acculturation and assimilation. In contrast, some Natives do speak their tribal languages, and there is a push to re-learn not only tribal languages but also to integrate traditional tribal values, practices and knowledge into contemporary family and community life. Before European contact, Native family and community organization were highly structured and complex with configurations that incorporated complex proscriptive behaviors and relationships; these served as protective factors to maintain order and respect. Further, cultural institutions such as societies and clan systems provided a safety net that provided for widows, orphans and those unable to care for themselves (Bowers, 1992; Wilson, 1981).

In contemporary society where human service agencies have been established to meet those needs previously met by relatives and community members, Native people are falling through the gaps as demonstrated by recent statistics. Overall, Native people have socioeconomic status far below the national level; for 1999–2001, the poverty rate for American Indians and Alaska Natives was 24.5%, higher than for other groups of color except blacks (Proctor & Dalaker, 2002). Nationally, the 2000 census reported an average Native household income of $31,064 during a two-year period; for all races during the same two-year period, the median household income was $42,168.

In the area of health and well being, Natives have the distinction of health problems far exceeding the national average. Posttraumatic stress disorder (PTSD) prevalence among American Indian and Alaska Natives is 22%, which is substantially higher than the 8% prevalence reported in the general population. Alcohol use is more prevalent among Native youth than in the general U.S. population, at 96% for Native males and 92% for females by the 12th grade (Oetting & Beauvais, 1989). The frequency and intensity of drinking is greater among Native youth, and negative consequences are more prevalent and severe, with a younger age at first involvement with alcohol (Oetting & Beauvais, 1989). The five top leading causes of death for all Native youth ages 5 to 14 years include suicide and homicide (Indian Health Service, 2000–2001). The overall mortality is twice as high as the rate for all U.S. races. On some Lakota reservations, the suicide death rate of 35.0 is more than three times the average for the U.S. population, and the suicide attempt rate is seven times higher. The alcohol-related death rate is more than seven times the national average (Indian Health Service, 2000–2001). South Dakota has nine reservations within its boundaries and can be viewed as representative of other rural reservation entities in demographics and needs. Urban communities located off the reservation also contain large Native populations. The 2000 state census shows a total Native population of 60,335 with a median family income of $19,371. In addition to poverty, social problems that exist in Native communities include high school dropout rates for First Nation youth in Rapid City of nearly 50% (South Dakota Dept. of Ed., 2002). Other major problems affecting these youth are domestic violence, homelessness, and teen pregnancy. The *2001 South Dakota Vital Statistics Report* demonstrates that the "average" homeless adult was between the ages of 25 and 44 years old, was probably a single female with children (40%), and Native American (47%) (*2001 South Dakota Vital Statistics Report,* 2003). In 1999, South Dakota reported 4,973 homeless children under age 18, a large number of these homeless youth are First Nations youth living in both urban and reservations settings (S.D. Dept. of Ed., 1999). Many clients in these groups are affected by more than one problem; for instance, homelessness affects a child's education, and substance abuse affects homelessness. Thus, social factors affect psychological and health status.

In 2001, women younger than 20 years of age accounted for 11.2% of total resident births; white women under age 20 constituted 8.4% total white births, and Native American women of the same age constituted 24.3 percent of total Native American births. Overall, Native mothers receive less prenatal care: 28.6 % native mothers had less than five prenatal care visits compared with 6.1% white mothers who had low birth weight babies (South Dakota Department of Education, 2002). A national study found that in general American Indian/Alaska Native women report significantly higher rates of intimate partner violence than do women of other racial backgrounds (Tjaden & Thoennes, 2000) Other research also reports that American Indian couples are significantly more violent than their white counterparts are (Brush, 1990, in Tjaden & Thoennes, 2000).

The trends in social, political and health issues of Native people in general are staggering; however, one must remember that Native people, like every other group, fall along a wide range of income, acculturation, and other characteristics. Native people are as diverse as the demography of their experience, education, and geography.

THE HISTORICAL OPPRESSION
AND SURVIVAL VALUES OF FIRST NATIONS PEOPLES

Survival and Cultural Values of First Nations:
Lakota (Teton Sioux) Culture

Despite the effect of colonization of the Americas by Europeans, many First Nations Peoples have been able to maintain a number of indigenous values to varying degrees. The social work practitioner must be sufficiently cognizant of traditional Native cultures and be able to recognize how these mores influence behavior and inform assessment and intervention with First Nations. These traditional cultural traits, behaviors, norms, beliefs, and practices all form the "survival values" for Natives, often providing strength and resilience for First Nations Peoples. At times, however, these values conflict with those imposed by the dominant European American culture and may create problems for Natives. This will be further discussed in the section on problem identification and assessment.

Among the Lakota, we have seven laws, *Woope Sakowin* (Kills Straight & Brave Heart, unpublished document), that traditionally governed our behavior and are still practiced to varying degrees among our people. These values are called laws, suggesting the traditional cultural expectation of strict adherence to these mores. The *Woope Sakowin* include generosity, compassion, respect for all of creation, developing a great mind (capacity to be patient, tolerant, and observant), humility (no one is above another), courage (capacity to be self-disciplined), and wisdom. The Lakota traditionally value interdependence and simultaneously embrace principles of non-interference and tolerance. Lakota children are placed at the center of the Nation; we carry the welfare of the Nation in our hearts, and our decisions are made with the next seven generations in mind (Brave Heart, 2001a). The good of the Lakota Nation traditionally is placed above that of the individual. Behavior that manifested traditional values included humility, respectful listening without interrupting, deliberation, silence and observance, politeness, deference, and reserve in front of strangers (Brave Heart, 2001a).

Traditional Lakota values embraced the sacredness of women and children, in contrast with European values at the time of colonization where women and children were considered the property of men and domestic violence was legal (Brave Heart-Jordan & DeBruyn, 1995). To our knowledge, among most First Nations, violence against women and children was not tolerated in traditional culture.

Active and ongoing communication with the spirit world and certain ancestor spirits were traditionally encouraged; all creation was considered sacred, and even the rocks were seen as having spirits, in contrast to Christian teachings that only humans have souls. This traditional Native belief has fostered traditional reverence for the earth and all it inhabitants. The value also resulted in conflict with Europeans who believed that they could own the earth, whereas the Lakota, for example, viewed themselves as being caretakers of the earth rather than owners.

Although we speak of traditional values in the past tense, many modern First Nations Peoples persist in practicing a variety of traditional values and behaviors in a variety of contexts while manifesting European American deportment. Social work practitioners must not make assumptions that a First Nations person with an assimilated dominant cultural style does not identify with and embrace traditional Native values (Brave Heart, 2001a). There may be value conflicts and contradictions within First Nations; as a result of colonization, non-Native values now influence First Nations including male domination, domestic violence, and child abuse. Each First Nations client should be seen as a unique individual within the historical context of oppression and traditional culture.

Historical Trauma and the Legacy of Genocide

The history of First Nations is fraught with genocide and massive traumatic group experiences (Brave Heart, 1998), including massacres such as the 1890 Wounded Knee Massacre of the Lakota (*Lakota Times,* 1990); starvation, displacement, war trauma, and prisoner of war experiences; and the compulsory removal of First Nations children and their placement in abusive boarding schools (Tanner, 1982). Tanner (1982) asserts that the United States never intended that the Lakota survive long-term but moved to negotiating treaties as a cheaper alternative to war. Policies for the extermination of First Nations are documented in congressional documents (Brave Heart, 1998; Brave Heart-Jordan, 1995). The genocide of Natives is chronicled in the literature (Legters, 1988; Stannard, 1992; Thornton, 1987); the history of First Nations meets the United Nations definition of genocide according to the 1942 Geneva Convention (Legters, 1988). For First Nations, the legacy of genocide has resulted in *historical trauma,* which we define as cumulative emotional and psychological injury, including the lifespan and across generations, that results from massive group trauma and ongoing oppression (Brave Heart, 1998).

Historical Trauma Theory and Its Implication in Practice with First Nations Peoples

Associated with the historical trauma for First Nations is the *historical trauma response* (HTR), first identified among the Lakota; it is a constellation of features associated with massive cumulative group trauma across generations and within the current lifespan (Brave Heart, 1998; Brave Heart, 1999a; Brave Heart, 2001a). HTR is analogous to traits found among Jewish Holocaust descendants (Brave Heart, 2001a; Danieli, 1998; Kestenberg, 1990). Characteristics of HTR include depression, self-destructive behavior, substance abuse, anxiety, poor affect tolerance, intrusive trauma imagery, survivor guilt, trauma fixation, identification with ancestral pain, somatic symptoms, and elevated mortality rates (Brave Heart, 1998; Brave Heart, 1999a). A component of the historical trauma response, *historical unresolved grief,* is the impaired mourning that emanates from generational trauma (Brave Heart, 1998). Historical trauma theory evolved from clinical experience, observations, and qualitative as well as quantitative research (Brave Heart, 1998, 1999a, b; Brave Heart & DeBruyn, in press; Brave Heart-Jordan, 1995).

One of the particularly traumatic episodes for First Nations Peoples that has strong implications for social work practice is the "boarding school era" beginning in 1879 (see Brave Heart & DeBruyn, 1998; Brave Heart, 2001a; Noriega, 1992; Tanner, 1982). First Nations children, under federal policy, were forcibly removed and placed in boarding schools, where they frequently experienced separation from family and tribal communities sometimes for years at a time, starvation, physical and sexual abuse, incarceration, and emotional deprivation (Brave Heart, 2001a). The boarding school legacy has resulted in a large number of elderly and mid-life First Nations adults possibly having had varying degrees of such traumatic experiences. Younger Native adults may be descendants of boarding school survivor parents or grandparents. Initial research suggests that the generational boarding school trauma has affected parenting and subsequently the current generation of both Native adults and children.

CULTURALLY COMPETENT KNOWLEDGE THEORY AND PRACTICE SKILLS FOR FIRST NATIONS PEOPLES

Social work practice with First Nations necessitates incorporating the cultural and historical information described in the preceding section. Culture shapes an individual's self-concept, identity, relationships with others, explanations of illness, symptom presentation, and response to the practitioner (Brave Heart, 2001a). In addition to consideration of culture, the HTR must be assessed. This will be discussed in further detail in the section on assessment. The culturally competent skills needed for effective practice with First Nations clients include contact skills, problem identification and assessment skills, and intervention as well as termination skills. Cultural congruence—that is, adapting one's behavior in practice in ways that complement the cultural behavioral manifestations and beliefs of the client—requires sufficient knowledge of the client culture, sensitivity, non-intrusive observation, and the capacity to adapt to changing behavior from the same client in different contexts (Brave Heart & DeBruyn, 1998; Brave Heart, 2001a). The concept of cultural congruence will be integrated throughout the following sections.

CONTACT SKILLS WITH FIRST NATIONS CLIENTS

Overcoming Communication Barriers, Relationship Protocols, Listening and Communication Skills

With First Nations clients, a number of potential barriers and pivotal points for resistance to emerge. A key underlying issue is the historically traumatic legacy of the relationship between the United States government (and European Americans) and First Nations Peoples. European American social workers have the challenge of establishing trust and rapport within this historical context. Further, the social work profession itself has a negative historical legacy among First Nations. In contrast to the "friendly visitor" heritage, social work with Natives evolved from the War Department, once home to the Bureau of Indian Affairs, which is now responsible for social services and progenitor of Indian Health Service under which mental health services are provided (Brave Heart, 2001b).

Developing rapport with First Nations clients can be more challenging if the social worker comes from a different cultural background, particularly if the social worker is non-Native. There will be greater cultural and perhaps social distance between the client and the worker; First Nations clients may behave with more reticence, seeing the European American social worker as an outsider with whom they must maintain more traditional, respectful reserve (Brave Heart, 2001b). Further, there may be incomplete and guarded disclosure of problems, family history, and references to traditional spiritual practices or phenomena, about which many Natives feel protective.

For First Nations social workers, establishing rapport and trust with First Nations clients are typically much easier because of shared experiences and often some shared values. There are three exceptions: (1) the worker's tribal ancestry is that of a traditional enemy Native nation or the traditional tribal cultures are too divergent, (2) there are significant phenotype (skin color and features) differences, and (3) the worker is from the same community and there are client conflicts with the extended family members. With the intertribal social work dyad, the historical tribal relationships and extended family kinship networks should be considered in assigning cases (Brave Heart, 2001a, b).

Within the First Nations social work-client relationship, barriers may exist because of the degree of acculturation, assimilation, traditionalism, or differences in tribal cultures. The Native client and Native social worker may hold divergent values and worldviews, possibly resulting in cultural conflict and miscommunication. Intragroup prejudice based on skin color, degree of traditional orientation, and Native language fluency exist among First Nations Peoples. For example, a Native social worker with a full-blood phenotype (skin color and features) may bring his or her own feelings of color consciousness and past experiences to a session with a light-skinned, mixed-blood client. A light-skinned, mixed-blood social worker may harbor underlying negative prejudices and stereotypes toward a full-blood client. Historically, overall, full-bloods faced greater racism and oppression, even at the hands of lighter-skinned, mixed-blood relatives. Discomfort and resentment from these past experiences could interfere with the therapeutic relationship. Simultaneously, during the resurgence of Native pride and identity particularly during the 1970s, some light-skinned, mixed-blood Natives experienced a sense of inferiority and shame about their Caucasian ancestry; some also experienced discriminatory treatment by full-bloods, often motivated by retaliation for past wrongs perpetrated by people with significant European ancestry. Both full-blood and mixed-blood Natives have been exposed to racism and oppression that has been internalized, to varying degrees. Both may harbor unconscious as well as conscious feelings of inferiority and self-hatred, particularly without some type of intervention or process of decolonization or a conscious, vigilant effort to combat the negative effects of genocide and colonization.

Language fluency and traditional spirituality can also become loaded issues in the therapeutic relationship. Those Natives who are fluent may feel superior to Natives who lack fluency; Natives who do not speak their own language may feel inferior and self-conscious. Although lack of language fluency is largely a function of boarding abuses and being deprived of the opportunity to learn and speak the language, it is often internalized and can be emotionally charged. Internal emotional conflicts about traditional spiritual practices, a function of the historical spiritual oppression of Native practices, may result in divergent views between Native social worker and Native clients. This conflict may result in distance and mistrust within the therapeutic dyad. To combat these potential pitfalls, social work values of respect and empathy must be promoted along with careful and sensitive exploration of these issues, without judgment (Brave Heart, 2001b).

Communication barriers may exist in the social work relationship. The European American style of direct communication is often experienced by First Nations clients as aggressive and intrusive (Brave Heart, 2001b). Cultural congruence will facilitate the social worker's handling of communication style differences. First Nations clients may manifest a more indirect communication style, and the social worker must listen closely for disguised requests. Content is often veiled in stories and metaphors (Brave Heart, 2001b). First Nations clients often respond indirectly to questions, and the worker must listen closely; the response may initially appear unrelated, but the answer is usually given in a disguised manner, in a story or through recounting a personal experience or that of another individual.

Additional barriers that may emerge include other interaction style differences. There is cultural diversity in eye contact, which is often governed by age and gender differences; avoidance of eye contact is common among some tribal communities as a sign of respect. Cross-gender interaction may also be limited among some First Nations Peoples where nonrelatives of the opposite sex are kept at an emotional, physical, and psychological distance (Brave Heart, 2001b). It is best to unobtrusively observe, respectfully proceed slowly, and maintain congruence in the communication style, for example, averting one's eyes periodically if the client does so (Brave Heart, 2001b). Social workers also need to consider the traditional tribal culture when working with gay, lesbian, and transsexual clients; there are often cultural explanations of the origin of transexuality and homosexuality as well as socially prescribed functional roles in a number of traditional Native societies. However, modern influences have also modified the degree of acceptance of homosexuality among First Nations.

Social workers need to develop comfort with silence, a state often comfortable for Native clients. The social worker will need to adapt to indirect communication styles, permitting time for silence, stories, and metaphors (Brave Heart, 2001b). More European American culture oriented First Nations clients may be assertive and use direct eye contact and direct communication. These clients may require the social worker to behave more similarly to working with non-Native clients while still maintaining awareness of the historical legacy and complex cultural issues. However, the social worker should be prepared to alter the communication when manifestations of more traditional Native communication patterns occur during a session (Brave Heart, 2001b).

Resistance in clinical settings may include medication management issues. There may be some suspicion of "white man's medicine" because of the historical legacy of genocide (Brave Heart, 2001b). Further, the absence of mind- or mood-altering substances in most indigenous cultures traditionally may further exacerbate resistance. We advocate the use of psychotropic medication only when biologically based mood and anxiety disorders cannot be managed through therapy, support groups, or traditional ceremonies. Many Native people manage such disorders without medication and without suicidal risk, provided there are sufficient therapeutic and community resources; ceremonies have been highly effective in resolving some depressions and psychotic symptoms that were misdiagnosed spiritual manifestations (Brave Heart, 2001a, b). If medication is needed, a clinical social worker may enlist the help of traditional spiritual leaders to facilitate client acceptance of medication and empower its effectiveness.

Barriers can usually be overcome across cultures. For European American social workers working with First Nations clients, the first step in the process of developing trust, rapport, and overcoming barriers is to internally acknowledge the legacy of genocide. This may not have to be verbalized to a client but it will be helpful for the social worker to hold this in her or his consciousness. A second recommendation is that practitioners should maintain cognizance of the collective racism toward and images of First Nations to avoid its interference and potency in the working relationship (Brave Heart, 2001a, b). There is an intransient, erroneous view of "the Indian" as "savage" and as one homogenous group (Berkhofer, 1979). These racist constructs permeate American society and are entrenched in the psyche of the general population. Hence, there is a potential that this collective image will bias every interaction with First Nations clients. Consciousness of this factor will facilitate its recognition in the social work relationship.

Patience, pacing, making some "small talk" about nonthreatening topics, and flexibility can be very helpful. Often, more traditional Native clients may view the sessions as "visiting" and may "drop by" unannounced early in the professional relationship; the social worker should make every effort to be available. Over time, some of these clients learn to keep appointments, but breaking appointments should not necessarily be interpreted as a resistance; the fluidity of time in traditional Native culture and the importance of relationships must be considered (Brave Heart, 2001b).

Establishing a Responsive Service Delivery System

The traditional western medical model of service has not proven to be effective with Native clients as exemplified by the continuing high rates of maladies demonstrated in the statistics presented earlier. Thus, paradigm shifts are required for worker approach, problem orientation, communication and relationship protocols, and treatment goals and intervention.

Native clients are private with their personal problems and rely on family or extended kin networks for accessing help in resolving their problems (Attneave, 1982). Many Natives rely on traditional healers or practitioners (medicine people) as the first choice in addressing physical problems, and frequently with emotional and family problems as well. Even Natives in urban settings arrange for a healer to travel to their homes or for the client to travel to the reservation to participate in traditional healing ceremonies. Further, Native pastors or lay clerics are sought out for counseling and guidance regarding relational and emotional issues. Thus, in many cases western doctors, social workers and therapists are the last service of choice for many Natives. Given this hierarchy of service selection, frequently when Native people arrive at a human service center, it may be a mandatory requirement after a serious violation of state standards of care. Consequently, the social worker may be met with suspicion and resistance.

One must be aware that suspicion and resistance are often well founded for Natives for a variety of reasons that will be addressed here. Further, in small reservation communities, mental health issues carry a stigma, as well as concerns of confidentiality and privacy. The U.S. government has carried the primary responsibility of providing care through the Indian Health Service and the Bureau of Indian Affairs, which have a reputation of oppression and are not trusted by Natives as acting in the best interest of Native people. (Horejsi, Heavy Runner-Craig, & Pablo, 1992). This impression of institutions filters into relationships with other helping systems such as social services, medical facilities, and schools. This attitude is even more prevalent when the issue is related to children and families because of forced removal of Native youth to government boarding schools and adoption to white families in the late 1800s through mid-1900s (Cross, 1986). For these reasons, any social service agency is suspect, even with Native workers involved (Horejsi et al., 1992).

A more sensitive approach is to be armed with general knowledge of Native history from their vantage point and information about Native resources in one's geographic proximity. Advocacy is frequently required to assist individuals in overcoming their fear of "the system" and developing comfort in asking for help. It may be beneficial to enlist a traditional or local intermediary in the early phases of therapeutic intervention (Attneave, 1982; Topper, 1992). However, the most crucial requisite is to be willing to view life from a perspective that is very different than from mainstream American and from other people of color who come to America as a place of refuge or seeking the American Dream. Native values are often diametrically opposed to those of mainstream America because of traditional teachings of community, generosity, respect, and compassion that influence decision making and choices.

PROBLEM IDENTIFICATION AND ASSESSMENT SKILLS WITH FIRST NATIONS CLIENTS

Gaining Problem Understanding

As with any population, cultural characteristics influence therapeutic models, including assessment, problem identification, and intervention. For the First Nations, a multidimensional approach has proven to be effective. This approach requires flexibility in all aspects of therapeutic work in which the therapist is able to view the client from a perspective incorporating different dimensions: medical, psychological, socioeconomic, and cultural-historical (Topper, 1992). This approach provides a goodness of fit with many Native cultures who understand their being as comprising four components: mental, spiritual, physical, and emotional. This model also allows intervention at various levels: the individual, group, or family level.

In summarizing important psychological factors exhibited among Native Americans, there is a 600-year history of displacement and oppression, and alienation in their own land. Natives are keenly aware and sensitive to this history and sensitive to difference. Any provider must recognize that assessment is a mutually occurring process between provider and client. The provider must be able to recognize and appreciate the strengths of Native families and cultures. Despite continual assault on their survival, Native Peoples have persevered in the struggle to retain traditional values and strengths. Despite many acquired maladaptive behaviors, the tenacity required to retain healthy traditions and cultural practices while adapting to a completely foreign lifestyle attests to their strength and resiliency. These strengths can be accessed in developing and planning successful models of intervention with Native clients.

In gaining understanding of the presenting problem, the clinician may be required to help the client extrapolate the identified problem from narrative content, as the client describes recent events, feelings, and thoughts that brought her to the service agency. Frequently, the problem may stem from an environmental or relational issue, or it may relate to conflicts between individual and group needs such as the client's inability to address personal boundary issues or resolve situations that require stepping around cultural mores. Because of close family and kinship ties, an identified problem that at first appears as limited to the individual may in fact originate with and include other family members and requires careful attention to determine this during the assessment phase. For example, a Native person will not directly state, "I am anxious/depressed because my spouse is overbearing and I am contemplating a divorce, and I am concerned about what my extended family will think." Instead, the situation will be presented as series of interactions and the client's experience of the interactions; the client may perceive himself or herself as being out of balance, as an ineffective communicator, or as an inadequate spouse. Hence, the assessment may require inclusion of other family members to gain a broader and clearer picture of the issue to determine whether the problem is individual- or family-based.

Clinical Assessment Issues

Assessment of First Nations clients by clinical social workers in mental health settings incorporates use of *the Diagnostic and Statistical Manual of Mental Disorders (DSM-IV)* (American Psychiatric Association, 1994). Although comprehensive discussion of this type of assessment is beyond the scope of this chapter, a few comments will be offered. (For a more detailed discussion of *DSM-IV* assessment with Native clients, see Brave Heart, 2001a). For Natives, tribal identity and the tribal cultural reference group are key issues. First Nations clients in urban areas may have a "pan Indian" identity—an amalgamation of diverse tribal traits that have become dominant in the region where they are living or that are representative of more well-known or common features of specific tribes that are easily identifiable by First Nations communities. First Nations clients who are more connected and closer to their tribes of origin typically embrace varying aspects of that tribal culture. First Nations clients who are living and working among other tribes may adopt the host tribal culture as their culture of reference. Other important issues include skin color and features, language fluency, involvement in traditional culture, and assimilation of European American customs (Brave Heart, 2001a).

In assessment, the extent of tribal cultural identification should be considered; this will facilitate correct problem identification and planning for services. Internal smaller cultural reference groups should also be considered, such as gender, sexual orientation, and age. Cultural explanations of illness are important because they inform the intervention. For example, First Nations clients view some disorders as conditions that can only be ameliorated by a traditional Native ceremony. The psychosocial environment affects assessment, that is, the degree of family and community support and resources, stressors in the environment including the lack of resources, and racism and discrimination.

To establish progressive communication with a client about the problem, the social worker must establish a rapport with the client, facilitate open communication, and accurately interpret what the client shares both verbally and nonverbally. Assessment and problem identification may take longer with First

Nations clients who may be reticent about sharing more emotionally laden material early on. Further, the indirect communication style and polite reserve of many First Nations clients makes assessment more challenging because the social worker has to listen carefully for disguised messages and metaphors. Enlisting the help of cultural informants can facilitate more accurate assessment, providing insight into relevant cultural traits and behaviors as well as important environmental factors about which the social worker may be unaware (Brave Heart, 2001a). Cultural informants can also shed light on traumatic tribal histories and ongoing communal trauma.

Assessment should include information about HTR, noting any features reported by the client. Exploration of the existence of boarding-school history both within the client's lifespan and in past generations can facilitate consciousness-raising about external historical and political factors (Brave Heart, 2001a). Eliciting detailed information and powerful emotions about traumatic boarding-school experiences should not occur until the client's ego strength and resources are assessed, just as one would do with any emotionally laden and traumatic content. This would occur after the assessment, during the intervention.

Building on client strengths can be enhanced by the attitude and approach of the social worker; the worker should value the client's culture, remembering that the client is the expert in her or his culture (Brave Heart, 2001b; Cox & Parsons, 1994). The social worker must also remain cognizant that First Nations traditionally have effectively used a variety of methods for healing mental, emotional, spiritual, and physical turmoil for generations (Brave Heart, 2001a). First Nations Peoples have their own assessment and intervention strategies through traditional ceremonies and cultural practices. However, generations of spiritual and sociopolitical oppression have resulted in the erosion, to varying degrees, of traditional healing practices. The current situation is that some Native clients do practice traditionally, but others may be conflicted about or ignorant of Native rituals.

As appropriate, facilitating client involvement in traditional interventions imparts a sense of mastery of the trauma and offers emotional containment (Brave Heart, 1998; Silver & Wilson, 1988). PTSD, alcohol and drug abuse, and mental health treatment programs also have contacts with spiritual leaders who provide purification ceremonies for Native clients (see Duran & Yellow Horse-Davis, 1997).

Gender issues need to be noted in the beginning phase. Cross-gender relationships may present difficulty for some traditionally oriented clients and clients who have been sexually abused or battered by the opposite sex. Trust issues and cultural mores surrounding interactions across genders must be considered. In rural settings, a clinical social worker might be the only available mental health professional in a geographically broad area. Therefore, the clinical social worker will have to develop particularly sensitive and competent behaviors to engage a client who otherwise might maintain a great deal of social distance.

Nonverbal cues and other forms of indirect communication are also important in assessment. A client may "hint" at an issue, indicating that he needs assistance in clarifying and presenting a topic that may be uncomfortable, such as sexuality. In some tribes, certain topics are not discussed with strangers, in mixed company, or at all. Likewise, young females do not have physical contact with male relatives after a certain age, or do not keep company with the opposite sex without supervision. In many Native groups, tribal mores prescribe sexual and age-appropriate relationships; for instance, men do not talk directly with daughters-in-law, and women do not talk directly with sons-in-law, and they often avoid being in the same room or alone with each other. These codes of conduct prevent people from becoming too familiar with, or meddling in adult children's marriages or problems. Sensitivity to these types of regulations requires attention and respect in the therapeutic milieu and in planning any family sessions. Making decisions toward "one's best interest" may conflict with family and group interest therefore presenting obstacles to developing and attaining therapeutic goals and progress, or may be perceived by the client as selfish or going against cultural values, thus creating therapeutic dilemmas. Likewise, other family members' support may be crucial to the client's continued treatment and should be considered in the assessment phase as well.

Reframing the Problem Orientation

A genogram is useful as an assessment tool and is helpful in working with Native families for a number of reasons; it opens dialogue by examining a family history instead of focusing on the individual, the process permits the client to approach the problem from a broad perspective that provides some distance from the issue and allows the client to tell her story, which can empower her as being an active and knowledgeable participant in the process. Most Natives are visual learners, so diagramming the family history helps the client visualize the historical legacy and provides cognition of the affect and role of the family environment on her current situation. A further benefit is that the development and examination of a family genogram gives the client some distance from and allows gradual review of what can sometimes be overwhelming loss, pain, and dysfunction across generations.

INTERVENTION SKILLS WITH FIRST NATIONS CLIENTS

As a traumatized population, First Nations clients may be appropriate for trauma intervention approaches. Following assessment of HTR, an intervention plan can be designed that may include techniques for working with PTSD (van der Kolk, McFarlane, & Weisaeth, 1996) or group historical trauma interventions (Brave Heart, 1998, 1999a, b, 2001a, b). Social worker flexibil-

CASE | # Case Study Integration Exercise on Contact, Problem Identification, and Assessment Skills

Case Vignette

Tanya is a 16-year-old Native American female who lives with her maternal grand-mother, Mary. Tanya and Mary live in a small town bordering the reservation, where Tanya attends high school as a sophomore. Tanya's birth mother lives in a nearby town on the reservation. She is remarried and has three younger children. Tanya visits her mother occasionally and sometimes stays over on weekends. Tanya's birth father is in a relationship and has one other child with this woman. Tanya knows who her father is but doesn't have a relationship with him or his extended family.

Recently, Tanya's grades have fallen, she has skipped classes, and missed numerous days of school. Tanya was evasive with her grandmother when asked about her absences. It was reported that Tanya was seen out late at night in a nearby town, and other information suggests that Tanya may be using alcohol and drugs.

Mary is concerned but evasive about Tanya's absences or skipping classes. Mary states that Tanya is a good and wholesome girl, helpful to Mary, whom Mary relies on for emotional support, and they are equal partners in decision making. Mary does not believe Tanya is drinking or using drugs and became angry that people would spread such lies. (Mary has expressed concern that Tanya could be removed from her care if social services learns of the recent developments).

Mary presents as a 52-year-old female, and her dress is conservative; she is a single grandmother, parenting her 16-year-old granddaughter. Mary's speech is soft spoken, and she tends to mumble. Mary is slightly overweight and her dress and mannerisms give her the appearance of being older than she actually is. Mary is cor-

---

ity is essential, allowing for narratives and client's use of stories and metaphors. Embedded in this flexibility is the need to incorporate theories and approaches that may seem incongruent to a clinical social worker from the dominant culture.

Among First Nations cultures, our approach to life in general is fluid and holistic. For example, we do not see spirituality as separate from physical, mental, and emotional health; all are interrelated in the cycle of life. In theoretical orientation, we incorporate a variety of frameworks and approaches to assist our clients. Although there appears to be a theoretical division between psychodynamic and empowerment or strengths-based theories, there is room for both in working with First Nations clients. It is well known that client outcomes and satisfaction have demonstrated that above all, the therapeutic relationship determines a successful experience between client and therapist. Rather than declaring one theoretical stance over another, we take the position that it is advantageous to have access to a sound and comprehensive assortment of therapeutic tools to apply with clients according to their needs, backgrounds, and situations. Not all tribes or individuals with the tribe have the same problems, education, or preferences—they may be as variable as in dial although she does not offer information unless it is impersonal, such as the weather or events that happen in the community. Mary avoids direct eye contact, as is in keeping with cultural show of respect. Mary is fluent in her Native tongue, but doesn't have the opportunity to converse in it except on occasions when she attends gatherings in reservation communities.

Mary changed her first name to the more religious sounding name of Mary at the time of her conversion and changed her legal name of Red Deer to a nondescript, anglicized name as well. Mary said it made her feel like she made a definite change from her old life style and gave her a fresh start. Recently, Tanya changed her first name from her given name that she perceived as a "stale" name.

While discussing family history for the genogram, Mary was matter-of-fact and forthcoming with information (see Figure 2.1). As the discussion progressed, Mary became somewhat pensive and quiet. As the discussion passed from Mary's current lifespan, to the previous generation, she became teary remembering her parents and other lost loved ones. Eventually Mary discussed the extensive alcohol usage in her family, how it affected relationships and her own usage and eventual recovery. Mary now gains strength from church and attends weekly Bible readings. Mary participates in Native social events such as naming ceremonies, dances, and feasts but does not participate in traditional spirituality, stating that she now believes in Christianity and that traditional spirituality is a thing of the past.

Application Exercise

1. What were the strengths of the individuals? Look at Mary's strengths for overcoming the cycle and trying to break the patterns of alcoholism and early death.
2. Focus more on strengths—what has Mary learned and done differently, and what can she pass on to Tanya?

any larger society. Further, we contend that emphasizing traditional First Nations cultures is congruent with both empowerment and strengths-based perspectives (see Brave Heart, 2001a). Indigenous concepts of power are delineated within the ecological framework of intimate relationships with the spirits, and all creation and all life dimensions are incorporated in empowering a First Nations person to function as an integral part of creation. A Native view of gaining or developing power, one definition of empowerment (Cox & Parsons, 1994), is through securing help from the spiritual and natural world for a higher purpose, to benefit one's community (Brave Heart, 2001a). A First Nations person's sense of self is defined by his or her relationship with the community, the natural world, and all creation. Traditionally, First Nations people invoked supernatural help to influence the natural world and life events, just as empowerment practice facilitates client influence on institutions affecting one's life (see Brave Heart, 2001a; Cox & Parsons, 1994). The prohibition of Native spiritual practices and the genocide altered the capacity of First Nations people to affect life and the government-regulated environment. A return to traditional empowerment promotes restoration of a positive sense of self and a healthy sphere of influence. Fostering collective goals, a tenet of

Figure 2.1 | Mary's Genogram

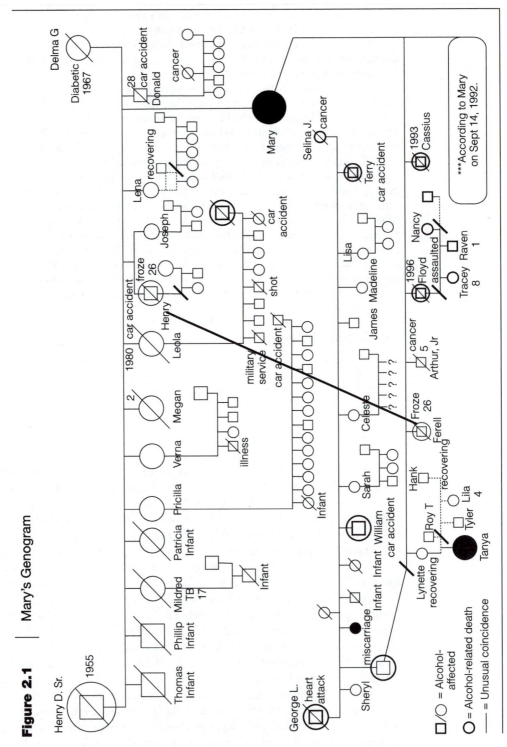

Based on genogram by Nallie Hall.

empowerment practice, is congruent with the inherent cultural collectivity of First Nations cultures.

Individual empowerment practice focuses on (1) egalitarian relationships with clients, (2) seeing the client as an expert in her or his culture as well as valuing that culture, and (3) consciousness-raising and engaging the client in an examination of external sociopolitical forces that impinge on her or his life circumstances while attending to intrapsychic or emotional issues (Cox & Parsons, 1994, as cited in Brave Heart, 2001a). Psychodynamic theory emphasizes the focus on intrapsychic or emotional issues. Much of the trauma literature, particularly related to massive group trauma such as that experienced by Jewish Holocaust survivors and descendants, is psychodynamically oriented. The Holocaust literature is some of the most relevant and meaningful literature for conceptualizing the effects of First Nations' intergenerational trauma as well as interventions to facilitate healing. One can incorporate an empowerment perspective into stages of individual psychodynamically informed clinical practice, including the beginning phase, transference and countertransference, the development of a therapeutic alliance and working through, and termination. Further, the nature of many First Nations clients' traditional manner of interacting lends itself well to some psychodynamic approaches and understanding, such as comfort with silence and nondirective styles of communication as well as the value of non-interference (Brave Heart, 2001a, b). For example, many First Nations clients find the directive style of some providers as intrusive and even rude; many clients prefer to take their time in sharing the intimate details of their lives. The psychodynamic manner of following the client's lead is often more comfortable for many Natives as is the psychodynamically oriented clinical stance of comfort with silences and the importance placed on symbolism in dreams. Psychodynamically oriented clinicians are trained to be comfortable with the use of metaphors and disguised or indirect communication and emphasize the importance of narratives, akin to storytelling in many First Nations cultures. In the beginning phase, questions about generational and current lifespan history of boarding-school attendance as well as communal trauma should be explored and can facilitate consciousness-raising about external historical and political factors, a focus of empowerment practice (Brave Heart, 2001a; Cox & Parsons, 1994).

In clinical interventions, the intensity of the social worker listening to a client's life story and deep feelings calls forth earlier significant relationships, particularly parental figures. Transference develops, which is the displacement and re-enactment of emotional issues, fantasies, and conflicts with early parental figures (Greenson, 1967; Hepworth & Larson, 1993). The social worker's feelings and reactions in response to the transference is the countertransference (Freud, 1910; Greenson, 1967; Hepworth & Larson, 1993). There is a misunderstanding about transference among many social workers; in contrast with the stereotypic view that dependency is deliberately fostered through transference, the phenomenon results from the experience and process of sharing one's life story with another who demands no personal relationship from you. This mirrors the archetype, in essence, of the ideal early childhood experience of unconditional love from a parent. Inherently, then, the clinical relationship holds a great deal of significance for the client, and the transference must be worked through (Brave Heart, 2001a). Transference can still take place in the empowerment-oriented practice of fostering an egalitarian relationship with the client because it is based on emotional significance rather than on power differences.

Managing both transference and countertransference can be challenging but important skills. Culture and historical experiences influence the character and quality of the transference and countertransference (Brave Heart, 2001b). European American social workers must acknowledge their relationship to the colonizers of this land who perpetrated genocide against First Nations Peoples; initially, feelings of guilt, resentment, victim blaming, and rationalization must be worked through so that it does not interfere with practice. This "collective historical countertransference" will compound any individual idiosyncratic countertransference that normally occurs in therapy. Further, the social worker must work with Native "collective negative transference" toward European American workers. Social workers can appropriately manage this by validating the feelings of the client.

More clinical intimacy develops after rapport is established with a client, and Native clients often begin to see the social worker as a trusted individual, despite race. This will be manifested in a decrease in indirect communication and an increase in openness, candor, humor, and warmth usually reserved for close friends and relatives (Brave Heart, 2001b). Emotionally charged memories are now shared; the social worker must maintain a balance between the discharge of powerful affects (emotions) and containment so that the client does not feel overwhelmed and leaves therapy. Timing, ending sessions with a debriefing time where the social worker communicates hope and reassurance, fosters client confidence in his or her ability to tolerate the emotions that emerge.

Transference does not foster dependency and still occurs in a therapeutic, egalitarian relationship fostered by an empowerment-oriented clinician, as it is based on early emotionally significant relationships in the client's life rather than power differences (Brave Heart, 2001b). Transference is complex and can involve the unconsciously induced feelings that early parental figures had toward the client, feelings the client has about the self, or the feelings that the client needs to induce in the social worker before emotional growth can occur. Transference can be positive or negative, depending on the unmet emotional needs of the client. One type of positive transference is the idealizing transference. Positive transference is compounded by identification with the aggressor or internalized oppression (Brave Heart, 2001a). What may appear as an idealizing transference of a European American or European American–oriented Native clinician might actually be identification with the aggressor or internalized oppression that should be handled differently, so that the client might begin to externalize the self-hatred that often results from oppression. Discernment of this internalized oppression versus an idealizing transference can occur if the social worker attends to any subtle self-deprecating or disparaging comments made by the client, particularly in reference to cultural themes, skin color, language, and traditions (Brave Heart, 2001a, b).

Persistent, culturally congruent, and sensitive intervention by the social worker can facilitate management of the transference and countertransference. After the therapeutic relationship is established, Native clients will become more candid, often humorous, warm, and may extend certain privileges normally reserved for close friends and relatives, even to a non-Native social worker (Brave Heart, 2001b). The social worker may be invited to Native social functions and even to ceremonies. Classically trained psychodynamically oriented social workers, taught to limit contact outside of the formal therapy session, must modify their stances to maintain culturally congruent therapeutic relationships. Accepting such invitations actually facilitates a greater therapeutic alliance with Native clients and in Native communities, particularly rural and reservation areas; too much formality and rigid boundaries are not feasible or desirable (Brave Heart, 2001b). The clinical social worker can attend powwows, community dinners, and even ceremonies if invited but can maintain professionalism by limiting personal disclosure of information and taking cues from the client about how open to be regarding their relationship. In small communities, everyone knows many details about the client and may already know who is in treatment with whom. However, it is not up to the social worker to disclose such information; despite more fluidity and less formality, the social worker must still maintain confidentiality. In response to an invitation to attend a traditional Native ceremony, the clinical social worker's own spiritual beliefs may prohibit attendance; this must be delicately communicated to the client. However, the social worker must understand that refusing to attend might cause irreparable damage to the therapeutic relationship. Being invited to a ceremony, which is often restricted to only Native Peoples, is one of the highest signs of honor and respect that a Native client can show another person. Social workers should support Native client participation in ceremonies, which provide safe, affective containers for the release of powerful emotions emerging during therapy (Brave Heart 2001a, b; Silver & Wilson, 1988).

If the social worker agrees to participate in a purification ceremony, professional neutrality can still be maintained. The social worker can pray for the client and other participants but reserve personal prayers for one's own spiritual functions (Brave Heart, 2001b). Native clinicians may be more comfortable with fluid boundaries, and Native clients may actually expect the Native social worker to actively participate in a ceremony; however, the Native social worker should still be cautions about inadvertently disclosing too much personal information through verbalized prayers.

As the therapeutic alliance develops, the client will begin to manifest an observing ego, which is the capacity to observe one's behavior with some objectivity and is akin to insight (Brave Heart, 2001b). Evidence of an observing ego includes the client's relating his behavior to the content of the sessions and referencing material from previous sessions. Once sufficient trust is established, Native clients are usually quite adept at using an observing ego, often using humor in their self-observations as well as narratives. During the working-through phase of the clinical social work intervention, content emerges, including dreams, and resistance emerges. Dreams provide further evidence of the therapeutic alliance, the transference, the observing ego, and the working through of repression as more material becomes conscious. Clients often report dreams that include the social worker and the session content. Some Natives are reticent about sharing dreams with the social worker because they may feel that describing the dream could lessen its spiritual power. However, others may share dreams even before they disclose the dream in a ceremony. Some Natives see all dreams as spiritual, but others see most dreams as psychological. The social worker must become comfortable with these diverse views and adjust her or his approach accordingly, that is, using non-intrusive exploration of dream content and respect. The social worker must simultaneously provide a climate of open acceptance for a client's sharing of dreams as well as space for a client to maintain privacy.

Dream content often includes cultural manifestations that may be misinterpreted by classically trained psychodynamic social workers. It is an error to assume that dreams of bodily flying represent grandiose fantasies suggesting a core narcissistic disorder (Brave Heart, 2001b). Instead, the social worker needs to recognize that such dreams are often spiritually significant and may not indicate psychopathology.

A major component of the clinical social work intervention is the cathartic release of affect and the lifting of repressions where emotionally charged memories and unresolved conflicts become conscious; this aspect of treatment can be uncomfortable for social workers and frightening for clients (Brave Heart, 2001b). The clinical sessions must provide emotional containment while providing a vehicle for the release of powerful emotions; the client must feel safe and competent to handle their affect. The social worker must attend to timing so that the client's ego is strong enough to handle the process and avoid letting the client feeling overwhelmed, which leads to them leaving treatment. Ending each session with some debriefing time is helpful, in which the social worker imparts hope and confidence that the client can handle the emotions that emerge (Brave Heart, 2001b).

During the working-through phase of treatment, acting out might occur, and sometimes depressed clients become greater suicidal risks. In addition to suicide prevention, efforts such as assessing lethality and reinforcing abstinence from drugs and alcohol are helpful because Native suicide is often substance-abuse related (Brave Heart, 2001b). Traditional Native culture fosters the norm for a clean and sober lifestyle. Not only should the social worker support the Native client's involvement in traditional culture, but he or she should assist the client in identifying social support networks and resources to strengthen abstinence.

Resistance is an inevitable part of treatment and social workers need to develop comfort with its presence. Resistance is motivated by the client's natural human inclination to avoid emotional pain. Traditional ceremonies often provide safe, affective containment for clients as well as facilitating cathartic release of emotions (Brave Heart, 2001b; Brave Heart-Jordan, 1995; Silver & Wilson, 1988). Social workers can promote the availability of ceremonies for

Native clients through contacts with Native cultural experts in the community. The clinical social worker may need to assist some clients in locating resources and making arrangements for a ceremony where family support is missing.

TERMINATION SKILLS WITH FIRST NATIONS CLIENTS

For many First Nations, the degree of interpersonal attachments is very strong; termination may magnify earlier loss issues to a greater degree than in the general client population, and suicidal behavior is often association with interpersonal loss (Brave Heart, 2001b). The clinical social worker must ensure that the client is connected to ongoing support networks and attend to suicidal risk factors. Referrals to support groups can be helpful. Group historical trauma interventions can also be helpful to Native clients, both during the intervention phase and the termination phase.

Historical Trauma Interventions

Historical trauma interventions focus on ameliorating the HTR through a brief intensive psycho-educational group experience (Brave Heart, 1998, 1999a, 2001b). Intervention goals include imparting a sense of mastery and control (van der Kolk, McFarlane, & Weisaeth, 1996) within a safe traditional context. Historically traumatic memories are stimulated; opportunities for cognitive integration are also provided, as are small and large group processing. Traditional Native culture and ceremonies are integrated throughout the intervention, which have been noted to have a curative effect on PTSD (Brave Heart, 1998; Silver & Wilson, 1988). Further, the inclusion of traditional Native spirituality and culture enhance protective factors against the development or exacerbation of PTSD (Brave Heart, 2001b). Increasing affect tolerance from mastery of trauma also serves as a protective factor against depression and other psychiatric disorders. The process of sharing trauma and grief affects within a traditional context provides cathartic relief.

Evaluation reveals that historical trauma interventions result in at least short-term amelioration of HTR features. The Takini (Survivor) Network, a collective of Lakota traditional spiritual leaders and service providers, is conducting further development of and researching the efficacy of historical trauma interventions in several First Nations communities. Research to date reveals that there is a reduction of trauma and grief affects over time, during and after the intervention, as well as significant changes in concepts such as more positive self-representation and group identification (Brave Heart, 1998; Brave Heart-Jordan, 1995). Historical trauma intervention participants affirm the utility of historical trauma response theory in facilitating a healing process. Historical trauma interventions have been incorporated in a parenting curriculum among the Lakota (Brave Heart, 1999a). Although more research is warranted, preliminary findings suggest that historical trauma interventions are experienced as helpful in the healing process and result in at least short-term amelioration of trauma response features.

Case Study Integration Exercise on Intervention and Termination Skills

The family genogram is a classic demonstration of conceptualization of historical trauma, and of cumulative trauma across generations. This family genogram reveals extensive grief and loss across generations. It also exhibits patterns of dysfunctions: alcoholism, tragedy, early death, and family disruption.

At once, one can identify profound loss in Mary's family of origin and in the extended family that include loss of lives and widespread alcoholism across generations. Of particular note are the repetitions: infant mortality, death by freezing, alcohol-related accidents and deaths, alcoholism, automobile accidents, cancer, cardiovascular disease, and diabetes. Also notable is that these illnesses and behaviors can be attributed to the characteristics of historical trauma response (Brave Heart, 1998, 1999a).

The case study provides an illustration of strategies that employ culturally competent assessment and treatment tools in working with a Native client. The use of genograms for assessment and engagement has been proven effective in addressing and sorting out individual and cross-generational behavior and experiences. The case demonstrated client confusion about problem identification, intergenerational and historical trauma effects on the individual, and family mental health. The case discussion addresses the therapeutic relationship, engagement, and empowerment in a culturally congruent manner. It is important to first acknowledge cultural differences between the client and therapist as well as to explain that the therapist will have to ask if she or he does not understand a culturally specific topic or reference. The therapist should use cultural consultants when appropriate, such as other therapists of color, preferably Native, or those who have knowledge and experience working with Native clients. In this case, the client is female with senior status in age and even a younger Native therapist would need to be aware of the communication and roles of this generation, as well as working with the opposite sex. Engagement would take longer because the client would need time to determine the competence of the worker before a therapeutic relationship, safety, and trust could be established. In all cases, the therapist must take time to get acquainted with the community/culture of the client as much as possible, perhaps by reading, participating in community events, or accessing cultural contents.

Application Exercise

The case of Mary exemplifies many of the clinical issues surrounding intervention and follow-up addressed to this point and is typical of circumstances often presented in helping situations in First Nations Peoples families and communities. Specifically, presenting problems involve reluctant clients, trauma and loss, extended family involvement, intergenerational issues, and an overtaxed support system. This case addresses assessment and treatment concerns from an individual and family perspective, as well as use of available resources within a cultural context.

If you were working with Mary, how would you help her reconnect to her community so that she can experience a sense of belonging and purpose? Discuss which of the following suggestions you think would help Mary reconnect to her community.

1. Have Mary participate in elders' organization.
2. Have Mary teach language and culture to youth.
3. Encourage Mary to expand the grandmother role with other grandchildren.

CLOSING THOUGHTS

Social work practice with First Nations Peoples must consider the traumatic history of genocide, racism, and oppression as well as diverse cultural traits. The history of Native Peoples has not been sufficiently recognized or acknowledged by the general population of the United States or the social work field. The collective representation of Native Peoples within the dominant cultural paradigm has erroneously been that of a homogenous group of people and is replete with negative stereotypes. The general population also lacks cognizance of and sensitivity to Native genocide. For effective social work intervention, the social worker must acknowledge massive group Native trauma and recognize the inherent rights of First Nations as the indigenous inhabitants of this land.

Validation of Native trauma, providing opportunities for testimony through narratives, and respect for First Nations cultures are all critical aspects of effective social work practice. Social workers can develop culturally sensitive and culturally congruent interventions with Natives. Incorporating an understanding of historical trauma theory and awareness of the promising effectiveness of historical trauma interventions, developed by the Takini Network, will empower social workers to facilitate healing within Native communities. Using key First Nations cultural informants is crucial. Social workers can also facilitate, through appropriate First Nations community contacts, the inclusion of spiritual and cultural resources when intervening with Natives.

An emphasis on traditional First Nations cultures is congruent with social work strengths and empowerment perspectives. Social workers must become sufficiently familiar with traditional cultural contexts for Natives, including indigenous values, normative behavior, and diverse styles of communication. Historical trauma responses must be assessed before the social worker can plan effective intervention strategies with First Nations Peoples. Cultural diversity among Native clients must be recognized while acknowledging the existence of some universal values and experiences. Varying degrees of assimilation to the dominant culture must also be addressed in interventions. Clinical cultural formulation and assessment are also germane to effective intervention. The social worker must have flexibility and the capacity to adapt her or his own behavior to achieve cultural congruence with First Nations clients

Special issues for Native social workers have been addressed in this chapter. Social distance between Native social workers and Native clients must be considered, particularly issues regarding skin-color differences, degree of assimilation, language fluency, and degree of traditional spiritual and cultural involvement. Further, intertribal issues must be included in assessment and interventions. Internalized oppression can be a difficult issue for both Native social worker and Native client and may impede effective social work practice.

Culturally congruent assessment and interventions with Native clients may be protracted. The historical legacy of genocide must be included in the development of social work practice strategies. Social workers must advocate for Native clients within the broader service system to ensure that time is provided for culturally congruent assessment and intervention of First Nations Peoples.

References

American Psychiatric Association. (1994). *Diagnostic and statistical manual of mental disorders* (4th ed.). Washington, DC: Author.

Attneave, C. (1982). American Indians and Alaska Native families: Emigrants in their own homeland. In M. McGoldrick, J. Pearce, & J. Giordano (Eds.), *Ethnicity and family therapy*. New York, Guilford Press.

Berkhofer, R. F., Jr. (1979, originally published 1978). *The White man's Indian: Images of the American Indian from Columbus to the present*. New York: Vintage, Random House.

Bowers, A. (1992, first published 1963). *Hidatsa social & ceremonial organization*. Lincoln: University of Nebraska Press.

Brave Heart, M. Y. H. (1998). The return to the sacred path: Healing the historical trauma and historical unresolved grief response among the Lakota. *Smith College Studies in Social Work, 68*(3), 287–305.

Brave Heart, M. Y. H. (1999a). *Oyate Ptayela*: Rebuilding the Lakota Nation through addressing historical trauma among Lakota parents. *Journal of Human Behavior in the Social Environment, 2*(1/2), 109–126; and in H. N. Weaver (Ed.), Voices of First Nations People: Human services considerations (pp. 109–126). New York: Haworth Press.

Brave Heart, M. Y. H. (1999b) Gender differences in the historical trauma response among the Lakota. *Journal of Health and Social Policy, 10*(4), 1–21.

Brave Heart, M. Y. H. (2001a) Clinical assessment with American Indians. In R. Fong & S. Furuto (Eds.), *Cultural competent social work practice: Practice skills, interventions, and evaluation* (pp. 163–177). Boston: Allyn & Bacon.

Brave Heart, M. Y. H. (2001b) Clinical interventions with American Indians. In R. Fong & S. Furuto (Eds.). *Cultural competent social work practice: Practice skills, interventions, and evaluation* (pp. 285–298). Boston: Allyn & Bacon.

Brave Heart, M. Y. H., & DeBruyn, L. M. (1998). The American Indian Holocaust: Healing historical unresolved grief. *American Indian and Alaska Native Mental Health Research, 8*(2), 56–78.

Brave Heart, M. Y. H., & DeBruyn, L. M. (in press). The historical trauma response among Natives: The Lakota example. In M. Y. H. Brave Heart, B. Segal, L. M. DeBruyn, J. Taylor, & R. Daw, (Eds.), *Historical trauma within the American experience: Roots, effects, and healing*.

Brave Heart-Jordan, M. Y. H. (1995). *The return to the sacred path: Healing from historical trauma and historical unresolved grief among the Lakota*. (Doctoral dissertation, Smith College School for Social Work, 1995). (Copyright by Author: reprints available through the Takini Network, P.O. Box 4138, Rapid City, SD 57709–4138)

Brave Heart-Jordan, M., & DeBruyn, L. M. (1995). So she may walk in balance: Integrating the impact of historical trauma in the treatment of Native American Indian women. In J. Adleman & G. Enguidanos (Eds.), *Racism in the lives of women: Testimony, theory, and guides to anti-racist practice* (pp. 345–368). New York: Haworth Press.

Cox, E. O., & Parsons, R. J. (1994). *Empowerment-oriented social work practice with the elderly*. Belmont, CA: Brooks/Cole.

Cross, T. (1986). Drawing on cultural tradition in Indian child welfare practice. *Social Casework, 67*(5), 283–289.

Danieli, Y. (Ed.). (1998). *International handbook of multigenerational legacies of trauma*. Plenum Press.

DeNavas-Walt, C., Cleveland, R. W., & Roemer, M. I. (2001, September) *Money income in the United States: 2000.*

Washington, DC: U.S. Census Bureau, Department of Commerce.

Duran, E., & Yellow Horse-Davis, S. (1997). Final research evaluation report: Evaluation of Family and Child Guidance Clinic Hybrid Treatment Model. Report to Indian Health Service.

Freud, S. (1910). The future prospects of psychoanalytic therapy. In *The standard edition of the complete works of Sigmand Freud, 11,* J. Strachey, Ed., (pp. 141–151). London: Hogarth Press.

Greenson, R. R. (1967). *The technique and practice of psychoanalysis.* New York: International Universities Press.

Hepworth, D. H., & Larson, J. A. (1993). *Direct social work practice: Theory and skills* (4th ed.). Pacific Grove, CA: Brooks/Cole.

Horejsi, C., Heavy-Runner Craig, B., & Pablo, J. (1992). Reactions by Native American parents to child protection agencies: Cultural and community factors. *Child Welfare, 71*(4), 329–342.

Indian Health Service. (2000–2001). *Regional differences in Indian health.* Washington, DC: U.S. Department of Health & Human Services.

Kestenberg, J. S. (1990, originally published in 1982). Survivor parents and their children. In M. S. Bergmann & M. E. Jucovy (Eds.), *Generations of the Holocaust* (pp. 83–102). New York: Columbia University Press.

Kills Straight, B., and Brave Heart, M. Y. H. (unpublished document) The *Woope Sakowin:* Seven laws of the Lakota. In M. Y. H. Brave Heart, J. Chase, B. Kills Straight, B. Sierra & J. James, *Tiwahe Asni Wicayapi (Healing the Family) Intervention Model.* Rapid City, SD: Takini Network.

Lakota Times (1990, December). Wounded Knee remembered. *Lakota Times (Special Edition).*

Legters, L. H. (1988). The American genocide. *Policy Studies Journal, 16*(4), 768–777.

Noriega, J. (1992). American Indian education in the United States: Indoctrination for subordination to colonialism. In M. A. Jaimes (Ed.), *The state of Native America: Genocide, colonization, and resistance* (pp. 371–402). Boston: South End Press.

Oetting, E. R., & Beauvais, F. (1989). Epidemiology and correlates of alcohol use among Indian adolescents living on reservations. In *Alcohol use among U.S. ethnic minorities,* NIAAA research monograph no. 18, Rockville, MD: U.S. Public Health Service.

Proctor, B. D., & Dalaker, J. (2002). *Poverty in the United States: 2001.* Washington, DC: U.S. Census Bureau.

Silver, S. M., & Wilson, J. P. (1988). Native American healing and purification rituals for war stress. In J. P. Wilson, Z. Harele, & B. Hahana (Eds.), *Human adaptation to extreme stress: From the Holocaust to Viet Nam* (pp. 337–355). New York: Plenum Press.

South Dakota State Department of Education and Cultural Affairs Office of Technical Assistance. (1999). *South Dakota's 1999 homeless report: Homeless not hopeless,* Pierre, SD.

South Dakota State Department of Education and Cultural Affairs Office of Technical Assistance, South Dakota Homeless Consortium. (2002). *Gaps analysis booklet,* Pierre, SD.

Stannard, D. (1992). *American Holocaust: Columbus and the conquest of the new world.* New York: Oxford University Press.

Stiffarm, L. A., & Lane, P., Jr. (1992). The demography of Native North America: A question of American Indian Survival. In M. A. Jaimes (Ed.), *The state of Native America: Genocide, colonization, and resistance.* Boston: South End Press.

Tanner, H. (1982). *A history of all the dealings of the United States government with the Sioux.* Unpublished manuscript. Prepared for the Black Hills Land Claim by order of the United States Supreme Court, on file at the D'Arcy McNickle Center for the History of the American Indian, Newberry Library, Chicago.

Tjaden, P., & Thoennes, N. (2000, July). *Extent, nature, and consequences of intimate partner violence, Findings from the National Violence Against Women Survey.* Washington DC: U.S. Department of Justice & Centers for Disease Control And Prevention.

Thornton, R. (1987). *American Indian Holocaust and survival: A population history since 1492.* Norman: University of Oklahoma Press.

Topper, M. D. (1992). Multidimensional therapy: A case study of a Navajo adolescent with multiple problems. In L. A. Vargus & J. D. Koss-Chioino (Eds.), *Working with culture: Psychotherapeutic interventions with ethnic minority children and adolescents* (pp. 225–244). San Francisco: Jossey-Bass.

van der Kolk, B. A., McFarlane, A. C., & Weisaeth, L. (Eds.). (1996). *Traumatic stress: The effects of overwhelming experience on mind, body, and society.* New York: Guilford Press.

Wilson, G. (1981, first published 1927). *Wahanee: An Indian girl's story.* Lincoln: University of Nebraska Press.

2001 South Dakota Vital Statistics Report: A State and County comparison of Leading Health Indicators. (2003, January). Data, Statistics and Vital Records South Dakota Department of Health, Pierre, SD.

Social Work Practice with African Americans

CHAPTER 3

Teresa C. Jones

African Americans represent an extremely diverse segment of the population with a unique place in the history of our country. During the hundreds of years that blacks have lived in this country, social and political forces have exerted tremendous influences on African American individuals, families, and communities. Contemporary life in African American communities has dramatically changed since slavery, but cultural vestiges of African traditions remain, as have particular cultural hallmarks that developed as survival mechanisms during slavery. This chapter presents, in the context of these historical and cultural realities, a description of the social work practice skills that are necessary to work effectively with African American individuals and families.

THE DEMOGRAPHICS OF AFRICAN AMERICANS

Current demographics from the U.S. Census Bureau (2003) suggest that even though some segments of the African American community are experiencing social and economic gains, significant numbers of African American individuals and families continue to struggle to meet their basic needs and to benefit from this country's prosperity.

Census 2000 was the first one in which individuals were able to choose more than one category to describe their racial identities. African Americans now number 36.4 million or 12.9% of the total U.S. population. This number includes those who reported their race as African American alone or in com-

59

bination with one or more other races. Once the largest group of people of color in the country, African Americans now rank second to the total Hispanic/Latino population, which now numbers 38.8 million (2004), a growth of 3.5 million since the 2000 Census. There are 8.4 million African American families with 11.8 million children under age 18. Among these children, 41% live in a home maintained by their mother, 34% in a home maintained by both parents, and 13% in a grandmother's home.

The majority of African Americans (55%) live in the south compared with 18% each in the Northeast and Midwest and 9% in the West. Within these major geographical regions, African Americans are more than twice as likely as whites to live in a central city within a metropolitan area (U.S. Census Bureau, 2003).

At $29, 470, the current annual median income for African Americans is just under the all-time high of $30,495 reached in 2000. By comparison, the national median income is $44,366. Thirty-three percent of all black families have annual incomes of $50,000 or more with married-couple families more likely to be in this income category. The number of African Americans who are poor stands at 8.1 million, a poverty rate of 22.7%. Fifty-seven percent of African American children are considered low income, down 3% from 2000, but the poverty rate is 30%, nearly twice the national rate for children under 18 (National Center for Children in Poverty, 2003).

High rates of unemployment continue to plague African American communities disproportionately. Despite a national unemployment rate of approximately 6%, the rate is 11.5% among African Americans. For black teenagers (age 16–19), the rate is 33.1%, compared with the national rate of 16.1% (National Jobs for All Coalition, 2002). Eighteen percent of black men and 26% of black women were employed in managerial and professional specialty occupations. Black men and women were more likely than whites to work in service occupations or as operators, fabricators, and laborers (U.S. Census Bureau, 2003).

There has been a steady rise in the percentage of African Americans age 25 and older who have at least a high school diploma from 51% in 1980 to 63% in 1990, and 72% in 2000. Fourteen percent of those age 25 and older have a bachelor's degree or higher, a statistic that could be negatively affected by the continued dismantling of college and university affirmative action programs. More black women (18%) than black men (16%) have earned at least a bachelor's degree (U.S. Census Bureau, 2003).

The median age for the African American population is 29.5, considerably younger than the median age of 35.3 for the total U.S. population. In 2002, 33% of all African Americans were younger than 18, compared with 23% of whites (U.S. Census Bureau, 2003). Only 8% of African Americans were 65 and older, compared with 14% of whites. Average life expectancy for black males and females is approximately 70 years, a figure that is six years less than the national average for all Americans. Although this is an increase over past years, disparities persist in access to adequate health care and to the incidence of disease between African Americans and others. Cardiovascular disease, strokes, and high blood pressure continue to be major health risks for blacks in this country at greater rates than for other racial and ethnic groups. Blacks are twice as likely as whites to die from diabetes and to die as infants (cbsnews.com, 2003).

These demographics present a mixed picture of hope and concern for the health, safety, and economic security of African Americans in our society. In many respects, the circumstances have improved over the years; however, the role of institutionalized systemic and structural inequities and discrimination and the persistence of the social problems that many blacks encounter cannot be discounted. The historical context helps explain both the existence of the inequities and the ways in which African Americans have demonstrated their abilities to survive and thrive in an atmosphere that has, more often than not, worked against their best interests.

THE HISTORICAL OPPRESSION AND SURVIVAL VALUES OF AFRICAN AMERICANS

An understanding of the structure and functioning of contemporary African American families cannot be accomplished without acknowledging and incorporating the historical context of black life in this country and its connection to African historical traditions. Although the history of blacks in North America dates as far back as the 1500s, the primary historical markers that have influenced present-day life for African Americans are slavery, emancipation, and the rural-to-urban migration of the early to mid-1900s.

The enslavement of an estimated 100 million Africans who were dispersed throughout South America, the Caribbean, and the plantations and cities of early America is characterized as one of history's largest and, for a time, most lucrative international business ventures. From the early 1500s through the mid-1800s, the forced removal of, primarily, West Africans from their homelands to America by Dutch, French, and English trading and shipping companies was viewed as the means by which cheap, captive labor could be used to build the fledgling agricultural economy of the southern states (Bennett, 1982; Franklin & Moss, 1988). Men, women, and children from many of the ancient tribes of West Africa were captured, packed in shackles in the holds of ships, and transported across the Atlantic. It is estimated that 10 to 15% of the Africans captured died during the Middle Passage, the long ocean journey from Africa to ports in the Caribbean and America. Deaths were caused by sickness, torture, and suicide.

Most of the slave ships destined for America landed at ports in Virginia and the Carolinas (Bennett, 1982). Here, African slaves were placed on auction blocks and sold to the highest bidder, thereby becoming slaves for life and the property of the bid-winning master. The slaves' status was that of chattel, property that could be sold at will and treated as the whims of the master dictated; slaves had no legal rights or protections. Although the vast majority of Africans were slaves on southern plantations, there were significant numbers of free blacks living in this country from the early 1500s when blacks who were born in Spain and Portugal accompanied Balboa, DeSoto, and other explorers to the New World. Many other blacks arrived here as indentured servants, bought their freedom, were born in free states, or escaped from enslavement. In the 1780s, of the estimated 757,000 blacks in America, 59,000 were free (Bennett, 1982). Despite the technical freedom these blacks had, they were still subject to the extreme oppression, marginalization, and violence toward nonwhites that was ingrained in American society by that time.

Ironically, as the right for freedom and separation from British colonial tyranny was being fought for and codified in this country, the lives of slaves were being legislated by the U.S. Constitution, the premiere law of the land, and other repressive policies. Article 1, Section 2 of the Constitution, which apportioned membership in the House of Representatives and determined levels of taxation based on a state's population, counted a slave as 3/5 of a person. Article 1, Section 9 forbade Congress from making slavery illegal until 1808. Escaped slaves were required to be returned to their owners by the provisions of Article 4, Section 2 (www.usconstitution.net). The Fugitive Slave Act of 1793 penalized any person who harbored or concealed an escaped slave. The Congressional debate in 1819 and 1820 about whether Missouri should enter the Union as a slave or a free state made it clear that the slavery issue would be a part of the political landscape for the foreseeable future (Bennett, 1982; Franklin & Moss, 1988).

With these and other policies creating legally sanctioned, life-long bondage for millions of slaves, an active abolitionist movement emerged in the early 1800s that attempted to achieve the immediate emancipation of all slaves and the ending of racial segregation and discrimination. During this time, many organizations, movements, and mutual aid groups were active in the abolitionist movement and in assisting and protecting blacks who were enslaved. Free blacks were a critical part of these movements. Slaves developed mutual aid and cooperative networks that were crucial to their survival. One of the most well known was the Underground Railroad, which flourished from 1830 to 1861 (Franklin & Moss, 1988). Martin and Martin (1985) write that these mutual aid networks were a manifestation of the helping tradition that was deeply rooted in traditional African society. Although aspects of African traditional life could not withstand the brutal impact of slavery, the helping tradition was such an integral part of tribal, communal life that it was impossible for it not to continue in the new environment of America.

By 1860, approximately 4.5 million blacks in the United States constituted 14% of the population (Bennett, 1982). The Emancipation Proclamation of 1863, the end of the Civil War, and the ratifying of the Thirteenth Amendment to the U.S. Constitution in 1865, which abolished slavery as a legal institution, brought fundamental changes to the lives of former slaves. Freedom that had been fought for was granted. The era of institutionalized enslavement that had lasted for nearly 250 years was over (Franklin & Moss, 1988). The country embarked on a period of rapid industrialization. However, the country remained bitterly divided and political disarray affected every state. The millions of newly freed slaves were in need, but debates raged over who would take responsibility for them. Despite their freed status, lobbying efforts by whites, especially in the South, called for distinctions to be made between the free blacks and whites and for laws to control this suddenly unshackled, large population of black men, women, and children. Black Codes were instituted in the 1860s as a means of ensuring that blacks continued to provide labor throughout the South. Although the specific laws varied from state to state, overall, the Codes included limitations on where blacks could purchase or rent property, penalties for vagrancy, prohibitions on blacks testifying in court, and fines and penalties for not working, violating curfew, making insulting gestures, and possessing firearms (Bennett, 1982; Franklin & Moss, 1988).

The oppressive denial of basic human rights for African Americans continued in the South and throughout the rest of the country culminating in successful campaigns for the disenfranchisement of blacks; the rise of the white supremacy movement and the Ku Klux Klan; periods of extreme violence against blacks in the form of lynchings, burning homes and neighborhoods, and murder; and the legalization of segregation through Jim Crow laws and the Supreme Court's *Plessy v. Ferguson* decision in 1896. From the 1880s to the 1960s, most states enforced segregation through Jim Crow laws. The most common laws forbade intermarriage and ordered businesses and public institutions to keep their black and white clientele separate (Franklin & Moss, 1988). The *Plessy v. Ferguson* decision upheld the legitimacy of Jim Crow laws by declaring that segregation was legal as long as the facilities provided were "separate but equal." The dismantling of institutionalized segregation did not begin until the landmark *Brown v. Board of Education* of Topeka, Kansas, Supreme Court decision in 1954 (Bennett, 1982; Franklin & Moss, 1988).

Reconstruction through the mid-1900s was also a time of advancement of civil rights, social justice, educational, and philanthropic organizations like the Freedman's Bureau, Atlanta University, the National Association for the Advancement of Colored People (NAACP), the National Association of Colored Women headed by Mary Church Terrell, and some labor unions that accepted African Americans as members. Despite the works of these and countless other organizations and the writings and advocacy of W. E. B. Du Bois and Booker T. Washington, the South, in particular, continued to view blacks as threats to the security of the region, thus justifying the need to control, remove, or eliminate them (Bennett, 1982; Franklin & Moss, 1988; Trotter, 1991).

Faced with the prospect of many more years of tyranny, oppression, and lack of opportunity, southern blacks, many of whom still lived in rural areas and on plantations as sharecroppers, started to move into southern cities and into the major industrial areas of the North, Midwest, and West. This Great

Migration occurred from approximately 1910 to 1950 and was responsible for more than tripling the African American populations of New York, Chicago, Detroit, Pittsburgh, Gary, Philadelphia, and the Richmond-Oakland area of California. It is estimated that as many as 5.5 million African Americans relocated in the hopes of fleeing the vestiges of slavery in the south and making new lives for themselves and their families in what were seen as more hospitable areas of the country (Bennett, 1982; Trotter, 1991).

Some historians (Bennett, 1982; Trotter, 1991) view the Great Migration as a revolt, a profound political statement by African Americans that continues to reverberate. This migration allowed African Americans to break away from the oppressive experiences of the South and forever changed the racial, political, economic, and social face of America. It led to the establishment of major African American centers of business and the arts and the renewal of the struggle for civil rights and political inclusion (Bennett, 1982; Trotter, 1991). Although the migration north presented new challenges for the families that came to the cities and for the local government and social service systems, it marked the beginning of new expectations by African Americans in this country and of the need for existing community and social service systems to consider the needs, culture, and ideas of blacks and their families when planning and offering services and programs.

The history of African Americans in this country has engendered a unique cultural framework that social workers need to be aware of to provide culturally competent services. To meet the needs of African American individuals, families, and communities, it is necessary to understand the value systems and norms of black communities and their importance in the lives of members of those communities. Those value systems and norms, which are based in the history of African American people in this country, are the foundation for many of the traditions, characteristics, and strengths that exist in African American culture today (Hill, 1997; Martin & Martin, 1985; McRoy, 1990). Although knowledge of the value systems and the cultural characteristics of African American individuals and families will not guarantee the success of a program or an intervention, when coupled with genuine sensitivity and cultural competence, it can set a positive foundation for meaningful interaction and mutually satisfying professional relationships. It is important, however, not to assume that all African American individuals, families, and communities will exhibit these cultural hallmarks in the same way. On the contrary, there is considerable diversity in African American life. With that diversity, however, are many cultural themes that have historically characterized the African American experience.

Though historical events and social and economic realities have contributed to the decline in the visibility of some of these cultural characteristics, some traditions that are still talked about, practiced, and valued within African American families and need to be acknowledged by professionals working within the community. The cultural traditions presented here are (1) the helping tradition, (2) extended families/elastic households, (3) race consciousness, (4) respect, and (5) spiritual life.

The Helping Tradition

Natural helping networks, which promoted the welfare of the community, were common in African traditional life and became an important and life-saving part of African American life during and after slavery (Hill, 1997; Logan, 2001; Martin & Martin, 1985; McRoy, 1990; Smith, 2001). From midwives to the Underground Railroad movement to the Freedmen's Bureaus to the NAACP, African Americans have valued the tradition of helping and providing mutual aid. Until the late 1920s, the primary responsibility for caring for African Americans rested with African American communities (Martin & Martin, 1985).

During the Depression, many African American organizations were stretched to their limits trying to respond to the needs of so many people. As the government responded to the economic crisis by instituting social welfare programs, more and more African Americans began looking to the federal government for survival. The community-based mutual aid network began to break down at this time. Urbanization and the migration of thousands of African Americans from the south during the late 1800s to the mid-1900s changed the focus of helping from rural to urban families. With the overwhelming needs of urban families, community-based helping organizations found that the problems were too massive for their resources. Again communities and individuals turned to the federal government for enactment of legislation and funding to solve the social problems of African American individuals and families (Martin & Martin, 1985).

Today, the problems facing poor, urban African American families are many. Unfortunately, there are those within the communities and in society in general who believe that communal resources have completely disappeared from the landscape of African American communities. However, many African American community organizations are sources of information, services, leadership, and support aimed at helping individuals and families. Community and professional organizations, churches, sororities, and fraternities remain part of the long-standing cultural foundation of natural helping networks. Social workers must identify and connect with these organizations and groups that, when asked, will respond for the benefit of the children and families in the African American community.

The Extended Family

The extended family is integral to the African American way of life and is characterized by an interaction network and kinship system of help and mutual support (Hill, 1997; Martin & Martin, 1985; Smith, 2001). It is not unusual for several generations of the same family to live together or for friends and distant relatives to be a part of a household. The extended family also transcends geographical boundaries. This phenomenon, like the helping tradition, is a carryover from traditional African family structures (Martin & Martin, 1985).

Most kinship structures among African Americans are rooted in blood ties. These blood connections are extremely important and form the foundation for relationships, family rituals, and self-identity (Sandven & Resnick, 1990). The raising of children and the care for the sick and the old occurs within these kinship and extended family networks. The pattern of taking in new family members in times of adversity has existed since slavery. This tradition of informal adoption or kinship care is also used to provide a child with opportunities not available at home, such as education, broader family connections, and a respite from city life. Referred to as elastic households by Hall and King (1982), this characteristic describes the ability of a household to expand and shrink in response to external and internal pressures. Parents, siblings, cousins, and so on may move in or out of a family member's household depending on personal circumstances. The children of friends or relatives are often informally adopted by a family, even if family resources are strained.

African American families often participate in extended family networks that pool resources to provide both economic and emotional security for individuals and, in turn, the family as a whole (Siegel, 1994; Smith, 2001). Often within the extended family, there are individuals whose roles are to provide leadership, counseling, security, group direction, or financial assistance (Martin & Martin, 1985). These networks provide important safety nets and supports for African American families and, for social workers, a source of understanding, connection, and direction.

Race Consciousness

Martin and Martin (1985) defined race consciousness as "the keen awareness by many black people of their history and condition as a people and their overwhelming desire to uplift their race to a state of dignity and pride" (p. 5). Race consciousness is the foundation for the helping tradition and is a key element in the existence and maintenance of extended families. Race consciousness is more than identifying as African American, although such identification is as integral part. Race consciousness also includes knowing about and respecting African American history and traditions, passing the history and traditions on to others, expecting the best from oneself, demanding equal treatment from others, being aware of the problems and oppression facing African American people, and deciding what one can do to help oneself, one's family, and the community.

Race consciousness was at its height in the 1960s during the civil rights struggle. As more and more African Americans assimilated into mainstream society and the African American middle class grew, race consciousness became a less visible and less vocalized part of the social movements in communities. In addition, according to Martin and Martin (1985), because race consciousness was not institutionalized in the 1960s, it has been difficult to maintain as time has progressed.

Even with its decline from the realm of active social movements, race consciousness is still a part of what drives many African Americans. Understanding the elements of race consciousness and the degree to which it is a part of an individual's or family's life is critical to working effectively with

African American families. Race consciousness can manifest itself in several ways that may affect a helping relationship, including a client's preferring to work with an African American social worker and the expectation that the unique cultural characteristics of African American families will be known or acknowledged by the social worker.

Respect

Although there may have been a decline in the aforementioned cultural characteristics, there has been no decline in the expectations surrounding respect. Respect from children and from strangers is paramount (Hurd, Moore, & Rogers, 1995; Jones, 1991). There are two primary ways that the characteristic is manifested in the African American community. One of those is in forms of address.

Many African Americans, particularly those who are older, expect to be addressed formally by strangers or by individuals who are younger than they are with the use of Mr., Mrs., Ms., or Dr. and their last name. To address someone by his or her first name, before being invited to do so, is often seen as disrespectful and as a serious breach of a relationship boundary (Jones, 1991). A relationship has to be established before less formal, more intimate interactions can comfortably occur. Overall, it is preferable to err on the side of formality.

The other major manifestation of respect involves the privacy of information or "minding your own business." Personal questions, particularly those about money, personal experiences, family situations, and health-related matters, from someone you have just met are often viewed with mistrust (Jones, 1991). Unfortunately, many of the questions asked during initial intake and assessment interviews fall into this category. Without an adequate explanation of the necessity for the questions to be asked, African American individuals and families faced with this situation may exhibit discomfort or anxiety and, in some cases, may not return for follow-up sessions. These actions may be inaccurately construed by the social worker as resistance or a lack of interest in available programs and services. Additional information about this topic is given later in the chapter.

Spiritual Life

For many African Americans, the church is a primary source of guidance, inspiration, and healing. Survey results have indicated that 84% of African Americans consider themselves religious. Eighty-two percent indicated that they believe the church is a very important influence in their lives. Most African Americans belong to a church (75%) and attend regularly (66%) (Billingsley, 1992; Hill, 1997). The way a person talks, behaves, dresses, eats, and so forth may all come from spiritual teachings of some kind. Even those who do not attend church as adults, but were raised in the church as children, may have a very strong connection to the church and its teachings (Billingsley, 1992; Chipungu, 1991).

In addition to providing spiritual guidance, black churches have served other important functions for African American communities as a whole. In particular, the churches have served as the hubs for community organizing efforts and as social service institutions, providing financial assistance and programs for children, families, and the old (Billingsley, 1992; Hill, 1997; Pinn, 2002). Being aware of a family's level of spiritual involvement and appropriately acknowledging it, primarily by allowing the family members to talk about it and to use their spiritual connections as part of a social work intervention, can help in the relationship building process between African American clients and social workers.

CULTURALLY COMPETENT KNOWLEDGE THEORY AND PRACTICE SKILLS FOR AFRICAN AMERICANS

Acquiring cultural competence is frequently viewed as a mysterious and unattainable process. Some assume, incorrectly, that cultural competence requires the gathering and remembering of numerous facts, histories, and norms of the many individuals and families a worker may encounter. From this view, becoming culturally competent would seem overwhelming and, perhaps, not worth the effort. However, the process of gaining and using culturally competent techniques is surprisingly simple. Much of it is predicated on one's willingness to reach beyond the boundaries of one's experience; to acknowledge the worthiness of other ways of thinking and being in the world. To a great extent, the foundations of culturally competent practice are rooted in common sense and sound social work practice. The core values of the social work profession provide a framework for the several models of culturally competent practice that have been researched and detailed in practice literature.

Devore and Schlesinger outlined assumptions and principles for what they call "ethnic-sensitive" social work practice:

- Individual and collective history has a bearing on problem generation and solution.
- The present is most important.
- Ethnicity is a source of cohesion, identity, and strength as well as a source of strain, discordance, and strife.
- Nonconscious phenomena affect individual functioning. (1996, pp. 155–156)

Green (1999), though acknowledging that it may be easier to define what cross-cultural sensitivity and cultural competence are not, describes the general features of cross-cultural capability including the following:

- Awareness of one's limitations
- Openness to cultural differences
- Having a client-oriented, systematic learning style
- Appropriately using cultural resources

Leigh (1998) describes a process for culturally competent communication in social work that has its foundations in ethnographic interviewing techniques developed in the field of anthropology. The techniques focus on the importance of learning from individuals and communities of color by listening to the stories and experiences.

Other models highlight similar values and features with an emphasis on open-mindedness, knowing oneself, and being aware of the influence of a particular group's history and position within our society. A primary key to successful culturally competent practice is the belief that everyone has strengths, limitations, and biases, including social workers. Although we are not required to agree with what clients present to us as the way they live their lives, we are required to honor people's right to self-determination, self-expression, and respect and to have the integrity to learn more about the things that we do not know and to excuse ourselves from situations that are beyond our ability to perform in an ethical and professional manner. Several basic principles can enhance the process of becoming a culturally competent social work practitioner:

1. Acknowledge that cultural differences exist and that they are important considerations for appropriate service delivery. Social workers who are comfortable with the differences that exist between them and their clients will avoid the trap of professing "color blindness," which, in effect, negates the uniqueness of people and sends a message that "we can get along if we are the same."

2. Be willing to form relationships with people of other cultures and backgrounds. Be aware of your own values, limitations, and biases and how they may affect your approach with culturally different clients.

3. Become comfortable with your own cultural background and identification. The more comfortable you are with your own, the more familiar you will be with the whole process of accepting your cultural heritage and the more willing you will probably be to allow others to express themselves culturally.

4. Remember that you are a stranger in each situation in which you work. It is important to curb the tendency to assume that you know what is going on, what people need, what a family's strengths are, what possible solutions are, and whether or not an individual or family actually needs help. In effect, you as the worker do not know anything that has not been told to you by members of that family or community. Placing the client as the expert means that you have a lot to learn from them. Your primary job is to listen and to become informed about what is going on from the client's perspective.

5. Promote mutual respect and the reduction of power disparities. Two of the most powerful tools social workers use are pens and paper. We record all of the things that we observe, think, and believe about the people with whom we work. These become indelible images of a particular client's life that can change that someone's experience positively or negatively. Putting aside the pen and paper and simply talking can lessen tension and the

power differential that may exist. For families to believe that you truly represent a process that is different from what they may have experienced with social workers in the past, you have to present yourself in a different way.

6. Believe that the process is important. The outcomes that you are hoping to achieve will not matter if the process is chaotic, adversarial, or interrupted.

7. Be aware of the likelihood of conflicts between the values of the individuals and families you are serving and the values of the agency that you represent. Agencies and social workers generally represent the dominant culture and its values. That means that, overall, efficiency, immediate response, timeliness, being organized, and linear thinking will be expected and valued by the worker and the agency. These values may directly conflict with the cultural patterns of your clients, a situation that you have to overcome. Ask yourself—Who is the client? Whose needs are paramount? How much latitude do I have as a worker in this situation? Am I willing to take a few risks on behalf of my clients? Your answers to these questions may help put the circumstances back in perspective.

8. Be knowledgeable of the sociopolitical system and its influences on individual, family, and community beliefs and actions. As the previous history of African Americans in this country illustrates, meso and macro level systems have a tremendous impact on the lives of individuals and families. Social workers need to be aware of these influences and their potential for affecting help-seeking, relationship building, and other aspects of the social work intervention process.

In contrast to the preceding, which can be characterized as traditional multicultural practice frameworks, is africentric social work practice. Based on the pioneering work of Nobles and Goddard (1984), an africentric perspective is a culturally based approach that uses African American history, culture, values, and worldviews as the context for understanding contemporary African American families and communities (Everett, 1991; Swigonski, 1996). This approach upholds the strengths and assets of African American families and communities and serves as a foundation and explanation for their social contexts, belief systems, coping strategies, help-seeking behaviors, and responses (Everett, 1991). The africentric perspective acknowledges the differences between African American and, in particular, European American culture without denigrating either one. While you set forth a context within which practice with African American families can be framed, you must understand that the degree to which the families participate in an africentric worldview will vary based on many factors, including class status, geography, and the level of connection with group history.

CONTACT SKILLS WITH AFRICAN AMERICANS

Overcoming Resistance and Communication Barriers

Tension and uneasiness are natural feelings that occur within any social worker-client interaction, especially during the initial stages of contact. Hesitancy to divulge information, silences, some lack of understanding regarding the course and purpose of the interventions, and similar behaviors are to be expected. The social worker's responsibilities during these earliest meetings is to set a tone of openness and calm and to make sure that the client is informed about the purpose, frequency, and course of the sessions and that any questions are answered to the client's satisfaction.

The term "resistance" is frequently used to label client behaviors that do not appear to be in line with the wishes and expectations of the social worker. What a worker may call resistance may take a number of forms—from not keeping appointments to disagreeing with worker recommendations to not informing the worker of changes and circumstances within the family. What, to some, may seem to be a particular problem that the worker needs to take care of may actually be a sign that the individual or family is realizing its power and responsibility in the context of the worker-client interactions. These moments of "resistance" need to be explored because they often signal the need for the worker to reexamine his or her approach, intent, direction, or attitude. Miley, O'Melia, and DuBois (2001) state that clients have the privilege to resist and that social workers who use an empowerment approach will acknowledge and respect these demonstrations of client power.

For African Americans specifically, seeking help from social workers and other helping professionals is an act that may be fraught with feelings of mistrust and reluctance because of historical discrimination and institutionalized racism. In general, the utilization rates of social services for personal and mental health concerns by African Americans are comparatively low (Griffin & Williams, 1992; McClennen & Glenn, 1997). The lack of services in neighborhoods, the cultural inappropriateness of existing services, past unpleasant experiences with helping agencies, limited financial resources, and the belief that family and individual problems should be handled within the family may all contribute to this reality. Once engaged in a helping relationship, African American clients may exhibit behaviors that workers view as resistance. Without an understanding of some of the experiences and societal forces that contribute to the worldview of black clients, these behaviors, which frequently have legitimate foundations, may lead to the premature termination of the helping process because of misinterpretations by the social worker.

Resistance, therefore, is not the client's problem. Rather, the social worker is responsible for exploring and addressing the breakdown in communication between the client and the social worker, within the context of the professional relationship and the cultural dimensions of the client.

The question of whether African American clients must work with African American social workers is a part of this topic, as well. For agencies to assume that client-worker race matching is a necessary prerequisite to a successful helping relationship is shortsighted and, in some cases, can be construed as racist. Many of the philosophical assumptions of culturally competent social work practice are directly in line with ethical social work practice. Therefore, the desires of the client are paramount. Preferences for African American social workers need to be openly explored early in the intake and assessment process. Some white social workers may be reluctant to broach the subject, but it may be in the forefront of the thoughts of an African American client. A simple "Are you comfortable with me as your social worker since I am not African American?" may be all that is needed to get the issue in the open and to show that the worker is at least cognizant of the possibility of cultural and communication differences.

African American social workers and other agency personnel cannot assume that, because they are the same race as their African American clients, the "goodness-of-fit" is automatic. In addition to the possibility of simple personality clashes between any client and worker, African American workers and clients may experience regional and class differences that can strain and inhibit an effective helping relationship. Although many African American individuals and families may prefer to work with same-race social workers, all clients are entitled to be asked about their preferences and to have those preferences respected.

Establishing a Responsive Service Delivery System

For the social service system to be responsive to the needs of African American individuals and families, it has to be comprehensive, accessible, affordable, well-staffed, and connected to the local community. Frequently, the agencies and organizations that have existed in the community for a long period and with which members of the community have had positive experiences are those that are trusted to deliver culturally sensitive and appropriate services. Social workers who are committed to culturally competent practice will learn as much as possible about the history of the local organizations and agencies through their own interactions with those service providers and through information provided by members of that community. Information and referral is a major part of social work practice with individuals and families. To be effective in this role, not just with African American clients, social workers need to "do their homework" and build relationships with community-based resources.

Practicing Relationship Protocols

As previously stated, respect is a primary cultural value in African American communities. Maintaining a sense of formality relative to forms of address and the general manner in which the social worker conducts himself or herself is critical to creating and maintaining a professional relationship. Titles (Mr., Mrs., Ms., Dr., Rev.) and last names should always be used unless and until the client gives permission for the worker to use first names. Some older African Americans, in particular, feel that they have worked long and hard and surmounted many obstacles to get where they are in their lives, so they are entitled to the respect that the use of a title engenders.

Another critical part of establishing relationship protocols is how the social worker explains his or her role and the role of the client in the helping relationship. This is a time for the worker to demonstrate respect for the client's view of the issues of concern and, in some cases, for the client's need or desire to have other family members become part of the social work intervention. If the client turns for help and advice to other family members, including these individuals in sessions and decision making can reinforce a critical social support structure and increase the likelihood of the long-term success of the individual or family. It is important to keep in mind that the sessions belong to the client. Whatever reasonable steps the social worker can take to make the sessions more meaningful, comfortable, and culturally proper will serve both the worker and the client well.

A question of some debate within the profession is whether it is appropriate to accept gifts or food from clients. This issue is raised here because of the cultural connection for African American individuals and families related to acknowledging someone's assistance and your regard for them. There is little, if any, social work literature on the subject. The limited literature that exists is primarily from the fields of psychiatry and medicine (Hundert & Appelbaum, 1995; Lyckholm, 1998; Smolar, 2002). The NASW Code of Ethics (1999) does not include any ethical standards directly pertinent to this topic, although some sections are related, including the following:

> 1.01 Commitment to Clients—Social workers' primary responsibility is to promote the well-being of clients.
>
> 1.05 Cultural Competence and Social Diversity—Social workers should obtain education about culture and diversity and their functions and have a knowledge base of their clients' cultures to provide sensitive and appropriate services.
>
> 1.06 Conflicts of Interest—Social workers should avoid conflicts of interest that interfere with professional discretion and impartial judgment and not take unfair advantage of any professional relationships or exploit others to further personal interests.
>
> 1.13 Payment for Services—Social workers should avoid accepting goods or services from clients as payment for professional services.

Applicable social work values include the following: (1) respecting the dignity and worth of the person, (2) recognizing the importance of human relationships, and (3) behaving in a trustworthy manner.

Lyckholm (1998) and Smolar (2002) suggest several factors that must be weighed when considering the appropriateness of accepting a gift from a client, for example the client's motivation for giving the gift, potential ethical problems and conflicts of interest, the best interest of the client, the cost and nature of the gift, the purpose and stage of the helping relationship, and cultural differences between the client and the worker. Given these considerations and the guidance provided by the NASW Code of Ethics, this is clearly a sensitive topic that is worthy of discussion and further research.

It may be safe to say that, overall, if the clients that most social workers serve were to present gifts, they would be small, of reasonable monetary value, and meant to show the clients' appreciation for the time and effort spent on their behalf. In the same way, food that is offered to the social worker during a home visit would, more than likely, be given with the same intent. For many African American individuals and families, offering food or small gifts can be a sign of welcome, respect, thanks, or inclusion in the family circle. Turning the gift or food down could be viewed as an affront, thus placing the maintenance of the professional relationship in jeopardy.

In the end, each social worker needs to judge the circumstances surrounding a client gift to determine if there are any ethical prohibitions to accepting it. Most of the time, the tokens of appreciation that clients offer complement the professional relationship. Although the risks and benefits of accepting or declining a gift need to be considered, understanding and respecting the cultural implications of the gift or food are critical to culturally competent practice.

Using Professional Self-Disclosure

Self-disclosure when working with African American individuals and families is another area where cultural considerations are important and where it is vital for the social worker to carefully consider the risks and benefits of relaying personal information to clients. Social workers have families, jobs, successes, failures, and wishes in their lives, so they may have relevant personal stories to relate to clients that may benefit them in some way. Although workers need to be selective about what to tell and when, sharing personal experiences helps to humanize and demystify the helping process and the social worker in the mind of the clients. Carefully chosen self-disclosure can lighten a tense situation and provide clients with immediately useable ideas.

Racial and cultural differences between client and worker may lead the client to ask personal questions of the worker. Generally, the questions asked are intended to help the client determine if there are areas of commonality or if the worker has experience with the clients' concerns. Questions such as "Do you have any children?" "Where do you live?" "Have you ever used drugs before?" or "How old are you?" may be posed to a social worker by a client who needs reassurance that the worker can actually understand what the client is going through and offer realistic suggestions and resources. Although some agencies caution their social workers not to divulge personal information, when helping across cultures, this advice needs to be tempered with the social worker's impressions of the motivation behind the questions and whether or not answering the questions will inhibit progress in the intervention. For some clients of color, avoiding or not answering the questions may be construed as disrespectful or may leave the client wondering if you can be trusted with their personal information when you will not disclose any of your own. Some pieces of information about a worker are clearly not to be revealed (e.g., home address). However, within the context of the professional relationship, social workers can and should exercise their own discretion about the level of self-disclosure that is appropriate with their clients.

Self-disclosure is a two-way street, the opposing direction being client self-disclosure in response to a social worker's questions. For some African American clients, the typical intake and assessment interview, which requires that clients reveal myriad pieces of personal information, is an uncomfortable situation that violates cultural values of privacy and respect. This necessary, but difficult, part of the social work intervention can be made easier if a full explanation of the need for the information and how confidentiality will be protected is provided at the outset. There are times when questions on agency forms gather information that is not germane to the immediate concerns of the individual or family or that may be viewed as intrusive. In these cases, it may be prudent to wait until a greater comfort level is established before asking these questions or to consider if the questions need to be asked at all.

Enhancing Listening and Communication Skills

The ability to enhance listening and communication skills is directly related to the ideas presented in this chapter. If you recognize the uniqueness of each African American individual and family along with the likelihood of discovering cultural similarities, keep an open mind, conduct your work in an honest manner, respect confidentiality, and educate yourself on the history and experiences of African Americans as a group, you will have the necessary foundation for appropriate and meaningful communication.

PROBLEM IDENTIFICATION SKILLS WITH AFRICAN AMERICAN CLIENTS

Gaining Problem Understanding

Similar to self-disclosure, problem identification has at least two perspectives—those of the social worker and of the client. What the social worker believes to be the problem might not be what the client identifies. For example, a social worker may believe that alcoholism is the primary problem when the client, though acknowledging concern about his or her alcohol use, states that the lack of adequate housing is the most pressing problem. In these cases, whether working with African Americans or others, the process is the same. From the generalist perspective, "problem" very broadly refers to an issue, need, question, or difficulty that is brought to the attention of the worker (McMahon, 1996). The problem or problems affecting a client need to be described and prioritized as a joint effort between the worker and the client. Social workers are not experts in the lives of the people who come to them for help, so the client's expertise and knowledge of his or her own circumstances has to be an integral part of the problem identification and prioritization process.

In acknowledging the reality of cultural differences, worldviews, and perceptions, the culturally competent social worker will create an atmosphere in which the opinions and feelings of clients are solicited and honored. Clients have the right to define problems as they see them. When problem identification occurs in an open, collaborative setting, it increases the likelihood that the clients will remain in and benefit from the helping relationship.

Reframing the Problem Orientation

Problems exist in all people's lives. For all clients, however, it is imperative that social workers refrain from viewing their clients solely as "presenters of problems." In what may seem to be the most intractable circumstances, the individuals and families involved in them have strengths, talents, knowledge, experiences, resources, and assets that can be mobilized to become part of the solution and intervention.

Historically, the lives, beliefs, and behaviors of African Americans have been evaluated based on a deficit model. This model, with white American values and behaviors as the standard, assumed that any variants from that standard were deficient, even deviant. Thus, African American family structures, child-rearing practices, speech patterns, beliefs, and values were automatically seen as lacking because, in many cases, they did not look like those of white Americans. In reframing the problem from an africentric or culturally competent perspective, the social worker will begin with the understanding that the cultural hallmarks of African American individuals and families are real, historically based, and valuable in their own right. This view at the outset will enable the worker to help the client identify strengths and resources that can be used to attain agreed-upon goals and, ultimately, have a successful experience in the helping relationship.

Viewing Micro, Meso, and Macro Level Problems

The question to be answered here is, "What is the actual source of the problem?" It is not uncommon for micro oriented social workers to focus on the individual and family systems as the location of the problem or problems to be addressed without considering other system levels and a more ecological view. Historical oppression and institutionalized racism have influenced the lives of all African Americans in this country, to one degree or another. Poverty, unemployment, educational underachievement, and other social conditions that seem to be overrepresented among African American communities have their roots in the neglect and maltreatment suffered by blacks throughout their existence in this country. Even though definite strides have been made to ameliorate these conditions, there remain large pockets of underserved African American communities. The difficulties that exist in these communities may be viewed by "outsiders" as caused or perpetuated by the people living in the communities. To the "insiders," however, the daily experiences of living life with inadequate resources despite efforts to change the situation reinforce the understanding that the realities of the meso and macro level systems have not changed. Many African Americans view the continuation of these community problems as verification that they still are not considered a true part of American society and that "the system" still does not function on their behalf.

Class differences can also play a role in individual's perceptions of problem causation, determination of what solutions are possible, and comfort working with social service agencies. Although there is no monolithic, homogeneous African American culture, commonalities and similar trends can be identified among blacks who may identify with particular regional areas or socioeconomic class groups. For example, Davis (1993) states that middle-class African Americans are as likely to identify with the mainstream culture as they are to identify with African American culture. Many middle-class African Americans are thought to have a bicultural worldview that manifests itself in the ability to deal effectively with mainstream culture without sacrificing African American cultural identification. Assuming the accuracy of this contention, middle-class blacks may be more likely to voluntarily seek help for personal or mental health issues and may experience less discomfort with the overall assessment and intervention process than would working-class or poor African American individuals.

Given the possible divergent perspectives on the same issues, it is incumbent on the social worker to fully explore micro, meso, and macro influences and the client's views on all these levels of influence.

ASSESSMENT SKILLS WITH AFRICAN AMERICAN CLIENTS

General social work assessment skills are fully applicable when working with African American clients. Attention must be given to the client's identification and definition of the presenting problem in addition to the information that the social worker has regarding what brought the individual or family to the agency's attention. During the assessment, the social worker needs to pay particular attention to the aspects of the biopsychosocial perspective—an ecological framework that seeks to gather information about client strengths, resources, connections, experiences, and concerns from as wide an array of locations as possible. Although this comprehensive assessment will help the social worker determine where and how to intervene, the extent of the assessment may be perceived as unnecessarily intrusive by some clients. A critical part of the social worker's role in this phase of engagement is to fully explain the reasons for the questions and how the information gathered will be used. Assurances of confidentiality need to be given and repeated. It is possible that for clients whose mistrust of social service and other bureaucracies is high, no amount of explanation about confidentiality will be sufficient to quell their fears. Culturally competent social workers will anticipate this possibility, be prepared to answer all the client's questions, and be able to genuinely hear the client's concerns. Assessment is, in effect, the gateway to the remainder of the helping process. If a foundation for honest communication is set here, both the client and the worker will have a more productive experience.

One of the pitfalls during the assessment phase is that of making assumptions about a new client based on limited or stereotypical information about a particular population. To avoid this, the worker will need to approach the assessment as a time for clarification and edification—questions for all parties involved can be answered, misconceptions can be cleared up, new knowledge can be gained, and a determination if the professional relationship will continue can be made. This is the time to ask if client resources include extended family, religious/spiritual associations, community or cultural organizations, and hobbies and interests and to what degree clients feel connected with the local community of color. Social workers can help clients identify resources through the use of tools such as eco-maps, graphic illustrations of the networks of micro, meso, and macro affiliations and connections individuals and families have, but may not be aware of. When clients are walked through this type of process, it can make apparent many sources of personal and cultural strength and support that may not have been recently used. Social workers should also be prepared to offer suggestions about local resources including services and organizations that are culturally appropriate so that the entire spectrum of the client's connections to what is available in the local community can be assessed.

INTERVENTION SKILLS WITH AFRICAN AMERICAN CLIENTS

Establishing Goals and Agreement

Social work interventions are intended to be collaborative processes that require the input of all involved parties. This value extends to establishing the short and long-term goals to be met during the intervention. As with the stages of problem identification and assessment, the client's opinions and perceptions of appropriate measurable and attainable goals are paramount. For any client, if the goals established are unrealistic or are imposed by the worker, there is little chance of the intervention being successful. Clients need and want to be the facilitators of their own accomplishments. For African American individuals and families who may have extended family members who serve as advisors and supporters, their inclusion in the goal setting process may be useful.

Many long-standing and well-respected African American organizations and agencies in communities throughout the country can become part of the intervention plan for African American clients. Black churches, community service and philanthropic organizations, private businesses, culturally focused schools, day-care centers, and neighborhood residents are among the many, and frequently untapped, indigenous resources within many African American communities. In the absence of these culturally focused organizations and resources, social service agencies need to make a commitment to having culturally diverse and well-trained staff who, despite the differences that may exist between them and clients, can provide appropriate services in an atmosphere of mutual respect, safety, and dignity. Green (1999) offers a Human Services Model of Cultural Competence that provides a framework for organizing one's thinking and professional behavior when engaging in cross-cultural practice. The components of the model and their application to social work practice with African Americans are as follows:

Case Study Integration Exercise on Contact, Problem Identification, and Assessment Skills

Angie Stewart is a home-based services social worker with a state-contracted, private, nonprofit agency. She received a new case today about the Williams family—a recently widowed, 40-year-old, African American mother and her five children. Originally, the family was reported to Child Protective Services (CPS) by a neighbor who was concerned because of hearing a lot of yelling coming from the home and seeing the younger children playing outside for long periods of time without any adult supervision. The CPS investigation determined that the children did not need to be removed from the home, but that home-based services for a six-month period would be helpful. When Angie received the case from the CPS worker, he warned Angie that the mother, Joyce Williams, is "loud, angry, and uncooperative" and wished her good luck working with the family.

Angie called the Williams home right away to set up an appointment. When Mrs. Williams answered the phone, Angie could hear lots of children's voices and the television in the background. Angie introduced herself, told Mrs. Williams that her case had been referred to her by CPS, and said that she wanted to make an appointment to come by the house to meet the family and to talk about the situation. All of this was met with stony silence from the other end of the phone. After a few seconds, Mrs. Williams said, "I don't know if I want you to come over. The last CPS person who came over here made me mad." Angie re-explained her position and her connection to CPS, clarifying the fact that she was not a CPS employee, but a social worker that CPS calls in when it looks like a family can use some extra help. Mrs. Williams told Angie that everything was a mess since the neighbor made the report and that no one would listen to anything she had to say. She felt like she was being treated like a child and she resented being told what to do. Sensing Mrs. Williams's frustration, Angie asked, "If you let me come over, what would you like me to do when I get there?" Mrs. Williams replied, "I just want someone to listen to me." Angie assured her that she could and would do that and an appointment time was arranged.

When she arrived for the appointment the next day, Angie was greeted at the door by Anita Williams, age 8. Anita invited Angie to sit down and told her that her mother would be right there. Mrs. Williams emerged from the kitchen, shook Angie's hand, and sat down. Angie thanked Mrs. Williams for letting her come over and told her how polite Anita was. After exchanging a few pleasantries, Angie reiterated her role, the types of services that she could offer the family, and the length of time she was allowed to work with the family. Angie added that although she ultimately did have to give a report to CPS about the family's progress, she and Mrs. Williams would be working together and, for the time being, the CPS worker would not be in contact with her. Mrs. Williams expressed her gratitude for that, stating that she did not think that the CPS worker liked working with African American families. She said that she did not like his tone of voice or the way he looked around the house when he came by. She said that she was a good mother, but that things had just been very hard since her husband died. Angie asked Mrs. Williams to tell her about her husband and how things had been.

(continued)

CASE | *continued*

Mr. and Mrs. Williams had been married for 20 years and had 5 children—Robert, 18; Alan, 15; Sandra, 10; Anita, 8; and Sammy, 2. The family had recently moved from the northern part of the city to their current home to be closer to potential job opportunities for Mr. Williams. He was a construction laborer, a seasonal job that required him to go wherever the work was. The family had been struggling, but usually managing to make ends meet until Mr. Williams's death from a sudden heart attack eight months ago. Other than a small insurance policy, the family had not received any other financial assistance since his death. Mrs. Williams had not worked full time since Sammy's birth. She worked part time at the community center nearby, a place where child care was available for Sammy while she worked. Her oldest, Robert, had just graduated from high school and was planning to attend the local community college until his father's death. He postponed entering college and took a full time job so that he could help the family. Mrs. Williams related that this situation distressed her since Robert was looking forward to going to college and she wanted him to continue his education now.

She said that all the children missed their father, but she was trying to pay extra attention to all of them to help them cope with the loss. She did notice some behavior changes in the children. Alan had become very quiet and sullen. He and Sandra were fighting with each other much more often. Anita had become "the little mother," helping to take care of Sammy and always asking, "Mommy, are you alright?" Mrs. Williams admitted that she really wasn't alright, but she didn't want the children to see her cry because it would just upset them more. Now that she had to be mother and father to the children, she had to be strong for all of them.

Angie asked Mrs. Williams what would help the family right now. Mrs. Williams said that besides money, her biggest concern was Robert. Because he had prepared for so long to go to college, she did not want him to delay it any longer. She understood his wanting to help the family and the money he brought home was definitely needed, but she was afraid that the longer he stayed out of college, the less likely it would be that he would ever go. After hearing this, Angie was concerned because the problems and goals outlined by the CPS worker were nothing like what Mrs. Williams believed was necessary. Angie mentioned to Mrs. Williams that

- *Ethnographic Knowledge Base—identifying what is salient in the client's culture with respect to issues that are routinely presented to social workers and being willing to work with and learn from others who can fill cultural knowledge gaps.* How can social workers most effectively get the cultural information they need to work with African American clients? Are there key informants in the local African American community who can assist agency staff with learning about the community's history, strengths, and priorities? Do agency programs and services support and strengthen the existing family and community systems?
- *Professional Preparedness—being willing to engage in continuous self-assessment and ongoing training and education related to cultural compe-*

the CPS worker had a different view of the situation, noting his concern about Mrs. Williams's level of anger, the fighting between Alan and Sandra, the fact that Sandra and Anita were frequently seen playing outside by themselves for long periods of time, and Anita's taking on tasks that were not age appropriate. The CPS worker recommended parenting and anger management classes for Mrs. Williams, relying less on Anita to fill adult roles, counseling for Alan, and a follow-up visit by CPS in six months to see if the situation had improved.

Mrs. Williams objected strongly to what she believed was a completely incorrect and biased characterization of her family. "I love my children and they love each other. Why couldn't he see that? My husband and I raised them to look out for themselves and each other. That's what brothers and sisters do. Yes, Sandra and Anita play outside, but someone else is always home in the evening and usually looking out the window to see where they are. Anita has always been a very caring and helpful child. If she wants to help with Sammy and do things around the house, what's wrong with that? That's the way it is in all of the black families that I know. Everybody pitches in and helps out. That's what family means." Turning to Angie, Mrs. Williams asked, "Wasn't it like that in your family?" Angie told her that she was an only child and, because of that, she was very independent as a child and helped out all the time around the house, so she understood Anita wanting to be involved in household chores. Angie suggested that she and Mrs. Williams go through the CPS worker's goals and recommendations and Mrs. Williams's concerns one at a time to get a complete picture and to create a priority list of what would be helpful to the family.

Application Exercises: Tools for Student Learning

1. What is your overall impression of how Angie approached this case? What would you do differently?
2. When Mrs. Williams commented that the CPS worker did not like working with African American families, Angie did not respond to that. Was that a good idea? If Angie were to respond, what might she have said?
3. Do you feel prepared to work with African American families? What additional knowledge do you need and how will you get it? Do you believe that it is necessary to have "specialized" skills to work effectively with African American families?

tence. Individual social workers must be willing to explore their own ideas, beliefs, values, myths, and misperceptions about African American families. Social service agencies must honestly assess their service delivery systems to fill service gaps and to ensure that clients are being served in a culturally appropriate manner. All aspects of client interaction and service delivery must be subject to evaluation and possible improvement. In addition, a commitment to understanding the effect of the broader sociopolitical environment on African American individuals, families, and communities is crucial to providing services that are appropriate and relevant.

- *Comparative Analysis—understanding the importance of and the variety of culturally focused worldviews.* This component of the model emphasizes the role of clients' worldviews and ways of thinking in the social work helping process. Are social workers individualizing their client interventions and remaining mindful of the myriad expressions of cultural hallmarks that exist among and between African American families? To what extent are workers and agencies joining with the local community to understand the issues and concerns of African American families from their perspective? Are the variations in worldviews, values, and norms viewed from a strengths-based framework?

- *Appropriate Intervention—keeping abreast of the racial, ethnic, and cultural changes in the local community to ensure that, as the population changes, interventions change.* The racial, ethnic, age, and socioeconomic compositions of neighborhoods are subject to change over the years. To be culturally competent and effective, social service agencies must keep abreast of changes in the local population and adjust programs and service delivery accordingly. A community that remains largely African American will still experience changes that will require a shift in approach from helping professionals. (Green, pp. 37–38)

Interventions that are based on an integrative approach and include a broad range of elements and ideas from the micro, meso, and macro levels are more likely to generate a positive response from African American clients and to reflect the ecological perspective. Following Green's (1999) model, an integrative approach will pay attention to the full scope of systems and influences that can affect African American families as they engage in a helping process. Culturally competent agencies will be prepared to support social workers in these endeavors and to provide the highest level of service possible.

The assumptions of strengths-based and empowerment intervention models direct attention to the need for a multifaceted approach that has its foundation in the acknowledgment of client strengths and the need to recognize and minimize power differentials both in professional relationships and in society as a whole. When working with African American clients, this means viewing the helping relationship as a collaborative partnership that may include extended family members in problem definition, goal setting, and interventions. A collaborative, inclusive approach begins with a social worker who focuses on what is right with the family—What resources are in place? Which existing family and community connections can be enhanced? What knowledge, assets, and talents do the family members possess that can be mobilized on their own behalf?

Viewing families from the standpoint of their strengths puts the power to change where it belongs—in the hands of the family members. Historically, African Americans have endured a paternalistic approach from government and social service agencies, a demeaning pattern of interactions that places the search for deficits above the acknowledgment of assets. Culturally competent practice hinges on recognizing this past approach and establishing a new framework that seeks to remove barriers, create equitable relationships, promote social justice, and advocate for the fair distribution of resources (Gutiérrez & Lewis, 1999; Logan, 2001).

TERMINATION SKILLS WITH AFRICAN AMERICAN CLIENTS

The termination skills used with African American clients are the same as for other clients. It is important to realize, however, that termination actually begins when workers and clients initially meet and begin the problem identification and assessment processes. Social workers should prepare clients not only for the steps to be taken during the helping process but also for the steps to be taken to end the professional relationship and for the feelings that might accompany termination.

Before the official end of the professional relationship, the social worker and the client should have time to review the goals that were set and the progress made in accomplishing them. An honest appraisal from both parties of what worked and what did not work can be valuable for the client's continued progress and for the social worker's continuing education in culturally competent practice. The worker and the client should discuss what the client will do if any follow-up sessions are needed and if it is appropriate for the client to stay in touch with the social worker. Clients who relate on a more personal level, even in professional relationships, may want to let the worker know how they are doing as time goes on.

CLOSING THOUGHTS

When providing services to African American individuals and families, social workers must consider several factors. In addition to providing the services that are an expected part of the agency's mission, social workers need to be aware of the effect of class and culture on the expectations, skill levels, and coping abilities of the clients. Social workers, by the nature of their jobs, should apply a multifaceted approach to their work. However, in working with African American individuals and families, that multifaceted approach needs to be informed by the realities of African American cultural and family life and the understanding of the possible difficulties African American families may have in working with white-dominated agencies and bureaucracies.

Social workers must recognize that, in general, for interventions with African American clients to be successful, clients need accurate information and professional service and a more personal approach that demonstrates respect and care for the person, the family, the values and traditions, and the knowledge and strengths that they bring to the helping process. As with all clients, African American clients want honest and open communication that demonstrates that the social worker values them and the contributions they are making to the well-being of their families and communities. Participating in a social work intervention process requires a significant investment of time, energy, and emotion. Social workers need to demonstrate their understanding of the level of investment African American families make to see their participation in the intervention to a successful termination. That understanding can come when social workers are aware of and acknowledge cultural traditions

Case Integration Exercise on Intervention and Termination Skills

Angie and Mrs. Williams continued their initial assessment conversation over three meetings. The details about the family that Mrs. Williams provided were helpful in creating a priority list of concerns with which Mrs. Williams agreed. Her top three concerns were Robert's education, Alan's unhappiness, and the family's financial situation. After meeting with the family, Angie told Mrs. Williams that she did not believe that either anger management or parenting classes were necessary. Angie allayed Mrs. Williams's fears that CPS would become directly involved again if she did not follow through with the recommendations. "My job is to meet with you and to make a plan that will help your family. If changes are needed in the CPS worker's recommendations, it's also my job to talk to him and to have adjustments made in his expectations."

Before talking about possible interventions, Angie asked Mrs. Williams if there was anyone that she wanted to have sit in on their discussion and to help with the decisions. She said no, but added that she might talk to some relatives later and get their thoughts.

In addressing Robert's education, Angie and Mrs. Williams had to discuss the family's financial situation. Up to this point, Robert's income was keeping the family afloat. Knowing that discussions of finances are personal, Angie mentioned to Mrs. Williams that she did not have to answer any questions that made her uncomfortable. Angie wondered if Mrs. Williams had a chance to review Mr. Williams's business papers to determine if there were other insurance policies or accounts. She had not reviewed them because of lack of time and because she had found it emotionally too hard to do. With Angie there, she felt that she might be able to look through them. After several minutes, Mrs. Williams discovered an additional life insurance policy and a small annuity account that she had forgotten about. While Angie was there, Mrs. Williams called the insurance company to determine how to submit a claim for the insurance benefits. This money would help establish a modest savings account to serve as a financial safety net in case of an emergency. Angie also put Mrs. Williams in contact with the local Social Security office to determine the family's eligibility for benefits.

Robert had strong objections to quitting his job and going to school full time because of his wanting to contribute to the family. During one meeting, Robert, Angie, and Mrs. Williams talked and determined that if Robert worked 30 hours a week, his income would be sufficient to help the family, and he would have time to take two evening classes each semester. Although financial aid through the community college was limited, Angie gave Robert the name of a financial aid counselor who helped him secure an aid package that defrayed much of the cost of his schooling. A welcome surprise for the family came in the form of an offer of financial help from one of Mr. Williams's cousins who found out about the family's struggles and wanted to support Robert's college education. This relative talked to Robert about the importance of going to college and helped him accept the compromise in his working hours.

Angie secured Mrs. Williams's permission to talk to the counselor at Alan's school. Alan was still doing well in school and had not come to the counselor's attention. After hearing the concerns, the counselor agreed to call Mrs. Williams and arrange a time to meet with her and Alan together. Two weeks later, Mrs. Williams told Angie that the meeting with the counselor went well. Alan not only talked about missing his father, but about missing the friends he had in their old neighborhood. The counselor also talked to Alan about his hobbies and interests and arranged for him to join the chess club and the afterschool basketball league as a way to make new friends. Alan and the school counselor met whenever Alan needed to.

Angie met weekly with the Williams family. Sometimes she would bring books or toys for the children. With Mrs. Williams's permission, Angie brought food baskets a couple of times when the family's food supplies were low. When Mrs. Williams told Angie that she was feeling better about how the children were doing, Angie asked, "Now, what about you?" Mrs. Williams assured her that she was doing fine. Angie pointed out that the family's move and her husband's death affected her, too. Mrs. Williams said that she stayed busy with the children and with her part-time job at the community center, but she was thinking about working full time. Angie asked her if she had a support system other than her children—friends, neighborhood organizations, church, clubs. Mrs. Williams admitted that the recent move had created a void in her life. She had lost contact with some of her friends and with the church she frequently attended. She said that now that the children were more settled, she might visit the local church. One of her neighbors, an older African American woman, had invited her a few weeks ago. That next Sunday, Mrs. Williams accompanied her neighbor to the church and met some other women who had lost their husbands. Talking to them helped her feel better, too. This also opened the opportunity for the Williams children to talk to other children whose fathers had died.

By the end of Angie's six months with the family, things had definitely improved. Robert was enrolled in the community college and working. Alan had become friends with two boys at his school. Although he still had days when he was withdrawn and unhappy, they were much less frequent. Angie informed Mrs. Williams that the option of more intensive counseling for Alan was open, if she felt it was necessary. Mrs. Williams was asked to increase her hours at the community center to three-quarter time, an opportunity she readily took. The family's financial situation was more stable. At the final meeting, Angie and Mrs. Williams reviewed the progress the family made. Mrs. Williams thanked Angie for all of her help and gave her a small, decorative candle. Angie accepted the candle. She briefly told Mrs. Williams what her final report would include and encouraged Mrs. Williams to call her if the family needed anything. Angie's final report to CPS detailed the family's strengths, and the changes the family had made, and stated that further home-based interventions were no longer necessary.

Application Exercises: Tools for Student Learning

1. In what ways did Angie demonstrate that culturally competent practice is often good, ethical social work practice?
2. What family strengths could Angie include in her final report?
3. What micro, meso, and macro level systems did Angie include in her interventions? What others would be appropriate for the Williams family?
4. What empowerment strategies did Angie use? What others would you use in this situation?

that affect individual and family beliefs and values and on their expectations of the social work helping process. Agencies that are committed to providing culturally competent services to African American clients will ensure that the composition of the staff is reasonably reflective of the clients served and knowledgeable about the cultural contexts in which African American clients live their lives.

References

Bennett, L. (1982). *Before the Mayflower.* New York: Penguin Books.

Billingsley, A. (1992). *Climbing Jacob's ladder.* New York: Simon & Schuster.

cbsnews.com (2002, April). Reducing the racial health gap. Retrieved August 8, 2003, from www.cbsnews.com/stories/2002/04/18/health/main506564.shtml

Chipungu, S. S. (1991). A value-based policy framework. In J. E. Everett, S. S. Chipungu, & B. Leashore (Eds.), *Child welfare: An africentric perspective* (pp. 290–305). New Brunswick, NJ: Rutgers University Press.

Davis, R. A. (1993). *The black family in a changing black community.* New York: Garland.

Devore, W., & Schlesinger, E. G. (1996). *Ethnic-sensitive social work practice.* Boston: Allyn & Bacon.

Everett, J. E. (1991). Introduction: Children in crisis. In J. E. Everett, S. S. Chipungu, & B. Leashore (Eds.), *Child welfare: An africentric perspective* (pp. 1–14). New Brunswick, NJ: Rutgers University Press.

Franklin, J. H., & Moss, A. A. (1988). *From slavery to freedom.* New York: McGraw-Hill.

Green, J. W. (1999). *Cultural awareness in the human services: A multi-ethnic approach.* Boston: Allyn & Bacon.

Griffin, L. W., & Williams, O. J. (1992). Abuse among African American elderly. *Journal of Family Violence, 7*(1), 19–35.

Gutiérrez, L. M., & Lewis, E. A. (1999). *Empowering women of color.* New York: Columbia University Press.

Hall, E. H., & King, G. C. (1982). Working with the strengths of black families. *Child Welfare, 61*(8), 536–544.

Hill, R. B. (1997). *The strengths of African American families: Twenty-five years later.* Washington, DC: R and B.

Hundert, E. M., & Appelbaum, P. S. (1995). Boundaries in psychotherapy: Model guidelines. *Psychiatry: Interpersonal and Biological Processes, 58*(4), 345–356.

Hurd, E. P., Moore, C., & Rogers, R. (1995). Quiet success: Parenting strengths among African Americans. *Families in Society, 76*(7), 434–443.

Jones, M. (1991). *Adoption and the African American child: A guide for agencies.* Rockville, MD: National Adoption Information Clearinghouse.

Leigh, J. W. (1998). *Communicating for cultural competence.* Boston: Allyn & Bacon.

Logan, S. L. M. (2001). A strengths perspective on black families. In S. L. M. Logan (Ed.), *The black family: Strengths, self-help, and positive change* (pp. 8–20). Boulder, CO: Westview Press.

Lyckholm, L. J. (1998). Should physicians accept gifts from patients? *Journal of the American Medical Association, 280*(22), 1944–1946.

Martin, J. M., & Martin, E. P. (1985). *The helping tradition in the black family and community.* Washington, DC: National Association of Social Workers.

McClennen, J. C., & Glenn, R. T. (1997). Use of social services by African

American families: A multivariate analysis. *Family Therapy, 24*(1), 39–53.

McMahon, M. O. (1996). *The general method of social work practice: A generalist perspective.* Boston: Allyn & Bacon.

McRoy, R. G. (1990). A historical overview of black families. In S. M. L. Logan, E. M. Freeman, & R. G. McRoy (Eds.), *Social work practice with black families* (pp. 3–17). New York: Longman.

Miley, K. K., O'Melia, M., & DuBois, B. (2001). *Generalist social work practice: An empowering approach.* Boston: Allyn & Bacon.

National Association of Social Workers (1999). *Code of ethics of the National Association of Social Workers.* [Brochure]. Washington, DC: NASW.

National Center for Children in Poverty (2003). Low income children in the United States. Retrieved July 23, 2003, from www.nccp.org/pub_cpf03.html

National Jobs for All Coalition (2002, December). December 2002 unemployment data. Retrieved February 13, 2003, from www.njfac.org/jobnews.html

Nobles, W. W., & Goddard, L. L. (1984). *Understanding the black family: A guide for scholarship and research.* Oakland, CA: Black Family Institute.

Pinn, A. B. (2002). *The black church in the post civil rights era.* Maryknoll, NY: Orbis Books.

Sandven, K., & Resnick, M. D. (1990). Informal adoption among black adolescent mothers. *American Journal of Orthopsychiatry, 21*(6), 705–727.

Siegel, L. (1994). Cultural differences and their impact on practice in child welfare. *Journal of Multicultural Social Work, 3*(3), 87–98.

Smith, H. Y. (2001). Building on the strengths of black families: Self-help and empowerment. In S. L. M. Logan (Ed.), *The black family: Strengths, self-help, and positive change* (pp. 21–38). Boulder, CO: Westview Press.

Smolar, A. I. (2002). Reflections on gifts in the therapeutic setting: The gift from patient to therapist. *American Journal of Psychotherapy, 56*(1), 27–45.

Swigonski, M. E. (1996). Challenging privilege through africentric social work practice. *Social Work, 41*(2), 153–161.

Trotter, J. W. (Ed.). (1991). *The great migration in historical perspective: New dimensions of race, class, and gender.* Bloomington: Indiana University Press.

United States Census Bureau. (2003). The black population in the United States: March 2002. Retrieved July 23, 2003, from www.census.gov

www.usconstitution.net. Retrieved August 14, 2003.

Social Work Practice with Latino Americans

Claudia L. Moreno and Marietta Guido

Immigration and fertility patterns of Latinos make them the largest minority[1] group in this country. Latinos are present in all 50 states in this country, with some areas being more populated than others. As a result, it becomes crucial for social work practitioners to be respectful of Latino individuals, informed of sociocultural and environmental influences on them, and knowledgeable of demographics and differences within subgroups if we are to provide competent, ethical, and responsive services.

The movement of diversity has taken us from cultural awareness, which implies cursory knowledge of a specific culture, to cultural competence, which involves the acquisition of specific knowledge and practice skills to work with specific groups. Imagine, for example, that a social worker is working with a Latina client whose husband died recently and that the client is going through the mourning process. The client is telling the social worker that her husband's spirit came to visit her. With a lack of cultural awareness and competence, the social worker might think that the client made this up or is seeing visions. On the contrary, a culturally competent social worker knows that this piece of information represents part of the belief system of this particular client. In a more comprehensive way, a culturally competent social worker should know that seeing the spirit of a dead person represents part of the belief system within the Latino culture and will explore how it is affecting the client's life and her mourning process in an effort to assist more effectively.

---

[1]The term *minority* refers to having unequal and inferior power and access to resources in comparison to the dominant majority.

This chapter will address a comprehensive view of Latinos' sociodemographic background, the history of oppression and survival that Latinos have endured, and cultural strengths. We will discuss the concept of cultural competence within the realm of practice with Latino Americans, from establishing initial contact to identifying a problem to assessment, intervention, and termination skills.

THE DEMOGRAPHICS OF LATINO AMERICANS

Latinos represent the largest minority group in the United States, with approximately 35.3 million of people representing 12.5% of the total population (U.S. Census Bureau, 2001). One of nine people in the United States is of Hispanic origin. In approximately two generations, the United States will be home to the largest number of Latinos other than Mexico (Suarez-Orozco & Paez, 2002). About 58% of Hispanics are concentrated in three states: California, Texas, and New York. Nationally, Hispanics are relatively young compared with other groups, one-third of Hispanics are younger than 18 and one in three Hispanics is aged 15 or younger. The mean age is 29, and the median age is 26.6, with almost equal numbers of males and females.

In the following section, we present an overview of socioeconomic indicators, such as foreign-born status, income bracket, educational attainment, and family composition. It is essential to note that the census figures (U.S. Census Bureau, 2001) provide a generic picture of Latinos without considering variability within and among Latino groups. Latinos in the United States are a very heterogeneous group that challenges generalizations.

- **Foreign-born status.** A large percentage (43%) of Latinos in the United States are foreign-born. During the last decade, immigration from Spanish-speaking Latin American countries increased from 37% to 46%. By 2000, Mexican immigrants accounted for 30% of the total population of immigrants (U.S. Census, 2001).
- **Origin.** Latinos of Mexican origin represent two-thirds (66%) of the U.S. Latino population, followed by 15% from Central America (the largest groups are Salvadorian, 43%, and Guatemalan, 20%) and South America (37% Colombian, 18.5% Ecuadorian, and 17% Peruvian), 9% from Puerto Rico, 6% from the Caribbean, and 4% from Cuba (U.S. Census, 2001).
- **Income bracket.** Income per capita and socio-demographic factors vary among the three major groups of Latinos (Puerto Ricans, Mexicans, and Cubans). Latinos are two times more likely to be unemployed than non-Hispanic whites, of those 8% were Puerto Rican, 7% Mexican and 5.8% Cuban (U.S. Census Bureau, 2000). A large number of Latinos live in poverty and have low educational skills, and a large majority hold low-skills jobs, which perpetuate their poverty. Latinos are three times more likely to live in poverty than are non-Hispanic whites, and the poverty rate for Latinos is 23% (U.S. Census Bureau, 2001). Puerto Ricans and

Mexicans have the highest rate of poverty. Among Latinos who live in poverty, 26% are Puerto Rican, 24% Mexican, 17% Central and South American, and 17% Cuban (U.S. Census Bureau, 2000). Thirty-four percent of Latino children live in poverty compared with 11% of non-Hispanic white children. The number of Latino children who live in poverty breaks down by subgroups as follows: 44% Puerto Ricans, 35% Mexicans, 32% other Hispanics, 27% Central and South Americans, and 16% Cubans (U.S. Census, 2001).

- **Educational attainment.** Educational attainment has been an issue of concern for the community because, despite progress, Latinos continue to lag behind in educational achievement compared with other groups. In 2001, about 56% of Latinos had earned a high-school degree compared with 88% of non-Hispanic whites (U.S. Census Bureau, 2001).

- **Family composition.** Latinos are also less likely to be married and more likely to have female-headed households than are non-Hispanic whites. Twenty-four percent of Latino households are headed by women, compared with 13% of non-Hispanic white families. Puerto Ricans are the largest group to have households headed by females (36%), compared with 21% for Mexicans, 25% for Central and South Americans, and 18% for Cubans (U.S. Census, 2001).

Hispanic or Latino?

The terms *Latino* and *Hispanic* did not exist 50 years ago and lack specificity regarding national origin. The terms are used differently geographically and in different arenas. Some Latinos are not aware of the political implications of both terms; such awareness varies by group, acculturation, sociopolitical identity, and geographic area. Ethnic awareness is a process of self-discovery, ethnic identity, and learning about one's own sociopolitical history in addition to engaging in the ethnic diaspora.

The term *Hispanic* was imposed by the Nixon administration on a group of people who come from Spanish-speaking countries. The term connotes colonization and a link to "Hispania" or Spain and does not acknowledge our native history. In the diaspora of Latino America, the term *Latino* embraces our indigenous African, Asian, Spanish, and Arabic ancestry. The terms *Latino* and *Hispanic* are used to make political statements, and both have different meanings. Both terms imply an ethnic background and not a race. Furthermore, the term *Hispanic* is a reminder of our history of colonization, whereas *Latino* reaffirms a mixed cultural and racial background. Most Latinos identify themselves by their country of origin, but when using a specific term, most Latinos prefer the word *Latino/a,* even though this term lacks specificity regarding national origin (Suarez-Orozco & Paez, 2002). For the purposes of the chapter, we chose the term *Latino* over *Hispanic* because we believe it evokes the indigenous cultures that have survived in the diaspora.

Detailed sociocultural information of Latino subgroups is slowly emerging. It is imperative to acknowledge the diversity among Latino subgroups: sociodemographic differences, and specific needs of each community such as linguistic and religious needs. To be culturally competent with Latino subgroups, social workers must acknowledge and understand these differences.

Latinos in the United States are a highly heterogeneous group in socio-economic factors such as income, education, marital and family composition, and employment. We also have different histories of colonization, immigration, and politics, as well as different experiences regarding class, race, and skin color, which affect our ethnic-identity development. Moreover, the composition of the Latino population in the United States changes over time. For example, during the 1970s, Cubans were among the three largest Latino subgroups, but today they only represent 4% of the Latino population. Today the third largest subgroup is South Americans according to the recent census estimates (U.S. Census Bureau, 1999). Latinos are often erroneously viewed collectively, and this has masked differences and vulnerabilities of certain groups (Zambrana & Dorrington, 1998).

THE HISTORICAL OPPRESSION AND SURVIVAL VALUES OF LATINO AMERICANS

We have witnessed more than 500 years of oppression and survival in Latin America. Although this oppression continues at different levels through Latin America, it has created in many Latinos a sense of resiliency and a survival code.

Historically, a number of groups have migrated to Latin America and left us African, Asian, Arabic, and European cultural influences. Different social classes and color lines emerged through colonization (Fortes de Leff & Espejel Arco, 2000). More specifically, most of Latin America was colonized by Spaniards, known as "the conquistadors." These *conquistadores,* as different from the colonizers in North America, mixed with the indigenous population and produced the mixed-blood "mestizo," who now is representative of most of Latin Americans (Blea, 1997). This colonization left religious, cultural, and language influences that have taken hold in various degrees within our indigenous groups.

The *conquistadores* who were mostly white, used their power to discriminate and oppress the indigenous peoples, *criollos* or *mestizos* (mixed), and slaves. These power structures are still prevalent and have created class and color divisions in Latin American societies that have resulted in economic and social differences across classes (Fortes de Leff & Espejel Arco, 2000). In the United States, there is prevalent oppression based on color, class, and socioeconomic status within Latino groups. Within the mainstream, this oppression has been translated into allocation of services and opportunities to certain groups but not to others.

The conquest of Latin America has been perceived as an act of sociocultural violence, through genocide and imposition of customs and belief systems, and as an act of sexual violence, through the raping of women (Fortes de Leff & Espejel Arco, 2000). It is believed that these historical events of violence, discrimination, and oppression have perpetuated continued violence, drinking, and other maladaptive behaviors among many Latin Americans.

The United States' involvement in Latin American governments has dictated the political behavior of Latino America, and many Latinos who arrive in this country come with the experience of being uprooted by socioeconomic forces in their homelands (Suarez-Orozco & Paez, 2002). The Latino experience has been shaped by immigration and the reallocation of the borders. The process of acculturation has profoundly affected Latinos in the United States at many levels. Such process involves the adaptation and adjustment of the individuals from the culture of origin to the mainstream culture. However, acculturation does not necessarily entail substituting the "new" culture over the culture of origin, but, rather, integrating the "old" and the "new" cultures. Biculturalism surfaces when the individual embraces dual visions and assesses aspects of both cultures and integrates them in a functional way. In contrast to other immigrant groups that settled in this country earlier, large numbers of Latinos are maintaining the languages, cultural values, and belief systems of their homelands (Marin, 1993). Many Latinos in this country have redefined the concept of double consciousness and transnationalism by being able to interact with the mainstream culture while maintaining strong ties with their countries of origin (Suarez-Orozco & Paez, 2002).

CULTURALLY COMPETENT KNOWLEDGE THEORY AND PRACTICE SKILLS FOR LATINO AMERICANS

Culture is an essential component in our work with clients. Culturally competent social workers need to know the history, geography, sociodemographic profile, and current sociopolitical issues of the population. Cultural characteristics of the population in addition to knowledge of cultural strengths are fundamental for a culturally competent social worker.

Cultural Strengths

Despite our violent history of colonization, Latinos have survived centuries of oppression, discrimination, and genocide. This survival is manifested in the resistance to lose the Spanish language, customs, and value system. Our presence has long sociohistorical roots and a legacy of racism that have influenced our relationships with and trust of institutions of power (Larkey, Hecht, Miller, & Alatorre, 2001). Furthermore, racism and oppression have defined Latinos from a cultural-deficit perspective without considering the social and economic disadvantages of many Latino groups. Socioeconomic disadvantages cannot be confused with "cultural disadvantages"; rather, social and economic injustices affect people's survival and create risk factors for many Latino families such as violence, substance abuse, and entering the child welfare system (Zambrana & Dorrington, 1998).

Like members of all cultures, Latinos transmit religious and spiritual beliefs, value systems, and traditions from generation to generation. Many cultural values such as *familialismo* (familialism), *personalismo, confianza* (trust), *respeto* (respect), *simpatia,* and fatalism guide and influence belief systems, attitudes, and behavior. Familialism is one of the most important factors that influence the lives of Latinos. Familialism emphasizes the priority of the family over individual needs and the importance of maintaining a strong kinship network (Marin, 1993). Strong familialism has been implicated as a preventive factor in child abuse (Coohey, 2001), substance abuse (Catalano et al., 1992), and family violence among Latinos (Gorman-Smith, Tolan, Zelli, & Huesmann, 1996). *Simpatia* is a basic social script that emphasizes positive and cooperative interpersonal relations (Marin, 1993).

Most Latinos place a lot of emphasis on the family as a unit that includes not only economic but also emotional and recreational sources of support. Family dynamics and gender roles vary from country to county and in relation to socioeconomic status, education, and exposure to the mainstream culture. Moreover, not all families are traditional but vary from conservative to liberal. We cannot assume that all Latino individuals cherish family to the same degree.

Cultural awareness, knowledge acquisition, skill development, and inductive learning are imperative to enhance competence for all social workers (Lum, 2003), especially at a time when the country is going through a tremendous renaissance of diversity and transformation. Globalization has brought greater recognition of other cultures and languages, particularly of Spanish, which is the second most frequently spoken language in the United States. People from Latin America represent a large percentage of clients for many social workers practicing in the United States today.

Knowledge of systems of care both in this country and Latin America is essential for assessment, planning, and intervention. Mental health services in Latin America do not function in the same way as those in developed countries do. For instance, Argentineans have been influenced by European traditions of counseling with a strong psychoanalytic influence that has permeated the society and cultural norms. European psychoanalytic counseling has created a system of established mental health care. In contrast, other countries in Latin America have a more salient medical model, where mental health issues are not dealt with within an established system of care but, rather, within nontraditional systems of care such as family members, friends, and community members who serve as mental health advisors. In addition to a nontraditional system of healers such as "curanderos," "spiritists," and "santeros" who has traditionally integrated indigenous, religious, and spiritual healing techniques. This system of care has existed for hundreds of years and has permeated the cultural beliefs and values of many Latino Americans. Nowadays, many Latinos integrate the traditional systems of care with the nontraditional. However, mental health systems in the United States have not integrated the nontraditional systems that have been part of our cultures for centuries. This dissonance increases distrust and low usage of traditional systems of care.

A culturally competent social worker is one who knows the cultural group with which he or she is working. Cultures differ in many aspects that include the perception of time orientation, social and personal space, and behavioral patterns of social scripts. In mental health, the manifestation, expression, and meaning of symptoms are part of the context of culture. When social workers fail to consider the shared beliefs, values, and practices of their clients' cultural groups, there is an increased danger of doing an improper assessment, planning, and intervention (Malgady, Rogler, & Costantino, 1987).

This notion is fundamental for understanding that the expression of stress and some clinical conditions are also cultural and can be misinterpreted. The problem with practice research with Latinos is that it takes an "establishment paradigm" perspective that is deductive and not inductive in the cultural context and, thus, does not produce knowledge of how culture might influence some cultural manifestations of psychopathology (Fabrega, 1990). There are, for example, Latino culturally bound syndromes, which are a particular way in which some people express psychiatric symptomatology. Furthermore, knowledge and competency skills give social workers a frame of reference from which to understand many dimensions of a client's symptoms.

Some researchers have mentioned that cultural values can serve as protective and risk factors for mental health problems. For instance, *fatalismo* can lead to a high incidence of depression (Mirowsy & Ross, 1984) and psychological distress (Roberts, 1980) in Mexican Americans. Fatalism is seen as an inability to change the self and master the environment. It is a sense of powerlessness to change things. Some mental health providers mention that *fatalismo* can have positive and negative effects because it can impair mastery of self and the environment, but as a cultural trait, *fatalismo* can protect some people from anxiety disorders (Mirowsy & Ross, 1984). Other risk factors that are not related to culture, but, rather, to socioeconomic status include economic distress and poverty, as well as factors present mainly in oppressed groups, such as prejudice, discrimination, and linguistic barriers.

COMMON CHARACTERISTICS OF LATINO CULTURES

- **Familialism** is a strong identification with the nuclear and extended family; a sense of responsibility and loyalty to the family—in some cases over spouses and children.
- **Respeto,** or respect, is shown to the elderly and those in position of power.
- **Confianza,** or trust, is a highly regarded value.
- **Traditional gender roles** place authority and power in male figures and allow them to exercise certain behaviors prohibited to females and characterized as *machismo* (the powerful, strong, and active man).
- **Collectivism** emphasizes the needs and importance of the group rather than the individual.
- **Simpatia,** the "good face," implies avoiding confrontation and anger towards others, hiding true feelings when they are negative, and creating smooth relationships.
- **Personalismo, or interest in another's personal situation,** is the preferred mode for social interaction. Some Latino clients might inquire about the social worker's well-being and expect a certain amount of disclosure.

CONTACT SKILLS WITH LATINO AMERICANS

The initial contact between the social worker and the Latino client is crucial and might determine whether the client will remain in treatment. The cultural values of *confianza, respeto,* and *personalismo* will affect the process of engaging clients. For instance, for many Latinos a handshake is establishing *personalismo, confianza,* and *respeto.* The use of formal language such as *usted* (formal word for *you*) instead of *tú* (informal word for *you*) is necessary, especially when working with older clients and parents.

Overcoming Resistance and Communication Barriers

There has been a long-standing controversy about whether there is ethnic bias in mental health service delivery. With the increase of immigrants from Latin America to this country, there are a large number of Spanish monolingual clients and a lack of social workers skilled in speaking Spanish. In addition, the established system of mental health services does not generally operate from a multicultural frame of reference. This creates a gap between mental health services and the needs of ethnic groups (Malgady & Zayas, 2001).

Three factors have been attributed to Latinos' underutilization of mental health services: (1) the lack of available and affordable mental health resources, (2) linguistic barriers, and (3) the strong reliance on family physicians and family members for mental health care (Karno, 1994). These factors, especially the language and the cultural gaps, interfere with the possibility of clients seeking and receiving services that would meet their needs.

Language for Latinos has become a symbol of resistance, and many Latinos from many generations in this country keep Spanish as an emotional and symbolic language of "heredity." The most common foreign language spoken at home in the United States is Spanish, which is used by more than 14 million people, followed by Italian. According to census figures (U.S. Census Bureau, 2000), about 69% of Latinos speak Spanish at home, and of those Latinos who speak Spanish, about 63% do not speak English very well. Latinos come from about 20 different countries, so we can find many dialect differences in the meaning and usage of words. For example, the word *guagua* for Caribbeans (Puerto Ricans, Dominicans, and Cubans) means *bus,* for Chileans it means *child,* and for Colombians and Ecuadorian, it means *dog.*

For proper assessment and intervention in clinical work with Latinos, it is essential to establish good verbal communication between client and clinician. Unfortunately, very few psychiatrists and other mental health professionals speak a foreign language. Communication barriers have been a cause of concern in the Hispanic mental health literature. Communicating meaning and understanding across cultures is a difficult task for any individual. Bilingual and bicultural as well as monolingual social workers need to consider that ethnicity and language might influence their diagnostic impressions of clients (Malgady & Zayas, 2001).

In one recent study (Arroyo, 1996), 56 non-Hispanic psychologists were asked to view and give their diagnostic impressions of two videotapes of a mock intake session. The content of the two tapes was identical except for the client's ethnicity. The researcher found that a Latino client was rated as more disturbed and in more urgent need of treatment than was the non-Latino client. A review of the literature on the evaluation of global psychopathology shows lack of agreement about whether the evaluation of limited English-speaking clients in English raises or lowers clinician ratings of these clients' severity of illness. Although reports indicate greater incidence of clinicians' reporting psychopathology in the primary language (Gonzalez, 1978), other studies show that Spanish-speaking clients with limited English-language skills are assessed as presenting higher levels of pathology when the language of interview is English rather than Spanish (Marcos, 1994).

Various aspects of language, such as intonation, speech, tone, emotional content, and the sense of self one feels when speaking a native but not a foreign language seem to play a determining role in the interaction between client and clinician. Monolingual Latino clients struggling with language barriers have difficulties expressing their emotions, feelings, and thoughts. Clinicians may interpret these difficulties as guarded behavior or uncooperativeness. A large number of Latino clients speak English and still struggle with the expression of emotions in a second language. For instance, some research (e.g., Marcos & Alpert, 1976) reveals that when people speak in a second language about emotionally charged experiences, the expression of emotion might be compromised.

Individuals communicating in a secondary language not only face having to deal with a different set of words but also in some cases may have a different sense of themselves and perceive themselves differently when speaking the nondominant language (Marcos, 1994). There are times when clients give different responses to the same questions in their primary and nondominant languages. According to Fishman (1960), this is a classic example of the language-relativity hypothesis, which postulates that language is not only a vehicle of communication but also a reality through which people identify and organize their worlds. These findings may be associated with the bilinguals' capacity to acquire, maintain, and use two separate language codes, each with its own lexical, phonetic, and emotional content.

Working with Latinos with limited English-language skills places important demands on the clinicians who must differentiate between verbal or nonverbal cues that are relevant for clinical impressions and those that are mere consequences of the language deficit.

Although communication is an essential ingredient for proper assessment and intervention, ethnic group membership alone does not account for communication barriers; socioeconomic factors also play an important role (Malgady & Zayas, 2001). For instance, some studies have found that socioeconomic factors influence the way people express and manifest mental health symptoms. A comparative study (Mirowsy & Ross, 1984) conducted with Mexican Americans found that those with lower socioeconomic status (SES) manifested more psychosomatic symptoms and more depression when interviewed in Spanish than did those with higher SES.

The ideal situation should involve clinicians able to communicate with clients in their primary languages. Reaching this point in a nation as ethnically diverse as ours is unlikely, so it is essential, at the very least, for clinicians to be sensitive to the linguistic implications and the impact of language barriers, which can substantially influence the clients' sense of identity, speech, and emotional content, as well as the clinicians' perception and interpretation of these. A potential misevaluation of the client's response could be minimized if the clinician can keep in mind the factors mentioned earlier. Besides these educational efforts, monolingual mental health professionals must consider having trained interpreters available to assist in situations where the low proficiency of clients in the English language could interfere with the accuracy of the work. Although this solution has potential, Marcos (1979) notes that translators without mental health training can minimize or normalize client's complaints and therefore mislead the clinician. The interpreter also might omit, condense, or change the focus of what was said. The need for more Latinos in the mental health field is evident. For social workers working with diverse Latino clients, it is imperative to account for differences in cultural identity, individual personality, and socio-economic factors, as well as how these components influence expressiveness, cultural manifestations, and language differences.

ESTABLISHING A RESPONSIVE SERVICE DELIVERY SYSTEM

Some studies suggest that use of services depends on many factors. As discussed earlier, Latinos have traditionally low usage of established mental health services both in Latin America and the United States.

Several studies of the prevalence of mental disorders among Hispanics have drawn mixed results, suggesting that Latinos have higher prevalence of symptom severity and are at a higher risk than are other groups for certain disorders, such as cognitive impairment, major depression, alcohol dependence, manic episodes, dysthymia, schizophrenia, and other affective disorders (Kessler et al., 1994). However, it may be that many Latinos encounter greater stressors than do members of other ethnic groups, stressors such as acculturation difficulties, low SES and education, general stress, immigration patterns, and use of alcohol and drugs, which exacerbate the incidence and prevalence of mental health problems (Rogler, Malgady, & Rodriguez, 1989). Given the current demographics of Latinos and their higher underutilization of established mental health care, Latinos are at high risk for having mental health disorders and for these disorders to remain untreated (Malgady & Zayas, 2001).

Recent movements in mental health have called for culturally appropriate and sensitive therapy, but despite this, Latinos continue to underutilize the traditional mental health centers. For those who use them, more than half terminate therapy after one session (Rogler, Malgady & Rodriguez, 1989). Furthermore, Latinos are disproportionately placed in programs that emphasize pharmacological rather than psychosocial interventions (Malgady & Rodriguez, 1989).

One of the probable causes of underutilization and early termination of services is the lack of understanding of culturally defined symptoms and disorders. For instance, some disorders or conditions are misunderstood outside of the Latino culture, such as *susto* (caused by a frightening event) (Weller, et al., 2002) and *ataque de nervios* (similar to a panic attack) (Lewis-Fernaandez, 1996). One of the difficulties in creating services that are sensitive to Latinos is that there is limited research on culture-bound syndromes that describe the phenomena within a cultural context rather than attempting to translate them into psychiatric diagnosis (Weller et al., 2002).

The system of mental health care for Latinos is also underrepresented by bilingual and bicultural mental health providers. These linguistic and cultural barriers exacerbate the high dropout rates of Latinos who are monolingual and do not continue services (De La Rosa, 1998). This lack of representation of professionals who resemble and understand the clientele creates a distance that interferes with the accuracy of the assessment, which leads to improper treatment and interventions.

A system of care that is responsive to the needs of Latinos is one that aims to create and deliver services while taking into consideration the heterogeneity of the Latino community. Key elements such as the similarity between the clinician and the client enhance the ability to identify cultural ways of identifying problems and expressing symptoms, to understand the meanings associated, and to understand the linguistic variation of words, thought, and expression (Malgady & Costantino, 1998). It is more important to create a responsive system of care that provides a cultural match than it is to create an ethnic match (Sue, 1988). In addition, a culturally responsive system of care should be based on relevant research and practice issues regarding the different groups of Latinos, should recognize that ethnicity and culture are important elements for understanding human behavior and psychological processes, and should respect variation in the roles of family members, community structures, belief systems, and values. Such a system should further demonstrate respect for Latinos' cultural beliefs and religious views and values, and their impact on psychosocial functioning, worldview, expressions of distress, and attitudes toward systems of care.

Using Professional Self-Disclosure

Some self-disclosure by the clinician could help in the process of engaging a client. Appropriate self-disclosure could include a discussion about clinician's areas of expertise and professional credentials. Latino clients could ask the Latino clinician about his or her country of origin. Non-Latino clinicians who speak Spanish could be asked where they learned the language. Information could be given in a brief manner without going into details about the clinician's personal life. For example, a clinician may want to disclose that his or her background is Ecuadorian, but it is not necessary to explain one's history in this country.

A clinician needs to educate clients about the importance of boundaries in the relationship by explaining the goals and objectives, not only of the clinical meetings, but also of professional ethics. It is important to explain why it is not therapeutic to mix professional relationships with personal relationships. In most cases, clients will honor these restrictions (Carrillo, 2001).

In general, some disclosure seems to give clients the feeling that clinicians are also human. In line with *personalismo,* a certain amount of self-disclosure facilitates openness and contributes to developing a sense of trust by the Latino client. However, a clinician who is asked a question that could be considered too personal should not feel compelled to answer it; instead, the clinician could redirect the client to the purpose of the meeting. According to Triandis, Marin, and Lisansky (1984), *personalismo* constitutes a style of communication that Latinos seem to feel comfortable with. Latinos tend to be more interested in knowing somebody as a person rather than assessing him or her on external variables such as occupational or socioeconomic status. This may translate to the need for the client to establish a personal connection with the clinician before establishing a working therapeutic relationship. For example, in our work we have found that clients sometimes asked for our marital status or whether or not we have children. We both agree that it is appropriate to answer these questions without giving further details. By making a personal connection between client and clinician, the *confianza* (trust) valued by the Latino client may be formed. The recognition of the importance of *personalismo* as a central component in interactions helps provide a culturally sensitive therapeutic alliance.

It is common for Latino clients to either invite clinicians to family gatherings or to bring them gifts as a sign of gratitude. Clinicians need to use good judgment about whether or not to accept gifts. Expensive or inappropriate gifts must be returned. The acceptance of food or any other inexpensive items may be therapeutic for the relationship (Carrillo, 2001). For example, an elderly female Cuban client whom one of us has been assisting for the last three years likes to prepare a Cuban lunch for me whenever she knows I will see her. Once a month, besides assisting her with what she needs, I also have lunch with her as part of our work. By doing this, I am helping this particular client, but also I am joining her, by using a cultural connection, which is the food. In this way, I am adopting an attitude that encompasses creativity and flexibility as part of the therapeutic process.

PROBLEM IDENTIFICATION SKILLS WITH LATINO AMERICANS

Gaining Problem Understanding

Given the collectivist orientation of Latinos, which stresses the importance of the group over individual needs and respect for traditional authority, many Latino clients might identify problems that relate to the group or family rather than the self. Some cultural theorists argue that people from collective cultures have a different conception of self than do those from individualist cultures (Coon & Kemmelmeier, 2001). On the other hand, the struggle between individual needs that comes from the values of the mainstream society and the cultural expectations, the referent culture, might be in conflict. However, recent evidence suggests that most cultures are not exclusively individualistic or collectivist but, rather, integrate elements of both, with each element appearing alone in different contexts (Ho & Chiu, 1994), and that individuals can be high and low in both elements without contradiction (Coon & Kemmelmeier, 2001).

For social workers working with Latino clients, it is imperative to understand these different orientations. Situating the Latino client as an autonomous actor rather than as an individual embedded in groups and relationships (Coon & Kemmelmeier, 2001) may result in misinterpretation of the feelings and problems the client is describing.

Viewing Micro, Meso, Macro, and Exo System Level Problems

To work effectively with Latino clients, social workers must view clients through a multisystemic perspective, examining the micro, meso, macro, and exo system levels of their experiences.

To begin, social workers must learn whether clients are immigrants or natives, how long they have been in this country, and what characterizes their histories of migration. For instance, clients coming from Puerto Rico are automatically American citizens and do not have legal entry issues as other groups might. Clients coming from war torn countries might present different issues, such as histories of trauma, persecution, and posttraumatic stress. Most Latin American clients come from countries fraught with corruption and economic problems and have emigrated for mainly economic reasons. Further, some clients bring distrust of the establishment and might have problems making ends meet.

ASSESSMENT SKILLS WITH LATINO AMERICAN CLIENTS

Using a biopsychosocial perspective allows the social worker to see various dimensions of clients. Because many health-related conditions have psychological and social manifestations, assessing biological aspects of clients' lives, such as health status, is imperative. Latinos continue to be overrepresented in selected conditions, such as HIV/AIDS; diabetes; cirrhosis of the liver; homicide; and cervical, gallbladder, and stomach cancer (Pérez-Stable & Nápoles-Springer, 2001). Some Latinos have a tendency to express psychological distress through physical symptoms; this phenomenon is known as *somatization* (Carrillo, 2001). The symptoms presented can include headaches, stomach problems, and gastric distress.

The literature advocates the importance of understanding culture in assessing the manifestations of mental health problems that include differences in response style and the cultural connotations to desirable behavior might increase symptom reporting among Latinos (Canino, 1994). For instance, *ataque de nervios* is a culturally bound syndrome, which is manifested by feeling heart palpitations, beginning to shout, and falling to the floor almost unconscious, and sometimes becoming aggressive. This symptom can be mistaken for a panic attack (Canino, 1994; De La Cancela, Guarnacci, & Carrillo, 1986).

Furthermore, a number of societal, political, and cultural factors can make the biopsychosocial assessment difficult. Latinos might be living or have a history of living under stressful circumstances, including alienation, prejudice, migration, immigration, poverty, living in high-crime areas, difficulties with English, and undocumented status.

The journey to this country usually involves gains and losses. Latino immigrants have left behind families, roles, statuses, a common culture, and, often, better weather. At the same time, they have gained a free educational system, more job opportunities, and so on. Latinos who have immigrated because of political oppression might have witnessed or survived brutal acts of war as well as social crime and violence, torture, and political and social oppression. Although they may be common to many Latinos, people can experience these phenomena differently. As part of the process-stage approach (Lum, 2003), social workers should try to identify these factors, and the client's responses to them, through a careful biopsychosocial assessment.

Social Worker's Self-Knowledge

Although culturally competent social workers must understand the values, beliefs, and sociocultural contexts of Latino cultures, it is perhaps even more critical to be sensitive to the individual variations. Having general knowledge of the culture without considering individual differences presents a danger of stereotyping.

Each of us must accept the influence of our process of socialization, which largely determines our biases, values, beliefs, assumptions, and stereotypes. Consciously or unconsciously, we tend to bring these factors into our work. Because there is a prevailing negative stereotype in the United States (dumb, lazy, uneducated, inferior, and so on) clinicians must engage in continual training to free themselves from these biases. Moreover, some professionals can perceive their own values as universal and assume pathology in the absence of such values. To prevent their beliefs and values from clouding their understanding of clients' experiences, social workers must maintain an awareness of the culturally bound origins of their own value systems.

In assessing a Latino client, it is important to evaluate the person's level of acculturation. *Acculturation* refers to the loss of traditional cultural attitudes, values, beliefs, customs, behaviors, and the acceptance of new cultural traits (Vega, et al., 1994). Acculturation is considered a complicated, multifaceted, and ongoing process, and research into who is acculturated and who is not has produced contradictory results. Generally speaking, however, people move along a continuum of acculturation at different points in their lives, and acculturation varies according to the individual's circumstances. A person might at times feel caught between two worlds. Intergenerational conflict is common in Latino families: In addition to "normal" generational differences, some families might experience huge differences in members' levels of acculturation, and these differences can result in a great deal of conflict (Carrillo, 2001).

Our society sustains values and beliefs that emphasize the importance of individualism over the group as well as autonomy, competition, progress, and future orientation, among others. These values are not universal values. A Latino/a client who identifies with the traditional Latino culture may hold opposite values. He or she may emphasize family or group over the individual, value extended family, and have a more present orientation. If so, the values of this particular Latino/a client may conflict with those values held by the professional. Similarly, a highly acculturated Latino/a client may show values, beliefs, and attitudes more similar to those of the majority of society, varying only in degree and manner.

As we begin the 21st century and the number of Latinos is growing in this country, we still need to find ways to develop more understanding of diversity. Despite the wide range of difference among people, diversity is not yet celebrated. We do not fully respect those who are different from us and often view them as a threat to the status quo. In fact, racism can be seen as a way to control diversity: the more monocultural we are, the safer many people within the majority feel.

Knowledge of Client

Obtaining information such as client's status of immigration, the experience of adjusting to a new culture, the experience and the history with oppression as well as the client's gender can help in the process of understanding this particular client. Along with this, it is important to bear in mind characteristics such as education attainment, employment, generation and immigration status, family income, family size, birth order, family deaths and divorces, childhood illnesses, type of parenting received, and language status. Never assume that a general finding for a particular Latino group applies to all Latino groups, or to all individuals within this particular group.

Latinos vary in flexibility of gender roles. Some families are still very traditional and are organized along hierarchical lines with strict gender roles. Some males are still seen as having more power and being the decision makers and providing financial support and protection for their families (Carrillo, 2001). Some females are still seen as the nurturers, and their main roles are usually rearing of children, managing the household, and providing emotional support for the family. In most countries in Latin America, however, many women are working full-time jobs, and the women's rights movement has penetrated into the diaspora society; thus traditional gender roles have also undergone changes. Many Latinas work outside the household, have attained higher education, and in some instances have more job security than men and demand equal rights and autonomy (Carrillo, 2001). Social service providers need to avoid assuming that all Latinos adhere to traditional gender roles.

For a social worker, it is essential to have enough understanding and curiosity to be able to open a dialogue with the client about the experience of being a Latino/a in this country. Identity formation is an important factor to consider here. We can talk about identity described as how one views oneself in qualities and values and how society perceives one's primary reference group. Identity formation is shaped by the interplay between these two aspects (the internal and the external). Externally, we can see how society portrays Latinos/as in a negative way: There are few positive images in the media and few positive role models in positions of power. This information coming from the outside is internalized by clients and affects their self-esteem. Similarly, if the clients' families do not affirm their good qualities, self-esteem can be hampered. If one has encountered strong positive messages about, and a sense of pride in one's own group, then one will likely not internalize negative messages to a great degree.

INTERVENTION SKILLS WITH LATINO AMERICAN CLIENTS

Culture has been a key element in the helping process, not only during the initial assessment phase but also at the intervention phase (Lu, Lum, & Chen, 2001). An approach that endorses the empowerment of Latino/a clients to engage in the process of change, rather than approaches that pathologize or blame the client, are welcome. The clinician needs to concentrate on and validate the client's strengths rather than weaknesses. In addition, showing a caring and respectful attitude tends to facilitate the development of trust in the working relationship. Perhaps most important, social workers working with Latino clients must demonstrate respect and an attitude that communicates admiration as well as delight for what is unique in that client. Believing in the Latino/a client can do a great deal to promote the confidence that has probably been damaged by the experience of life in this society.

An effective social worker validates the qualities of care and nurturing toward others present in the Latino/a clients as well as teaching clients to develop the same kind of principles for themselves. Discouraging a Latino/a client from caring for others, especially members of the family, can be quite confusing. Instead, an important learning experience for this client can be to validate his or her care for others and to help find ways for this client to recognize when giving "too much" to others violates his/her own needs.

Because of the collectivist nature of Latino cultures, concepts such as "power over" or "power for oneself" often leave the Latino/a clients unable to act. Miller (1994) defines *power* as the capacity to move or to produce change and as the internal process of constructing meaning. A social worker can assist a client by exploring healthy ways of being powerful and by empowering through awareness and expression of feelings, reactions, and needs.

Latinos might differ in what form of therapy will be most appropriate. Some research has found that because of the strong *familialism* and *personalismo* (interpersonal relationships) of Latinos, family work seems to be the most viable modality of treatment (Bean, Perry, & Bedell, 2001). It is important for the social worker to act as advocates for the family and familiarize Latinos with entitlements and services available. It is important to develop interventions within the context of the culture. For instance, Latinos might perceive assertiveness in women as negative. Assertiveness needs to be assessed within the context of the culture. Social workers should avoid forcing changes, should provide concrete suggestions that Latinos can quickly implement, and should engage the family warmly and with *personalismo* (Bean et al., 2001).

Group intervention has long been the model of choice for subgroup populations. Group process helps individuals validate and support one another in dealing with issues of ethnic identity. The group leader should promote and encourage the interaction that can create connections and enhance individual power.

The development of intervention programs for Latinos needs to account for the sociocultural worldview of Latinos. This sociocultural view is permeated by the prevalence of myths that influence behaviors, attitudes, and social relationships (Fortes de Leff & Espejel, 2000), in addition to the interpretation of social reality and expectations of family members and others. It is important to maintain attention to intergroup, intragroup, and individual differences as well as to the set of shared values and beliefs most Latinos hold. The family is the cornerstone of the Latino culture, and it serves as the source of emotional support, identity, self-esteem, and sense of security for many Latinos—known as *familialismo* (Gloria & Perogy, 1996). Given the importance of the family, family therapy and family interventions that stress the responsibility of each family member for the stability and health of the family as a whole can be an effective tool—albeit one that contradicts messages coming from mainstream U.S. culture. As an intervention strategy, although it might be appropriate to stress individualism with some clients, most Latinos value familialism and derive strength through their bonds with relatives. The cultural emphasis on *simpatia* (smooth relationships) discourages Latinos from engaging in interpersonal conflict and can impede or enhance conflict resolution. In mental health situations, *simpatia* can be misunderstood as the client avoiding conflict and denying feelings of anger. In the worst cases, *simpatia* can result in enduring abusive, conflictive, and dysfunctional situations. Interventions that are sensitive to the notion of *simpatia* can help clients explore actions and behaviors that maintain and change the meaning of *simpatia* (Gloria & Peroy, 1996).

TERMINATION SKILLS WITH LATINO AMERICAN CLIENTS

Different studies have shown the effect of termination on clients as well as on practitioners. The termination phase is usually perceived as a period tinted with feelings of loss and inevitable mourning. Clients generally express feelings that resemble the period of grief subsequent to the loss of a loved one: a time of denial of the actual termination followed by anger, feelings of being abandoned and perhaps acting out as a way of trying to reestablish the relationship, reexperiencing previous losses, and finally, if grief work is successful, the acceptance of the ending of the treatment. Termination can be a difficult phase not just for the Latino client but also for the culturally competent social worker. When the therapeutic relationship is characterized by *personalismo,* termination can present a conflict. *Personalismo* (the informal) and professional role (the formal) constitute part of the therapeutic process. *Personalismo* can bring conflict to the relationship; for instance, *personalismo* can be at times in the forefront and professional etiquette will be in the background and vice versa. Because *personalismo* calls for an informal and smooth relationship between client and clinician, ending the relationship can feel inappropriate to the client and result in hurt feelings. Furthermore, the practitioner might experience sadness, feelings of loss, denial, anger, and the reliving of previous losses.

Ideally, however, during the termination phase, practitioner and client evaluate their work together and the accomplishments made through the treatment. In addition, those areas that need more work are discussed, and the social worker helps the client think about how to use newly discovered skills to address these issues. The clinician also helps the client focus on experiencing pride, joy, excitement, and a deep sense of gratitude for the process of growth and enrichment. Moreover, the practitioner can focus on feelings of pride in the clients' success, pride in his or her own effectiveness, and gratitude for the growth attained and for each having learned from the other. The culturally competent social worker thus turns the termination process into an act of celebration for the work accomplished together. Further, as an extension of *personalismo,* the culturally competent social worker conveys during the termination a message that the social worker can be of use in the future if need be.

The reactions mentioned earlier constitute responses that take place in successful treatments. But the reactions elicited by an abrupt or premature termination are stronger, depending on the circumstances. In such abrupt terminations, the practitioner might feel guilt, anger, and a sense of failure. Both parties leave feeling frustrated, with the therapeutic process left unresolved.

CLOSING THOUGHTS

In working with Latinos, it is important that social workers acquire knowledge of the history and the geographic and subtle cultural differences among Latinos. In addition, factors such as socioeconomic level, gender roles, language barriers, and level of acculturation make the work with this ethnic group complex—but at the same time enrich clinical work.

Social workers face the difficult task of integrating all the elements involved in assessment and intervention with Latinos. In the *initial phase,* it is crucial to establish respect and a comfortable environment for the client. Although similarities (ethnicity, among others) with clients can facilitate the development of trust and respect, they are not sufficient, and we need to constantly strive toward developing a relationship that will lead to trust and respect. Clients whose native language is not English might feel more at ease

CASE

Case Study Integration Exercise on Assessment and Intervention Skills

Problem Identification

The setting is a community-based agency that works with children who are chronically ill, disabled, or both and their families. Pascual is a 4-year-old boy who came to the agency referred by the Head Start social worker for family-supportive services. The chief complaint is that Mrs. Mendez is under a lot of stress, and the family needs assistance to understand and deal with Pascual's condition and learn effective management of his disability. Pascual suffers from encephalitic metabolic seizures. As a result of constant seizures, this condition has impaired his nervous system and has left him barely able to move and eat. Pascual lives with his parents and two younger brothers, ages 3 years and 18 months, in a rundown apartment in a dangerous neighborhood. The family came from Ecuador on a lottery visa and has no relatives in the area. They moved to this country about six months ago. Both parents demonstrated little command of the English language and have a third-grade level of education. Mr. Mendez works six days a week as a construction worker and spends most of the day out of the household.

Mrs. Mendez is the caregiver of their children. The family lives in a two-bedroom apartment, and although Mrs. Mendez says she likes where they live, she wishes they could have more space. Pascual is currently receiving occupational, speech, and physical therapy, as well as neurological and neurodevelopmental treatment through the agency. Pascual needs to be seen on a regular basis by a neurologist for follow up and antiseizure medication management. Mrs. Mendez' interview was conducted in English by a social worker and a translator. Although both Mrs. Mendez and the social worker felt comfortable and able to somewhat break the ice, Mrs. Mendez asked to work with a Spanish-speaking social worker.

Initial Contact

The Spanish-speaking social worker greeted the family in Spanish and welcomed them to sit down as she offered toys to the children. At the initial contact, the social worker commented about the weather since it had been extremely cold and initiated the session with small talk. Mrs. Mendez immediately asked the social worker what country she was from, and the social worker answered. As Carrillo (2001) noted, some self- disclosure can facilitate the process of engaging a client. Mrs. Mendez proceeded to express a sense of relief because the social worker spoke Spanish. At the same time, Mrs. Mendez mentioned that she had requested a Spanish-speaking social worker because she needed someone who could understand her culture and speak her language. She mentioned feeling uncomfortable at the intake because English is not her first language and she had difficulties explaining some events and talking about feelings in English. As Marcos (1994) postulates, bilingual clients experience themselves with a "dual self," and feel their identity change depending on which language they are using. Marcos adds that expressing emotion in a non-native language might result in a higher stress situation for the client.

Along with the engagement phase, the culturally competent social worker has the enormous task of bringing awareness of the unique cultural maps, not only the client's, but also her own (Falicov, 1998). Bringing awareness of such maps, the social worker needs, along with the client, to understand the similarities and differences between these cultural maps. For example, Mrs. Mendez came from the same country, spoke the same language, and had the same sociohistorical background and religion as the social worker; however, there were differences in acculturation, the immigration journey, and social class. The similarities fostered connections between Mrs. Mendez and the social worker. Because of the potential areas of difference, however, the culturally competent social worker must show interest in learning about the experiences and worldview of the client as a way of creating a better understanding and demonstrating respect. An ability to compare those cultural maps enhances connectedness with the client, shows an empathic understanding by the social worker, and most importantly, diminishes stereotyping.

With the Mendez family, the social worker validated Mrs. Mendez's feelings by saying, "It must have been hard to convey your emotions." The social worker then talked to the family about services, entitlements, and resources available for Pascual within the agency.

Assessment

After meeting with Mrs. Mendez and her children, the social worker's impressions of the overall situation were related to the difficulties of raising two small children in addition to a third demanding child with severe developmental problems. Pascual requires constant care as well as medical and rehabilitative therapies. Mrs. Mendez seemed to be overwhelmed with the whole situation. She reported some working history in her country before Pascual's birth and missed not having the opportunity to work and earn some money of her own. Because of his work schedule, her husband was generally unavailable to help with the children. According to the information provided by Mrs. Mendez, her husband appeared to have limited involvement with their children. Furthermore, Mrs. Mendez appeared to be dealing with several difficulties: the loss of her financial and emotional independence, the process of adjustment to a new country, isolation from her family and relatives, and the struggle of dealing with a disabled child with very little support from her husband. All these factors seemed to have contributed to Mrs. Mendez' sense of sadness and high level of stress. She expressed desires to go back to her native country of Ecuador.

During a series of sessions, the social worker explored Mrs. Mendez' feelings about having a child with a disability. Mrs. Mendez mentioned feeling guilty about her child's condition and mentioned that she felt God was punishing her. With tears in her eyes, Mrs. Mendez explained that she had become pregnant with Pascual in a moment where they were facing financial difficulties. Subsequently, Mrs. Mendez thought about terminating the pregnancy and now she believes she is suffering the consequences of what she considers an immoral wish. She stated with sadness, "I have been punished by God. My punishment represents my child with a disability."[1] According to Moreno (2001), some Latino parents trying to deal with the process of accepting their child's disability may attribute causation by using cultural explanations in an effort to understand the etiology of the disability. Mrs. Mendez continued by expressing shameful wishes of wanting to abandon her children and run away but felt guilty for having those thoughts.

---

[1] I am assuming that the reason Ms. Mendez felt she was being punished was that she had thought about terminating the pregnancy. I think this needs to be made explicit for the reader; I've tried to do that here.

(continued)

CASE | *continued*

As a result of the process of exploring these issues, Mrs. Mendez openly mentioned that all these factors made her feel overwhelmed, inadequate, and perhaps depressed. The social worker validated Mrs. Mendez' cultural and religious beliefs by allowing her to express them openly and by reaffirming her feelings. The use of respectful questioning by the social worker allowed Mrs. Mendez to open up about her feelings of having a child with a disability and also her cultural explanation's of her child's condition. All these factors allowed Mrs. Mendez to open new perspectives, within her own cultural map.

Intervention

First, and because of the family's legal status, the social worker referred Pascual to the Social Security office to apply for supplemental security income (SSI). Second, in an effort to address Mrs. Mendez' high levels of stress, the social worker referred her for respite care services. At the same time, a referral was made to the board of education's special needs services for a complete educational evaluation and placement for Pascual. If Pascual is placed in a special class, he will receive therapies and perhaps a wheelchair, which would help alleviate Mrs. Mendez's stress level. In addition, a social worker will continue to see Mrs. Mendez to help her cope with all her losses. A referral to a support group for parents of children with encephalic metabolic seizures will also be made.

A culturally competent social worker is one who knows the client's cultural context (Marin, 1993). In this case, Mrs. Mendez expressed feeling responsible for her child's disability and linked her situation to her religious beliefs, and the social worker openly explored the meaning of this experience from both emotional and cultural perspectives.

Application Exercise

1. What cultural elements were present in Pascual's case?
2. What areas would you describe as part of the belief systems of Mrs. Mendez's culture?
3. As a culturally competent social worker, what might you have done differently?
4. Was the social worker culturally sensitive in disclosing information about herself?

expressing themselves in their native languages, especially when they have to talk about emotionally charged material. Raising the issue of self-disclosure applied with caution is advisable, especially in the crucial process of engaging, as a way of establishing a connection.

Some studies have provided evidence of how culture and socioeconomic status affect the perception of well-being in mothers of children with disabilities (Moreno, 2001). Latinos as a group have high rates of depression compared with the general population, with contributing factors being immigration, difficulties integrating into society, underemployment, low socioeconomic status, and belonging to an ethnic group (Blazer et al., 1994).

A comparative study conducted with 249 Latina mothers with and without children with mental retardation found that Latina mothers of children with mental retardation had higher rates of depression.

It is important to assess for family cohesiveness because that often relates to the concept of "familialism." In our case, factors contributing to Mrs. Mendez feeling overwhelmed may include her lack of support systems in this country and of support from her husband. Her desire to go back to her native country is a way of seeking this family support. In cases that involve children with disabilities, it is also important for social workers to assess the severity of the child's disability and how this factor has affected the caregivers. Disabled children who require constant care might place higher stressors on mothers than do those who have more mild disabilities. Religious beliefs might also promote a sense of guilt in parents who are struggling to understand the meaning of having a disabled child.

A competent social worker is the one who considers the uniqueness of clients as well as the multidimensional factors that make work with Latinos fascinating. Successfully working with this population depends on establishing proper training based on culturally and ethnically valid research. It is critical to make policy makers aware of these issues and to work toward a system change that includes training programs on cultural awareness, Spanish immersion programs, community advisory boards, recruitment of bilingual and biculturally competent staff, and culturally sensitive mental health programs.

References

Arroyo, J. A. (1996). Psychotherapist bias with Hispanics: An analog study. *Hispanic Journal of Behavioral Sciences, 18*(1), 21–29.

Bean, R., Perry, B., & Bedell, T. (2001). Developing culturally competent marriage and family therapists: Guidelines for working with Hispanic families. *Journal of Marital and Family Therapy, 27*(1), 43–54.

Blazer, D. G., Kessler, R. C., McGonagle, K. A., Swartz, M. S. (1994). The prevalence and distribution of major depression in a national community sample: The national comorbidity survey. *American Journal of Psychiatry, 151*(7), 979–986.

Blea, I. I. (1997). *U.S. Chicanas & Latinas within a global context: Women of color at the fourth World Women's Conference.* Westport, CT: Praeger.

Catalano, R. F., Morrison, D. M., Wells, E. A., & Gillmore, M. R., et al. (1992). Ethnic differences in family factors related to early drug use initiation. *Journal of Studies in Alcohol, 53,* 208–217.

Canino, G. (1994). Psychiatric conditions among Puerto Ricans. In C. Telles & M. Karno (Eds.), *Latino Mental Health: Current research and policy perspectives.* Monograph, National Institute of Mental Health & Neuropsychiatric Institute, University of California, Los Angeles.

Carrillo, E. (2001). Assessment and treatment of the Latino patient. In A.G. Lòpez, & E. Carrillo (Eds.). *The Latino Psychiatric patient: Assessment and treatment.* Washington, DC: American Psychiatric Publishing.

Coohey, C. (2001). The relationship between familialism and child maltreatment in Latino and Anglo families. *Child Maltreatment, 6*(2), 130–142.

Coon, H. M., & Kemmelmeier, M. (2001). Cultural orientations in the

United States: (Re) examining differences among ethnic groups. *Journal of Cross-Cultural Psychology, 32*(3), 248–364.

De La Cancela, V., Guarnacci, P. J., & Carrillo, E. (1986). Psychological distress among Latinos: A critical analysis of Ataques de Nervios. *Humanity and Society, 10,* 431–447.

De La Rosa, M. R. (1998). Prevalence and consequences of alcohol, cigarette, and drug use among Hispanics. *Alcoholism Treatment Quarterly, 16*(1–2), 21–54.

Fabrega, H. (1990). Hispanic mental health research: A case for cultural psychiatry. *Hispanic Journal of Behavioral Sciences, 12*(4), 339–365.

Falicov, C. J. (1998). *Latino families in therapy: A guide to multicultural practice.* New York: Guildford Press.

Fishman, J. A. (1960). A systematization of the Whorfian hypothesis. *Behavioral Sciences, 4,* 323–339.

Fortes de Leff, J., & Espejel, Arco, E. (2000). Cultural myths and social relationships in Mexico: A context for therapy. *Journal of Family Psychotherapy, 11*(4), 79–92.

Gloria, A. M., & Perogy, J. J. (1996). Counseling Latino alcohol and other substance users/abusers: Cultural considerations for counselors. *Journal of Substance Abuse Treatment, 13*(2), 119–126.

Gonzalez, J. R. (1978). Language factors affecting treatment of bilingual schizophrenics. *Psychiatric Annals, 8,* 68–70.

Gorman-Smith, D., Tolan, P. H., Zelli, A., & Huesmann, L. R. (1996). The relation of family functioning to violence among inner-city minority youths. *Journal of Family Psychology, 10*(2), 115–129.

Guarnaccia, P. J., Pelto, P. J., & Schensul, S. L. (1985). Family health culture, ethnicity, and asthma: Coping with illness. *Medical Anthropology, Summer,* 203–224.

Ho, D. Y., & Chiu, C. (1994). Component ideas of individualism, collectivism, and social organization: An application in the study of Chinese culture. In U. Him, C. H. C. Triandis, S. Kagitcibasi, C. Choi, & G. Yoon (Eds.), *Individualism and collectivism: Theory, method, and applications* (pp. 137–156.). Thousand Oaks, CA: Sage.

Karno, M. (1994). The prevalence of mental health disorder among persons of Mexican birth or origin. In C. Telles & M. Karno (Eds.), *Latino mental health: Current research and policy perspectives* (pp. 1–16). Rockville, MD: National Institute of Mental Health (NIMH).

Kessler, R. C., McGonagle, K. A., Zhao, S., Nelson, C. B., Hughes, M., Eshleman, S., Wittchen, H. U., & Kendler, K. S. (1994). Lifetime and 12-month prevalence of DSM-III-R psychiatric disorders in the United States. *Archives of General Psychiatry, 51,* 8–19.

Lewis-Fernaandez, R. (1996). Cultural formulation of psychiatric diagnosis: Case No. 02. Diagnosis and treatment of nervios and ataques in a female Puerto Rican migrant. *Culture, Medicine & Psychiatry, 20*(2), 155–163.

Larkey, L. K., Hecht, M. L., Miller, K., & Alatorre, C. (2001). Hispanic cultural norms for health-seeking behaviors in the face of symptoms. *Health Education and behavior, 28*(1), 65–80.

Lu, Y. E., Lum, D., & Chen, S. (2001). Cultural competence and achieving styles in clinical social work: A conceptual and empirical exploration. *Journal of Ethnic and Cultural Diversity in Social Work, 9*(3/4), 1–32.

Lum, D. (2003). *Culturally competent practice: A framework for understanding diverse groups and justice issues,* 2nd ed. Pacific Grove: Brooks/Cole.

Malgady, R. G., & Costantino, G. (1998). Symptom severity in bilingual Hispanics as a function of clinician ethnicity and language interviews. *Psychological Assessment, 10*(2), 120–127.

Malgady, R. G., Rogler, L. H., & Costantino, G. (1987). Ethnocultural and linguistic bias in mental health evaluation of Hispanics. *American Psychologist, 42,*228–234.

Malgady, R. G., & Zayas, L. H. (2001). Cultural and linguistic considerations in psychodiagnosis with Hispanics: The need for an empirically informed process model. *Social Work, 46*(1), 39–49.

Marcos, L. (1994). The psychiatric examination across the language barrier. In C. Telles, & M. Karno (Eds.), *Latino mental health: Current research and policy perspectives* (pp. 129–138). Rockville, MD: National Institute of Mental Health (NIMH).

Marcos, L. R. (1979). Effects of interpreters on the evaluation of psychopathology in non-English speaking patients. *Archives of General Psychiatry, 136,* 171–174.

Marcos, L. R., & Alpert, M. (1976). Strategies and risks in the psychotherapy with bilingual patients: The phenomenon of language independence. *American Journal of Psychiatry, 133,* 1275–1278.

Marin, D. (1993). Defining culturally appropriate community interventions: Hispanics as a case study. *Journal of Community Psychology, 21,* 149–161.

Miller, J. (1994). A family's sense of power in their community: Theoretical and research issues. *Smith College Studies in Social Work, 64*(3), 221–241.

Mirowsky, J., & Ross, C. (1984). Mexican culture and its emotional contradictions. *Journal of Health and Social Behavior, 25*(1), 2–13.

Moreno, C. L. (2001). Developmental disabilities. In A. Gitterman (Ed), *Handbook of social work practice with vulnerable and resilient populations,* 2nd ed. (pp. 205–223). New York: Columbia University Press.

Pèrez-Stable, E. J., & Nàpoles-Springer, A. M. (2001). Physical health status of Latinos in the United States. In A. G. Lòpez & E. Carrillo (Eds.), *The Latino Psychiatric patient: Assessment and treatment.* Washington, DC: American Psychiatric Publishing.

Roberts, R. E. (1980). Prevalence of psychological distress among Mexican Americans. *Journal of Health and Social Behavior, 21,* 135–145.

Rogler, L. H., Malgady, R. G., & Rodriguez, O. (1989). *Hispanics and mental health: A framework for research.* Melbourne, FL: Krieger.

Suarez-Orozco, M., & Paez, M. M. (2002). The research agenda. In M. Suarez-Orozco, & M. M. Paez (Eds.), *Latinos: Remaking America* (pp. 1–37). Berkeley: University of California Press.

Sue, S. (1988). Psychotherapeutic services for ethnic minorities: Two decades of research findings. *American Psychologist, 43,* 301–308.

Triandis, H. C., Marin, G., & Lisansky, J. (1984). Simpatia as a cultural script of Hispanics. *Journal of Personality and Social Psychology, 47,* 1363–1375.

U.S. Census Bureau. (1999). *Hispanic Population in the United States: Population Characteristics, March 1999.* (Current Population Report P20–527). Washington, DC: U.S. Government Printing Office.

U.S. Census Bureau. (2000). *The Hispanic population in the United States: March 2000.* Current Population Reports, P20–535. Washington, DC- U.S. Government Printing Office.

U.S. Census Bureau. (2001). *Hispanic population in the United States: March 2000.* (Current Population Report P20–535). Washington, DC: U.S. Government Printing Office.

Weller, S. C., Baer, R. D., de Alba Garcia, J., Glazer, M., Trotter, R., Pachter, L., & Klein, R. E. (2002). Regional variation in Latino descriptions of susto. *Culture, Medicine & Psychiatry, 26*(4), 449–472.

Zambrana, R. E., & Dorrington, C. (1998). Economic and social vulnerability of Latino children and families subgroup: Implications for child welfare. *Child Welfare, 77*(1), 5–27.

CHAPTER **Social Work Practice with Asian Americans**

*Paula T. Tanemura Morelli**

All phenomena are interdependent. When we think of a speck of dust, a flower, or a human being, our thinking cannot break loose from the idea of unity, of one, of calculation. We see a line drawn between one and many, one and not one. But if we truly realize the interdependent nature of the dust, the flower, and the human being, we see that unity cannot exist without diversity. Unity and diversity interpenetrate each other freely. Unity is diversity, and diversity is unity. (Hanh, 1993, p, 129).

Cultural competence, "the capacity to function effectively within the context of culturally integrated patterns of human behavior defined by the group" (National Association of Social Workers [NASW], 2001), is fundamental to social work's mission, ethical principles, and core values of engaging and providing services to clients through respectful, just, and effective means (NASW, 1999, 2001). Despite this deep commitment, social workers continue to be challenged by the actual implementation of culturally competent practice. It seems we talk a great deal about cultural competence, but we are slow to put it into practice.

The applications lag is often attributed to the lack of cultural competency training methods, research on practice efficacy, limited resources and time, and resistance to change. These explanations notwithstanding, we cannot afford to

*The author gratefully acknowledges the participants of the Cambodian American Health-Seeking and Social Networks Project and the National Research Center on Asian American Mental Health for their support of this work.

ignore the critical need for culturally competent practice emphasized by the United States Surgeon General and the Research and Training Center on Family Support and Children's Mental Health. These practice-guiding authorities have charged health and social service systems, and the professionals working in them, with the responsibility of delivering effective services to our culturally diverse clients (Cross, Bazron, Dennis, & Isaacs, 1989; U.S. Department of Health and Human Services [DHHS], 2001).

By social work's own definition, denying or withholding culturally competent practice constitutes unethical and incompetent practice. Thus, however unintentional, postponing or ignoring the necessary training, process, and application of awareness, knowledge, and skills that constitute cultural competence contributes to oppression of the very people we serve (Morelli, 2001).

Throughout their history in the United States of America, Asian American and Asian immigrants and refugees have endured and continue to experience oppression via persistent racism, prejudice, and discrimination (Chan, 1998; Takaki, 1989). Asians in America are poorly understood (Fadiman, 1997); their cultural values of deference to authority and acceptance of what "cannot be changed" increases the likelihood that their needs are neglected and that they are denied culturally competent services. The U.S. Surgeon General has identified Asian Americans among the minorities that (1) use services infrequently, (2) receive poorer quality of care, (3) have a higher proportion of unmet need, and (4) are overrepresented among the nation's vulnerable, high-need groups (DHHS, 2001). Within this group, Asian refugees have greatest socioeconomic, physical, and mental health needs, intensified by the effects of war.

Written contributions from practitioners and scholars toward the development of culturally competent practices with Asians and Asian Americans are considerable (some examples: Berg & Miller, 1992; Fong, 1994; Fong & Furuto, 2001; Kagawa-Singer & Chung, 1994; Kim, 1995; Kitano, 1989; Lu, Lum & Chen, 2001; Lum, 1982, 2003; Mokuau, 1991; Morelli, Fong, & Oliveira, 2001; Okazaki, 1998; Richards & Browne, & Brokerick, 1994; Root, Ho, & Sue; 1986; Sue & Sue, 1987; Sue & Sue, 1999; Takeuchi, Uehara, & Maramba, 1999; Uehara, Morelli, & Abe-Kim, 2001; Yuen & Nakano-Matsumoto, 1998; Zane & Sue, 1991); this is a humble offering to that effort. This chapter synthesizes specific aspects of culturally competent practice with Asian immigrants, refugees, and Asian Americans (the term *Asian American* will refer generally to Asians residing in the United States) primarily from the Far East and Southeast Asia; examines systemic oppression based on discriminatory immigration policies; provides a case example of the assessment and intervention processes with a Cambodian refugee; and suggests guideline questions to evaluate client progress. The information and skill framework will be useful to begin collaboration or therapeutic alliances with Asian Americans. The great diversity within the Asian populations, however, poses limitations in generalizing this information.

As a start, all practitioners who work with Asian clients regardless of skill level should engage in a process to understand their clients' cultural context and experiences. Preparation, engagement, and direct collaboration with families, social networks, and communities are necessary parts of developing culturally competent working alliances. An often-neglected critical piece of cultural competence is the practitioner's willingness to develop awareness regarding the strengths and limitations of her or his own cultural perspectives and values. Let us be mindful that the journey to becoming culturally competent is a lifelong process that belongs to all of us.

THE DEMOGRAPHICS OF ASIAN AMERICANS

Asian Americans are a fast-growing, but relatively small group in comparison with other racial designations in the United States. Individuals who identify as Asians constitute 4.2% (11.9 million) of the population reported via the United States Census 2000. This number includes 3.6% (10.2 million) who reported being Asian alone, and 0.6% (1.7 million) who reported Asian as well as one or more other races (U.S. Census Bureau, 2002). With the increase in Asian immigration into the United States after the Vietnam War, the term *Asian American* has evolved to include individuals who have ethnic and cultural origins in countries of the Far East, Southeast Asia, or the Indian subcontinent, for example, Cambodia, China, India, Japan, Korea, Laos, Malaysia, Pakistan, the Philippine Islands, Thailand, and Vietnam.

In 1960, Asians alone numbered 877,934, one-half of one percent of the U.S. population (Takaki, 1989). By 1990, the U.S. census counted 6,908,638 Asians, a 99% increase from the 1980 census count of 3,466,847 (U.S. Census Bureau, 1993). The Asians in the 1990 census included the following: Chinese, 23.8%; Filipino, 20.4%; Japanese, 12.3%; Asian Indian, 11.8%; Korean, 11.6%; Vietnamese, 8.9%; Laotian, 2.2%; Cambodian, 2.1%; Thai, 1.3%; Hmong, 1.3%; other Asian, 4.4% (Pakistani, 1.2; Indonesian, 0.4; Malayan, 0.2; Bangladeshi, 0.2; Sri Lankan, 0.2; Burmese, 0.1; all other Asian, 2.1) (U.S. Census Bureau, 1993).

Between 1990 and 2000, Asians alone or in combination with one or more other races increased by nearly 4.9 million, or 72% (6,908,638 to 11,898,828) (U.S. Census Bureau, 1993, 2002). The Asian alone population increased by 3.3 million or 48% between 1990 and 2000. In comparison with the general U.S. population, which increased by 13% (248.7 million to 281.4 million), the Asian population increased from 48 to 72% during the same period (U.S. Census Bureau, 2002).

THE HISTORIC OPPRESSION AND SURVIVAL VALUES OF ASIAN AMERICANS

Racism, bigotry, discrimination—ranging from verbal abuse to personalized acts of violence and vandalism—and public proliferation of negative stereotypes were part of the torment and suffering Asians of all ages faced for the better part of their first one hundred years in the United States (Takaki, 1989). Asian Americans were politically powerless in the face of Federal and state legislation that prevented foreign-born Asians from becoming naturalized citizens because of race (1790 U.S. federal law), and thereby denied them the right to vote; exclusionary U.S. immigration laws; alien land laws (California Alien Land Laws, 1913, 1920, 1923; similar laws passed in Washington, Arizona, Oregon, Idaho, Nebraska, Texas, Kansas, Lousiana, Montena, New Mexico, Minnesota, and Missouri; U.S. Congress, 1924 Immigration Act) prohibiting land ownership based on ineligibility to become a naturalized citizen; restrictive, short-term land leases (2–3 years); state laws prohibiting Asians from working in specific occupations; anti-miscegenation laws; and race-based school and housing segregation (Ng, 2002; Takaki, 1989). The most egregious of these discriminatory policies was Executive Order 9066 issued by President Franklin D. Roosevelt ordering the removal and incarceration of more than 120,000 Japanese Americans in concentration camps without the due process guaranteed by the Fifth Amendment of the U.S. Constitution or writ of habeas corpus (Conrat & Conrat, 2003;Hata & Hata, 1995; Ng, 2002; Takaki, 1989).

The following brief discussion of U.S. immigration policies and Executive Order 9066 captures a small portion of the historic context in which Asian Americans and immigrant and refugee Asians were singled out for discriminatory, exclusionary policies and denial of their civil rights under the U.S. Constitution. It offers a foundation for understanding the Asian American experience in this country.

Oppression via Immigration Policy

U.S. immigration policy, as applied to Asians for more than 150 years, has been ruthlessly discriminatory. The extent and nature of the discrimination can be established by examining U.S. immigration policies beginning in late the 19th century. To appreciate the extent and ongoing pattern of discrimination toward Asian Americans, these policies must also be viewed within the historic geopolitical context of the times.

Before the mid-19th century, Asian immigration to the United States was rare. Beginning in the 17th century, the Japanese, Koreans, and Chinese enforced formal isolationist policies by execution of émigrés upon their return (Hing, 1993). The Japanese, fearing the encroachment of foreign governments, prohibited emigration until 1868 when they entered a program of industrialization and modernization (Ichihashi 1915, pp. 1–3, cited in Hing, 1993; Takaki, 1989). Korea was known as the Hermit Kingdom during two and a half centuries of self-imposed isolation following the invasion of the Manchus in 1627 and 1636 (Choy, 1979, p, 19; Kim, 1971, p. 3; Kitano & Daniels, 1988, p, 107, all cited in Hing, 1993). China under the Qing dynasty (1644–1911) banned emigration or exiles until the Burlingame Treaty in 1868[1] (Hsu, 1975, p. 4; Tsai, 1986, pp. 8–11, both cited in Hing, 1993).

---

[1] In the Burlingame Treaty between the U.S. and Chinese governments, China agreed to permit her citizens to emigrate. The U.S. Congress was exceptionally pleased with this agreement, anticipating the benefits of free trade and insinuating that, "the removal of surplus population of China" would be of mutual benefit to both countries (Hing, 1993, p, 22).

The isolation of China, Japan,[2] and Korea[3] did not last long because of political, economic, and external forces. In China, isolationist policies were eroded by a dramatic increase in population (275 million in 1779 to 430 million in 1850), which led to scarcity of food, the ravages of the 1839–1842 Opium War with Britain, and the cession of Hong Kong to Britain at the end of the war in 1842 (Hing, 1993). The 1850–1864 Taiping Rebellion eventually opened China to trade and travel.

The discovery of gold and expansion of the American West fueled demand for labor that the Chinese were able to provide cheaply and abundantly. As long as a critical need for exploitable labor existed, the Chinese were welcomed and encouraged to settle with state legislative support and promises of land grant incentives (Hing, 1993; Takaki, 1989). They were prized as cooks, laundry workers, and servants and found to be indispensable in the completion of the transcontinental railroad. Thus, by 1882, approximately 300,000 Chinese had been brought in to work on the West Coast.

Almost immediately, however, exploitative labor practices that bought Chinese labor for two-thirds the cost of white labor became the source of racial animosity between nativists and all foreign labor. Irish and German miners in California demanded the passage of a foreign miners' tax, which required all non-native born to pay an exorbitant license to mine and effectively forced the Latinos out (Hing, 1993; Takaki, 1989). As the largest remaining group of foreign laborers, the Chinese were attacked through anti-Chinese newspaper editorials, "Anti-coolie" clubs, and miner and merchant tax laws specific to them.

By 1870, nativist demands denied Chinese the right to citizenship through an amendment to the Nationality Act of 1790. In this amendment, Chinese

---

[2] Nineteenth-century Japan was open to foreign trade by the ships and guns of Commodore Perry in 1853. In the years before his visit, Japan remained isolated from foreign influence under a policy imposed by the Tokugawa shogunate. In 1868, a group of samurai from western Japan succeeded in overthrowing the Tokugawas and began the restoration of an imperial government (Meiji Restoration) ending the rule of samurai and the feudal economy (Tamura, 1994, p. 9).

Aware of China's inability to control foreign influences, Japan's leaders began a program to transform the country into an industrial and military power capable of repulsing Western imperialism. To fund this ambitious program, in 1873 the government imposed heavy taxes based on land value of the past year's crops. This had a devastating effect on farmers; between 1883 and 1890, more than 367,000 farmers were financially ruined and lost their land for failing to pay taxes (Tamura, 1994, p. 9).

[3] Between 1903 and 1920, approximately 8,000 Koreans left their homeland for the islands of Hawaii (Takaki, 1989, p. 53). These immigrants came to escape Japanese imperialism and persecution, poverty, famine, and drought. Many Korean immigrants found opportunities in Hawaii limited and re-immigrated to the west coast states. There they faced many of the discriminatory practices confronted by the Chinese and Japanese: racism, exclusion from services, disrespect, cruelty, physical violence, hatred, exclusion from citizenship, restricted employment opportunities, and exclusion from landownership. The first generation of Koreans in America found solidarity in their emotional commitment to liberating their country from Japanese oppression. They considered themselves exiles rather than immigrants (Takaki, 1989, p. 285).

were described as having "undesirable qualities" (Hing, 1993). They were also heathen, morally inferior, savage, childlike, and lustful, which made them unsuitable for citizenship through naturalization (Takaki, 1989). Furthermore, to be certain that any doors in family immigration policy were closed, in 1875, Congress passed the Page Law, which forbade the entry of Chinese women thought to be "prostitutes"; interpreted to an extreme, this law practically excluded all Chinese women from entering the country.

The furor and fear contrived around the presumed evils of Chinese immigrants culminated in the passage of the Chinese Exclusion Act on May 6, 1882. This law prohibited the entry of Chinese laborers for 10 years, and with the exception of a small quota of professionals, effectively ended Chinese immigration. The scope and effectiveness of this law notwithstanding, unrelenting fear and paranoia led anti-Chinese movement leaders to press for more legislation to further protect themselves from the "yellow peril." For example, the Scott Act of 1888 prohibited the reentry of all Chinese laborers who temporarily left the United States regardless of whether they held a valid reentry certificate. The Geary Act of 1892 extended the exclusion laws for 10 more years, and required the registration of all Chinese laborers because they were perceived as all looking alike and it was necessary to distinguish those who were illegal entrants. Furthermore, the law denied bail in habeas corpus proceedings and, in its original form, required that an illegal Chinese immigrant be imprisoned to hard labor for as long as a year. In 1904, after the Chinese government refused to renew their acceptance of the Geary Act, concessions to the Scott Act were rescinded and an indefinite ban on Chinese immigration was enacted. Anti-Chinese sentiment ran high and further exclusionary laws were passed; during the same period, the presence of European foreigners was not considered a threat (Hing, 1993; Takaki, 1989).

Succeeding Asian immigrants—for example, Japanese, Koreans, Filipinos, and East Indians—all encountered short-lived welcomes followed by anti-immigration protest from nativist, exclusionist, and racist elements. By 1884, the Japanese government, yielding to internal economic pressures, began allowing her citizens to fill the need for cheap labor on Hawaiian sugar plantations.[4] In 1888, the first Japanese labor was introduced in Vacaville, California, to pick fruit (Takaki, 1989). The success of Japanese farming in California again led nativists and xenophobes to clamor for exclusionary policies. Groups like the Japanese and Korean Exclusion League (later known as the Asiatic Exclusion League), Anti-Jap Laundry League, and the Anti-Japanese League of Alameda County sprang up in California (Hing, 1993; Takaki, 1989) to fan the flames of anti-Japanese hysteria and resurrect immigration as a political issue.

The progression of anti-Asian immigration policies reached its zenith in the 1930s and remained that way through 1952. In *United States v. Singh*

---

[4] The Meiji Restoration (1868) government of Japan passed the first modern emigration law in 1885, which permitted government-sponsored contract laborers to work on Hawaiian sugar plantations (Hing, 1993).

Thind (1923), the court determined that Asian Indians, like Japanese, were not considered white, and therefore, were not permitted to become citizens. In 1924, the National Origins Quota Act, aimed at limiting the large numbers of immigrating Jews, Italians, Slavs, and Greeks, curbed immigrants from any particular country to 2% of their nationality in 1890 (Hing, 1993). The Act further barred any "alien ineligible to citizenship." Asians were ineligible under the 1870 law and were, thus, excluded from entry indefinitely.

The repetitive pattern of welcoming exploitable immigrants and rejecting them as soon as their tendencies toward resourcefulness or capitalism appeared, played itself out again with Filipinos, the only Asians not affected by the National Origins Act. In 1934, the Tydings-McDuffie Act, supported by exclusionists, anti-colonialists, and Filipino nationalists, limited the Filipino immigration quota to only 50 visas (Hing, 1993; Takaki, 1989).

Policy makers did not began to seriously reflect on the implications of such practices in the climate of the communist-capitalist cold war until the United States, having assumed leadership in the United Nations after World War II, received glaring world criticism for its domestic and immigration policies. Thus, despite postwar anxieties about enemy aliens and after much consideration, the McCarran-Walter (Immigration and Nationality) Act was enacted by Congress in 1952. Its primary achievement was reversal of the 1924 National Origins Quota Act's prohibition of Asian naturalization. The McCarran-Walter Act abolished the Asiatic barred zone, and limited immigration to 2,000 within the Asia-Pacific triangle; it was repealed in 1965, but retained country quotas of 20,000 under the auspices of family reunification.

Following the Second Indochina War, since 1975 an estimated 2 million Cambodians, Laotians, and Vietnamese have fled their homelands (Karnow, 1991). More than 1.75 million refugees were resettled in other countries, 80% of these in Western Europe, North America, and Australia. By 1992, some 200,000 Indochinese refugees remained in first-asylum countries in Southeast Asia. And 370,000 Cambodians were encamped on the Thai-Cambodian border as displaced persons waiting for repatriation. In their attempts to escape to Thailand, an estimated 60,000 Cambodians, 15,000 Hmong, and 5,000 Laotians perished. An estimated 30,000 to 100,000 Vietnamese boat people also met death while trying to escape. These Southeast Asian refugees, our "allied aliens," are foreigners to whom the nation promised to extend protection because of their voluntary or coerced allegiance to America's foreign policy objectives. The United States is responsibly linked to the Indochinese arena because of failed attempts to control communism in their homelands from the 1930s to 1975.

Discriminatory immigration policies were perpetuated in decisions regarding Southeast Asian refugee resettlement. As was the case with Asian immigrants entering the United States in the late 19th century, Southeast Asian refugees had their employment, geographic location of residence, the likelihood of family members joining them, and deportation determined by prevailing public sentiment and government policy designed to identify and expel undesirables (Hing, 1993, 2002).

Executive Order 9066: Denial of Japanese Americans' Civil Rights

Even before World War II and the attack on Pearl Harbor, anti-Japanese sentiment was part of a larger anti-Asian movement beginning with the Chinese in the late 19th century (Daniels, 1968, cited in Ng, 2002; Takaki, 1989). From 1868, the time of their first entry into the United States, Japanese were subjected to verbal and physical attacks, vandalism and threats of violence, discriminatory immigration policies, laws preventing ownership of property, prohibition from engaging in particular professions, anti-miscegenation laws, school and housing segregation (Ng, 2002; Takaki, 1989). Despite these persistent forms of rejection and abuse, Japanese Americans managed over a 70-year period to steadily establish their lives and lay claim to their U.S. citizenship.

On December 7, 1941, Japan's surprise attack on Pearl Harbor was a calamity felt by all Americans and U.S. residents. In the days that followed, it became the touchstone for reprisal and continued discrimination against Japanese Americans and their *issei* (first generation Japan-born, not eligible for naturalized citizenship) parents. Despite federal investigative reports that Japanese living in the United States posed no real threat to national security, on February 19, 1942, President Franklin D. Roosevelt issued Executive Order 9066, which effected the swift military round up, removal and incarceration of more than 120,000 Japanese Americans into 16 concentration and isolation camps throughout the United States (Hata & Hata, 1995; Ng, 2002; Takaki, 1989).

The primary rationale for internment was "military necessity" for reasons of national security. Executive Order 9066 was a blatant denial of Japanese American citizens' civil rights, but mainstream Americans made no significant protest against it. In four separate cases (*Hirabayashi v. United States; Korematsu v. United States; Endo v. United States; Yasui v. United States*), young Japanese Americans challenged Executive Order 9066 and race-based curfew all the way to the U.S. Supreme Court, where their basic civil rights were denied because they were not white (Hata & Hata, 1995).

The magnitude of disruption and trauma caused by Executive Order 9066 in the lives of Japanese Americans cannot be given the just and appropriate discussion it deserves here. The reader is encouraged to learn more about the experiences of Japanese American families during World War II (see Chin, 2002; Daniels, Taylor, & Kitano, 1991) because the effects on families are widespread and have important implications for social work practice.

On August 10, 1988, the U.S. government provided an official apology and monetary compensation to Japanese survivors of the concentration camps. Despite this national acknowledgement of wrongdoing, most Americans remain uninformed about Executive Order 9066 or other discriminatory U.S. policies and their effects. More important, there is no nationally sustained effort to recognize the crippling effects of racism and discriminatory policies in our country. What are the implications of ignoring the dynamics of racism and bigotry in our society? How and why do we (citizens and the government) tacitly condone racism and bigotry?

Survival Values

Racism and discriminatory policies have not prevented Asians from overcoming the odds against their survival in the United States. Why? What factors have contributed to Asian American perseverance?

An essential feature of developing cultural competence in working with Asian Americans is acquiring knowledge of and respect for their traditional values (Fong & Furuto, 2001; Lum, 2003), ways of knowing, belief systems, and the historic geopolitical context of their immigration to this country. Concepts of individualism and collectivism aid us in understanding the values central to Asians. Individualism is a cultural pattern identified with most northern and western regions of Europe and North America (Chan, 1998). Collectivism, the degree to which a culture facilitates conformity, compliance, and striving for harmony (Gardiner, Mutter, & Kosmitzki, 1998), is a cultural pattern most common in Africa, Asia, Latin America, and the Pacific (Triandis, 1995, in Chan, 1998).

The collectivist perspectives of Asians are rooted in the philosophies of Confucianism, Taoism, and Buddhism. For the past 2,000 years, these "three teachings" have contributed to commonalities in the worldviews, ethics, social norms, values, folk beliefs, and life styles of Asians (Chan, 1998).

Confucianism (Confucius 551–479 B.C.) is a philosophy that suggests that social harmony and good governance are based on individual virtue and reciprocal social obligations. Individual virtue can be developed through practice of the "five virtues": (1) *ren* or *jen,* benevolence and humanism (primary virtue); (2) *yi,* righteousness or morality; (3) *li,* proper conduct; (4) *zhi* or *chih,* wisdom or understanding; and (5) *xin,* trustworthiness (Chan, 1998). The five virtues were exemplified in *xiao,* filial piety, duty to one's parents, that is, unquestioning loyalty, obedience, care, concern, and anticipation of parental needs (Chan, 1998). This reverence extended to one's ancestors and authority figures defining moral, social, and moral obligations.

Lao Tzu, an ancient Chinese philosopher, is considered the major proponent of Taoism, the way or path. In this philosophy of life, "one must cultivate inner strength, selflessness, spontaneity, and harmony with nature and man" (Chan, 1998). Taoism differed from Confucianism in its focus away from societal rules of conduct and instead emphasized a reality that appreciates nature, avoids interference with nature, and seeks a balance between yin (submissive, receptive) and yang (dominating, creative) forces.

Buddhism founded by Prince Siddhartha Gautama (560–480 BC), is based on the four noble truths:

1. All life is suffering;
2. Suffering is caused by desire or attachment to the world;
3. Suffering can be extinguished and attachment to all things including the self can be overcome by eliminating desire;
4. To eliminate desire, one must live a virtuous life by following the Middle Way and the Eightfold Noble Path. (Chan, 1998)

The central tenets of Buddhism urge practitioners to free themselves of attachment to limiting concepts or dualities such as birth and death; being, non-being; high and low; more beautiful and less beautiful—such concepts are the source of suffering and limit our ability to be happy (Hanh, 2002). The practice of breathing and mindfulness of the impermanence of all things frees one to live happiness and fulfillment in the moment without limits; according to Buddhist teachings there is no way to happiness, rather, happiness is the way.

Confucian, Taoist, and Buddhist teachings were blended and practiced during centuries of cultural history among Asians. These philosophies and their associated practices are the core of Asian survival values. The practices of thinking and being are often so integrated into socialization and daily life patterns that most Asians are unaware of their connection to the "three teachings."

CULTURALLY COMPETENT KNOWLEDGE THEORY AND PRACTICE SKILLS FOR ASIAN AMERICANS

Gathering information about Asian American family ways requires a keen sensitivity to communication styles, relationship protocols, and spiritual beliefs. These characteristics and ways are mediated by the time of their arrival in the United States and degree of acculturation.

Lee (1997b) proposes five hypothetical family types that are useful when examining the complex factors that need to be considered when working with Asian American families. The *Traditional Family* (Type 1) consists of members who were born and raised in their country of origin. Individuals are recently arrived immigrants and older unacculturated immigrants who live in predominantly Asian communities such as Chinatown or Koreatown and have limited contact with the mainstream U.S. society.

Cultural Conflict Family (Type 2) members who hold varying cultural values, are more acculturated than other members, or differ by religious, philosophical, or political beliefs. Typically, intergenerational conflicts arise between the parents and grandparents who honor traditional beliefs of family interdependence, common values and goals, and their more Westernized third-generation children.

Members of the *Bicultural Family* (Type 3) are well-acculturated. Parents in these families may have grown up in large Westernized Asian cities, came to the United States at very young ages, or were American-born and raised in traditional families. These families tend to be middle- or upper-class, bilingual, and bicultural, with a shift from patriarchal to egalitarian familial relationships.

The *Americanized Family* (Type 4) consists of members who were born and raised in the United States. In these families, English is the primary language, traditions of their cultural of origin may be disappearing, and their orientation tends to be more individualistic and egalitarian.

Interracial Families (Type 5) among Asian Americans are the result of steadily increasing interracial marriages, an estimated 10 to 15% of all marriages. These families experience successful adaptation as well as conflicts. Much like the other family-types described, interracial families need to work through values, cultural and religious beliefs, language, and numerous other areas of difference.

Such general typologies are a helpful framework to begin the process of understanding a family's background. It is important to note that the Asian families we encounter may consist of characteristics from several family types. For example, a typical Asian American family in Hawaii will be Americanized, often interracial, may still hold to Asian values and traditions, yet the relational orientation may be egalitarian.

CONTACT SKILLS WITH ASIAN AMERICAN CLIENTS

Enhancing Communication and Listening Skills

Cultures in which people are deeply involved with one another, where information is widely shared and commonly understood, and where relatively simple messages convey deep meanings are considered to be "high context"; such cultures are "rooted in the past, slow to change and highly stable," and may become "overwhelmed by mechanical systems and lose their integrity" (Hall, 1977). In contrast, low-context cultures are characterized by relatively shallow involvement between people, high individualization, need for large amounts of detailed information, alienation, and fragmentation (Hall, 1977). The high-context nature of Asian cultures contrasts with the low-context nature of Northern European and North American cultures.

High-context Asian cultures place maximum value on human relationships and preservation of harmony and face. Unity and harmony are more important than staying on task, being goal directed, or getting the job done at all costs. The goal of communication is to promote harmonious, unifying relationships. The intricate rules of communication that are based on social status, age, sex, education, occupation, family background, and marital status determine what is communicated and how it is communicated, thereby ensuring harmonious social interaction (Chan, 1998).

Thoughtful, intuitive, indirect communication styles that preserve balance and accord are valued within high-context Asian cultures as opposed to the open, direct communication styles of low-context cultures such as the United States. One does not openly contradict, criticize, or cause discomfort to another; it is better to say "yes" if saying "no" would be offensive. The ability to sense and nonverbally determine what is going on without being told is encouraged in children and important in all interactions. Nonverbal communication conveys more information than verbal communication does in high-context Asian cultures. Silence is more powerful in controlling a conversation, communicating acceptance or nonacceptance, and in conveying attitudes of interest and respect: "He who knows, talks not; he who talks, knows not" (Chan, 1998).

Even third- and fourth-generation Asian Americans, born and raised in the United States maintain high-context communication styles with little awareness of their bicultural communication patterns, going back and forth from high to low-context communication patterns. The main point is that understanding cultural context can aid in determining what is important to the individual/cultural community, for example, what is attended to or not attended to.

Culturally competent communication with Asian Americans can be developed with practice. Begin this practice with the attitude of a learner; observe nonverbal and indirect communication styles of those around you; listen more than speak, even when you think you have something to say; observe your own feelings about being silent, and how you communicate nonverbally; and be patient as well as alert—the answers you seek will be provided within the context of verbal and nonverbal communication. Practice observing the essences of the "three teachings" as they are embodied in the Asian ways, outlook, and understanding about the meaning of life.

Practicing Relationship Protocols

Beginning the process of developing a working relationship with Asian American clients requires ongoing attention to one's own trustworthiness. How do you demonstrate you can be trusted in your relationships? For Asians, credibility begins with standing by your word, not saying what you don't mean, and not promising what you cannot deliver: "talk is cheap" and "actions speak louder than words." Consistent, reliable behavior, coupled with respect and humbleness are part of continuous trust building.

An Asian American client's access to services will mostly likely begin with a relative, trusted friend, or respected authority making a referral or verifying the reliability of the service provider (Leung, 1988, in Chan, 1998). When social workers initiate contact, proactively identify, seek out, and respectfully recognize family members, community elders, and social networks, they demonstrate commitment to developing a trusting relationship.

Role of the Professional, Overcoming Resistance, and Communication Barriers

Asian Americans will typically expect that consultation or intervention by professionals such as social workers will be practical, structured, and prescriptive and provide specific answers and recommendations (Behring & Gelinas, 1996, Kim, 1985, both in Chan 1998). A professional who assumes a nondirective or neutral stance may be perceived as disinterested, uncaring, or incompetent (Uba, 1994). Thus, it is important to carefully assess from the onset an individual or family's range of needs and establish the temporal order in which they realistically can be met. Such timely, credible provision of services can enhance and maintain the client-social worker relationship and client follow-through (Sue & Zane, 1987).

Traditional Asian parents, in accordance with practices of filial piety, view allegiance proceeding from governmental authority to teacher to parent and assume a "dependent" orientation of deference, noninterference, and delegation of responsibility to school authorities and professionals (Chan, 1986; Cheng, 1987; Uba, 1994, all in Chan 1998, p. 329). Social workers, using their cross-cultural awareness, can mediate the confusion Asian families experience regarding policies that sanction client rights, responsibilities, and entitlements. For example, attempts at collaborative assessment and treatment planning may be threatening if parents believe that they are being held accountable for their special-needs child's difficulties (Chan, 1998).

Many of the barriers to cross-cultural communication are inadvertently posed by social workers or other service providers for whom cultural competency is not established as the foundation of practice. For example, in all cases where the client's English-speaking ability is limited, a competent interpreter should be provided. Even when the client speaks English as a second language but may have difficulty understanding policies or complicated issues, a trained, adult interpreter should be provided. We need to be aware of clients who may deny themselves the service of an interpreter because they feel it will cause inconvenience or expense to authorities.

PROBLEM IDENTIFICATION AND ASSESSMENT SKILLS WITH ASIAN AMERICAN CLIENTS

As we have reviewed, social work practice with Asians involves inclusion and understanding of multiple perspectives (historic, geopolitical, personal, etc.), systems, and processes. Social work practice in general should begin with worker and systemic self-evaluation of cultural values and competencies. Although a detailed discussion of the cultural competency self-evaluation process is beyond the scope of this chapter, Lum (2003) and others (Acevedo & Morales, 2001; Leung & Cheung, 2001) have developed guidelines to examine competency. As depicted in Figure 5.1, self-evaluation of cultural values and competencies mediates the subsequent processes of engagement, assessment, development of agreed-upon interventions, and ultimately, the effectiveness of interventions. The discussion that follows will examine cultural competence in assessment, intervention, and the inclusion of cultural intervention options, evaluation, and service termination.

Public disclosure of family problems or requesting help is very difficult for many Asian families. Such disclosure may be considered shameful, a betrayal of family trust, an act of weakness, a disgrace of family honor, or an act of disrespect even if information is provided to a helping professional (Chan, 1998). Therefore, social workers must understand the importance of saving face and how to aid families in maintaining their dignity, honor, and self-respect.

Chan (1998) describes some key principles that can assist the assessment and intervention planning process. Briefly, we need to remind ourselves to go slow, reframe, pay attention to details, and be flexible; in other words: (1) Take time to establish a connection with the family or individual even if the conversation seems unrelated to the referral issue, and avoid moving

Figure 5.1 | Culturally Competent Social Work Practice Process

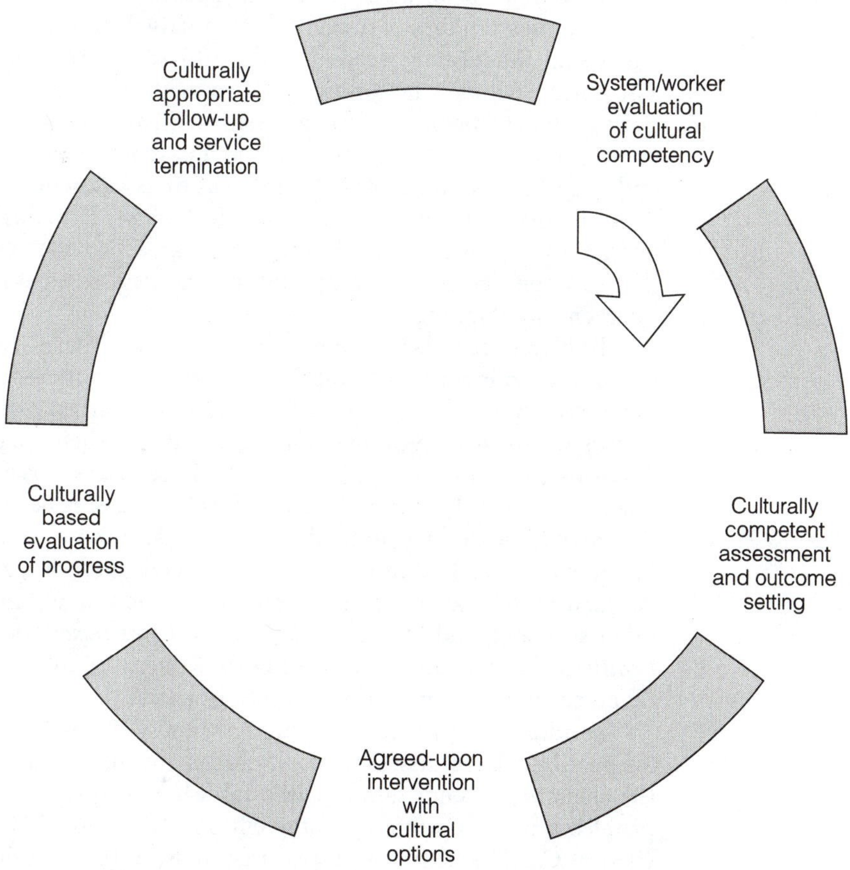

Culturally
appropriate
follow-up
and service
termination

System/worker
evaluation
of cultural
competency

Culturally
based
evaluation
of progress

Culturally
competent
assessment
and outcome
setting

Agreed-upon
intervention
with
cultural
options

quickly into frank discussion of specific problems; (2) reframe problems and approach them indirectly, in a round-about manner, allowing mutual respect and trust to develop; (3) pay careful attention to what may appear to be minor issues that the family defines as important, which helps establish your continuing concern for their general well-being; and (4) accommodate and be flexible about meeting times and places that are familiar to them and, when possible, accompany them to important meetings or show up in support.

Leung and Cheung (2001) describe the importance of involving Asian clients from the very beginning in defining issues and problems because of factors that mediate use of services such as "losing face," cultural norms relating to handling problems on one's own, and fear of being misunderstood by the host culture. By collaborating to reframe the helping process to a learning process, the social worker can aid Asian clients in identifying problems and developing achievable solutions with measurable outcomes.

Using a Biopsychosocial Perspective in Assessment

The biopsychosocial assessment is a process and product that provides an overall understanding of a client's life situation and biological, psychological, and social functioning needs (Sands, 2001). The traditional biopsychosocial assessment includes the following: (1) a medical assessment; (2) psychological testing, which includes rapid assessment instruments and functional assessment; (3) psychosocial history; and (4) a psychiatric evaluation, mental status, and diagnosis (Sands, 2001). These areas of assessment have been described in detail by others (Hepworth, Rooney, & Larson, 1997; Sands, 2001) and will not be addressed here. Each assessment area provides essential information that can contribute to a comprehensive needs assessment and client-centered intervention planning.

To better serve Asian American clients, a multilevel assessment that examines and accounts for cultural heritage, migration issues, acculturation, experiences with racism and discrimination, war stress, societal, and cultural factors will provide a more complete and comprehensive database toward the development of interventions. Lee (1997b) provides a useful assessment guideline to capture: (1) *family dynamics* based on assessment of the *internal family system,* including individual members, family subsystems, life cycle, hierarchy, leadership, communication, behavioral styles, and norms and *external factors,* such as war trauma, migration, racism, and financial, housing and other stressors; and (2) *mental health problems based on a holistic concept of health and illness.* In this model, both Western biomedical and Eastern holistic perspectives are incorporated into practice.

In addition to identifying internal family dynamics and external factors, an overall cultural assessment developed through negotiated consensus with the client and client's family will establish a client-centered perspective of the problems and appropriate interventions (Castillo, 1997). Kleinman (1996 cited in Castillo, 1997) proposed that steps in the overall cultural assessment should include the following: (1) Assessment of cultural identity, (2) use of cultural sources to understanding meaning system of the client; (3) assessment of cultural meanings associated with symptoms; (4) assessment of family explanatory models of illness; (5) assessment of social environment on client's illness; (6) assessment of social stigma associated with the illness; (7) assessment of ethnocentric biases of the clinician or service provider; and (8) negotiation of the clinical reality and treatment plan with client, family and clinician (Kleinman, 1996, pp. 21–24).

Similarly, Lee (1997b) proposes discussion questions to help the social worker develop a database that reveals the client's perspectives about the cause of problems, past coping behaviors, health-seeking behavior, and treatment expectation.

- What symptoms and problems are perceived by each family member?
- What would be the diagnostic label given in the client's home country?
- What are the family's cultural explanations of the causes of the problem?

- What kind of treatment would the family get if they were back in their home country?
- Where did the family go for help before they came to see the clinician?
- What is the family's experience with herbal medicine and indigenous healers?
- What was the family's previous experience with Western health and mental health care systems?
- What are the family's treatment expectations? (Lee, 1997b, p. 23)

Identifying and Mobilizing Client's Cultural Strengths in Intervention

Asians are said to live by their strengths on a daily basis; their centuries-old cultural ways are rooted in values and traditional practices evolved within high-context (slowly changing), collectivist group-oriented cultures. Among their strengths are the family, which serves as a major source of guidance and protection; the "three teachings," which stress harmony in all relationships including nature and divergent forces; and the reinforcement of personal characteristics such as industriousness, self-sacrifice, thrift, patience, determination, humility, endurance, tolerance, and accommodation (Chan, 1998).

The influence of traditional cultural ways as a source of strength for Asian American individuals and families can only be determined through careful assessment, given the considerable variation of Asian experience and acculturation patterns. Our Western culture often obscures and invalidates a minority culture through its vast media resources. For example, a second- or third-generation Asian youth who strives to become Americanized will idealize the norms and values of our low-context, individualistic culture, and then suffer internal conflict because of inability to reconcile the differences between her or his instinctive Asian ways and the unattainable ideal. The culturally competent social worker can creatively provide this youth with opportunities to use her or his cultural strengths; one such opportunity may involve reeducation and rediscovery of the origins and strengths of her or his cultural roots.

INTERVENTION SKILLS WITH ASIAN AMERICAN CLIENTS

The accompanying Case Study of Chanda's narrative and history permits us the privilege and honor of viewing a portion of the complex data gathered from the historic, geopolitical context, and ensuing stressful events at the macro level; cultural norms, beliefs, and meanings attributed to illness by society at the meso level; and at the micro level, knowledge of her strengths, resources, and priorities. This data, in combination with relevant biopsychosocial information, when formulated into a comprehensive, culturally informed assessment establishes a foundation for posing the next question: How are culturally relevant, effective interventions developed for Asian American clients?

CASE | # Case Study Integration Exercise on Contact, Problem Identification, and Assessment Skills

Valid data gathering empowers a client to tell her or his story unimpeded by the listener's underlying goals or cultural set. In actual practice, assessments do not develop in a linear fashion. The practitioner must patiently listen to accounts, and develop ongoing analysis of meanings based on collaboration with the client.

Although the prospect of listening to a cross-cultural account may appear daunting, it is helpful to approach the arena with an attitude of discovery. The use of Kleinman's (1988) and Lee's (1997b) cultural assessment guidelines may greatly facilitate this process. As you read the case history of Chanda, a Cambodian refugee, keep in mind the cultural context discovery questions presented here as you gather information for the multilevel assessment.

CULTURAL CONTEXT DISCOVERY QUESTIONS

1. What specific historic, geopolitical, or personal events and experiences have contributed to the client's issues or problems over time?
2. What are the recurring issues, themes, or problems in the client's account?
3. From the client's perspective, why have these events or problems happened specifically to her or him? What meaning do these occurrences/events/symptoms have for her/him, her/his family now and for the future?
4. What are the client's strengths and resources?
5. As the assessor, what conclusions do you tentatively draw, and what personal/cultural assumptions are they based on?
6. What are the implications for developing assessment and intervention plans?

Critical Elements of the Cambodian Historic Geopolitical Perspective

A beginning point in establishing a relationship with immigrants or refugees is to learn about the historic geopolitical context that families have survived. For Cambodian refugees, knowledge of Cambodia's complex history is an essential prerequisite to understanding what families experienced during the war and why. For more than 400 years, foreign governments such as Thailand, Vietnam, France, China, Japan, the Soviet Union, and the United States were either directly involved in Cambodia's affairs or conducted "proxy wars" within its borders (Haas, 1991). These intrusions, along with complex internal factors, eventually unleashed the rage of the Pol Pot regime. Anthropologist E. T. Hall (1977) has observed, "Powerlessness and lack of self-affirmation lead to aggression." The rage that engulfed so many millions in forms of barbarism unparalleled in modern times was the experiential context that shaped the lives of Cambodian refugees residing in the United States. This history is a critical part of their lives, and their truths must guide our work.

In April 1975, Khmer Rouge revolutionaries effectively defeated the U.S.-backed forces of Lon Nol and entered the capital of Phnom Penh to take control of Cambodia. Their seemingly peaceful entry into the city gave rise to some brief rejoicing in the streets. But the atmosphere quickly turned to fear, terror, and panic as expressionless, intense, young Khmer Rouge, barely in their teens, dressed in black, carrying grenades and assault guns moved door to door directing residents to leave their homes immediately (Ponchaud, 1977). The entire city was emptied; thousands of Cambodians were forced to relocate on the pretext that they would return in a few days because "Americans were going to bomb the city." In reality, the Khmer Rouge intended to eliminate their "enemies" and relocate the population to villages for work and reeducation for Angkar (the organization, party and state).

Many died during the forced removal as a result of starvation, illness, and murder. Terrorized at gunpoint, children were forcibly separated from their parents, the infirm were forced to leave hospitals regardless of their condition, and those that refused were killed. An escapee recounted the march out of Phnom Penh:

> Here and there we could see the bodies of villagers who had been killed by the Khmer Rouge, presumably because they didn't want to leave their homes.
>
> On April 19, at ten in the morning, I saw the Khmer Rouge arrest about twenty young men with long hair; they shot them before our eyes. Everybody was terrified and had their hair cut at once, even in the middle of the night.
>
> When we got to Ang Long Kagnanh (10 kilometers from Phnom Penh) the road was blocked by Khmer Rouge who searched us, tore off wristwatches, and took away radios, necklaces, and gold rings. They told us the Angkar needed them and was only borrowing the jewels for a while but would give them back later. From there we were made to turn back to Highway 5. We reached Prek Phneuv on April 25 . . . (Ponchaud, 1977, p, 26).

This reign of terror under Pol Pot's direction sought to eliminate "enemies" of the Khmer people. These enemies were capitalists (shopkeepers and traders), feudalists (Buddhists), intellectuals, royalty, imperialists, ethnic minorities, and anyone who dressed or spoke differently from the Khmer (Haas, 1991). These designated enemies of Angkar were hunted down and systematically executed; entire families were tortured and murdered.

Conservative estimates are that over 1 million Cambodian men, women, and children died as the result of murder, torture, starvation, and disease during the purge of Pol Pot's killing fields (Jackson, 1989), but other estimates suggest as many as 3 million Cambodians died (Kinzie, 1989). Thus, less than 6 million of the 7.3 million Cambodians alive on April 17, 1975, when the Khmer Rouge took over, remained alive after the Khmer Rouge departed in 1979 (Jackson, 1989, p. 3). The horror and devastation of the Cambodian holocaust remained largely out of the American consciousness until 1984 when the movie *The Killing Fields* brought the atrocities to our attention.

More than 150,000 Cambodian refugees have resettled in the United States since 1975. At extreme peril to their lives, Cambodians fled on foot, in many cases over half the breadth of the country (200 miles), to the Thai and Vietnam borders. These survivors of the Cambodian holocaust endured a wide range of life-threatening and traumatic experiences. They were dislocated from their homes, forcibly separated from their children and other family members, watched family members taken to their death, given little or no food, denied medical care, tortured, and raped and witnessed mass executions or the murder of individuals who did something minor, like covertly eating a grasshopper (Martin, 1994, p. 194).

(continued)

CASE | *continued*

Pain No One Understands: The Case History of Chanda

This case history is from a study of social networks and health-seeking efforts of Cambodian refugees (Morelli, 1996). In 1983, Chanda was resettled in the United States after fleeing the ravages of war and genocide. Her narrative details complex life-events, cultural beliefs, and self-questioning that yield critical clues to aid a collaborative problem-identification process and development of a viable assessment.

Chanda believed that she survived the Pol Pot era because she did good deeds in her previous life. Her story suggests that resourcefulness, strength of character, and strong maternal instincts were factors responsible for her family's survival. Chanda actively used Western medical services but did not find relief from the physical and mental suffering. From a Western psychiatric perspective, she continues to suffer from posttraumatic stress disorder. Why didn't she continue to adhere to Western treatment for optimal results? From Chanda's lived experience and perspective, traditional healing practices provided relief from suffering, albeit at times inconsistently. As you read this case history, focus on Chanda's perspectives and seek awareness about why she preferred traditional Cambodian healing practices.

Chanda's Story

In 1975, Chanda was 25 years of age. Her extended family consisted of 23 people all residing together in the same village outside of Phnom Penh. Her father was an investigator and was pursued by the Khmer Rouge as soon as they came to power. He was shot to death after several escape attempts. At the end of the Pol Pot era, the entire family, with the exception of Chanda, her daughter, and two younger brothers, had either been killed by the Khmer Rouge or died of starvation.

Chanda's family of origin consisted of herself and four siblings. Her older brother died before the Pol Pot era in an auto accident, and one of her younger brothers died for lack of medical care in 1975. Both her parents were ethnically part Chinese and part Khmer. Her mother had been married previously; thus, Chanda also had an older stepsister and stepbrother living with their biological father's family.

Chanda's entire extended family lived together and made their living as various types of merchants, selling rice, groceries, and other items. She went to school for six years, and recalls being 17 or 18 when she first got married. Chanda was working in a cloth-weaving factory when the Khmer Rouge took over the government.

Chanda has been pregnant 12 times: six resulted in miscarriages: one before Pol Pot and five during that era; two children that were born during the Pol Pot era died from starvation as infants. She currently has four children ranging from 8 to 16 years of age. Her oldest child, a daughter, was the only one who remains alive from the Pol Pot era. The second child was born in a refugee camp, and the last two in the United States.

Chanda's first husband was executed by the Khmer Rouge just before the Vietnamese invasion. Her second husband died of an illness while they were awaiting resettlement in the refugee camp. Her third husband left with another woman, and she separated from her fourth husband.

Initially, when her family was evacuated from Phnom Penh, they lived in the woods without food or shelter. Because of her family's background, they were rationed only one can of rice and a spoon of salt for a month.

Forced Labor, Starvation, and Death

Chanda was moved from village to village by the Khmer Rouge group leader in charge of their area. She finally ended up farming in Svay Dangkham. The living and working conditions caused thousands to die; she recalled of that time:

When I first got off the truck, I was made a rice farmer. There were four groups that came to this area. When we first arrived there, there were 19,000 people. Then, by the time the Vietnamese invaded there were only 1,800 people left. They all died. They usually died by the families; [by] starvation, because some families have 80 people and only one can of rice. And some even had 100 people. Sometimes there was nothing, we had to drink the water as broth without any rice.

Then when the floods came, we had nothing to eat at all. Living there, you know? And from working and over exhaustion, having nothing to eat. Some months, when there was no rice at all, they would make soup out of rice peel (husk) for us to eat.

There were even people who ate their own children. There was a lady who ate her dead baby, too hungry! If you don't believe me, go see for yourself, and you'll see that this village is full of skeletons.

In our group, at first, the men agreed to farm, but as time went on they all died off. . . . Sometimes they were rushed and forced to make seven tons of rice per one acre of land, people were then forced to work all day and night. From seven in the morning until twelve, then from one until five o'clock in the evening. Then would work from seven in the evening until eleven at night, again.

Yes, only two hours for rest! A lot of people would die because of not enough sleep also. There wasn't enough to eat, people's stomachs were big. When there was flooding, there was nothing to eat at all. We would walk around looking for food, even one little plant; we left no leaves on it. We were even eating vegetables that would give us diarrhea. In that village, nothing grew only morning glory vegetable and sdauw [a bitter vegetable]. It was too much, there was nothing and as far as we can see there were no trees around. There was nothing to shelter under, no trees. You had to make your own shelter or else you had nothing.

Young children, ages six, seven had to go around picking up cow dung. They weren't allowed any free time. Living in that village, there was a lot of hardship. There was never a moment to sleep easy during Pol Pot times. We had to dig irrigation ditches. There was a group of people sent from Svay Reang to dig irrigation ditches, when they were done, they were beaten to death.

They beat them line by line. They were all tied together in a line. Yes, they beat them. We would ride out in wagons in the morning you could smell the stench. These were the people that were accused of being traitors, so they brought them over and killed them. Ooooh . . . it was scary!

In 1979, three days before the Vietnamese invasion, Chanda's first husband was taken away and beaten to death. Pregnant at the time, she gave birth alone and found herself needing to be on-guard that the child would not be taken from her. She described the first of these situations:

(continued)

CASE | *continued*

> When I gave birth, I did it by myself. When my stomach hurt, I called out for the midwife, I was going crazy. I had to build a fire and boiled water on my own. When the water was about boiled, I went and sat up on the bed. Then the midwife showed up, but by that time, I had already given birth. . . .
>
> It was after I had given birth that there was a Vietnamese person [soldier] that took care of us. . . .
>
> The Vietnamese kept asking me for my baby. He said he would give me 10 units of gold. But I wouldn't give up my baby; after all I had been through. I would not trade my child for anything.

Chanda was on her own after her husband's death, and she needed to support her child. During this period she walked from village to village, carrying her baby and following the movement of people headed toward Battambang (a city closest to the Thailand border). She described herself as having bountiful energy and help from an unknown source:

> Back then, my strength was like something was helping me, I never ran out of strength. I would go get water for people, wash people's clothes for them, as long as they gave me enough rice for two meals. Then, I kept praying for my life and to take care of my baby's life, to help me live, and I never was sick back then. It was as though something was helping me the entire time, back then.

Along the way Chanda was shown kindness and generosity by several strangers, who shared food. She was given work in exchange for food by a woman who took her in for about five months after seeing Chanda was trustworthy and industrious. Then, she continued following the exodus of people toward Camp Tmeay, where she was reunited with a younger brother, and later met her second husband.

Both families moved to Khao-I-Dang camp when their children became ill and needed medical care. They were advised that medical care would be available at the camp's clinic. There, Chanda's second husband fell ill; he died after they were moved to Srakeo, just before the birth of her second child. After the birth of her second child in Thailand, Chanda became totally blind for three months, after warming herself over a charcoal fire, which she believes may have caused the blindness.

Illness and Suffering

Since 1983, after resettling in Washington State, Chanda has suffered continuously from various forms of illness, physical pain, constant coughing, feeling that something was stuck in her throat, allergies, hearing voices, and seeing spirits. In one of her first encounters with the health system, she had uncontrollable shaking in reaction to drinking coffee and eating jauf kway [fried bread]. She had to be taken to the hospital on three separate occasions because of this reaction. Chanda is also allergic to the ingredients in Nyquil and develops a severe rash when she takes it. Unbeknownst to the doctors treating her for coughing up blood, she was prescribed medication containing such ingredients, which resulted in the unpleasant rash.

In 1992, Chanda and her family were robbed at gunpoint in their home by a group of four robbers who spoke Cambodian, English, Laotian, and Vietnamese. They tore the place apart and physically abused, threatened, and terrorized Chanda and her family for almost an hour. After the robbery, Chanda and her children were so frightened of being at home that they slept at her sponsor's home every night for a year. When they returned to sleeping at home, Chanda began to be sick. She described occurrences at that time:

> When I was driving, I saw stop lights . . . red lights, I saw green lights. I looked and didn't see any cars, so I kept driving on. My child yelled, "It's a red light!" When the light was green, I came to a stop. At that time, I thought I was going crazy. When it kept getting worse, I was extremely worried, because everything I owned was all gone. . . .
>
> It was an illness related to the mind, thinking. I kept thinking that these things that I had collected from a long time ago were all gone with a blink of an eye. I was thinking that, you know?
>
> Then, I was sick and was unable to drive or anything anymore. I drove and got lost in downtown [laughter]. I was in downtown and asked the police which way to downtown. The police would look at me and shake his head. My child that was in the car was scolding me that it was downtown, but I wasn't able to understand my child anymore. Then, I was sick and began to have a fever. I had fever to the point of losing my consciousness and my children were scared. Then, I took some medicine. I was sick and was hot to the point of confusion. My child made rice soup for me to eat. I was eating rice soup and it seemed like the rice soup was stuck in my throat.

Chanda was taken to the hospital, where X rays were taken, but the medical people were unable to determine the cause of her problem because nothing showed up in the photos. Her pain persisted, as she reported it:

> I went to Harborview Hospital; I told them that I had a fever and things. As soon as I came down with a fever, it was like "a hundred ghosts took over my body." I was sick on that day. Within one hour, it was like I was sick with 10 different types of illnesses. I would sit there and I would hear ringing.
>
> Then, I went to the doctors, I told them that this hurt and that hurt, because it really did hurt inside my body. My arm hurt, to this day it hurts where I extend my arm and the pain won't go away. If I don't take painkillers I would "sleep in tears" every night. I have to take it continuously.

Chanda also experienced spirit visitations. She says these spirits keep telling her things, and she keeps seeing something from another world. She described these experiences:

> In my ear, I would hear somebody telling me things the entire time. And when I went to tell the doctors, they took me and put me in "hand cuffs" and said I was "crazy." And I said, I told them, "That I'm not crazy." But since I was sick, I have this thing, like people are telling me things.
>
> They wear something like a king's crown or a beautiful angel, they tell me things. My eyes were open, you can't see it, but I can see it. I told them, when I was in the hospital, I told them, "He is coming to me again." The doctor said I was crazy and they put me in cuffs and things. I said I wasn't crazy, that people were calling me to go.

(continued)

CASE | *continued*

They don't come to harm me or anything, they are good people. I would see my grandfather, like from the time of the Republic, like from before. I wasn't asleep; I saw it like I was really there. Then when I went to the hospital, I tell them that I see these things . . . speaking based on what I saw. . . .

Sometimes, I would see . . . but it became worse after I was robbed. It's related to "the way of my mind." Because I have sinned in the past and when I've lost everything from my body . . . these things are related to each other. I don't think about it. I just think that these are little things, as long as I am alive and find a way to live it's okay, right?

Chanda's descriptions of her visitations from spirits caused her to be hospitalized for a week. Doctors wanted her to stay there longer, but she was released because she insisted, and she planned to travel to Cambodia.

Chanda's suffering also manifests itself in severe, uncontrollable anger, which she has unleashed on her children. In the past, she has thrown a knife at her daughter and scarred her face. She says they are too big now, but she still attempts to hit them when she becomes angry or has problems with them.

Application Exercises: Problem Identification and Assessment

Developing a client-centered tool for organizing factors within a client system can facilitate problem identification, client's priorities, and client-worker communication. Using Chanda's case history and the Cultural Context Discovery Questions (see p. 128) here is an example of an approach one might take.

• After reading Chanda's case history, identify the external events or stresses, internal/personal dynamics or effects, and her strengths over time.

It bears repeating that cultural explanations of illness need to be given sincere respect and attention, and the client's desire for traditional healing practices should be accommodated when feasible and appropriate. For newly immigrated Asian families, it may be important to identify respected elders within the extended family or kinship system who are consulted before major decisions are made. Collaborative alliances with family members can help to create a client-centered balance between traditional cultural practices and Western practices.

Intervention Models

Two social work practice models are particularly suited to serve as frameworks in collaborating with Asian American clients, and to customize interventions for maximum efficacy: the strengths perspective (Saleebey, 2002), and

- In collaboration with the client, sketch a simple table such as the one shown here to view these contextual factors; this allows the client, family, and service provider to acknowledge the multiple stressors the client has endured and how strengths were successfully used.
- Use a client-centered tool as a starting point to identify problems in an indirect, nonconfrontative manner. In this way, the client and social worker as a team can identify needs and move toward negotiating intervention priorities in the assessment process.

Example of Client-Centered Tool

	1975	1979	1982	1992
External factors	Khmer Rouge control Cambodia	Vietnamese liberate the country	Chanda resettles in the United States	Robbed at gun point at home
Internal factors (personal/ family events and dynamics)	Father killed by Khmer Rouge; family members separated sent to work camps	Chanda flees with family to Thailand and refugee camps	Started having illness, pain, constant coughing, heard voices, saw spirits	Disoriented, physically disabled, angry
Strengths	25 years of age lives with 23 extended family members; nuclear family: parents and 4 siblings	Chanda strong and energetic	Seeks out Western medical care and traditional healing practices	Syncretically utilizes Western, traditional self-care, and spiritual healing; motivated to seek well-being

the empowerment practice model (Parsons, Gutierrez & Cox, 1998). Both invite us to affirm cultural identities, cultural ways of being and knowing, to provide opportunities for cross-cultural education, and to create flexible approaches in the collaboration and development of interventions with clients. Used in conjunction with each other, these practice models may increase the likelihood for behaviors and actions that support positive outcomes at micro, meso, and macro levels.

Strengths Perspective   The strengths perspective draws its power from grounding in the concepts of liberation, empowerment, and a clear commitment to the people we serve. Saleebey (2002) articulates the principles of strengths-perspective practice in ways that enable us to be creative in facilitating liberation and empowerment. Using Saleebey's framework, examples of issues to be aware of when developing interventions with Asian Americans are discussed at the micro, meso, and macro levels:

- *Every individual, group, family, and community has strengths*—When developing interventions, practitioners need to interact with families and communities in ways that acknowledge, respect, and affirm Asian cultural values, traditions, and other resources unknown to us. Their strengths have sustained Asians through difficult times and continue to serve them. Learning about cultural ways we are unfamiliar with, and acting in ways that demonstrate genuine concern for clients' well-being are at the heart of establishing trust and providing culturally competent services. Interventions may draw on strengths from micro, meso, and macro levels of practice; the following questions aid in directing the focus:

  - Micro level: What strengths does the individual or family bring? How might these strengths serve them in dealing with a current problem?
  - Meso level: What strengths can the community offer to intervene in this situation? How can they be mobilized?
  - Macro level: What existing policies apply to or facilitate the current problem or issue?

- *Trauma and abuse, illness, and struggle may be injurious, but they may be also sources of challenge and opportunity*—For Asian refugees, acknowledging and affirming family, individual, and community resilience already demonstrated by their survival is vital to healing and adjustment within a new cultural context. Developing intervention plans with Asians who have suffered trauma requires awareness that pain and suffering are understood to be part of what one must endure in life, that emotional suffering from trauma may be manifested in bodily illness, or what Western medicine terms *somatic illness*, and that belief systems around the causes of illness must be respected while clients are educated about Western concepts and complimentary intervention options. Potential questions to pose include:

  - Micro: How has the individual or family coped with changes, death, trauma, or injury in the past and currently?
  - Meso: How has the community provided support in the past and presently? Who are the facilitators, leaders, and elders within the community who could be approached to initiate support of the family?
  - Macro: What resources are available at the state, federal, or other levels?

- *Assume that you do not know the upper limits of the capacity to grow and change and take individual, group and community aspirations seriously*—We need to keep the parameters of possibility open and not base assessments on past performance.

  - Micro: What does the individual or family desire or perceive as its goals or outcomes?
  - Meso: What are the community and leadership perspectives of their potential?

- Macro: What has the community identified as policy needs? How can they be addressed? Who can be mobilized?

- *We best serve clients by collaborating with them*—The wisdom of practice comes from our clients.

  - Micro: How are families, individuals, and social networks included in assessment, intervention planning, and evaluation?
  - Meso: How are communities included in these processes?
  - Macro: How can communities and families affect needed policy?

- *Every environment is full of resources*—Individuals are the substance of communities, and individual strengths may be amplified through community action. Asian communities have demonstrated their abilities to develop a wide range of resources.

  - Micro: What are the resources, traditional practices, and so on? How do they apply to the problem/situation? How can these micro-level resources be mobilized?
  - Meso: What community organizations or entities can Asians rely on for specific resources? Who are the key people, leaders, and so on? What are the specific resources?
  - Macro: What policies or governmental representatives may be of service in this situation?

- *Caring, caretaking, and context*—Caring and caretaking within the context of traditional Asian families is a source of strength. As Asian families have become westernized, traditional practices have weakened. We may pose the following question:

  - How are cultural norms of caring and caretaking continued or prevented within families and communities and through policies?

Empowerment   Empowerment practice focuses on developing "within individuals, families, groups or communities the ability to gain power" (Parsons, Gutierrez & Cox, 1998, p. 4). The empowerment process involves (1) a critical examination of one's attitudes and beliefs about self and one's sociopolitical environment, (2) validation of one's experience, (3) increased knowledge and skills for critical thinking and action, and (4) action for personal and political change (Parsons, Gutierrez & Cox, 1998).

How can empowerment practice be used in developing interventions with Asians? At first glance, the somewhat individualistic nature of this model may appear to pose cross-cultural limitations. However, the historic oppression of Asians makes empowerment practice a particularly salient model. Empowerment practice can aid practitioners and clients to target intervention areas and, based on readiness, to develop potentially effective interventions. As Leung and Cheung (2001) have pointed out, reframing problems toward a vision of change can aid Asian clients to redefine problems from a positive perspective, and concretize attainable solutions. Reframing problems and perspectives with the objective of empowerment can enable a family to view its problems as a challenge that can ultimately produce positive energy and good health. Using the empowerment process for intervention development, the practitioner may explore the following:

- *Attitudes, values, and beliefs*—What attitudes and beliefs limit the client or family options to health or healing? How may attitudes or beliefs be reframed to include more options for interventions?
- *Validation through collective experience*—How can the individual or family benefit from collective validation? What sources of validation does the client desire or may be appropriate?
- *Knowledge and skills for critical thinking and action*——How can critical thinking knowledge and skills be applied as an intervention in this situation?
- *Action taken for personal and political change*—Relative to the situation and cultural context, what actions or interventions are appropriate now?

Collaboration with clients to identify and mobilize strengths at the individual, family, community, and policy levels empowers clients and practitioners to develop creative, effective interventions. In this way, the strengths perspective and empowerment practice enable Asian Americans to accept their rightful place as contributors in this society and reduce barriers to service and participation.

TERMINATION SKILLS WITH ASIAN AMERICAN CLIENTS

The professional's evaluation of client-progress and follow-up would be an unspoken expectation of many Asian Americans. A trusted individual's credibility relies on an Asian belief that "your word is your bond"; thus, professional follow-through demonstrates genuineness and competence. The process of review and evaluation of agreed-upon goals at regular intervals also develops client readiness for service closure. These reviews must include systems accountability by coming full circle and evaluating how effective the system and worker have been in implementing culturally competent, empirically based, best practice interventions; optimizing clients' well-being; and thereby progressing toward planned termination of services as depicted in Figure 5.1 (see p. 125).

The client-progress evaluation framework (see Figure 5.2, p. 141) suggested here attempts to learn about: (1) the implementation of culturally competent practice, (2) the outcomes of agreed-upon interventions, and (3) follow-up and readiness for service termination. The first question focuses on whether cultural competency is supported and implemented at systems and practitioner levels and to what extent. The second question addresses the progress of the client in achieving outcomes or meeting goals. And the third area of inquiry examines follow-up and readiness for termination of services.

Case Study Integration Exercise on Intervention Skills

Chanda's story raised our awareness about some of the ways culturally competent practice skills could have facilitated her healing process. The major points from previous sections are brought together here to remind us of ways to implement cultural competence with Asian Americans. In this excerpt from Chanda's story, examine how service providers might have intervened in a culturally competent manner. For example, what does Chanda identify as important factors to her healing? How might these factors be important in determining an intervention with the client?

Culturally Competent Ways with Asians

1. Go slowly, allow the client to tell you her story, from her perspective, even if it seems like a digression from the focus—the indirect path is often more direct; this demonstrates respect.
2. Take time to hear and understand the client's belief system; this demonstrates humbleness, patience, and a willingness to learn.
3. Research the geopolitical history of refugees or the history of oppression this specific Asian American family has faced; this demonstrates accommodation and preparation.
4. Understand and practice respectful indirect, nonverbal communication styles; this demonstrates respect for harmony and accommodation.
5. Pay attention to the details of what matters to the client; this demonstrates genuineness and competence.
6. Recognize clients' strengths in many ways, especially in subtle ways that indicate your appreciation for who they are and what they've been through; this demonstrates compassion.
7. Provide clear recommendations or intervention options, that consider the client's cultural beliefs and ways; this demonstrates flexibility and competence.
8. Use trained language interpreters whenever you sense that there may be misunderstanding; this demonstrates competence and accommodation.

Attempts to Heal: Using Whatever Helps

In revisiting the case history of Chanda, we can observe that much of her suffering is associated with the experiences and losses of the Pol Pot era and exacerbated by the armed robbery in her home in the United States. Physical ailments such as her coughing seem to be triggered by things she worries about, depression, not feeling well, and stress.

Chanda used many forms of traditional treatment in addition to Western medicine. She says she tried, "Kru Khmer and Khmer medicine, Chinese medicine, anything that was supposed to be good. I went to American doctors, Vietnamese doctors." She also tried acupuncture, chiropractors, and exercise at a fitness center. From her perspective, "everything" offered some help toward her healing.

Chanda also performed self-treatment or had the family help her with coining, suction, bleeding, bruising of her neck, and drinking herbal potions. Here she described some of the practices:

(continued)

CASE | *continued*

I had heating rub [tiger balm] on my head with a bandage wrapped around it for 30 days in a month. The headaches, I had suction done to the forehead for it until it didn't bruise [bruising means it's working, bad air is being taken out].

At first, it helped. But later, it became not as effective.

I do the suction everyday, now it doesn't even turn red anymore. It stopped turning red, so, I would take a razor blade and make a small incision and create a small opening until black blood runs down.

Headaches, I've tried everything. When I go the doctors and it would hurt so bad, I would do this with my hands. The doctor would ask what I was doing. When he pulled my hand away and saw the bruise there, he would ask if it was hurting again [headaches]. I said it was hurting again. He said I shouldn't be so tense. When it hurts so bad and the doctor would come and ask about it, I wasn't happy, I would even get into arguments with the doctor. When I go there, I would be loud at the clinic, when it hurts so bad.

In special Buddhist ceremonies, Chanda had her head shaven regularly. In 1992, she went to Cambodia and had her head shaved in such a ceremony. As a result, her condition was better for more than a year. This ceremony had special significance as she explained:

During Pol Pot times, they took me to be beaten to death [execution]. I prayed to Buddha and said that if I survived that I would go and shave my head, just so they wouldn't beat me to death. So I wouldn't die and if I was alive, I would be able to meet up with my aunt and uncle and shave my head and have a ceremony.

Doctors, social workers, and other health care professionals diagnosed and treated Chanda's symptoms solely from the Western biomedical perspective without benefit of knowledge about Cambodian spiritual beliefs, health beliefs, and healing practices. Western treatment attempts ignored Chanda's belief system and explanations for the illness. They assigned pathological meanings to Chanda's spirit visitations that she found offensive. She recalled,

After Harborview . . . they sent me to University Hospital. But before they sent me to University Hospital, they cuffed my hands and ankles together. I kept arguing with them, saying, "I'm not crazy, why do you treat me like this." At that time, it was like something was coming again. I said, "Here they come again." They came and said this and that to me. The interpreter interpreted like I said it, from what I could understand. Then, when the doctor came, they made me lay on the bed and they put cuffs on my wrists and cuffed my ankles together. I said, "How come you are putting cuffs on my wrists and ankles? I'm not crazy."

Unfortunately, Western medical service providers were uninformed about Chanda's cultural beliefs and historic geopolitical background. Her determination to heal and survive proved to be powerful. She creatively brought together Western and Cambodian healing ways to deal with her suffering. Like many survivors of the Cambodian Killing Fields, she continues to endure physical pain, social dislocation, and the difficulties of adjustment to a foreign culture.

Figure 5.2 | Culturally Competent Implementation and Evaluation of Client Progress

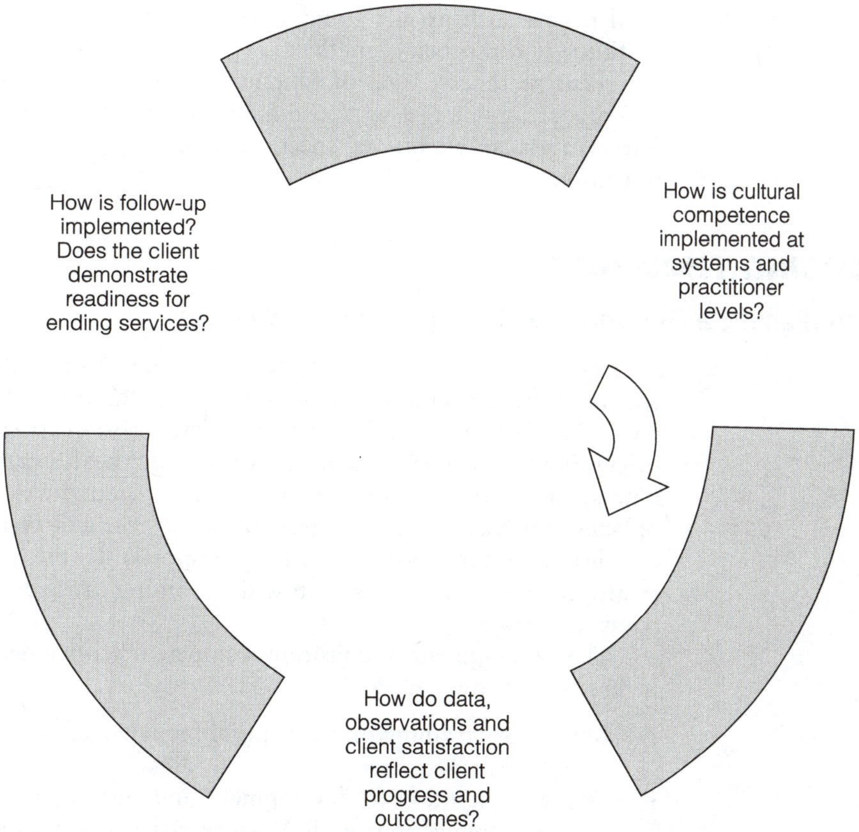

How is cultural competence implemented at systems and practitioner levels?

How is follow-up implemented? Does the client demonstrate readiness for ending services?

How do data, observations and client satisfaction reflect client progress and outcomes?

Analysis of the answers to these questions can potentially provide a clearer picture of where adjustments may be needed within systems and processes to promote client progress. Longitudinal data analysis may contribute to understanding whether culturally competent practice mediates outcomes and how it mediates outcomes.

Classic termination is the "ending stage of the social work process" (Lum, 2000, p. 315). When working with Asians, especially in communities where one may meet clients publicly with some regularity, termination in the classic sense may be acknowledged; however, the relationship between the giver of services and the receiver continues to exist. Asian American clients feel a moral obligation, indebtedness, and need to reciprocate to a "superior" who has provided services (Chan, 1998). Thus, to partially repay the "debt," the client will offer the professional a personal gift or an invitation to a family gathering.

Rejection of such a gift may be viewed as rejection and failure to give face (Behring & Gelinas, 1996, in Chan, 1998).

Preparation for terminating services involves our own awareness of cultural rituals such as gift giving and of how we can respectfully reciprocate gratitude without being unethical. The ending of services will involve assessing client readiness, level of functioning, the availability of social supports, and preparing linkages to housing and other services. We can learn from our Asian American clients' perspectives what will aid them in making optimal transitions.

CLOSING THOUGHTS

Establishing a Responsive Service Delivery System

A responsive service delivery system for Asian Americans embodies and mirrors the culturally competent ways and values discussed throughout this chapter. It understands and anticipates the cross-sections between Western orientations and Asian orientations regarding health care, mental health and illness, and societal norms. The responsive system develops mutual education policies that teach Asian refugees to use services and systems freely and without discriminatory restrictions. Most importantly, the system should demonstrate commitment to systemwide training and practice of culturally competent ways.

The development of culturally competent service delivery systems should include the following:

- Mandatory training on the general knowledge, values, and skills of Asian Americans.
- Ongoing attention to development and sustainability of cultural competence via connections with Asian service organizations, and communities.
- Training for language interpreters that focuses on cultural competency, nuances of meaning, cultural norms, ethics of professional care, and other areas of care delivery.
- Partnerships with Asian communities, organizations, and other interested parties to strategically plan for competency needs as community needs change. Such partnerships have the potential for long-term benefits to all cultural groups and communities.
- Financial support and availability of traditional forms cultural intervention.

Culturally competent practice is a step toward ensuring that cultural, ethnic, and racial minorities are accorded the same respectful treatment, rights, and services as all people in this country. The development and practice of cultural competence benefits people who struggle for social justice and quality of life nationally and internationally. Our willingness to risk the discomfort of learning about ourselves in relation to individuals from diverse cultural contexts with mutual respect, collaboration, and affirmation of all cultures will in time reveal that we are different and yet not different.

References

Acevedo, G., & Morales, J. (2001). Assessment with Latino/Hispanic communities. In R. Fong and S. Furuto (Eds.), *Culturally competent practice: Skills, interventions, & evaluations* (pp. 147–162). Needham Heights, MA: Allyn & Bacon.

Berg, I. K., & Miller, S. D. (1992). Working with Asian American clients: One person at a time. *Families in Society, 73*(6), 356–363.

Castillo, R. J. (1997). *Culture and mental illness: A client-centered approach.* Pacific Grove, CA: Brooks/Cole.

Chan, S. (1998). Families with Asian roots. In E. W. Lynch & M. J. Hanson, *Developing cross-cultural competence* (pp. 251–354). Baltimore: Brookes.

Chin, F. (2002). *Born in the USA: A story of Japanese America, 1889–1947.* Lanham, MD: Rowman & Littlefield.

Conrat, M., & Conrat, R. (2003). *Executive Order 9066: The Internment of 110,000 Japanese Americans.* Los Angeles: UCLA, Asian American Studies Center.

Cross, T. L., Bazron, B. J., Dennis, K. W., & Isaacs, M. R. (1989). Towards a culturally competent system of care. *A monograph on effective services for minority children who are severely emotionally disabled.* Rockville, MD: National Institute of Mental Health.

Daniels, R., Taylor, S., & Kitano, H. (Eds.) (1991). *Japanese Americans from relocation to redress.* Seattle: University of Washington Press.

Fadiman, A. (1997). *The spirit catches you and you fall down.* New York: Farrar, Straus & Giroux.

Fong, R. (1994). Family preservation: Making it work for Asians. *Child Welfare, 73*(4), 331–341.

Fong, R., & Furuto, S. (Eds.). (2001). *Culturally competent practice: Skills, interventions, and evaluations.* Boston: Allyn & Bacon.

Gardiner, H. W., Mutter, J. D., & Kosmitzki, C. (1998). *Lives across cultures: Cross-cultural human development.* Boston: Allyn & Bacon.

Gutierrez, L., Parsons, R. J., & Cox, E. J. (1998). *Empowerment in social work practice.* Pacific Grove, CA: Brooks/Cole.

Haas, M. (1991). *Genocide by proxy: Cambodian pawn on a superpower chessboard.* New York: Praeger.

Hall, E. T. (1977). *Beyond culture.* Garden City, NY: Anchor Books.

Hanh, T. N. (1993). *Love in action: Writings on nonviolent social change.* Berkeley, CA: Parallax Press.

Hanh, T. N. (2002). *No death, no fear: Comforting wisdom for life.* New York: Riverhead Books.

Hata, D., & Hata, N. (1995). *Japanese Americans and World War II: Exclusion, internment and redress.* Wheeling, IL: Harlan Davidson.

Hing, B. O. (1993). *Making and remaking Asian America through immigration policy 1850–1990.* Stanford, CA: Stanford University Press.

Hing, B. O. (2002). Deported for shoplifting. *Washington Post,* December 29, B07. Washington, D.C.

Jackson, K. D. (1989). *Cambodia 1975–1979: Rendezvous with death.* Princeton, NJ: Princeton University Press.

Kagawa-Singer, M., & Chung, R. C.-Y. (1994). A paradigm for culturally based care in ethnic minority populations. *Journal of Community Psychology, 22*(2), 192–208.

Karnow, S. (1991). *Vietnam: A history.* New York: Peguin Books.

Kim, Y.-O. (1995). Cultural pluralism and Asian Americans: Culturally sensitive social work practice. *International Social Work, 38*(1), 69–78.

Kinzie, J. D. (1989). Therapeutic approaches to traumatized Cambodian refugees. *Journal of Traumatic Stress,* 2(1), 75–91.

Kitano, H. H. L. (1989). A model for counseling Asian Americans. In P. Pedersen, J. Draguns, W. J. Lonmer & J. E. Trimble (Eds.), *Counseling across cultures* (pp. 139–151). Honolulu: University of Hawaii Press.

Kleinman, A. (1988). *The illness narratives: Suffering, healing and the human conditions.* New York: Basic Books.

Kleinman, A. (1996). How is culture important for DSM-IV? In *Culture and psychiatric diagnosis: A DSM-IV perspective* J. E. Mezzich, A. Kleinman, H. Fabrega, & D. Parron (Eds.) (pp. 15–26). Washington, DC: American Psychiatric Press, Inc.

Lee, E., (Ed.) (1997a). *Working with Asian Americans: A guide for clinicians.* New York: Guilford Press.

Lee, E. (1997b). The assessment and treatment of Asian American families. In E. Lee (Ed.), *Working with Asian Americans: A guide for clinicians.* New York: Guilford Press: 3–36.

Lee, E., & Mokuau, N. (2002). Meeting the mental health needs of Asian and Pacific Islander Americans. National Technical Assistance Center for State Mental Health Planning. Washington, DC.

Leung, P., & Cheung, M. (2001). Competencies in practice evaluations with Asian American individuals and families. In R. Fong & S. Furuto (Eds.), *Culturally competent practice: Skills, interventions, and evaluations* (426–437). Needham Heights, MA: Allyn & Bacon.

Lu, Y. E., Lum, D., & Chen, S. (2001). Cultural competency and achieving styles in clinical social work: A conceptual and empirical exploration. *Journal of Ethnic and Cultural Diversity in Social Work,* 9(3–4), 1–32.

Lum, D. (1982). Toward a framework for social work practice with minorities. *Social Work,* 27(3), 244–249.

Lum, D. (2000). *Social work practice and people of color: A process-stage approach.* Pacific Grove, CA: Brooks-Cole.

Lum, D. (Ed.) (2003). *Culturally competent practice: A framework for understanding diverse groups and justice issues.* Pacific Grove, CA: Brooks/Cole.

Martin, M. A. (1994). *Cambodia: A shattered society. Berkeley:* University of California Press.

Mokuau, N. (Ed.). (1991). *Handbook for social services for Asian and Pacific Islanders.* New York: Greenwood Press.

Morelli, P. T. T. (1996). Trauma and healing: The construction of meaning among survivors of the Cambodian holocaust. Unpublished doctoral dissertation. School of Social Work, University of Washington, Seattle.

Morelli, P. T. (2001). Culturally competent assessment of Cambodian American survivors of the Killing Fields: A tool for social justice. In R. Fong & S. Furuto, *Culturally competent practice: Skills, interventions, and evaluations,* (196–211). Boston: Allyn & Bacon:.

Morelli, P. T., Fong, R., & Oliveira, J. (2001). Culturally competent substance abuse treatment for Asian/Pacific Islander women. *Journal of Human Behavior in the Social Environment,* 3(3–4), 263–280.

NASW (1999). National Association of Social Workers Code of Ethics. Retrieved from http://www.naswdc.org

NASW (2001). NASW Cultural Competence Standards. Retrieved from http://www.socialworkers.org/sections/credentials/cultural_comp.asp

Ng, W. (2002). *Japanese American internment during World War II: A history and reference guide.* Westport, CT: Greenwood Press.

Okazaki, S. (1998). Psychological assessment of Asian Americans: Research agenda for cultural competency. *Journal of Personality Assessment,* 70, 54–70.

Ponchaud, F. (1977). *Cambodia Year Zero*. New York: Holt, Rinehart & Winston.

Richards, M., Browne, C., & Broderick, A. (1994). Strategies for teaching clinical social work practice with Asian and Pacific Island elders. *Gerontology & Geriatrics Education, 14*(3), 49–63.

Root, M., Ho, C., & Sue, S. (1986). Issues in training of counselors for Asian Americans. In H. Lefley & P. Pedersen (Eds.), *Cross-cultural training for mental health professionals* (pp. 199–209). Springfield, IL: Thomas.

Saleebey, D. (Ed.) (2002). *The strengths perspective in social work practice*. Boston: Allyn & Bacon.

Sands, R. G. (2001). *Clinical social work practice in behavioral mental health: A post modern approach to practice with adults*. Boston: Allyn & Bacon.

Sue, D., & Sue, S. (1987). Cultural factors in the clinical assessment of Asian Americans. *Journal of Consulting & Clinical Psychology, 55*(4), 479–487.

Sue, D. W., & Sue, D. (1999). *Counseling the culturally different: Theory and practice*. New York: Wiley.

Sue, S., & Zane, N. (1987). The role of culture and cultural techniques in psychotherapy. *American Psychologist, 42*, 37–45.

Takaki, R. (1989). *Strangers from a different shore: A History of Asian Americans*. New York: Penguin Books.

Takeuchi, D. T., Uehara, E., & Maramba, G. (1999). Cultural diversity and mental health treatment. In A. V. Horowitz & T. Scheid (Eds.), *A Handbook for the Study of Mental Health* (550–565). New York: Cambridge University Press.

Tamura, E. H. (1994). *Americanization, acculturation, and ethnic identity: The Nisei generation in Hawaii*. Urbana: University of Illinois Press.

Uba, L. (1994). *Asian Americans: Personality patterns, identity, and mental health*. New York: Guilford Press.

Uehara, E., Morelli, P., & Abe-Kim, J. (2001). Somatic complaint and social suffering among survivors of the Cambodian Killing Fields. *Journal of Human Behavior in the Social Environment, 3*(3–4), 243–262.

U.S. Census Bureau (1993). *We the Americans: Asians*. Washington, DC: U.S. Department of Commerce, p. 7.

U.S. Census Bureau (2002). *The Asian Population: 2000*. Washington, DC: Author.

U.S. Department of Health & Human Services (2001). *Mental health: Culture, race, and ethnicity—A supplemental to mental health: A report of the Surgeon General*. Rockville, MD: U.S. Department of Health and Human Services.

Yuen, F., & Nakano-Matsumoto, N. (1998). Effective substance abuse treatment for Asian American adolescents. *Early Child Development & Care, 147*, 43–54.

Zane, N., & Sue, S. (1991). Culturally responsive mental health services for Asian Americans: Treatment and training issues. In H. Myers, P. Wohlford, L. P. Guzman, & R. J. Echemendia (Eds.), *Ethnic minority perspectives on clinical training and services in psychology* (pp. 49–58). Washington, DC: American Psychological Association.

Social Work Practice with Multiracial/ Multiethnic Clients

Rowena Fong

Social workers are today ever more frequently engaged with children and families formed in complex blends of interracial and interethnic sexual relationships and marriages. Added to this are families and children coping with transracial and intercountry adoptions. This multiethnic population increased from fewer than 150,000 in 1960 to more than 1,260,000 a mere 30 years later (DeBose, 2003, p. xii).

Census 2000 tried to accommodate this diversity by offering, in addition to its six distinct racial categories (white, black or African American, American Indian and Alaska Native, Asian, Native Hawaiian, and Other Pacific Islander), options for multiracial and multiethnic people to identify themselves by choosing two races or even a third category of "three or more." Heeding the additional complexities of ethnic identification, the Census added categories for Hispanic or Latino (of any race) and White alone, not Hispanic or Latino, allowing individuals to choose whether to link Hispanic and Latino with white (U.S. Census Bureau, 2001b).

To clarify, in this chapter multiracial clients are "people who are of two or more racial heritages" (Root, 1996, p. xi). Multiethnic clients, on the other hand, are people who are of two or more ethnic heritages. The distinction is critical because the two groups do share some problems and issues, but we cannot assume that all the issues will be identical. Even in identifying a population as multiethnic, it must be noted that individuals may identify with one ethnic group more than another. Wehrly, Kenney, and Kenney mention that Latinos see themselves as being "varied in gradations and shades of color"

(1999, p. 11) and cite Root (1996), who reports that Filipinos have considered themselves a mixed-race people. In Hawaii, within the single-race classification of "Asian," many youth have multiethnic identity struggles with blood lines embracing Hawaiian, Chinese, Japanese, Portuguese, and northern European ancestry in both parents.

These multiracial and multiethnic populations are found in interracial and interethnic marriages, but their problems and issues frequently appear also in families involved in transracial and international adoptions. McRoy and Hall write about the racial/ethnic identity of black children adopted by non-black parents: "Black children adopted by white families know they are African American but may not know how to interact (language, common experience) with other black people comfortably. This discomfort may lead to limited interaction with blacks while the need for identification remains great" (1996, p. 75). Fong and Wang interviewed Caucasian parents who had adopted infants from the People's Republic of China about instilling pride in Chinese identity and found that "racism, minority status, stereotypes, and integration into the non-adoptive community were all issues parents might have to contend with in instilling pride in their daughters' Chinese identity and helping them create their own versions of being adopted Chinese Americans" (2001, p. 25). Consequently, in this chapter multiracial clients will also include those whose family systems involve more than one race either through biological or adoptive parentage.

The majority of the literature, sparse as it is, refers to the multiracial client without distinction from the multiethnic client. The same emphasis prevails for interracial marriages and the identity formation for multiracial persons. For convenience, this chapter will do likewise, except in cases where conditions for multiethnic and multiracial clients diverge.

In this chapter, we will discuss demographics, historical oppression, survival skills of multiracial people; culturally competent theory and assessment, intervention, and termination skills in working with this population, and case examples to integrate these practice skills. Closing thoughts will reiterate the main points, especially the need for intersectionality and greater attention to issues such as transracial and intercountry adoptions that need to be considered when working with multiracial and multiethnic clients.

THE DEMOGRAPHICS OF MULTIRACIAL PEOPLE

The categorization of races and ethnicities has evolved. Morning reports that the Census before the year 2000 had two types of multiracial ancestry, the "combination of black and white referred to as *mulatto* and American Indian in combination with others referred to as *mixed blood* (2003, p. 43). According to Root (1992, p. 1), multiracial populations have increased in Arizona, California, Hawaii, South Florida, New Mexico, New York City, and Texas. In her more recent work, Root states, "The particular configurations of interracial marriage may vary by state and region. In California, where more than a quarter of all interracial couples live, all mixtures are present. With the numerically largest Asian American population in the United States, California is home to the largest proportion of interracial marriages involving Asian Americans. In Oklahoma, most intermarriages occur between American Indians and whites. In Texas, black/white and Chicano, Latino/white intermarriage prevailed" (2001, pp. 7–8).

The multiple-choice categories evident in the Census 2000 reflect the changing demographics and growth in numbers of multiracial individuals. According to Census 2000, 6.8 million or 2.4% of the total U.S. population marked two or more races (Morning, 2003). The 15 combinations in the two-race category in the Census 2000 data (shown in Table 6.1) are by descending order of numbers and percentage.

There have been many difficulties with racial categorization, especially with the one drop rule for African Americans and quantum blood for Native Americans (Davis, 2000; Nagel, 2000). For example, Morning recounts the quandary of Native Americans' and Latino and Mexican Americans' struggle with the census classification system:

> One of the earliest signs that traditional census classification overlooked significant dimensions of racial identity was the puzzling post 1960 growth in the American Indian population that could not be explained by fertility and mortality factors alone. Instead, demographers discovered that part of the increase was due to the "new Indians," people who had previously identified as belonging to another race (actually white) but switched to identification as Indian . . . These ideas about the fluidity and malleability of ethnic and racial identities ran counter to the system of classification used on the census, which assumed individuals' identities were fixed and easily described by a handful of categories. (2003, p. 56)

There is much variability for classification and self-identity as is manifested by terminology. Root describes five identity choices for mixed-race people:

1. Accept the identity society assigns, which usually refers to the "hypo-descent or one drop rule,"
2. Choose a single identity,
3. Choose a mixed identity,
4. Choose a new race identity, or
5. Choose a white identity (2003, pp. 13–16)

This option for self-definition is open to individuals whether they grow up with biological parents or adoptive parents with different ethnic backgrounds. A new race identity may be what clients strive for as they try to sort through the many factors to consider and seek professional assistance. Multiracial clients may also seek help with concerns over racism and discrimination, confusion in identity, incompatibilities in foster care or adoptive homes, or anxieties in blended and divorced families. In working with this population, social workers need to examine their own attitudes about ethnic groups to avoid unconscious biases about the mixing of races in mating or family making.

Table 6.1 | Two-Race Population

Race	Number	Percentage of Total Population
Two race	6,368,075	2.26
White and some other race	2,206,251	0.78
White and American Indian	1,082,683	0.38
White and Asian	868,395	0.31
White and black	784,764	0.28
Black and some other race	417,249	0.15
Asian and some other race	249,108	0.09
Black and American Indian	182,494	0.06
Asian and Native Hawaiian	138,802	0.05
White and Native American	112,964	0.04
Black and Asian	106,782	0.04
American Indian and some other race	93,842	0.03
American Indian and Asian	52,429	0.02
Native Hawaiian and some other race	35,108	0.01
Black and Native American	29,786	0.01
Asian Indian and Native Hawaiian	7,328	0.00

Source: Morning, A. (2003). New faces, old faces: Counting the multiracial population: Past and present. In L. Winters & H. DeBose, *New faces in a changing America: Multiracial identity in the 21st century.* Thousand Oaks, CA: Sage, p. 58.

The usual classification of the multiracial client is based on the marriage or union of opposite sex individuals to produce offspring who are of mixed blood and heritages. The terminology for multiracial persons, according to Dhooper and Moore (2001, p. 215), includes terms such as "bicultural, intercultural, multicultural, interracial, half-breed, mixed, mixed-race, mélange, multiracial, rainbow, racially/culturally blended, transracial, *mulatto, mulatta, mestizo, mestiza, hapa, hapa haole,* cosmopolitan, Eurasian, Afroasian, Amerasian."

This chapter will primarily address issues related to interracial marriages, but a plethora of other interracial and intercultural relationships also appear among multiracial clients. Some multiracial clients struggle with identity because they have been adopted into families of different racial backgrounds from their own. (Dorow, 2000; Fong & Wang, 2001; McRoy, 1994; McRoy & Hall, 1996; McRoy, Oglesby, & Grape, 1997). Single parents and gay and lesbian couples are adopting special needs children from different racial backgrounds (Feigelman & Silverman, 1997; Groze & Rosenthal, 1991). Some clients are struggling to blend families of divorce from different racial and ethnic backgrounds. Intermarriages between foreign-born immigrants and refugees and American-born individuals of the same race and ethnic grouping are yet another variation social workers encounter. Though not the focus of the chapter, these relationships will also be addressed as needed.

THE HISTORICAL OPPRESSION AND SURVIVAL SKILLS OF MULTIRACIAL PEOPLE

Although African Americans, Asians, Latinos/Mexican Americans, and Native Americans have all experienced discrimination, the history of oppression and discrimination for multiracial people has basically focused on the major facets of (1) societal attitudes about hierarchy in races and (2) hostile laws and policies and racist attitudes against people of color and interracial marriage.

Societal Attitudes about Hierarchy in Races

Supported by societal attitudes about white supremacy and theories and myths about racial mixings, anti-miscegenation laws forbade interracial marriage or any kind of mixing. Root asserts that the "anti-miscegenation laws were developed not to prevent any interracial marriages but to protect 'whiteness'" (2001, p. 35). White supremacy dictated social policies and societal approaches to nonwhite people (Dhooper & Moore, 2001; McLemore, Romo, & Baker, 2001). The "one drop rule" was used to define a black person, which ultimately cast the individual into a "hypodescent" or subordinate group (Dhooper & Moore, 2001; Spickard, 1989).

Williams wrote, "black and white miscegenation dates back to the early colonial period; it became widespread and took place within the socioeconomic context of southern American slavery under thoroughly unequal and brutally coercive circumstances" (1996, cited in Dhooper & Moore, 2001, p. 217). Black women were raped and exploited on southern plantations by their white slave masters. Black male slaves were also exploited by white women.

Native Americans, on the other hand, also experienced sexual exploitation but in another way. "The white man, on arriving for a stay in an Indian settlement, would approach the parents of a girl and seek her domestic and sexual services" (Dhooper & Moore, 2001, p. 218). The injustices based on racial hierarchal inequities were imposed on persons of color because of the belief that one race was superior to others. This and similar attitudes spilled over to both sanctioned and unsanctioned sexual relationships. Legal and formalized interracial marriage relationships were not accepted by white society because in doing so it would create major threats to political, economic, and social statuses.

Racist Attitudes toward People of Color and Interracial Marriages

Both before and after the Civil War, states prohibited marriage between whites and non-whites (DeBose & Winters, 2003; Gibbs, Huang, & Associates, 1989; Gibbs, Huang, & Associates, 2003; Rockquemore & Brunsma, 2002; Spickard, 1989). Racial intermixing was common nonetheless. Black slave women were forced into sexual relations with their white owners and, according to Henriques, "Rejection of intermarriage with the Indian co-existed with unrestrained promiscuity with Indian women" (1975, cited in Dhooper & Moore, 2001, p. 219). Sexual mingling and marriage with Asian Americans were also publicly abhorred: "Were the Chinese to amalgamate at all with our people, it would be the lowest, most vile, and degraded of our race, and the result of that amalgamation would be a hybrid of the most despicable, mongrel of the most detestable that has ever afflicted the earth" (Takaki, 1989, p. 101). Regardless of ethnic background, there was strong resistance to sanctioning sexual intermingling between whites and people of color in practice and in law.

Hostile Laws and Policies

The first law to forbid interracial marriage appeared in 1661 in Virginia. Three centuries later, Virginia still had severe penalties for interracial marriage when its miscegenation laws were repealed in 1967. In the 1940s and 1950s, American soldiers returning with Asian war brides collided with old laws that had "followed the waves of immigration by various Asian groups, first the Chinese, then the Japanese. Because of Filipinos' multiracial background, California passed additional legislation that classified them as Malays and included them in the existing antimiscegenation laws" (Root, 2001, p. 34).

State courts heard several challenges to these laws, yet as recently as 1960, 29 states had laws prohibiting interracial marriage (Root, 1996). The challenges were based on the equal protection clause of the Fourteenth Amendment of the U.S. Constitution, which declares that states cannot deprive any persons born or naturalized in the United States of life, liberty, or property without the process of law. The landmark case was *Loving v. Virginia,* in 1967, when Richard Loving married Mildred Jeter, part black and American Indian in Washington, D.C. The marriage was declared illegal when they returned to Virginia, and although they were prosecuted and jailed briefly, the Supreme Court finally ruled in their favor, overturning all the existing state antimiscegenation laws.

Survival Skills

The survival skills of multiracial people have manifested themselves in many ways—at the macro level with multiracial activism, at the meso level by resisting community and family prejudice, and at the micro level by individual determination to overcome discrimination. The Multiracial Movement in the

1990s occurred during a time when the Census' racial classifications incited objection (Williams, 2003). In 1995, Project RACE (Reclassify All Children Equally) was established to promote national recognition that multiracial/multiethnic persons deserved their own classification. These multicultural activists, believing that "they are entitled to determine identity for themselves . . . fight for 'choice' in racial identity rather than determination by the logic of hypodescent. Rejecting the idea that a monoracial identity could accurately reflect their racial identity, multiracial activists do not reject the idea of racial authenticity itself. Rather, they argued that one-drop ideology forced them into racial categories that could not describe their authentic inner self" (DaCosta, 2003 p. 79).

The Association of Multiethnic Americans (AMEA) has as its primary goal to educate and "to promote a positive awareness of interracial and multiethnic identity, [for ourselves] and for society as a whole" (Williams, 2003, p. 95). AMEA's mission statement asserts, "multiracial people should have a right to claim or incorporate their entire heritage, and enhance their total identity" (p. 95). DeBose and Winters note, "Over the past 30 years, attitudes towards interracial marriages have changed dramatically. However, people who marry outside their race and their offspring continue to experience prejudice, discrimination, and stereotyping. . . . Although acceptance in these [interracial] marriages appear to be creeping into the American psyche, life is not necessarily easy for children of mixed parents" (2003, p. 143).

CULTURALLY COMPETENT KNOWLEDGE THEORY AND PRACTICE SKILLS FOR MULTIRACIAL CLIENTS

In working with the multiracial and multiethnic clients, culturally competent knowledge and theory are needed. Practice skills are needed in making contact, relationship building, problem identification, assessment, intervention, and termination. Most multiracial/multiethnic persons have experienced racism, discrimination, and marginalization because of their backgrounds. Arredondo maintains that culturally skilled counselors "possess specific knowledge about the groups with which they are working. They are aware of the life experiences, cultural heritages, and historical backgrounds of their culturally different clients and clients from the marginalized groups in that community. . . . Culturally skilled counselors understand and have knowledge about sociopolitical influences that impinge on the lives of individuals from marginalized groups by limiting access and further dehumanizing of individuals" (2002, p. 247).

The marginalization Arredondo refers to is a disempowerment process that counselors and social workers need to help multiracial clients reverse so they can be justly validated by society, family, or even themselves. Marginalization occurs when an invalidation process tells the individual he or she is not accepted in a group or situation. Maslow's (1962) work on the hierarchy of human needs (physiological needs, safety needs, belonging needs, esteem needs, and self-actualization needs) is pertinent. Multiple forces intrude to prevent multiracial persons from having these needs met. Physiological needs are usually met, but safety needs—psychological and emotional safety—are often unmet. According to Maslow, the need to belong to some group, whether a social group or even family, must be resolved before self-esteem and self-actualization can occur.

CONTACT SKILLS WITH MULTIRACIAL CLIENTS

Many multiracial persons have struggled with acceptance issues either with racist strangers or rejecting parents or family members. Because the multiracial person has many issues to sort through, particularly in identity formation and development, a trusting relationship must be built between the social worker and the client. The initial contact—taking time to build the relationship and listen carefully—is important. There are many facets of multiple identity development, so the therapist must listen without notions based on previous experiences with similar clients or personal acquaintances. Listening is the critical contact skill because communication barriers are easily raised.

Leigh advocates that practitioners communicate for cultural competence:

> Communication can only occur when the agendas of those in the communicative process are the same. When each person's status is mutually accepted, communication occurs. A fellowship must be present; if not, contacts tend to express themselves in unsympathetic understanding without the healing spirit and energy of each person. With fellowship, suspicion is allayed, and intentionality pervades the communication process. Without fellowship, the communication process becomes an arena where each moves around in a world of shadows. (1998, p. 12)

To remove the communication barriers practitioners should, as Leigh (1998) says, first try to accept each person's status. With multiracial clients, practitioners need initially to accept the confusion, struggles, and complexity of that client's dilemma. As the practitioner listens, she or he has to resist hasty conclusions about the problem. Many variables need to be sorted through, not least of which is the practitioner's own stereotypes and conscious or unconscious racist attitudes that can thwart accurate communication in the helping relationship.

Resistance, for the multicultural client, may be the result of the frustrations of being misheard and misunderstood. Clients may be angry at being prematurely or incorrectly categorized. The LatiNegra (African Latina) client, Comas-Diaz reports, "is caught between three diverse worlds—black, Latino, and white—and racially excluded from all. Her marginality binds her in a conflict of ethnoracial loyalties without a satisfactory resolution of her identity. . . . the LatiNegra often suffers from identity conflicts and needs to integrate her fragmented identity with her cultural and familial contexts in order to combat guilt, shame, and feelings of inferiority engendered by her combined racial-ethnic and gender status. The denial of one aspect of her identity implies denial of her self, her mixed race heritage, and her cultural continuity" (1996, p. 190). Interrupted attempts to articulate their problems may totally alienate them from the social worker and even from the attempt to seek professional help.

To overcome resistance, practitioners should be attentive to collecting all the data and understanding the nuances of the intersecting issues complicating the client's situation. The practitioner ought to have a contextual and intersectionality framework to approach social work practice. Fong speaks of culturally competent practice to include "the intersection of ethnicity and race with gender, sexual orientation, religion, social class, and physical and mental abilities" (2003, p. 281). This facilitates understanding the context and social environments of the client's background (Fong, 2004a). Because multiracial clients need help at the macro, meso, and micro levels, social workers need this framework and approach, which will help in establishing a responsive service delivery system.

The culturally competent contextual social work practice approach is grounded in the belief that multiple variables intersect in the clients' lives. The social worker's challenge is to learn from the multiracial client how these intersections sort themselves out. Lum categorizes intersectionality by internal and external factors related to "multiple social group memberships that are interconnected and interrelated" (2003, p. 42). He includes race, ethnicity, sexual orientation, gender, age, and physical and mental abilities as intersecting variables with individuals, families, groups, and social group memberships. Fong (2004b) speaks of intersectionality as social services, cultural values, and indigenous treatments and strategies. She advocates that "one approach to intersectionality is to consider the following components that all intersect in the assessments, intervention planning, and implementation of culturally competent practice: a) societal level/cultural values; b) social environments; c) ethnicity/gender/religion/politics; d) legal statuses; and e) indigenous strategies biculturalization of interventions."

For example, in doing culturally competent contextual social work practice with a multiethnic female youth who is struggling with her sense of belonging, a social worker would (1) determine the most meaningful cultural values and traditions from all the ethnic groups influencing the youth's functioning, (2) determine in which ethnic social environments the youth feels most comfortable, (3) explore the multiple identities the youth has (based on her gender, sexual orientation, religion beliefs, political beliefs), (4) determine which of her various ethnic group associations makes her feel accepted or marginalized, and (5) find a meaningful intervention (e.g., talking, art, journaling) that the female youth is comfortable using to express her thoughts and fears.

Practicing Relationship Protocols

The National Association of Social Work (NASW) in 2001 passed 10 Standards for Cultural Competence in Social Work Practice. The first four standards focus on ethics and values, self-awareness, cross-cultural knowledge, and cross-cultural skills. For ethics and values, social workers are to "recognize personal and professional values [that] may conflict with or accommodate the needs of diverse clients" (p. 2). This may be a problem when a social worker tries to establish relationship protocols. For example, the social worker from outside the African American culture may not be practicing the respectful manner or protocol in addressing a black person as Mr. or Mrs. or Dr. because of personal prejudicial or racist attitudes.

The NASW Standards on self-awareness and cross-cultural knowledge call for social workers to "develop an understanding of their own personal, cultural values, and beliefs as one way of appreciating the importance of multicultural identities in the lives of people. . . . [and] develop specialized knowledge and understanding about the history, traditions, values, family systems, and artistic expressions of the major client groups that they serve" (2001, p. 2).

This specialized knowledge would also include protocols of the ethnic cultures of the clients served because protocols reflect cultural values and dictate human behaviors. For example, if the client is part Asian and is reared in a traditional home, the client may have been reared to be particularly respectful to the elders and to defer to all decisions made by males. This could have protocol implications in that a young Japanese-Chinese female client may have difficulty asserting herself to an older male Asian therapist conducting family therapy sessions.

Relationship protocols are dictated by traditional cultural values. In some Pacific Islander cultures, elders are often consulted in problem solving situations. Relationship protocols would have the Hawaiian *kupuna* be consulted in the treatment planning. Such would also be the case in traditional Tongan culture where the chief *matai* has an esteemed role in family and community affairs. In Puerto Rican culture, traditional healers are important. In some Asian cultures, the mental health of clients will be manifested in the form of physical symptoms. If the multiracial client is an older client, there may be some hesitation to visit a therapist because the client's emotions are internalized or somaticized. There may be a preference for a *kupuna,* or *matai,* or traditional healer depending on the client's ethnic background. It would be very important for helping professionals to know the cultural values and preferred treatment modalities in helping the multiracial client establish a trusting relationship so he or she could pursue professional help.

Using Professional Self-Disclosure

The term "use of professional disclosure" is usually associated with the social worker's dilemma: How much of one's personal life experiences should a social worker reveal to the client?

The professional social worker is to use discretion in self-disclosure. The helping relationship is based on trust, and too much self-disclosure may evoke pressure for both the client and therapist to create an inaccurate or inauthentic sense of self. Helms and Cook reiterate that self-disclosure is a normal and important part of being trusted and establishing safety in the cross-racial therapy relationships but warn, "Some clients are mistrustful of therapists who belong to a different socioracial group than their own. Typically, stereotypes are negative and inhibit the development of a trusting relationship. However, even positive stereotypes may mar the relationship by requiring the client or therapist to conform to standards that do not fit" (1999, p. 193). For example, if an Asian American therapist is working with a multiracial adolescent male with an Anglo and Mexican American father and an Asian mother, the model minority stereotype held of Asians may lead the client and his mother to have expectations about the therapist being a model minority role model that may not be totally accurate.

The NASW Code of Ethics advocates that social workers be self-reflective in personal prejudices, ethnic identity, and racial stereotyping, which will be described.

Personal Prejudices

In working with multiracial clients, social workers must engage in ongoing self-evaluation to examine personal prejudices about different racial groups. Does the social worker harbor prejudicial attitudes toward a mixed couple, either consciously or unconsciously? Lingering biases must be examined and dealt with in order to be effective with the couple's problems.

Ethnic Identity Recognized   Social workers need to be comfortable with their own ethnic identity so they can help the multiracial client, but professionals from Euro-American backgrounds are often not aware of their ethnic identity or its importance to them. Rather, there may be a more readily identified affiliation to being a Midwesterner, Texan, or Bostonian. Geographic identity may not be an important variable to a multiracial person so the white social worker needs to have some sense of understanding his or her own ethnic identity to be empathetic to the struggle of the multiracial client.

Internalized Racial and Ethnic Stereotypes   The social worker needs to examine the racial and ethnic stereotypes that he or she has about certain racial and ethnic groups of people. What does a female white Jewish social worker feel or think about a Jewish father's and Hispanic mother's decision not to raise their children following Jewish customs? How would a Catholic Filipino social worker feel if a Filipino wife decided not to raise her children Catholic but, rather, Buddhist because of the Japanese father's preference? Each social worker's personal beliefs, stereotypes, and expectations about ethnicity, religion, and sexual orientation may be retained, and yet not imposed on the client seeking help.

Problem Identification Skills with Multiracial Clients

Although the common theme for multiracial clients seems to be focused on self-validation and identity formation, each multiracial client will have a unique set of issues with which to grapple. Even when there are two individuals in interracial marriages, who are of the same age and gender, both from Asian ethnic heritages, the experiences and concerns can be different. For example, there are many within-group differences among the Chinese depending on whether the families are from America, Hong Kong, or China. For example, if a Chinese woman whose mother was a traditional Chinese woman from Hong Kong or China were to marry a Caucasian man, the young woman might be worried about producing a male heir to continue her husband's family line because of pressure from her mother and the upholding of traditional cultural values (Sung, 1990). However, a multiracial woman whose mother was a traditional Japanese mother might put pressure on the multiracial daughter to maintain Japanese traditions and produce children who were academically or economically successful. In the Asian grouping, intergroup and intragroup variability affects the expectations and identity of the multiracial individual.

Differences within groups probably apply to all the ethnic groupings. The First Nations Peoples culture has more than 100 tribal groups (Weaver, 2003), and they identify themselves according to affiliation "in a band, nation, confederacy, tribe, or village"(Yellow Bird, 2001, p. 62). The intragroup variability within the Native tribes can be distinguished also by matriarchal and matrilineal descent or patriarchal and patrilineal descent. If a multiracial client has two tribal backgrounds (one matrilineal and one patrilineal) and a Caucasian mixing, the individual may have three cultures to grasp for identity formation. Herring writes, "The difficulty that Native American Indian youth experience in establishing a positive ethnic self-identity is made all the more difficult by the extreme political, socioeconomic, and cultural diversity among Native American Indians. . . . Many Native American Indian adolescents also experience the complexities of biracial and multi-ethnic identity development. This additional developmental task may be assisted (or hindered) by the degree of acculturation present in their immediate family and the degree of biculturalness inherent in their socialization. Membership in an interracial family brings additional conflicts and potential problems" (1994, p. 176). The culturally competent social worker needs to have awareness of the intragroup and intergroup differences and conflicts among the tribal groups and skills to help the multiracial Native youth identify the impact of these conflicts on his or her development and functioning.

Often to accurately identify the conflict or problem, it is important to discern the contexts of the problems and use an intersection model. O'Melia and Miley (2002) describe the importance of contextual social work practice and its empowerment possibilities. This knowledge and approach to social work practice through contextualization empowers both the social worker and the multiracial client. For the multiracial client, the context is the explanation of the problematic past, the conflictual present, and fearful future.

Problem identification skills need to include the discernment that for multiracial individuals there is diversity within, as Dhooper and Moore mention the "subgroup and intragroup differences among biracial/mixed-race

Americans" (2001, p. 226). These differences are based on "different combinations of part-white heritage, different combinations of part-black heritage; needs of the ethnic community associated with the person's heritage, gender of the biracial person" (pp. 228–229).

Gaining Problem Understanding

In working with multiracial clients and their issues, it is critical that social workers use a framework of intersectionality. The concept of intersectionality (Fong, 2003, 2004a; Lum, 2003) plays a critical role in the work with multiracial clients because most of their lives may be about sorting through intersecting variables. Social workers need to learn certain skills about interesectionality to become an effective and culturally competent social worker. Social workers will need to work on all three levels of macro, meso, and micro assessments and interventions. Many variables—such as multiple races and ethnicities, race and sexual orientation, race and disability, and race and religion—need to be addressed.

Family situations will vary, and the professional needs to be prepared to contextualize their social work practice to address the following:

1. Two biological parents of different races
2. Multiracial and gay and lesbian issues
3. Multiracial in foster-care and adoption placements
4. Multiracial and divorce and blended families

The constellation of multiracial clients will continue to diversify and social workers need to be prepared to work with the complex situations the multiracial clients face in the United States. With the increase of immigrants and refugees in America, interracial problems may be mono- or multiracial or related to multicontextual and multienvironmental transitions to the United States. Table 6.2 identifies the intersecting issues at the three macro, meso, and micro levels.

At the micro level, people normally address issues related to their gender, age, abilities, and sexual orientation. However, if someone is multiracial he or she then adds the complexities of examining how their combinations of racial and ethnic identities (macro level) are affecting their approach to handling the normal developmental issues related to age, gender, abilities, and sexual orientation (micro level). This is further compounded when the multiracial person's environmental context reflected by macro level societal values and customs through religious beliefs and practices (macro level) dictates how the multiracial person should be behaving and functioning according to the societal expectations about age, gender, and sexual orientation (meso level). At the meso level, family, friends, peers, coworkers, and neighbors may support societal expectations about behaviors related to normal developmental functioning dictated by age and gender. Caution needs to be heeded when the multiracial/multiethnic person's struggle to interact with all these intersecting

Table 6.2 | Racial Issues at the Macro, Meso, and Micro Levels

Macro	Meso	Micro
Same race/same ethnicity	Family	Gender
Same race/different ethnicity	Friends	Sexual orientation
Different race/different ethnicity	Coworkers	Age
Religions/politics	Neighbors	Abilities

variables seems very overwhelming but the therapist fails to realize this complex burden.

In understanding the multiracial client's problems, there are frequently many intersecting variables, such as race, gender, religion, sexual orientation, and ability. It is important that the therapist see the interaction between the variables and help the client to sort through the interactions because problems for multiracial clients focus on all three—macro, meso, and micro—levels.

At the macro level, the problems focus on rejection, marginalization, discrimination, oppression, the stress of socialization, the appearance to "pass" and identification, the lack of social networks, and people putting them in racial categories they don't want to be in (Kerwin & Ponterotto, 1995; Spickard, 1989). Other problems are the reception or rejection from other ethnic groups (majority and minority), social and institutional racism, and historical associations that lead to social isolation or rejection as experienced by Amerasians in America after the Vietnamese War.

Multiracial persons may also have prolonged health problems because they can't get treatment because of the lack of accurate multiclassification systems. Dhooper and Moore (2001) cite Graham (1996), who gives the example of medical institutions not allowing "multiracial" as a race code for their records resulting in inaccurate records and inappropriate treatment: "It is much more likely for people of the same racial or ethnic background to match as bone marrow donors, because human leukocyte antigens (HLAs) follow racial background. . . . No donor drives have been directed toward multiracial people, as they have other racial and ethnic groups, therefore the donor pool for our children is inadequate. . . . How many multiracial children will suffer or die as a result of inadequate medical classification?" (p. 231).

At the meso level, multiracial people may receive questionable help from family friends and neighbors. Families may be unwelcoming to the multiracial member because the interracial marriage is with another ethnic grouping that is not as acceptable. Family members may not understand the loyalty dilemmas multiracial persons have when choosing parental heritages. Gibbs reports, "Relatives sometimes treat the [multiracial] child in an ambivalent, demeaning, or rejecting manner, or they may express their ambivalence by teasing the child or making racist statements about either parent's racial background" (1989, p. 342). Gibbs also found in her research on biracial and multiracial adolescents,

> There has been a partial or complete failure to integrate both parental racial backgrounds into a cohesive racial/ethnic identity. These teenagers may identify with the White parent as the symbol of the dominant majority, rejecting the Black parent even if there is a closer physical resemblance. . . . As a consequence of incorporating negative attitudes and stereotypes about Blacks, they often try to distance themselves from Black peers in school and social situations, and they may reject any identification with Black culture as it is expressed in the music, dance, and dress styles of those peers. When biracial teens have overidentified with their Black parents, the similar phenomenon of rejecting White culture and White friends is played out. (1989, p. 342)

Gibbs speaks to the dilemmas of biracial youth, but multiracial youth face the same struggles and dilemmas of choosing an ethnic culture over others, sometimes to the consternation of family members and friends. The multiracial person's struggle to choose one, both, or all heritages may seem substandard in family members' opinions because of the erroneous belief that being multiracial cannot equal the true whole of a single ethnic heritage.

At the micro level, multiracial clients experience problems with self-validation, have a great need to have pride to be empowered, and struggle with questions about self-esteem. The terminology of "what do you call yourself" is an ongoing battle. Most multiracial persons battle with problems at the macro, meso, and micro levels, but those multiracial clients who are also gay or lesbian may have additional struggles because of biases and discrimination because of their sexual orientation.

Dhooper and Moore (2001) suggest that the many variables that influence the lives of multiracial clients can be sorted through questions that are characteristic of commonalities of culture and worldviews, such as

1. Which parent's culture dominated the family of the biracial individual? That determines which culture the child would identify primarily.
2. If one of the parents was white, was that parent the father or mother?
3. Where did the family live during the biracial child's childhood, in terms of the size and type and dominant culture of the community?
4. What role did the extended family on both sides of the family play in the life of the biracial person?
5. What was the perceived acceptance of the biracial person? (Dhooper & Moore, 2001, pp. 223–224)

Dhooper and Moore also indicate that the "answers to several pertinent questions and the various combinations of those answers suggest all kinds of experiences of biracial individuals and their families" (2001, p. 223).

Reframing the Problem Orientation

Social workers need to view the multiracial client's micro-, meso-, and macrolevel problems simultaneously because in working with this population, it is almost as if all the problems work in tangent with each other. Even if a clinical social worker works very hard on building the individual's self-esteem but does not deal with family biases because of gender or sexual orientation preferences in some races, whatever gains the social worker may have been able to obtain with the client may be only short-term because family rejection may continue to perpetuate the client's problem. Low self esteem and family rejection need to be addressed simultaneously. For example, Wehrly, Kenney, and Kenney report, "The major issues for these couples [gays and lesbians of Asian, Latino, and African American backgrounds] include the acceptance of the gay or lesbian individual's sexual preference by the individual of color's family and cultural community and the acceptance of the interracial relationship by family and community. Of salient concern here is the extent to which the partner of color not only experiences acceptance from the cultural community but feels supported by the White partner for his or her efforts to maintain connectedness to the culture and cultural community" (1999, p. 46).

Gay and lesbian multiracial individuals also battle with racism, bigotry, and loyalty issues. Wehrly, Kenney, and Kenney warn,

> As racism and bigotry is just as prevalent in the gay and lesbian community as it is outside them, the extent to which the person of color feels comfortable navigating within the gay and lesbian community becomes significant as well. . . . The extent to which the person of color feels supported and validated in his or her experiences by the White partner is important. In a relationship with a lesbian of color, for example, a White lesbian may encounter racism for the first time. How the White person deals with it often affects the relationship. A White partner who is naïve about comments that are racist in origin may experience her partner's anger as inappropriate. The White partner may overreact and criticize her partner for being complacent in her response to situations that are racist in nature. She may also be presumptuous or patronizing and assume the role of rescuer, a role that her partner may not want or need. Other reactions White lesbian partners have exhibited that manifest in the relationship are feelings of guilt about White racism and political hypervigilence. Additionally, both partners in the interracial relationship may have to deal with shaming questions regarding their individual loyalties to their own cultural group. (1999, pp. 46–47)

To battle with macrolevel discrimination or other kinds of problems, it is important that social workers have knowledge and access to macrolevel organizations to pass on to the multiracial client. The multiracial client must be empowered and encouraged to network or tap into those resources. For example, the Biracial Family Network in Chicago, Illinois, formed in 1980, is committed to combating racism and discrimination, offering support to parents of multicultural children, and educating people and communities about multiracial experiences (Brown & Douglass, 2003). The Interracial Family Circle in Washington, D.C. was first conceived in 1984 to address the social isolation interracial couples were experiencing. It has evolved to commemorating historical decisions such as the 1967 Supreme Court *Loving v. Virginia* decision and honoring figures such as Dr. Martin Luther King, Jr., who stood for issues involving social justice (Brown & Douglass, 2003). These and many other organizations are resources for clients to get help in reframing problems experienced because of their multiracial backgrounds, which are ignored or minimized.

ASSESSMENT SKILLS WITH MULTIRACIAL CLIENTS

In assessing the multiracial client, a biopsychosocial and cultural perspective is necessary. In using a biopsychosocial perspective, the social worker needs to consider the factors in the context of the ethnic cultures and discern where additional assessments are necessary because of complexities.

Biological Assessment

In the biological assessment, social workers may find multiracial persons concerned with their appearance, particularly physical features that may influence the identification of races the multiracial person has. There may be questions related to sexual orientation factors or hereditary factors with which multiracial clients have to grapple. In some instances, such as in intercountry adoptions, there may be medical situations where multiracial families cannot access medical information. For example, infants adopted from the People's Republic of China have been abandoned by biological parents, and adoptive parents whose child has health problems with hepatitis B are not sure of the child's medical background because of inaccessibility and unavailability of medical records (Fong & Wang, 2001).

Psychological Assessment

Major issues for many multiracial individuals center on self-esteem and self-validation. How the multiracial thinks about himself or herself and feels about himself or herself will vary from individual to individual. But also within the same individual, it will vary depending on the age and stage of life of the individual. Spencer, Icard, Harachi, Catalano, and Oxford (2000) reiterate that in Phinney's (1996) stages of adolescent ethnic identity formation, multiracial adolescent individuals can go through the three stages of diffusion or foreclosure, moratorium or exploration, and ethnic identity achievement repeatedly because "individuals might examine their ethnicity throughout their lifetime and might reexperience earlier developmental stages" (p. 368). For example, a multiracial school-age boy may early on identify with his Native American maternal culture and heritage but change his ethnic identity more toward his

Caucasian/Mexican father as an adolescent, eventually settling into a Mexican American community as an adult.

Explorations have to be made with the multiracial client about where and when the negative images of self developed because the early childhood years and adolescent years may have been very difficult. Wehrly, Kenney, and Kenney write,

> The most significant issue faced by children with more than one racial heritage is the development of a positive multiracial identity. Some multiracial children face pressures to identify with only one of their racial heritages. When individuals only identity with one of their multiracial heritages they do not integrate the other heritages into their racial self-identity. Sooner or later the individual will feel the loss of the missing part(s) of their identity and will suffer because of their loss. When multiracial children are not accepted by relatives of both their paternal and maternal heritages and when the family does not live in a multiracial community, the challenge to identify with all of their racial roots may be magnified. (1999, p. 56)

Social Assessment

Social assessments involve family members, peers, and support groups focusing around social acceptance. Social acceptance has to be explored within the family system. Wehrly, Kenney, and Kenney warn, "Extended family members sometimes treat multiracial children differently based upon the appearance of the children" (1999, p. 57). Parents and family members of interracial couples may have to address fears, spoken and unspoken. Many of the fears revolve around unfulfilled expectations. Parents are disappointed with the dreams they had of their children's marriage and future. An assessment about fears and unmet expectations needs to be addressed.

Cultural Assessment

Cultural assessments can focus on what was emphasized in childhood and the importance placed on which ethnic culture. Questions to ask are these: Was one ethnic heritage emphasized more than the other? Was the other ethnic heritage ignored or minimized? What was meaningful to the multiracial client from the cultural upbringing? Root (2003) offers an ecological framework on racial identity formation, which is also helpful in including the historical, geographical, and gender lenses as well as generational, family, and community influences.

Although there are these biological, psychological, social, and cultural assessments, some generic skills are also necessary in doing assessments. In working with multiracial clients, Dhooper and Moore recommend these general assessment skills:

1. Make the assessment comprehensive.
2. Make the assessment process a multipurpose activity.
3. Explain the racial-cultural identity of the client system.

4. Explore how biracial clients use their identity and how they feel about it.
5. Explore the vulnerability of mixed-race clients.
6. Make assessments the basis for client strengths. (2001, pp. 236–237)

The process of conducting assessments with a multiracial client is not linear; as it is stated, personal, biological, and sociocultural variables related to ethnicity are complex and interactive. McLemore, Romo, and Baker state,

> Although the concept of ethnicity usually emphasizes a person's sociocultural heritage, a biological connotation sometimes adheres still to "ethnic," but even when a person's appearance or behavior is generally acknowledged to derive exclusively from culture, there is a common tendency to treat the characteristic as a fixed, all or none matter to miss entirely the flexibility of group boundaries thus created. (2001, p. 12)

Client Strengths

Identifying and mobilizing client cultural strengths is critical in helping the multiracial client sort through all the issues and cling to the ones he or she can identify. Too often the focus is on the deficits or weakness and not the strengths of the multiracial client. To identify and fortify the strengths can empower the multiracial client. Multiracial clients need to consistently, not occasionally, identify strengths and incorporate and solidify these strengths into the clients' identity formations. For example, Wehrly, Kenney, and Kenney suggest that professional workers "listen for the strengths that multiracial individuals and families bring to counseling. Give feedback to individuals and families on their strengths. Help the individuals see how they can use the strengths in everyday living and problem solving" (1999, p. 73). Helping multiracial clients see their strengths and use them in problem solving will eventually help the clients with a positive identity formation. Wehrly, Kenney, and Kenney's research found multiracial clients reporting "many advantages to being multiracial, such as having increased sense of uniqueness; having more variety in their lives; enjoying the best of both worlds; experiencing opportunities to relate to people in the cultures of both their parents; being able to move freely between the two groups as well as other groups; and being more open, accepting, tolerant, and sensitive to others" (1999, p. 64). These many advantages can easily be converted to strengths and positive skills.

INTERVENTION SKILLS WITH MULTIRACIAL CLIENTS

The National Association of Social Workers' 2001 Cultural Competence Standards require that social workers "use appropriate methodological approaches, skills, and techniques that reflect the worker's understanding of the roles of culture in the helping process. . . . [and] be knowledgeable about and skillful in the use of services available in the community and broader society and be able to make appropriate referrals for their diverse clients" (p. 2).

CASE | ## Case Study Integration Exercise on Contact, Problem Identification, and Assessment Skills

Born into a Caucasian/Asian family as the oldest of three children, Mei, age 15, is the only daughter with two younger brothers, Jonathan and David, ages 11 years and 9 years. Her 37-year-old mother Lin is an immigrant Chinese woman who married Mei's 65-year-old Jewish father, Ben. A lonely widower with two grown children, Miriam and Caleb, ages 36 and 34, Mei's father sought the company of his cleaning lady, Lin, to the consternation of his children, family members, and Jewish friends. Despite opposition, Ben married Lin when she became pregnant. Two more children, Mei's younger brothers, were born into this strife-ridden family, meshed with alcoholism and financial burdens.

Mei's homeroom teacher at this middle school in Minnesota reported Mei's recently teary-eyed, depressed, fearful, and withdrawn behavior to the school social worker. Mrs. Smith, the 54-year-old, white, school social worker, meets with Mei to find out what the problems are at home. Mrs. Smith finds out that Mei's father has been drinking heavily because of financial strains and has been abusing her mother and making sexual advances toward Mei at night.

In working with this case in the contact, problem identification, and assessment phases, it would be important for the social worker to ask Mei the following questions.

Application Exercises

1. What is Mei's relationship with her parents like, and will they be supportive if she talks to them?
2. Does she have someone in the family that she can talk to? Is there someone who is supportive of her?
3. What problems does she see existing between her mother and father?
4. Are the problems because of differences in cultural background?

Intervention with the multiracial client depends on the situation of whether the client is from an intact, adopted, or divorced family. Although the interventions may be the same in all three contexts, most likely there are differences because of the situations.

Dhooper and Moore offer several suggestions for intervention-related practice principles and approaches:

1. Be aware of your own opinion and biases about interracial marriages, racial identity of biracial persons, and your own personal identity and be aware of internalized racial and ethnic stereotypes.
2. Understand and be sensitive to the biracial's sense of being "different" and "special" but not in a positive way . . . sense of not belonging anyway, feeling lonely, confused, and victimized.

3. Use a nonoppressive theoretical perspective in working with biracial-multiracial clients.
4. Mix and match therapeutic techniques in order to attain the best fit between the client's needs and your intervention. (2001, pp. 237–238)

Interventions at the macro level have to address the racism and oppression that multiracial clients experience. Multiracial clients may be encouraged to join national organizations such as the AMEA or I-Pride, whose missions are to educate people about multiracial experiences and fight racism and prejudice around interracialism (Brown & Douglass, 2003).

Interventions at the meso level may include finding support groups and organizations, such as Interracial Family Alliance, Multiracial Asians of Southern California (MASC), IMAGE (one of the 14 charter member organizations forming the Association of Multiethnic Americans [AMEA]), Interracial Network, or Parents of Interracial Children, that meet the needs of the multiracial individual and families. Supportive family members are also important.

Interventions at the micro level may include therapy, self-reflective journaling, support groups, or individual friends to help process issues. For male persons, interventions may mean creating family histories and genealogies to understand roots or visiting the countries and places of origin. Interventions should be individualistic, tailored to the preference and need of the multiracial individual.

Whatever intervention is chosen, the approach to treatment needs to have a "nonoppressive" theoretical approach and effect on the client. Dhooper and Moore suggest using theoretical approaches such as feminist theory (if appropriate to the client's gender and sexual orientation) because it makes an effort to separate pathological and nonpathological behaviors (2001, p. 238). Helms and Cook warn,

> Just as therapists are socialized by their life experiences to adopt certain cultural and racial perspectives, they are also socialized to adopt certain theoretical orientations by their therapist training experiences. Further, just as the therapist's racial and cultural perspectives shape his or her perceptions and conceptualizations of her or his client's dynamics, a therapist's orientation shapes his or her conceptualization of the dynamics of the therapy process, from the beginning to end. . . . The therapist must remember to compensate for the theories' lack of attention to cultural or racial dynamics or potential aspects of the therapeutic process at every phase including her or his conceptualization of therapy goals, assessment, and selection of therapy intervention." (1999, pp. 133–134)

Establishing Goals and Agreement

The goals need to be what the multiracial client is most concerned about now. Rapport building will allow the client to trust the professional so the social worker can suggest other problems that may exist but that might not be evident to the multiracial client at the time. The professional may suggest issues to work on, but the social worker has to understand that it is not his or her discomfort with the client's confusion or ambiguity that dominates the work agreement.

Because issues may be complex and changing, the social worker needs to be flexible in allowing the client to choose issues as they arise. However, summarizing each issue's interrelatedness to the myriad of problems would be necessary.

Using Indigenous and Social Work Intervention Strategies

Indigenous social work strategies are those preferred by the multiracial client. Because there may be more than one ethnic culture in the multiracial client's background, there may be several to choose from. It is also important to know how familiar the multiracial client is with his or her ethnic heritages and cultural backgrounds. The social worker should also be able to discern what interventions are important to the multiracial client. Because the social worker may need to be prepared to help the client become familiar with an indigenous intervention, the social worker himself or herself would have to obtain some knowledge about the indigenous cultures. In Vietnamese culture, the *shaman* or medicine man is involved in problem solving, but a non-Vietnamese social worker may not be familiar with this indigenous intervention or recognize the importance in using these medicine men in the treatment. To apply culturally competent practice, the social worker would have to learn.

In some cultures, indigenous intervention may involve cultural values and belief systems. For example, Asian interracial couples may have cultural norms that social workers need to know, for instance, the Asian concept of not "losing face." In working with clients where the cultural value is the family—as in Asian and Pacific Islander and Latino and Mexican American cultures—the practitioner would normally include family members in the therapeutic work. Where there are family tensions about racism, however, it may be difficult to have all the family members participate in a helpful way. The Hawaiian family problem-solving process of *Ho'oponopono* has a stage where the family members in conflict need "to make things right" before they can get to healing (Mokuau, 1991). An integrative approach of using micro, meso, and macro interventions would be important to incorporate with the indigenous interventions.

TERMINATION SKILLS WITH MULTIRACIAL CLIENTS

Terminations skills usually focus around ending the relationship and work accomplished between the client and worker. Lum (1996) speaks of termination as destination, recital, and completion. The destination is the "endpoint," the recital is the "retelling of major events that brought the worker and client to the destination," and the "completion is the sense of accomplishment" (1996, p. 282).

| CASE | **Case Study Integration Exercise on Termination** |

Mrs. Smith, the white social worker, tries to call Mei's parents, but the mother does not understand English very well and the father refuses to come in to see her. Mrs. Smith tries to find a Cantonese-speaking interpreter but can only find one who speaks Mandarin. Mrs. Smith also tries to find out about Mei's brothers David and Jonathan to see how they are doing. She finds out from the boys' teachers that they are not doing well because they do not turn in their homework but are smart enough to keep up with what is going on in class.

Mrs. Smith tries to get Mei to talk about her father's older children. But Mei says she is afraid of them because they do not like her because she is not as Jewish as they are. Although they come to visit their father, Ben, sometimes, they really do not interact with Mei, her mother, or brothers. What should Mrs. Smith the social worker do?

Application Exercises

1. Should Mrs. Smith try to use the Mandarin-speaking interpreter?
2. Should she try to see the older children, Miriam and Caleb, anyway to try to help the situation despite their rejection of Mei because of her Asian background?
3. Should Mrs. Smith be worried about the younger brothers Jonathan and David?

In the destination or endpoint phase, several issues will arise such as attachments, and unresolved grief and loss. Developing a close relationship and making attachments may be difficult with multiracial clients. Termination may trigger losses and unresolved grief. There may be anxiety in ending an important relationship that was meaningful to the client, especially if the multiracial client felt like the social worker really understood him or her.

In the recital part of the termination process, it would be good to review client progress, retell the major events that brought the worker and client together, and summarize the progress made in each area. In the completion part of the termination process, it is helpful to evaluate the present and the future and outline follow-up strategies.

CLOSING THOUGHTS

The challenges for the social worker helping multiracial and multiethnic clients and their families address their problems at the societal, familial, and individual levels are complex. The social worker needs to know about historical discriminatory laws and practices. Racist attitudes from even friends and family members need to be confronted. Individual struggles with fears and low self-esteem may couple identity confusion and lack of belongingness. Problems of domestic violence and substance abuse may add to the complexity and challenges. Social workers need to equip themselves to help multiracial/multiethnic clients. Considering that the rights of multiracial persons can be the basis on which you can initiate empowerment strategies. Whatever the situation and environment of multiracial clients, they have the right for a better life and treatment as summarized by Root in "A Bill of Rights for Racially Mixed People":

1. I have the right not to justify my existence in this world.
2. I have the right not to keep the races separate within me.
3. I have the right not to be responsible for people's discomfort with my physical ambiguity.
4. I have the right not to justify my ethnic legitimacy.
5. I have the right to identify myself differently than strangers expect me to identify myself.
6. I have the right to identify myself differently than how my parents identify me.
7. I have the right to identify myself differently than my brothers and sisters.
8. I have the right to identify myself differently in different situations.
9. I have the right to create a vocabulary to communicate about being multiracial.
10. I have the right to change my identity over my lifetime—and more than once.
11. I have the right to have loyalties and identify with more than one group of people.
12. I have the right to freely choose whom I befriend and love. (1996, p. 7)

Social workers have a pivotal role in helping multiracial clients achieve these rights that they deserve and to which they are entitled. Having culturally competent knowledge, values, and skills is mandatory in accomplishing this important feat.

References

Arredondo, P. (2002). Counseling individuals from marginalized and underdeserved groups. In P. Pedersen, J. Draguns, W. Lonner, & J. Trimble (Eds.), *Counseling across cultures* (pp. 233–250). Thousand Oaks, CA: Sage.

Brown, N., & Douglass, R. (2003). Evolution of multiracial organizations: Where we have been and where we are going. In L. Winters & H. DeBose (Eds.), *New faces in a changing America: Multiracial identity in the 21st century* (pp. 111–126). Thousand Oaks, CA: Sage.

Comas-Diaz, L. (1996). LatiNegra: Mental health issues of African Latinas. In M. Root (Ed.), *The multiracial experience: Racial borders as the new frontiers* (pp. 167–190). Thousand Oaks, CA: Sage.

DaCosta, K. (2003). Multiracial identity: From person problem to public issue. In L. Winters & H. DeBose (Eds.), *New faces in a changing America: Multiracial identity in the 21st century* (pp. 68–84). Thousand Oaks, CA: Sage.

Davis, F. (2000). Black identity in the United States. In P. Kivisto & G. Rundblad (Eds.), *Multiculturalism in the United States: Current issues, contemporary voices* (pp. 101–112). Thousand Oaks, CA: Pine Forge Press.

DeBose, H. (2003). Introduction. In L. Winters & H. DeBose (Eds.), *New faces in a changing America: Multiracial identity in the 21st century* (pp. xi–xxi). Thousand Oaks, CA: Sage.

DeBose, H., & Winters, L. (2003). The dilemma of biracial people of African American descent. In L. Winters & H. DeBose (Eds.), *New faces in a changing America: Multiracial identity in the 21st century* (pp. 127–157). Thousand Oaks, CA: Sage.

Dhooper, S., & Moore, S. (2001). *Social work practice with culturally diverse people.* Thousand Oaks, CA: Sage.

Dorow, S. (2000). Narratives of race and culture in transnational adoption. In P. Kivisto & G. Rundblad (Eds.), *Multiculturalism in the United States: Current issues, contemporary voices* (pp. 135–148). Thousand Oaks, CA: Pine Forge Press.

Feigelman, W., & Silverman, A. (1997). Single parent adoption. In H. Merindin (Ed.), *The handbook for single adoptive parents* (pp. 123–129). Chevy Chase, MD: National Council for Single Adoptive Parents.

Fong, R. (2003). Cultural competence with Asian Americans. In D. Lum (Ed.), *Culturally competent practice: A framework for understanding diverse groups and justice issues* (pp. 261–281). Pacific Grove, CA: Brooks/Cole.

Fong, R. (2004a). Culturally competent contextual social work practice and intersectionality. In R. Fong (Ed.), *Culturally competent practice with immigrant and refugee children and families.* New York: Guilford Press.

Fong, R. (Ed.). (2004b). *Culturally competent practice with immigrant and refugee children and families.* New York: Guilford Press.

Fong, R., & Wang, A. (2001). Adoptive parents and identity development in Chinese infants. In N. Choi (Ed.), *Psychosocial aspects of the Asian American experience: Diversity within diversity* (pp. 19–33). New York: Haworth Press.

Gibbs, J. (1989). Biracial adolescents. In J. Gibbs, L. Huang, & Associates. *Children of color* (pp. 322–350). San Francisco: Jossey Bass.

Gibbs, J., Huang, L., & Associates. (1989). *Children of color.* San Francisco: Jossey Bass.

Gibbs, J., Huang, L., & Associates. (2003). *Children of color,* 2nd ed. Somerset, NJ: John Wiley & Sons.

Graham, S. (1996). The real world. In M. Root (Ed.), *The multiracial experience: Racial borders as the new frontier* (pp. 37–48). Thousand Oaks, CA: Sage.

Groze, V., & Rosenthal, J. (1991). Single parents and their adopted children: A psychosocial analysis. *Journal of Contemporary Human Services, 72*(2), 130–139.

Helms, J., & Cook, D. (1999). *Using race and culture in counseling and psychotherapy: Theory and process.* Boston: Allyn & Bacon.

Kerwin, C., & Ponterotto, J. (1995). Biracial identity development: Theory and research. In J. Ponterotto, J. Casas, L. Suzuki, & C. Alexander (Eds.), *Handbook of multicultural counseling* (pp. 199–217). Thousand Oaks, CA: Sage.

Leigh, J. (1998). *Communicating for cultural competence.* Boston: Allyn & Bacon.

Lum, D. (1996). *Social work practice and people of color.* Pacific Grove, CA: Brooks/Cole.

Lum, D. (Ed.). (2003). *Culturally competent practice: A framework for understanding diverse groups and justice issues.* Pacific Grove, CA: Brooks/Cole.

Maslow, A. (1962). *Toward a psychology of being.* Princeton, NJ: Van Nostrand.

McLemore, S., Romo, H., & Baker, S. (2001). *Racial and ethnic relations in America,* 6th ed. Boston: Allyn & Bacon.

McRoy, R. (1994). Attachment and racial identity issues: Implications for child placement decisionmaking. *Journal of Multicultural Social Work, 3*(3), 59–74.

McRoy, R., & Hall, C. (1996). Transracial adoptions: In whose best interest? In M. Root (Ed.), *The multiracial experience: Racial borders as the new frontier* (pp. 63–78). Thousand Oaks, CA: Sage.

McRoy, R., Oglesbly, Z., & Grape, H. (1997). Achieving same-race adoptive placements for African American children: Culturally sensitive practice approaches. *Child Welfare, 76*(1), pp. 85–104.

Mokuau, N. (1991). *Handbook of social services for Asian and Pacific Islanders.* New York: Greenwood Press.

Morning, A. (2003). New faces, old faces: Counting the multiracial population: Past and present. In L. Winters & H. DeBose, *New faces in a changing America: Multiracial identity in the 21st century* (pp. 41–62). Thousand Oaks, CA: Sage.

National Association of Social Work. (2001). *NASW standards for cultural competence in social work practice.* Washington, DC: Author.

Nagel, J. (2000). The politics of ethnic authenticity: Building Native American identities and communities. In P. Kivisto & G. Rundblad (Eds.), *Multiculturalism in the United States: Current issues, contemporary voices* (pp. 113–124). Thousand Oaks, CA: Pine Forge Press.

O'Melia, M., & Miley, K. (2002). *Pathways to power: Readings in contextual social work practice.* Boston: Allyn & Bacon.

Phinney, J. (1986). When we talk about American ethnic groups, what do we mean? *American Psychologist, 51,* 918–927.

Rockquemore, K., & Brunsma, D. (2002). *Beyond Black: Biracial identity in America.* Thousand Oaks, CA: Sage.

Root, M. (Ed.). (1992). *Racially mixed people in America.* Thousand Oaks, CA: Sage.

Root, M. (Ed.). (1996). *The multiracial experience: Racial borders as the new frontier.* Thousand Oaks, CA: Sage.

Root, M. (2001). *Love's revolution: Interracial marriage.* Philadelphia: Temple University Press.

Root, M. (2003). Five mixed-race identities: From relic to revolution. In L. Winters & H. DeBose (Eds.), *New faces in a changing America: Multiracial identity in the 21st century* (pp. 3–20). Thousand Oaks, CA: Sage.

Spencer, M., Icard, L., Harachi, T., Catalano, R., & Oxford, M. (2000). Ethnic identity among monoracial and multiracial early adolescents. *Journal of Early Adolescence, 20*(4), 365–387.

Spickard, P. (1989). *Mixed blood: Intermarriage and ethnic identity in the twentieth century.* Madison: University of Wisconsin Press.

Sung, B. (1990). *Chinese American intermarriage.* New York: Center for Migration Studies.

Takaki, R. (1989). *Strangers from a different shore: A history of Asian Americans.* New York: Penguin Books.

U.S. Census Bureau. (2001a). *The two or more races population: 2000.* Census 2000 Brief, November 2001, Washington, DC: Author.

U.S. Census Bureau (2001b). *Population by race and Hispanic or Latino origin for the United States, regions, divisions, and states, and for Puerto Rico: 2000.* Washington, DC: Author.

Weaver, H. (2003). Cultural competence with First Nations Peoples. In D. Lum (Ed.) *Culturally competent practice: A framework for understanding diverse groups and justice issues* (pp. 197–216). Pacific Grove, CA: Brooks/Cole.

Wehrly, B., Kenney, K., & Kenney, M. (1999). Counseling multiracial families. Thousand Oaks, CA: Sage.

Williams, K. (2003). From civil rights to the multiracial movement. In L. Winters & H. DeBose (Eds.), *New faces in a changing America: Multiracial identity in the 21st century* (pp. 85–98). Thousand Oaks, CA: Sage.

Yellow Bird, M. (2001). Critical values and First Nations Peoples. In R. Fong & S. Furuto (Eds.), *Culturally competent practice: Skills, interventions, and evaluations* (pp. 61–74). Boston: Allyn & Bacon.

Social Work Practice with Women of Color

Valli Kalei Kanuha

CHAPTER 7

The courageous organizing efforts of African Americans and white allies in the U.S. Civil Rights movement, now more than six decades old, could not have foretold the extensive legal, economic, and social reforms that many Americans now take for granted. Interracial couples now constitute a significant proportion of marriages, but such cross-ethnic relationships were once illegal in numerous states. Spanish-speaking students in many school districts across the country can now study math and social studies in their native language, while learning English as a second language. African American and Asian employees occupy key positions in major corporations and government, having attained such opportunities through affirmative action initiatives, educational scholarships, and training programs specifically targeted to increasing the number of ethnic minorities in all aspects of American social life.

The success of the Civil Rights movement, however, was partly the result of the engagement of citizens from different regions and constituencies who shared a moral imperative about freedom for black Americans. This tradition of broad constituency organizing was also seen in the 1800s when the women's suffrage movement joined with anti-slavery advocates, and during the 1960s when white middle-class college students galvanized African American civil rights leaders, labor organizations, and women's groups to protest the Vietnam War. Parallel strategies were employed by other

U.S.–based social movements advocating for women's equality, the environment, disability rights, and lesbian, gay, bisexual, transgender, and queer (LGBTQ) liberation (Darnovsky, Epstein, & Flacks, 1995; Elder, 1985).

The history of cross-issue and cross-constituency organizing in the United States reflects the true nature of diversity in this country. The focus of this chapter on women of color represents a century of gains from the Civil Rights, women's, and LGBTQ movements in the United States. Through those macro level mobilization efforts we understand better the challenges faced by people of color, women, lesbians and gay men, and other marginalized populations in this country. And because of the extensive impact that such social change efforts have had on the media, government, education, health, and legal systems, we live in a transformed society infused by people at the margins becoming more visible, and for some, moving toward the center of American social life.

Culturally competent social work practice with women of color requires understanding the historical conditions that precipitated our American-based social movements for liberation and empowerment, and the ways such movements have influenced how women of color are now viewed in everyday society. It means that we analyze and appreciate the complex intersections of race, sex/gender, class, nationality, ability, age, sexuality, and other identities that have structured how we know ourselves, how we are known to others, and how we join with like- and different-others to make meaning in our individual lives and in our communities.

This chapter will notably diverge from the other chapters in this compilation on culturally competent social work practice. This chapter begins with an overview of four theoretical frameworks that undergird professional practice with women of color, each framework offering critical and analytical perspectives, but all still rooted in the best traditions of social work. As with the other chapters in this text, the second section describes the histories of resistance and survival that contextualize the social-cultural-political lives of women of color. In the third section of the chapter, we focus on deconstructing and offering alternative paradigms for some of the key concepts, perspectives, and premises underlying our knowledge and skill-practice sets with women of color. The fourth section centers on an integrative approach to intervention wherein issues such as practitioner self-reflection, colonization, and spirituality are discussed as key concepts in social work practice with women of color. Finally, a case study will be used to illustrate the theoretical and practice frameworks, perspectives, and principles outlined in the chapter, following Lum's (2000) process-stage approach for culturally competent social work.

Although the chapter will probably present more conundrums than "best practices," I hope readers will gain another perspective on the traditional ways we approach culturally competent social work practice, a view that focuses on critical thinking and self-reflection as keys to intervention with women of color.

THEORETICAL FRAMEWORKS FOR CULTURALLY COMPETENT PRACTICE WITH WOMEN OF COLOR

Any discussion about "women of color" must be prefaced with the analytical and conceptual foundations underlying the term. Is "women of color" a political classification? Is it an "identity"? Who *are* women of color? What constitutes cultural competence as an approach to working with women of color? In this section, I present four analytical and theoretical frameworks that inform the ways I understand, conceptualize, and approach practice with "women of color" as a social category of interest for social work practice. These frameworks are (1) Omi and Winant's model of racial/ethnic categorization (1986), (2) Ewing's multiple representations of the self (1990), (3) critical race feminism, and (4) Warrier's model of cultural competence (2002).

Omi and Winant's Analysis of Racial Categorization

Omi and Winant (1986) and other political scientists (Delgado & Stefancic, 1999; Webster, 1992) have traced the political origins of racial/ethnic minority categories that suggest that such groupings are not necessarily related to genetic, phenotypic, or even blood quantum measures but, instead, to historical and political mobilization by racial/ethnic minorities. The groupings suggest that our collective understanding of what constitutes race is formulated almost entirely by political and ideological motivations; that is, "the effort must be made to understand race as an *unstable and 'decentered' complex of social meanings constantly being transformed by political struggle*" (authors' italics) (Omi & Winant, 1986, p. 68).

Omi and Winant argue that the concept of race in contemporary American life is derived by a pattern of conflict and accommodation between the state and social movements such that, for example, in the early 1960s as Asian American communities organized to gain power and resources relative to the state, they were able to mobilize by forcing the state (federal/national) to begin to count them as a distinct category rather than as "other." However, this shift was more than just one of nomenclature; rather, where literally no Asian Americans once existed, as governmental entities created a category of "Asian American," wherein citizens could actually be counted, a heretofore invisible and low-power constituency almost overnight became a power broker within a political arena. This accommodation by the state resulted in increased power and resources for the social group, and in an emergent personal identity for individuals who now claimed this new category of Asian Pacific Islander.

With the ever-growing diversity and "multicultural" blending of race, ethnicity, and nationality in the United States today, we must question whether the nomenclature and attributes we associate with the various minority racial/ethnic groups are truly meaningful for the ways we structure our social relations with each other and, subsequently, our social work practice with constituents from those groups.

Ewing's Multiple Representations of the Self

Anthropologist Ewing (1990) has proposed an alternative framework for understanding identity and "the Self" that is situated first in a critique of Western anthropological field research, but that she extends into a critical examination of concepts of the self as "whole and timeless." Integrating the work of Mead (1934) and Kohut (1971), Ewing argues that "self-representation" more accurately describes the work of knowing and presenting the self in social contexts.

Ewing's work (1990) has four primary and interrelated aspects:

1. "People construct *a series of self-representations* that are based on selected cultural concepts of persons and selected chains of personal memories." (p. 253) [italics are author's]
2. "In all cultures people can be observed to project *multiple, inconsistent self-representations that are context-dependent.*" (p. 251)
3. Because of these constant and "shifting selves" that people must construct and enact, *most people are "unaware of these shifts and inconsistencies,"* which may, however, be "clearly *observed during negotiation and argument among situationally located actors.*" (p. 251)
4. "As long as an individual is able to maintain contextually appropriate self-representations in interaction with others, he or she may experience *a sense of continuity despite the existence of multiple, unintegrated or partially integrated self-representations.*" (p. 273)

Ewing's framework is particularly relevant to understanding practice with women of color because she suggests that all humans know and enact themselves in complex ways, and that those enactments are largely context-driven and, more important, are filled with contradictions that human beings are still able to manage relatively well. This fits with my view of the complexity of identities or self-representations as lived by women of color who must balance being women, nonwhite, middle class, immigrants, lesbians, old, and the myriad of characteristics that compose who we are and how we are known.

Critical Race Feminism

Critical race feminism (CRF) is an outgrowth of critical race theory (CRT), a postmodern critique of civil and legal strategies to address race-based inequities that first emerged among radical legal scholars in the 1970s. CRT is grounded in a few key principles from which CRF evolved.

CRT proponents (Bell, 2000; Crenshaw, Gotanda, Peller, & Thomas, 1996; Delgado & Stefancic, 1999), who have been critical of most mainstream legal initiatives to overturn racist policies and practices, suggest that the strength of the law should be concerned with the underlying conditions that maintain racism as an institution of oppression. CRT scholars argue that most of the law is inherently racist and discriminatory and that legal tenets such as "neutrality," "objectivity," and even "color blindness" are problematic.

Women of color in the law began CRF (Crenshaw, 1994; Williams, 1992; Wing, 1997a, 1997b) as an offshoot of CRT in response to the male-dominated and sometimes sexist perspectives of their black, Latino, and Asian brothers in the profession. As CRF scholar Wing notes, "Women of color are not simply white women plus some ineffable and secondary characteristic, such as skin tone, added on" (1997b, p. 3). In fact, some of the most influential and well-used concepts in the field of cultural competence come from CRF theorists. Crenshaw's *intersectionality* (1994) and Matsuda et al.'s *multiple consciousness* (1993) both describe the complex and additive identities through which women of color make meaning of race, class, sex, gender, sexuality, and other aspects of their lives. CRF scholars are particularly critical of essentialist perspectives that propose singular or static ways of understanding the phenomenology of women's experiences.

Warrier's Model of Cultural Competence

Warrier's (2002) cultural competence framework was devised for and is primarily employed with domestic and sexual violence workers in the United States. However, some key concepts and principles that are unique in her approach to cultural competence are central to the framework for culturally competent practice with women of color as presented in this chapter:

1. Culture is not a static set of beliefs, values, and traditions; rather culture intersects "in different ways for different individuals in the same groups, as well as for different groups at different times and differently over different spaces." (Warrier, 2002, p. 7)
2. Values, beliefs, and practices of cultural groups are often contradictory; aspects of all cultures are positive in some contexts and problematic in others.
3. Learning about one's "authentic" or "real" culture is a privilege, and not necessarily a naturally occurring process because of the structures of misinformation and power that control how we know ourselves and each other.
4. Cultural competence "recognizes that diversity exists both *within* and *between* cultures." (Warrier, 2002, p. 19)
5. The process of becoming culturally competent "does not mean learning as many 'characteristics' as possible" about a given cultural group.

Warrier describes a "world traveling" approach to cultural competence synonymous with the act of traveling to places and spaces out of our own local realm. That is, when we travel to another "place," we are out of our everyday element and comfort zone; we must learn a new language and nuances of communication. At best, we must not be arrogant travelers who pretend to know everything or even a few key "facts" about a group of people gained from a guidebook (the most recent edition, of course). Warrier recommends instead that we "shift from being one person in the world to a different person in another world" (2002 p. 28).

A Note on Statistical Profiles on Women of Color

Although facts about high rates of cancer, diabetes, domestic violence, and all manner of social ills often accompany our knowledge building with women of color, such facts underscore the centuries of resistance, resilience, and accomplishments that women of color have achieved despite historical oppression. Cultural profiles that describe collective, nurturing matriarchal structures in First Nations and Latina families run the risk of being generalized across tribes, countries of origin, language groups, historical periods, sexualities, current place of residence, and literally hundreds of other variables that could render such a profile moot at an operational level.

Therefore, although it may be comforting for the reader to have "facts" about women of color by racial and ethnic category, I will refrain from including this type of information in this chapter because it risks reinforcing stereotypes and generalizations that are generally irrelevant when we should be relying instead on more complex thinking and skills in our helping relationships. Instead, I will provide select data and narratives throughout the chapter to illustrate certain knowledge, skills, and practices in the professional relationship with women of color across specific process stages in culturally competent social work. For more information about population, health, and other race- or ethnic-specific data on women of color, readers are referred to the wide range of sources currently available on these topics. [1]

THE HISTORICAL OPPRESSION AND SURVIVAL SKILLS OF WOMEN OF COLOR

The historical context for women of color must always be situated in the intersection of at least three major oppressive systems: sexism, racism, and classism. Certainly other factors such as age, ability, sexuality, gender identity, and national origin are also salient in the lives of women of color; however, most women of color understand their social-cultural status—and, more important, how others view and treat them, particularly in the United States—through the lens of sex, race, and class. In this section, descriptions of institutional oppression based on race, sex, gender, class, and other factors are coupled with resistance and survival in the her/stories of women of color.

---

[1] Population data are available from the U.S. Census Bureau (United States Census Bureau, 2003). A comprehensive source of health data on women of color is *The Women of Color Health Data Book* published by the U.S. Office of Women's Health (Office of Research on Women's Health, 2002).

Struggle and Survival of First Nations and Indigenous Women

Perhaps the most significant blight in U.S. history is the systematic genocide of the people and culture of the First Nations. As the first and host peoples of the American continent, indigenous tribes were subject to the intentional theft of their lands by the United States and other nations. With land as a sacred and spiritual aspect of First Nations people, the loss of land foretold the subsequent death of hunting, gathering, fishing, language, myths, and all social practices linked to Mother Earth. The Christian-based boarding home movement, in which Native children were taken from their families to be socialized into "civilized" Americans is only now being exposed in the mainstream as a horrific example of racist policy against indigenous people of this country. In March 1954, the U.S. government detonated the largest nuclear bomb in history, 1,000 times that of Hiroshima, on the Bikini Atoll in the Marshall Islands. A half century later, Marshallese women have cancer rates five times those of white women, and Micronesian women are diagnosed with cervical cancer 75 times more often than are white women (Office of Research on Women's Health, 2002).

For First Nations women, racist and sexist attitudes of white men were reflected in most governmental social policies, military incursions into Native lands, and the rape and killing of indigenous women and children. Smith (Oklahoma) (1999), a longtime violence against women activist, has documented the flagrant physical and sexual violations of Native women from the early 1600s through the present. In an 1867 report to the U.S. Congress, one white officer describes cavalry who "cut a woman's private parts out" (cited in Smith, 1999, p. 36), and displays of women's excised genitals on saddles and hats of soldiers.

Despite these travesties, First Nations women have always resisted attempts to destroy their people and culture. Stories of the nobility and courage of tribal people were shared with Native children in the quiet and furtive embraces of their grandmothers and on rare visits home from boarding schools. The first language of the Sioux, Ojibwe, Patowatomi, and Oklahoma were spoken in private at home, even while mothers encouraged children to speak English in public. Indigenous healing practices and medicine people were known to Native people on every reservation and among urban First Nations peoples displaced in large cities across the United States. The various nations of indigenous people know the strength of women in their own traditions, such as the White Buffalo Calf Woman who symbolized truth and courage for the Sioux, Papa or Mother Earth for the Kanaka Maoli, and Sky Woman in the Seneca. Women leaders not only sat beside men in key decision-making councils, but also were the touchstone on which future generations rest. Today, while domestic and sexual violence abound in the First Nations as in all communities around the globe, Native women are reclaiming their traditional roles as healers and leaders through programs that integrate Native spirituality, community accountability, and empowerment (Allen, 1986; Minnesota Program Development, 1989; Mousseau & Artichoker, no date;

Sacred Circle National Resource Center to End Violence Against Native Women, 2000).

Immigrant Women of the United States

Unlike First Nations women, who are the original peoples of the Americas, most other categories of women of color are not indigenous to the United States. From that common starting point, women of African, Asian, Pacific Island, Latino, Arab, or West Asian descent are survivors of displacement and estrangement from their home lands. Whether first arriving in the United States in slave ships from Africa, as mail order brides from the Philippines, escaping torture from Pol Pot in Thailand, or seeking a better life for themselves from Cuba, Mexico, or India, U.S. immigrant women of color have faced the triple burden of being women, racial/ethnic minorities, and ex-patriots in their new homeland of America.

For many women of color, their lack of skills and, for more recent immigrants, their restricted English language fluency have contributed to intergenerational histories of poverty and educational barriers. They are generally underskilled and underemployed, working in sweatshops, as domestic workers, in factories, or in small businesses (Kuo & Porter, 1998; Office of Research on Women's Health, 2002). They are trafficked in the sex/drug industries across continents, and they are the single mothers and grandmothers of children, lacking community infrastructure and economic support to help families survive (Foo, 2002). Even the relatively few women of color in positions of power and prestige are victims of the "plastic ceiling" wherein job promotions beyond a certain level are limited, and the small number of women of color colleagues on whom they can rely for mutual support make success and job satisfaction even more challenging.

The racist and sexist histories that most women of color have survived have also contributed to poor health and socioeconomic indices across the various ethnic groups. Hawaiian women are 50% more likely to be overweight than are all women in the United States and have a diabetes-related death rate of 37 per 100,000 (Office of Research on Women's Health, 2002). Vietnamese women have the highest rate of cervical cancer among all women in the United States (43 per 100,000), and more African American women die from cerebrovascular disease than any other group of American women (Office of Research on Women's Health, 2002). Women of color are disproportionately the single heads of their families and the victims of intimate partner violence and sexual assault (Office of Research on Women's Health, 2002; Tjaden & Thoennes, 1998).

In all people of color communities, however, women have also been the sustainers and life-givers of culture and history. Because of their gendered relationships with children, mothers, aunts, grandmothers, and women friends often retain the first languages and cultures of a people, which they pass on to the next generation. Native women have been at the forefront of sovereignty movements and serve in leadership roles in Kanaka Maoli organizing in Hawai'i (Kame'eleihiwa, 1999). African American women developed mutual aid and support associations, culminating with Josephine Ruffin's extensive black women's club movement in the late 1800s that provided material aid to black families and organizing efforts against racial discrimination (Streitmatter, 1994). The first Asian American of either gender in Congress was Patsy T. Mink, the daughter of Japanese immigrants. After arriving in the United States post–Vietnam era, Hmong women were instrumental in mobilizing community associations to serve women, men, and children in their new American communities (Lie, 1999).

Triple Jeopardy for Lesbians of Color

Lesbians of color face three interconnected oppressions—sexism, racism, and homophobia. These three institutions are systematically reinforced through male domination against women, white racism against communities of color, and heterosexism rooted primarily in white male patriarchy against lesbians of color.

Lesbians of color must be constantly vigilant to protect themselves from being fired as teachers because of unwarranted fears they may "recruit" children into homosexuality and from being expelled from their religious institutions. In their intimate relationships, lesbians lack hundreds of legal rights afforded other heterosexual couples, such as insurance benefits and estate protections.

The most significant loss for lesbians of color is their estrangement from their ethnic communities. In a racist world, people of color seek a safe haven in their racial/ethnic communities or identities; for lesbians, their ethnic communities can be the most dangerous place of all because of the psychological and cultural weight placed on our ancestral connections and the fear of being detached from them. Narratives and personal testimonies abound of lesbian daughters leaving home because of shame and fear of rejection that propel them away from parents and extended family (Greene, 1997; Kanuha, 2003).

In this challenging environment, however, lesbians of color have continued to survive and thrive. Lesbians of color have been at the forefront of most social movements organizing for peace, Civil Rights, women's rights, disability rights, and lesbian and gay rights (Vaid, 1995). Lesbians of color in the Combahee River Collective articulated the first radical statement to frame the interconnections between racism, sexism, classism, and other forms of oppression particularly affecting women of color (Combahee River Collective, 1983). The women's anti-violence movement to end sexual assault and domestic abuse has changed the landscape of American life regarding women's rights to safety and security, largely because of the work of lesbians of color in grassroots organizing, social policy making, and the academy (Burns, 1986; Crenshaw, 1994; Kanuha, 1996; Richie, 1996; Smith, 2001).

DECONSTRUCTING AND RECONSTRUCTING KEY PRACTICE CONCEPTS IN SOCIAL WORK

In this section, some fundamental concepts in social work practice are reconstituted in the context of culturally competent practice with women of color. Most of these concepts figure significantly throughout the practice process, from contact through evaluation. Therefore, each of these concepts is presented in the order in which they might be most relevant to the stage-process approach to practice, that is, beginning with help seeking and ending with termination.

Although each of the stages of the practice process requires distinctive knowledge, theoretical frameworks, and skill sets, I suggest that the entire helping relationship should be foregrounded in each of the concepts discussed here regardless of stage or client group. The goal of this section is to critically reflect on many of the concepts and principles in social work practice that we so often take for granted, and that in practice may not necessarily serve the best interests of those most vulnerable to the power of the profession.

Reconceptualizing Help Seeking and Problems

Throughout this text, the reader analyzes both the client and worker's dual and simultaneous tasks as they move through the helping process. However, the basis of any professional helping relationship is the prerequisite that the client is the help-seeker and the social worker is the help-giver. The implicit foundation and nature of the professional relationship is one of unequal power wherein the client enters the social service system in a state of vulnerability delivered voluntarily, by mandate, or by literally "wandering" into the helping arms of the social worker whose function is to help "normalize" them or their situation.

In their challenging deconstruction of social work, Chambon and colleagues suggest that a fundamental function of social work similar to many institutions of a capitalist democratic state is to assist in organizing the populace to "maintain the performance of the economy, preserve civil order and the welfare of the citizens" (1999, p. 8). Therefore, the nature of social work practice is always one whose interest is in reinforcing the status quo in which "normal" society should or does in fact exist. Batterers are helped to stop their abusive behavior, drug abusers curb their addictions "one day at a time," welfare mothers learn job skills and leave the doles, and sexually active youth use condoms more often than not.

The way practitioners help clients and client systems fit better into social life is by helping them view and construct their problems and troubles through our lens, the lens of the trained professional. For all of social work's celebration of and adherence to strengths and empowerment perspectives, the field continues to be dominated by a problem-solving approach that still reflects a medical and, therefore, pathological viewpoint about the purpose of help seeking and, therefore, of help seekers.

De Jong and Berg (2002) and Weick and colleagues (1989) suggest that overlaying knowledge and skills of multicultural practice on a problem-solving model still reinforce the social worker as expert, albeit a newfound culturally competent one. Instead, they propose as an alternative the solution-building approach of truly starting wherever each client enters the helping relationship. By honoring the client's framing of his or her own presenting issues and problems, and listening to how clients describe and bring meaning to their racial, sexual, gender, age, class, and other identities in unique and dynamic ways, De Jong and Berg (2002) suggest that the practitioner need not know specific cultural facts or generalized traits about certain subgroups. Outcome evaluations of solution building appear to bear out the effectiveness of the approach across racial/ethnic, gender, class, and other categories (De Jong & Berg, 2002).

Reframing the Problem Orientation

Appleby argues that oppression is "a by-product of socially constructed notions of power, privilege, control and hierarchies of difference" (2001, p. 37). That power, control, and differences of all kinds in human relationships are understood and acted on based on how such concepts are defined and by whom they are defined is a social constructionist perspective. As theorized by Spector and Kitsuse (1973), Berger and Luckman (1966), Best (1989), and Loseke (1999), the social construction of social problems is an important framework for social workers to consider as they establish a helping relationship with clients. The social constructionist perspective helps us understand why and how some troubles and issues get named as "problems," and understand why some people become associated with certain problems and subsequently become clients seeking help for those problems.

One premise of the social constructionist approach to social problems is that "a social problem doesn't exist until it is defined as such" (Loseke, 1999, p. 13). For example, when white missionaries systematically removed Native children in the United States from their homes in the 1800s, such a concerted effort to eradicate Native ways with "civilizing" strategies was not viewed by white people at the time as "a problem." The "problem" lay in the Native people and their "primitive ways," not in taking away their language, cutting their hair, and forcing them to wear the clothes of their oppressors. When Asian women are battered by husbands they've met through mail-order bride services, the problem is often defined as the domestic abuse of Asian women, rather than as the mail-order or trafficking business.

This illustrates a key aspect of the social constructionist approach, which is that problems come to our attention because they resonate with some subjective value (moral beliefs or righteousness, for example) in people who express those interests. These people are known as claims makers. Importantly, claims makers need an audience; that is, someone to hear and give credence to their claims that some phenomenon is indeed a problem. The believability of claims makers varies based on their subjective and objective positions of power, prestige, and control, called a hierarchy of credibility. Therefore, if a low-ranking child welfare worker states that battered mothers cause harm to their children by staying with their batterers, such an opinion probably holds little weight. However, when a congressman or family court judge has intoned the same recommendation through legislative mandate, public policies have been created to jail battered women for failure to protect their children. An entirely new category of "problem" has just been created.

How does the social constructionist perspective affect our professional relationship with women of color? As stated earlier in this chapter, regardless of the mission or function of a social service setting or how ardently one believes in a strengths-based approach to practice, all social workers inherently have more power than their clients in the helping relationship. The client is "by definition . . . *a person in need;* to be a person in need is to be a *weak person*" [author's italics] (Loseke, 1999, p. 160). And particularly, if there are differences in gender, race, class, ability, age, and other factors wherein the worker is likely to have a more elevated status than her clients on the hierarchy of credibility, power differentials are marked. Therefore as Loseke (1999) describes in her analysis of "the troubled persons industry," social workers are compelled by the nature of our roles to both reinforce claims that certain people are troubled, or that troubles (that is, problems) must have certain dimensions, characteristics, and variables associated with them.

If an African American woman first comes into the office, we "scan" her and, based on "facts about African American women" we have learned (or not learned), we may expect her to enact certain roles or behaviors. Depending on our work context or locale, we may also have some preconceived expectation about what her "presenting problem" might be. However, an alternative self-reflective strategy from both a social constructionist *and* culturally competent perspective suggests that we ask ourselves such questions as these:

- Where did I get this image of African American women?
- Where did I get the image of African American women relative to this particular client?
- What do I know of her or how shall I treat her if she does not typify or fit my image of what African American + woman is? Or if she does not fit my image of African American + woman + "expected problem"?
- "What are these claims encouraging me to *think?* What are these claims encouraging me to *feel?*" [author's italics] (Loseke, 1999, p. 187)
- What investment do I have in establishing the power of my role in our working relationship? Do I have to be "expert?" What if she does not agree with my assessment or intervention plan? What if she is uncooperative with treatment?

The social constructionist perspective helps us understand why we view social problems in certain ways and, more important, those persons Loseke calls the villains and victims in the social problem matrix. For example, when we imagine *a person* living in an urban area who neglects and abuses children in his or her care, what does that image look like? I suggest that it is never (or perhaps rarely): (1) a man, (2) a white man or woman, (3) an older white man or woman, (4) a middle-class man or woman, (5) a gay man or lesbian, or (6) a happily married Latina professor.

The social construction of woman of color as urban child abuser is so commonplace because claims makers in the media, social policy, and helping professions have focused our attention and resources on urban women of color as "villains" relative to their children. I am not arguing that we ignore the "problem" of child abuse and neglect in the context of mothering and motherhood. Rather, the social constructionist perspective asks us to critique and reconfigure those types of "problems" that we apply differentially to certain kinds of people and contexts that are implicitly racist, sexist, and classist. And overwhelmingly, the types of social problems that come to the attention of social work professionals implicate women and women of color who are often typified as clients, consumers, villains, and vixens.

The social constructionist perspective also questions the need for practitioners, clients, and laypersons alike to seek simple solutions to complex issues. We would indeed be reassured as practitioners if we not only understood all the cultural nuances of various women of color groups, but that our cultural knowledge was well-integrated with the various problem sets that women of color are likely to experience. By constructing, embracing, and reinforcing social constructions of social problems as represented by "a South Asian woman with HIV" or "a Palestinian activist who is being deported," we fail to appreciate the unique and dynamic individualism reflected in the human spirit of every woman we meet.

Reconceptualizing Resistance

Epstein (1999), Chambon et al. (1999), and others (Chambon & Irving, 1999; Foote & Frank, 1999) who have analyzed the field of social work from a Foucauldian perspective suggest that the predominant nature of social work is "more and more to regulate and control conduct" (Chambon & Irving, 1999, p. 94). In fact, many of the "populations at risk" defined by the Council of Social Work Education (CSWE) are from those communities that are disproportionately engaged in a mutually dependent-conflictual relationship with the social welfare state. They are those adolescents engaged in unsafe sex, they are immigrants, and they are so many poor women of color living in urban and rural areas.

Under this pretext, thousands of women of color in the United States initiate contact with social workers. For many women whose racial/ethnic cultures value problem solving within the family or community, seeking help outside the home/community is a signal of failure accompanied by shame in exposing one's vulnerabilities. For lesbians of color who legitimately fear the repercussions of societal homophobia, walking into a social worker's office requires courage and often desperation. For immigrant women, the threat of losing what little autonomy and well-being they have may render them reticent during their first encounters with a social work professional.

Behavioral characteristics such as reluctance to disclose, hostility, passivity, or incongruity of affect (laughing at a sad story) can often be construed by social workers as resistance, the psychological defense mechanism first identified by Freud (Bonaparte, Freud, & Kris, 1954). Viewed as defensiveness and client unwillingness to positively engage in the helping relationship, client resistance is rarely seen as a deficit in the helper but, rather, is viewed as another problem in the client. These "tough to work with" clients are considered noncompliant or even ungrateful, implying that the client owes a certain degree of cooperation and even appreciation toward the worker for providing assistance.

De Shazer and colleagues (De Jong & Berg, 2002; de Shazer, 1985) have developed a practice strategy rooted in the strengths perspective known as solution building. Some fundamental concepts and beliefs in solution building include the client as expert (versus the practitioner), emphasis on the client's dreams, wishes, and priorities for their lives, and "drawing on clients' frames of reference" (De Jong & Berg, 2002, p. 19) throughout the helping process. According to de Shazer, client resistance is neither defiance nor client ego defense from therapist intrusion but, instead, is the result of practitioner resistance in allowing clients to determine what they want and how to get it (1984, p. 72). As De Jong and Berg state,

> In solution-building, we do not seek to enhance client motivation by overcoming client resistance but by quieting our own frames of reference, so that we listen with solution building ears and invite clients to participate in solution-building conversations. (2002, p. 73)

This alternative conceptual and strategic approach to client resistance coheres in many ways with culturally competent practice with women of color. Based on centuries of race and gender-based oppression, women of color know too well how raced and gendered social institutions have forced them to be self-protective and "resistant."

I suggest that in our work with women of color we replace the psychoanalytic, pathologized concept of client resistance with the empowered and survival-based concept of *resistance as struggle against oppression*. African American scholar Lewis emphasizes that recognizing the long history of resistance "helps us to understand that the women of the African diaspora are not passive victims of the social, political and historical circumstances they are born in" (1999, p. 157). In my work with lesbians of color, I suggest that the strategy of "passing"—wherein, for example, a lesbian of color enacts a covert role as a married heterosexual—is in fact an act of resistance caused by societal homophobia (Kanuha, 1997).

Therefore, throughout the case process stages, instead of focusing on what the client should do to overcome *their* resistance, perhaps we must examine what we must do to overcome *our* resistance at not being in control of the client or helping process. As Lowery (Laguna-Hopi) recommends, we should view our "role as one of contribution not domination, as being one of many with power, not the only bearer of knowledge" (1999, p. 149).

Women's Relationships with Men of Color

For many women of color, their loyalties first to their children and families are linked closely to their relationships with men of color. Women of color are often the buffers for the differential racism that men of color experience in society-at-large. As more men of color leave their families, homes, and workplaces for jails and prisons, women of color have to "hold it together" by maintaining childrearing, income, and other family roles. When men of color are unable to get work, women of color are often able to get at least menial labor in the pink-collar industries of waitressing, housekeeping, and factory work.

Thus, women of color must often acquiesce to the needs of a larger racial agenda, particularly the upholding and protecting of men of color in their communities. Hill Collins states about African American women, "the overarching emphasis on racial solidarity often promotes a paradigm of individual sacrifice that can border on exploitation. Many Black women encounter punishment if they are seen as too individualistic, especially those Black women who put themselves first" (1998, p. 29). Lie describes a strikingly similar predicament in her discussion of Asian American women and empowerment, stating, "As Asian American women became more active in their communities, they encountered sexism. They began to realize that equal participation in community organizations could never be realized as long as the traditional dominance of men and the gendered division of labor continued" (1999, p. 201). And finally, Afro Caribbean lesbian Makeda Silvera echoes, "There is another struggle: the struggle for acceptance and self-definition within our own communities . . . we have all at one time or another given support to men in our community, all the time painfully holding onto, obscuring, our secret lives" (1991, p. 24).

In this culturally engrained deference to one's racial/ethnic community as viewed through the dominance of male perspectives, many women of color must decide to break free to seek attention for themselves. The strength of this disinclination to solicit the services particularly of a social worker is also bound in the historical experiences and stereotypes women of color have about the social work profession. Significantly, those stereotypes are also reinforced by men of color who are often viewed as Loseke's (1999) "villains" to women's "victims" in the social construction of family problems because men of color are often required to pay child support, are detained or deported, or are served with protective orders to refrain from hurting their wives or children.

The reluctance of women of color to engage in the helping process is partly related to the gendered roles and functions of women within their racial and ethnic minority communities. Because women of color are viewed as more responsible for maintaining their families, and therefore more defective when they do not do so effectively, this double bind is a significant deterrent to help seeking, particularly when it must be sought from professionals in the dominant society. As long as institutional racism and sexism prevail, women of color will also bear the burden of sexist treatment by men of color within their racial/ethnic families and communities.

Resistance against Social Oppression

It is a testimony to the strength and agency of the human spirit that acts of resistance have always co-existed with individual and institutional acts of oppression. In notable and insignificant ways, defiance against interpersonal coercion appears to be an authentic response in even the most downtrodden. In her writing on empowerment with women of the African diaspora, Lewis argues, "resistance to the extensive segregation and discrimination experienced by people from the African diaspora have remained constant, and the role of women here has been stellar" (Lewis, 1999, p. 156). Lewis goes on to suggest that acts of resistance may be *overt,* as with African American women putting pieces of glass in food prepared for their slave masters, or *covert,* such as women's positive self-affirmations after experiences of racist oppression. Resistance must also be characterized as acting against or in response to deeds perpetrated against another, and I would add when the human object of such acts is in a position of less power relative to the perpetrator.

Overt acts of resistance can involve many or a few people, with dramatic or undisclosed effects:

- Mobilization during the Civil Rights era starting with Mrs. Rosa Parks's ride in the whites-only section of a bus to thousands of black women domestic workers walking instead of taking the bus to work in Montgomery, Alabama.
- Audre Lorde (1992), Cherrie Moraga and Gloria Anzaldua (1983), Barbara (1985) and Beverly (1983) Smith Urvashi Vaid (1995), Joanna Kadi (1994), Beth Brant, Gloria Anzaldua (1990), Chrystos (1989), Beverly Greene (1990; 1994; 1997), Oliva Espin (1987), Kitty Tsui (1983), and the many lesbians of color who give voice to and nurture those at the borderlands.

Acts of resistance by women of color are frequently more covert to mediate explicit retaliation against women and their families:

- A New York-based Puertoriquena saving a bit of money each month from an abusive husband's monthly paycheck as preparation for her flight from violence.
- Anita Hill telling the first person in confidence that her boss, now a Supreme Court justice, was sexually harassing her.

Resilience in the Face of Social Oppression

One of the main strengths to be affirmed with women of color throughout the practice process is their resilience as women and as people of color. Extensively studied in children and youth, *resilience* describes children "who achieve positive outcomes in the face of risk" (Kirby & Fraser, 1997, p. 14). Masten, Best, and Garmezy (1990) suggest that there are three types of resilience. The first refers to those people of children who achieve some success despite the odds. The second type of resilience is the daily type of lived stress in which certain people have the unusual ability to cope and sometimes thrive under stressful conditions. The third type refers to the ability to recover from trauma-related stress such as sexual assault or unexpected death of a loved one.

Resilience assumes the power of women to recover from life challenges; the directional movement toward recovery, healing, and surviving and not necessarily toward despair is another fundamental necessity of life as a woman of color. In many ways, the ability of women of color to recover from trauma reminds us that they are inherently full of strengths, resources, skills, abilities, and beauty. They are neither inferior nor inadequate; rather, despite or perhaps because of race, gender, and class oppression, they are uniquely positioned to know the world as Hill Collins (1986) posits, "from the outside within."

Resilience in women of color is exemplified in the following affirmations of cultural assets and strengths:

- Poor women from Latin America have long and more recent histories of radical community organizing and social movement-building in worker rights, human rights, and anti-violence issues. (Safa, 2000)
- Lao women have established battered women's programs and other women's organizations within their own communities. (Zaharlick, 2000)
- Lesbians of color across all racial/ethnic groups are in leadership and other positions of prominence as academicians, community organizers, poet laureates, CEOs, social service administrators, and entertainers. Unfortunately, because of societal homophobia, many still risk censure if they are open about their sexuality.

There are many narratives of resilience about women of color in the United States that every culturally competent social worker should become familiar with. However, the very concept of resilience as an alternative paradigm in assessing client "problems" is what cultural competence offers to practitioners who want to approach women of color with integrity, hope, and respect.

The Illusion of Termination

The notion of "termination" as the final stage in the professional helping relationship is encumbered with many and complex meanings for women of color. For poor women of color, for immigrant women of color, for elderly women of color, and for others who because of their citizenship status, age, or financial needs must interface with social services on an ongoing basis, one never ends their helping relationships with "the system." As such, women may terminate their work with us as battered women's advocates when they leave a shelter, but it is rare that battered women who have once entered the system never reconnect again.

Although many women of color are able to terminate a helping relationship with one helper or helping agency, their reliance on public and private systems of care—often without choice because of the disparity of race, class, gender, sexuality, and other marginal statuses—enforces a permanent role of

dependency from which termination may be unlikely. From a social constructionist perspective, this forced dependency results in a number of disturbing
contradictions and dynamics. First, women of color become typified as dependent on the system, reinforcing not only that they are unable but, more importantly, unwilling to "launch" themselves into autonomous, "productive"
citizenship. The image of the welfare cheat and multigenerational welfare mothers is a feminized, classed, and raced one. We expect women to extricate themselves from dependence on the system, but we prevent them from doing so
through repressive welfare-to-work policies, lack of safe and accessible child
care, and underfunding of race- and gender-sensitive substance abuse treatment.

Another illusory component of termination with women of color is that
the "usual" steps taught to practitioners and codified in many social service
settings do not fit the ways many women of color culturally approach transitions in their relationships. The very linear method of the helping relationship
from engagement to termination/follow-up epitomizes a major drawback of
Western-based interventions. All these steps ideally should be recurring
throughout the practice process; however, the orderly progression of such topics indicates an approach to ending that does not always coincide with the
phenomenological experience of women of color.

For many women of color whose communal group cultures include extensive and long-lasting relationships across miles, generations, and even with
those who've passed into another life force in death, "termination" is not only
illusory, it is almost incomprehensible. In a rural substance abuse program with
Native Hawaiian women, some stated that even though they may no longer be
"clients," what was most important is that they always knew their workers
were now part of their families (Kanuha, Mueller, & Goh, 2003). In addition,
women reported that it was the unconditional positive regard expressed to them
by their workers that created trust in their helping relationships and reinforced
that they could always contact their workers for help.

Who's Terminating Whom?

When clients terminate before the evaluation and follow-up planning stages,
such action constitutes a conundrum for the practitioner. Many of us are left
to ponder and speculate about the reasons for ending, usually focused on what
went wrong. Even the term "premature termination" implies that the intervention process was incomplete. Whether or not the practitioner terminates or
the client terminates, it seems that it is usually the client who is "blamed" for
the unmet goals and lack of follow-through with treatment.

Lum (2000) suggests that premature termination by a client may be less
the result of resistance as a reaction to being confronted about resistance from
a provider. Perhaps it is in the value and act of confrontation that cultural
competence is truly tested. As stated throughout, respect for self-determination, autonomy, and agency in our clients means that we honor their decisions
to do what they believe is best, including that they might terminate contact
before we as clinicians believe they "should."

As Lum further suggests, client mistrust of the worker or worker mistrust of the client, or practical resource issues such as child care, fees, or transportation may also be causes for termination. If we have pushed clients beyond the point that they are able, are willing, or have the skills to handle, perhaps we must reconsider the ways we have used our power or skills inappropriately. It is particularly important to remember that women have histories of power being used against them in intimate, familial, and social relationships. Social workers must be vigilant about not replicating those same hierarchical systems and relationships as helpers.

AN INTEGRATIVE INTERVENTION APPROACH

Addressing the multiple identities, cultural histories, political contexts, and micro, meso, and macro systems in which people and communities interact requires a complex toolbox of knowledge and skills to practice competently as a social worker. In their model of stress over the family life cycle, Carter and McGoldrick (1999) highlight the interface of individuals, families, and society as influenced by past and current factors that evolve and age through time. At the micro (individual), meso (family and community), and macro (societal or cultural) levels, all those systems have their own historical and present-day issues (such as genetic makeup, family histories, domestic violence, and racism), along with daily and mostly unpredictable stressors such migration, unemployment, wars, and natural disasters that affect their functions and structures. Carter and McGoldrick posit that only as we understand how humans progress and interact simultaneously through the multileveled systems of everyday life in a political-social environment can we intervene effectively.

In the preceding sections of this chapter, I offered alternative paradigms on "traditional" frameworks, concepts, knowledge, and skills attending social work practice with women of color. This section builds on the earlier content elaborating on and extending our practice considerations to include topics such as practitioner self-reflection, contextualizing oppression issues, focusing on the helping relationship, and addressing spirituality in our work with women of color. As suggested throughout, an integrated approach that includes multiple identities, narratives, social-political histories, and institutional-structural critiques as they affect women of color is not only culturally competent, it is perhaps the only ethical and effective strategy with this or any population seeking help from social workers.

Practitioner Self-Assessment, Reflection, and Critique

Standpoint theory, as developed initially by feminist Sandra Hartsock (1983), proposes a situated worldview that those who are oppressed have of social relations, such that lesbians would understand and experience homophobia as a system of oppression in ways that heterosexual men and women could not. This worldview is constructed and enacted through "minority" group membership, and oppression is analyzed, critiqued, and resisted through such standpoints.

African American scholar Hill Collins (1986) designed a more intricate analysis of power relations in her work on black feminist thought, arguing that the standpoint perspective does not incorporate the multiple stations in a dominant hierarchy in which women of color reside. Instead, she suggests that we view the position or standpoint of African American women and perhaps all women of color as "one of a heterogeneous commonality embedded in social relations of intersectionality" (Collins, 1990, p. 234). That is, there is a dynamic quality and meaning to oppression when viewed through the constantly evolving life experiences of gender, race, class, age, nationality, sexuality and the various dimensions we call identity. We cannot, any of us, think of ourselves as "just" women or lesbians or Hawaiian or "just social workers," for that matter. Instead, as culturally competent practitioners, we must always consider the multiple ways of understanding the self and society in hierarchies of oppression, power, and domination.

Beth Richie and I (Kanuha & Richie, 2000) developed a six-step model for multicultural practice that focuses primarily on practitioner knowledge and skill development. The first step is self-reflection and self-critique about our own positionality relative to the world, our place of work, our ways of knowing and practicing, and most importantly, how we view our clients and collaborators. Step two requires a deliberate and conscientious commitment to expose oneself to cultural sets and experiences that are different from our own paradigms. In step three, practitioners should conduct a power analysis of our own positionality and the effect of our status in the U.S. power hierarchy on our values and conduct.

Step four requires that practitioners inventory their current practice paradigm, knowledge base, and skill set in the context of the preceding power analysis. We call step five the practitioner shift in practice paradigm, in which praxis (reflection and action) occurs. Step five puts the previous four steps into practice. With step six, the model culminates in monitoring, evaluating, and modifying one's practice paradigm; however, this step is recapitulated throughout our practice lives as we make mistakes, reflect, revise our paradigm, and try again. For in acknowledgment of not knowing we begin the wonderful journey of discovery, of knowing about those so different and so similar to us.

Colonization, Decolonization and Conscientizacao

A second knowledge and practice emphasis among integrative approaches to practice is to focus on consciousness-raising and dialogue about social and historical manifestations of oppression. Although the concept and practices of oppression suggest a general hierarchical system of power relations and resource allocation, Comas-Diaz prefers the term *colonization* to *oppression* when considering the U.S. situation because "people of color are obliged to adapt to the norms of the dominant culture" (1994, p. 298). She suggests that a key practice skill in working with women of color is to engage them in a three-step process that includes (1) regaining the self through self-affirmation, (2) claiming one's worth and dignity through self-determination, and (3) acting to change oneself or the conditions of society through critical consciousness or *conscientizacao* as described by Brazilian educator and scholar Paulo Friere (1972). Similarly, one of the key steps in Lewis's and Guitierrez's empowerment approach to social work with women of color is consciousness-raising (Gutierrez & Lewis, 1999a, 1999b), in which women of color join to analyze the social conditions that contribute to personal or individual problems.

Emphasis on Relationship

Almost every approach to working with women of color emphasizes the unique challenges we face because of the multiple identities and subsequent forms of oppression we experience daily. The notion of relationship and connection has been noted repeatedly as a common characteristic of women's lives, particularly for women of color who must traverse the various roles and expectations attributed to them by their partners, children, families, communities, and most important, the generations who have preceded them.

Therefore, practitioners must tread carefully and thoughtfully in the helping relationship to prevent replicating the same burdens and blames that are often placed on women of color even by those who love and care about them the most. Such qualities of the professional helping relationship are

- Encouraging and listening authentically to their stories, particularly of the almost contradictory challenges of joy and strife in their lives
- Understanding and honestly communicating empathy about the daily and ongoing challenges of being women of color in the United States
- Placing personal and interpersonal struggles reported by women into a larger social and historical framework of oppression
- Remaining nonjudgmental about the choices, beliefs, and expectations women have had placed on them, have placed on themselves, or have enacted
- Asking about other family members; remembering elders, grandparents, and those who have passed on as significant influences on women's lives
- Respecting and enforcing confidentiality
- Employing various theoretical and practice methods, always engaging and involving women in the decision to do so
- Suggesting and using culturally relevant and appropriate rituals such as prayer, blessings, herbs, or celebrations of special occasions as guided by women clients themselves
- Believing and knowing that you are not the expert about the lives of all women of color; each woman is unique, each meaning of her life is distinct from all that you have read about "women of color"

Case Study Integration Exercise on Contact, Problem Identification, and Assessment Skills

This case study is divided into two sections that separate the initial relationship-building and assessment phases from the intervention and termination phases of the stage process of helping. Key issues and practice skills for each of the helping stages are suggested following the case narrative.

Contact, Problem Identification, and Assessment Stages

Maile is a 45-year-old woman of Hawaiian and Caucasian ancestry, born and raised in a small rural area in the state of Hawai'i. Her Hawaiian mother has roots in the Hawaiian Islands, where she and many generations of family members have resided all their lives. Maile's father is from Duluth, Minnesota, descended from Swedish immigrants.

Two years after graduating from high school in Maui (one of the islands in the Hawai'i), Maile met and married Tony, who was born and raised in Los Angeles, the son of Mexican migrant workers. Within a year, Maile was pregnant, an unplanned event that resulted from failed birth control. Although both were serious about their relationship, the pregnancy was not only a surprise but also a stressful event. Neither of them wanted to follow through with the pregnancy; however, abortion was also unacceptable to them.

At the same time as the birth of Michael Alika (Alan in Hawaiian, named for Maile's father), Tony's mother became very ill. Maile, Tony, and the baby moved to L.A. to help care for her. The first months of the transition to urban life in California were difficult for Maile. She had never lived outside of Hawai'i and was very homesick. Caring for Tony's mother and a new baby, on top of moving, was challenging and exhausting for the young couple. Finances were tight because Maile was not working, Tony's salary was going to help support his mother's financial and other needs, they had a new baby, and expenses in L.A. were higher than in Maui.

Maile and Tony began to disagree on little things such as who would wake up to care for Alika or run errands for Tony's mother. Tony's work pattern as a flight attendant was five days flying, when he was rarely at home, followed by four days of being almost constantly around the house. Maile would begin a schedule to manage daily living while Tony was gone, only to find it disrupted when he returned home. Maile also started feeling guilty for not contributing to their finances because she had worked since she was young. Both started to spend more time apart, creating physical and emotional distance to avoid conflict and disappointment.

One night after hanging out with friends, Tony returned home drunk and belligerent. He and Maile began to argue, which escalated with loud voices, name calling, and accusations, culminating in Tony shaking, pushing, and slapping Maile. This was the worst argument they had ever had, and neither of them had physically hurt the other before. Maile was in shock, as was Tony. She went into their bedroom, slamming the door. Tony left the house, feeling a confusion of feelings from anger to shame to resentment to hurt. The next morning, Maile awoke to mild bruising on her face and arms, a headache, and some back pain. Feeling hurt but not afraid of Tony, Maile called for an appointment at her community clinic, apprehensive about seeking help but in pain.

The nurse practitioner sensed that Maile was hesitant about explaining the details of the pain she was experiencing. She asked, "Have you and your son been abused by your husband? Is that what happened?" Immediately, Maile felt afraid, ashamed, and defensive because she didn't want to get Tony into trouble. She replied that the bruises occurred when she slipped and fell at home. This response appeared to frustrate the nurse practitioner, who asked Maile to wait while she asked the social worker to join them. Despite Maile's protestations that she didn't need to talk to anyone else, a few minutes later a young Caucasian woman entered the room, introducing herself as Joan, one of the clinic social workers.

Contact Issues

Following is a list of intervention issues that the social worker should consider in working with Maile:

1. Maile's displacement from her homeland; living in an urban area, on the U.S. continent, with racial, ethnic, classed, and cultural differences different from her own homeland
2. Precipitating events for contact—immediate and crisis-related physical and emotional trauma, as well as in-depth issues such as couples communication, financial problems, childrearing, and extended family responsibilities
3. Ambivalence about seeking help because of shame about "presenting" issues, as well as confusion and complexity of feelings/thoughts; fear of losing Alika to child protection; possible fear of retaliation from Tony for revealing the source of her injuries
4. Cultural differences between Maile and her service providers, agency setting, and cultural practices
5. Lack of practice and cultural sensitivity of nurse practitioner, e.g., direct confrontation about possible domestic violence
6. Abrupt and nonconsensual nature of referral to social worker

Problem Identification Issues

1. Knowledge of and assessment skills for domestic violence
2. Listening and attending to nonverbal cues
3. Self-reflection on stereotyping associated with women of color who use public health care, and stereotyping associated with battered women of color
4. Understanding and situating the presenting crisis in the context of long-term or complex issues

Assessment Issues

1. Knowledge and skills to prevent blaming the victim of abuse, or for the victim not taking action, such as talking to social worker
2. Looking for strengths, resilience, and survival skills, such as the multiple stressors of caring for a newborn child and a sick parent, moving to a different cultural setting, social isolation, financial pressures, role changes from independent single woman to mother, partner, caretaker
3. Focusing on assessing for safety, protection, and collateral needs separate from but related to the presenting problem (such as financial problems, couples communication issues, lack of family support)

(continued)

CASE | *continued*

Intervention and Termination Stages

Maile has been involuntarily referred to meet with Joan, the clinic social worker. Before entering the clinic examination room, Joan was briefly oriented to the case by the nurse practitioner, who suggested it was a possible domestic violence situation. As Joan made initial contact with Maile, she smiled and introduced herself, extending a handshake to Maile. Joan had been to Hawai'i once before and had a few college friends who were from Honolulu.

Joan began by asking whether "Maile" was a Hawaiian name, stating that it sounded Hawaiian to her. Maile appeared comforted by this question, more so because it was the first question Joan asked her. Joan proceeded to ask additional questions about where in Hawai'i Maile was from, how she got to southern California, and how she liked living there compared with living in Hawai'i. Joan self-disclosed that she knew a little bit about Hawai'i from her one visit and college friends, but admitted that from her limited knowledge she would think life in Los Angeles might be quite different from Hawai'i. This particular opening allowed Maile to begin talking about the challenges and difficulties of leaving home, and some aspects of her current living situation.

More than ten minutes had passed in the interview and Joan had not followed up about the possible domestic violence situation. Joan continued by asking about Alika and his developmental milestones, more with genuine interest and ease in his teething, eating, and elimination patterns than in assessing for possible child abuse/neglect. She made contact with Alika and asked to hold him when he appeared comfortable with her. Joan self-disclosed about her own parenting challenges with her two young children, connecting with and affirming the similarities she and Maile shared as mothers.

Ten more minutes had passed, after which Joan asked about Maile's relationship with Tony, linking it to their shared parenting responsibilities of Alika. It was in this context that Maile began sharing small pieces about the conflicts they had had in their marriage, and the various transitions and stressors they faced everyday. Joan proceeded carefully and with sensitivity about how Maile and Tony managed the stress, and whether they had "disagreements that were sometimes hard for her." Maile affirmed the difficulties, and admitted that her clinic visit was due to an argument they had had the previous night.

Joan allowed Maile to talk about whatever she wanted regarding the abusive episode with Tony, not following any agenda to force Maile toward disclosure.

Spirituality

The final theme to consider in working with the diversity of women of color is spirituality. Too long ignored by social work educators and practitioners, there is an emerging emphasis on the importance of religion and spirituality in the lives of our clients. For women of color in particular, religion and spirituality are protective factors that help them resist the intolerable effects of

Maile's perception is that she had "egged Tony on," which resulted in his abusive outburst. Joan responded with, "When we have arguments in our relationships, sometimes women think we're responsible for the fact that our husbands hurt us." Their dialogue continued for another ten minutes after which time Joan suggested that maybe they should get together to just talk some other time since it seemed that Maile was a little lonely for company.

Maile consented and returned for three more sessions in which she talked about a range of issues and concerns. Joan's assessment of the domestic abuse incident is that it did not fit the pattern of a violent relationship, which was affirmed by Maile's willingness to speak about the situation and her apparent lack of fear that Tony would be angry with her for discussing the situation. The approach was very unstructured, with Joan listening and learning about the losses Maile felt about leaving Hawai'i but the hope she had for repairing and building her relationship with Tony. Joan affirmed the strengths in Maile with her many transitions and stressors, and worked on here-and-now solutions to issues raised by Maile at each session. After the third session, Maile decided that she was feeling better for now and did not think she needed to come in on a regular basis. However, she asked if she could call Joan on an as-needed basis since she felt they had a connection that she didn't want to end permanently.

Intervention Issues

Following is a list of intervention issues that the social worker should consider in working with Maile:

1. Using self-disclosure appropriately to connect on a relational level on issues particular to women, such as parenting and childrearing, carrying the baby
2. Using self-disclosure appropriately to connect on a relational level on issues particular to race/ethnicity, for example, Hawai'i context
3. Sensitive approach to assessment of and intervention with domestic abuse, that is, the primary purpose should be engagement for safety, and not confrontation for safety
4. Affirming the social and cultural context for Maile's well-being, e.g., stressors of displacement from Hawai'i, new baby, lack of social support
5. Intervention from a solution-focused approach, with less predetermined structure or expectations from the social worker's perspective

Termination Issues

1. Allowing termination to be impermanent, that is, leaving the door open
2. Allowing termination to be determined by the client's needs and perspectives

racism, sexism, and classism. For First Nations Peoples, Native Hawaiians, and Pacific Islanders, whose cosmological roots are fundamentally linked to more powerful forces than human psychological workings, the importance of linking distress to the healing power of the *'aina* (land), our connections to all things in nature, and our ancestors is a useful strategy. Lewis (1999) and Greene (1994) discuss the important roles of the church, prayer, and meditation in the lives of women of African descent, particularly in their journey to empowerment in the company of other black women. West Indian women in their home countries and in the United States use such spiritual practices as *obeah, Santeria,* and *espiritu* to address their problems within a culturally relevant, community environment (Brice-Baker, 1994). Finally, Comas-Diaz (1994) suggests that spirituality is a central concept in the ways women of color understand and strengthen their sense of self, as individuals and in relation to others.

CLOSING THOUGHTS

Cultural competence is a now ubiquitous perspective in professional social work, business, and government. In many ways, however, the "field" of cultural competence has replicated or at best reconstituted many of the prevailing and dominant paradigms that precipitated its very origins. We say we need to be well-informed about people of color while inadvertently perpetuating stereotypes that "Asian Americans are. . . ." We intone goals of sensitivity about the plight of sexism and women's experiences while expressing frustration at an Iranian battered woman who doesn't successfully fulfill her intervention goal to leave a violent partner. "Sexual diversity" shall be celebrated in our new culturally competent profession, but only if a Latino transgendered youth is willing to actively engage in sharing the painful details of his family history during the assessment phase. We must continue to challenge, honor, and reflect on the best of social work practice and, by so doing, continue our journey toward the best of culturally appropriate, respectful, and growthful practice.

References

Allen, P. G. (1986). *The sacred hoop.* Boston: Beacon Press.

Anzaldua, G. (Ed.). (1990). *Making face, making change (Haciendo caras): Creative and critical perspectives by women of color.* San Francisco: Aunt Lute Books.

Appleby, G. A. (2001). Dynamics of oppression and discrimination. In G. A. Appleby, E. Colon, & J. Hamilton (Eds.), *Diversity, oppression, and social functioning: Person-in-environment assessment and intervention* (pp. 36–52). Needham Heights, MA: Allyn & Bacon.

Bell, D. A. (2000). *Race, racism and American law* (4th ed.). Gaithersburg, NY: Aspen Law and Business.

Berger, P. L., & Luckmann, T. (1966). *The social construction of reality.* Garden City, NY: Anchor.

Best, J. (1989). *Images of issues: Typifying contemporary social problems.* New York: Aldine de Gruyter.

Bonaparte, M., Freud, A., & Kris, E. (Eds.). (1954). *The origins of psychoanalysis* (translated by E. Mosbacher & J. Strachey, eds.). New York: Basic Books.

Brant, B. E. (1994). *Writing as witness: Essay and talk.* Toronto, Canada: Women's Press.

Brice-Baker, J. R. (1994). West Indian women: The Jamaican woman. In L. Comas-Diaz & B. Greene (Eds.), *Women of color: Integrating ethnic and racial diversities in psychotherapy* (pp. 139–160). New York: Guilford Press.

Burns, M. (Ed.). (1986). *The speaking profits us: Violence in the lives of women of color.* Seattle: Center for the Prevention of Sexual and Domestic Violence.

Carter, B., & McGoldrick, M. (1999). *The expanded family life cycle: Individual, family and social perspectives* (3rd ed.). Needham Heights, MA: Allyn & Bacon.

Chambon, A. S., & Irving, A. (1999). Social work, social control and normalization: Roundtable discussion with Michel Foucault. In A. S. Chambon, A. Irving, & L. Epstein (Eds.), *Reading Foucault for social work* (pp. 83–97). New York: Columbia University Press.

Chambon, A. S., Irving, A., & Epstein, L. (Eds.). (1999). *Reading Foucault for social work*. New York: Columbia University Press.

Chrystos. (1989). *Not vanishing*. Vancouver, British Columbia: Press Gang.

Collins, P. H. (1986). Learning from the outsider within: The sociological significance of Black feminist thought. *Social Problems, 33*(6), 14–32.

Collins, P. H. (1990). Black feminist thought: Knowledge, consciousness and the politics of empowerment. New York: Routledge, Chapman & Hall.

Collins, P. H. (1998). *Fighting words: Black women and the search for justice*. Minneapolis: University of Minnesota Press.

Comas-Diaz, L., & Greene, B. (Eds.). (1994). *Women of color: Integrating ethnic and racial diversities in psychotherapy*. New York: Guilford Press.

Combahee River Collective. (1983). A Black feminist statement. In C. Moraga & G. Anzaldua (Eds.), *This bridge called my back: Writings by radical women of color* (pp. 210–218). New York: Kitchen Table: Women of Color Press.

Crenshaw, K., Gotanda, N., Peller, G., & Thomas, K. (Eds.). (1996). *Critical race theory: The key writings that formed the movement*. New York: New Press.

Crenshaw, K. W. (1994). Mapping the margins: Intersectionality, identity politics and violence against women of color. In M. A. Fineman & B. Mykitiuk (Eds.), *The public nature of private violence* (pp. 93–120). New York: Routledge.

Darnovsky, M., Epstein, B., & Flacks, R. (Eds.). (1995). *Cultural politics and social movements*. Philadelphia: Temple University Press.

De Jong, P., & Berg, I. K. (2002). *Interviewing for solutions*. Pacific Grove, CA: Brooks/Cole.

Delgado, R., & Stefancic, J. (Eds.). (1999). *Critical race theory: The cutting edge* (2nd ed.). Philadelphia: Temple University Press.

de Shazer, S. (1984). The death of resistance. *Family Process, 23,* 79–93.

de Shazer, S. (1985). *Keys to solution in brief therapy*. New York: Norton.

Elder, K. (1985). The "new social movements": Moral crusades, political pressure groups, or social movements? *Social Research, 52*(4), 869–900.

Epstein, L. (1999). The culture of social work. In A. S. Chambon, A. Irving, & L. Epstein (Eds.), *Reading Foucault for social work* (pp. 3–26). New York: Columbia University Press.

Espin, O. M. (1987). Issues of identity in the psychology of Latina lesbians. In B. P. Collective (Ed.), *Lesbian psychologies: Explorations and challenges*. Urbana: University of Illinois Press.

Ewing, K. P. (1990). The illusion of wholeness: Culture, self, and the experience of inconsistency. *Ethos, 18,* 251–278.

Foo, L. J. (2002). *Asian American women: Issues, concerns and responsive human and civil rights advocacy*. New York: Ford Foundation.

Foote, C. E., & Frank, A. W. (1999). Foucault and therapy: The disciplining of grief. In A. S. Chambon, A. Irving, & L. Epstein (Eds.), *Reading Foucault for social work* (pp. 157–188). New York: Columbia University Press.

Freire, P. (1972). *Pedagogy of the oppressed*. London: Penguin Books.

Greene, B. (1990). What has gone before: The legacy of racism and sexism in the lives of Black mothers and daughters. In L. S. Brown & M. P. P. Root (Eds.), *Diversity and complexity in feminist therapy* (pp. 207–230). New York: Harrington Park Press.

Greene, B. (1994). African American women. In L. Comas-Diaz & B. Greene (Eds.), *Women of color: Integrating ethnic and racial diversities in psychotherapy* (pp. 10–29). New York: Guilford Press.

Greene, B. (Ed.). (1997). *Ethnic and cultural diversity among lesbians and gay men* (Vol. 3). Thousand Oaks, CA: Sage.

Gutierrez, L. M., & Lewis, E. A. (1999a). *Empowering women of color*. New York: Columbia University Press.

Gutierrez, L. M., & Lewis, E. A. (1999b). The empowerment approach to practice. In L. M. Gutierrez & E. A. Lewis (Eds.), *Empowering women of color* (pp. 3–136). New York: Columbia University Press.

Hartsock, N. (1983). The feminist standpoint: Developing the grounds for a specifically feminist historical materialism. In S. Harding & M. B. Hintikka (Eds.), *Discovering reality* (pp. 283–310). Boston: Reidel.

Kadi, J. (Ed.). (1994). *Food for our grandmothers*. Boston: South End Press.

Kame'eleihiwa, L. (1999). *Na wahine kapu: Divine Hawaiian women*. Honolulu: 'Ai Pohaku Press.

Kanuha, V. (1996). Domestic violence, racism and the battered women's movement in the United States. In J. Edleson & Z. Eisekovits (Eds.), *Future interventions with battered women and their families* (pp. 34–50). Newbury Park, CA: Sage.

Kanuha, V. (1997). *Stigma, identity and passing: How lesbians and gay men of color construct and manage stigmatized identity in social interaction*. Unpublished doctoral dissertation, Order No.

9819258, University of Washington, Seattle.

Kanuha, V., Mueller, C., & Goh, S. S. (2003). *An evaluation of Pulama Na Wahine Ola Hou: An outreach and treatment readiness program for Native Hawaiian women in three rural areas of Hawaii*. Honolulu: Salvation Army Family Treatment Services.

Kanuha, V. K. (2003). *Violence in Asian and Pacific Island queer women's relationships*. Unpublished report.

Kanuha, V. K., & Richie, B. E. (2000). *Creating and maintaining culturally diverse social work practice: A six-step model*. Unpublished manuscript.

Kirby, L. D., & Fraser, M. W. (1997). Risk and resilience in childhood. In M. W. Fraser (Ed.), *Risk and resilience in childhood: An ecological perspective* (pp. 1–9). Washington, DC: NASW Press.

Kohut, H. (1971). *The analysis of the self*. New York: International Universities Press.

Kuo, J., & Porter, K. (1998). *Health status of Asian Americans: United States, 1992–1994: Vital and health statistics*. Centers for Disease Control and Prevention. Atlanta, GA.

Lewis, E. A. (1999). Staying the path: Lessons about health and resistance from women of the African diaspora. In L. M. Gutierrez & E. A. Lewis (Eds.), *Empowering women of color* (pp. 150–166). New York: Columbia University Press.

Lie, G.-Y. (1999). Empowerment: Asian American women's perspectives. In L. M. Gutierrez & E. A. Lewis (Eds.), *Empowering women of color* (pp. 187–207). New York: Columbia University Press.

Lorde, A. (1992). *Undersong: Chosen poems, old and new* (rev. ed.). New York: Norton.

Loseke, D. (1999). Thinking about social problems: An introduction to constructionist perspectives. New York: Aldine de Gruyter.

Lowery, C. T. (1999). The sharing of power: Empowerment with Native American women. In L. M. Gutierrez & E. A. Lewis (Eds.), *Empowering women of color* (pp. 137–149). New York: Columbia University Press.

Lum, D. (2000). *Social work practice and people of color: A process stage approach* (4th ed.). Belmont, CA: Wadsworth.

Masten, A., Best, K. M., & Garmezy, N. (1990). Resilience and development: Contributions from the study of children who overcome diversity. *Development and Psychopathology, 2,* 425–444.

Matsuda, M. J., Delgado, R., & Lawrence, C. R. (Eds.). (1993). *Words that wound: Critical race theory, assaultive speech, and the first amendment (New perspectives on law, culture, and society)*. Boulder, Co: Westview Press.

Mead, G. H. (1934). *Mind, self and society*. Chicago: University of Chicago Press.

Minnesota Program Development Inc. (1989). Mending the sacred hoop: Addressing domestic violence in the American Indian community. In *Mending the Sacred Hoop Domestic Abuse Intervention Program*. Duluth: Minnesota Program Development Inc.

Moraga, C., & Anzaldua, G. (Eds.). (1983). *This bridge called my back: Writings by radical women of color*. New York: Kitchen Table: Women of Color Press.

Mousseau, M., & Artichoker, K. (no date). *Violence against Oglala women is not Lakota tradition* (handbook). Pierre, SD: Cangleska, Inc.

Office of Research on Women's Health. (2002). *Women of color health data book* (02–4247). Bethesda, MD: U.S. Department of Health and Human Services.

Omi, M., & Winant, H. (1986). *Racial formation in the United States*. New York: Routledge.

Richie, B. E. (1996). *Compelled to crime: The gender entrapment of battered Black women*. New York: Routledge.

Sacred Circle National Resource Center to End Violence Against Native Women. (2000). *Role of batterers' program: Ending violence against Native women training institute*. Rapid City, SD.

Safa, H. I. (2000). Women's social movements in Latin America. In M. B. Zinn, P. Hondagneu-Sotelo, & M. A. Messner (Eds.), *Gender through the prism of difference* (pp. 467–477). Boston: Allyn & Bacon.

Silvera, M. (Ed.). (1991). *Piece of my heart: A lesbian of colour anthology*. Toronto: Sister Vision Press.

Smith, A. (1999). Sexual violence and American Indian genocide. *Journal of Religion and Abuse, 1*(2), 31–52.

Smith, A. (2001). Special report: The colors of violence against women. *ColorLines, 3*(4), 5–14.

Smith, B. (Ed.). (1983). *Home girls: A black feminist anthology*. New York: Kitchen Table: Women of Color Press.

Smith, B. (1985). Home truths on the contemporary black feminist movement. *Black Scholar, 16*(2), 4–13.

Smith, B., & Smith, B. (1983). Across the kitchen table: A sister-to-sister dialogue. In C. Moraga & G. Anzaldua (Eds.), *This bridge called my back: Writings by radical women of color* (pp. 113–127). New York: Kitchen Table: Women of Color Press.

Spector, M., & Kitsuse, J. (1973). Social problems: A reformulation. *Social Problems, 21,* 145–159.

Streitmatter, R. (1994). *Raising her voice: African American women journalists who changed history*. Lexington: University Press of Kentucky.

Tjaden, P., & Thoennes, N. (1998). *Prevalence, incidence and consequences of violence against women: Findings from* the National Violence Against Women survey. Washington, DC: U.S. Department of Justice, Office of Justice Programs, National Institute of Justice.

Tsui, K. (1983). The words of a woman who breathes fire. San Francisco: Spinsters Ink.

United States Census Bureau. (2003). U.S. Census Bureau, United States Department of Commerce. Retrieved March, 2003, from the World Wide Web: http://www.census.gov/

Vaid, U. (1995). Virtual equality: The mainstreaming of gay and lesbian liberation. New York: Anchor Books.

Warrier, S. (2002). "It's in their culture": Culture, competency and violence against women. San Francisco: Asian and Pacific Island Institute on Domestic Violence, Asian Pacific Islander American Health Forum.

Webster, Y. O. (1992). The racialization of America. New York: St. Martin's Press.

Weick, A., Rapp, C., Sullivan, W. P., & Kisthardt, W. (1989). A strengths perspective for social work practice. Social Work, 34, 350–354.

Williams, P. J. (1992). The alchemy of race and rights. Cambridge, MA: Harvard University Press.

Wing, A. K. (1997a). Brief reflections towards a multiplicative theory and practice of being. In A. K. Wing (Ed.), Critical race feminism: A reader (pp. 27–34). New York: New York University Press.

Wing, A. K. (Ed.). (1997b). Critical race feminism: A reader. New York: New York University Press.

Zaharlick, A. (2000). Southeast Asian-American women. In M. Julia (Ed.), Constructing gender: Multicultural perspectives in working with women (pp. 177–204). Belmont, CA: Wadsworth.

Social Work Practice with Lesbian, Gay, Bisexual, and Transgender People

CHAPTER 8

Nancy M. Nystrom

THE DEMOGRAPHICS OF LGBT PEOPLE

Unlike any other group that is considered "minority," communities of lesbians, gay men, bisexuals, and transgender people (LGBT) span all other spectrums of identity. We cannot create a simple dichotomy of "gay/straight" and neatly define who does or does not fit into these ascribed roles because LGBT communities are composed of individuals whose differences encompass every other societal dimension including race, ethnicity, gender, age, class, lifestyle, and locale (Seidman, 1993). Although this text recognizes the diversity of communities within LGBT identities, it can rely only on the most established and empirically valid data, which until recently focused almost exclusively on lesbian and gay people; more recent research offers long-ignored insights into the lives and experiences of bisexual and transgender people, but it is still scarce within the larger body of queer-related literature.

Although it is widely believed that roughly 10% of the population is gay or lesbian, this figure is largely misunderstood. The famous Kinsey reports on human sexuality estimated that approximately 10% had been exclusively homosexual for an extended period of time; far fewer actually identified themselves as exclusively homosexual; however, far more (37% of men and 19% of women) reported having had same-sex relations at some time in their adult lives (van Wormer, Wells, & Boes, 2000). Practitioners must be wary of using these figures as established facts, however, given the prevalence of homophobic and heterosexist attitudes and beliefs throughout a society in which disclosing an attraction to someone of the same sex is an unthinkable act for many. Moving past these barriers to disclosure to gain more accurate data is, for now, an unlikely accomplishment.

A 1997 survey conducted by *The Advocate* indicated that approximately 42% of LGBT people seek mental health services, versus roughly 10 to 12% of the general public (van Wormer et al., 2000). Meanwhile, studies on the attitudes of social workers indicate that although a small number could be defined as homophobic, many more express beliefs about heterosexuality as a "natural" or "superior" identity. At the same time, practitioners with higher amounts of social contact with LGBT people typically express less heterosexist views than do those with low exposure to communities of sexual minorities. We must keep in mind also that LGBT people make up a significant client population, and many are practitioners themselves (van Wormer, Wells, & Boes, 2000). Social workers will likely benefit personally and professionally from recognizing that a sexual minority status does not indicate a deficiency or barrier to growth and happiness but, rather, for many is a common characteristic among service recipients and providers alike.

A brief description is offered here of each community to facilitate a basic understanding. There are issues, concerns, and experiences that are of interest to all of these communities: gay, lesbian, bisexual, and transgender. There are also issues, concerns, and experiences that are unique to each (Hunter, Shannon, Knox, & Martin, 1998). For a deeper understanding of each community, it is necessary to engage in further reading of available literature and to come to know about the communities themselves.

Gay men identify and affiliate with other men. This affiliation is partly a process of identity formation, which is largely influenced by experiences and behaviors. Gay men have been affected by the institutionalization of heterosexism and masculinity in our society. Based on one's experiences of stigmatization and oppression, issues of concern will vary widely for gay men.

Lesbians constitute a different community from gay men, not only because of gender, which plays an important role, but also because of issues of concern. Lesbians are affected by sexism, an experience they share with heterosexual women. As Hunter and colleagues describe,

> One's gender is a powerful influence on how one is socialized and, consequently, on one's identity. Because of the power of gender socialization, lesbians are generally more similar to heterosexual women than to gay men, who are more similar to heterosexual men. Lesbians also share with other women the institutional oppression of sexism. (Hunter et al., 1998, p. 43)

THE HISTORICAL OPPRESSION AND SURVIVAL VALUES OF LGBT PEOPLE

For all LGBT people, the right and opportunity to develop a healthy self-image and a positive sense of identity is constrained by a long history of hostility, rejection, and marginalization directed by society toward LGBT individuals and communities (Silverstein, 1991; Warner, 1993; Whitam, 1991). This history is a result of persistent oppression by the dominant culture, based on intolerance of the difference between heterosexual norms and LGBT norms. This section is not intended to serve as a comprehensive history of LGBT people in America but, rather, to provide an overview of their struggles, barriers, and accomplishments in American social, legal, political, and cultural institutions. This basic history offers social service providers greater insight for understanding the assets, needs, and survival values of LGBT service recipients in the context of their own experiences, and the larger experiences of gay Americans.

Since the advent of Christianity, LGBT people have been vilified as sinners by various religious leaders (Victor, 1994). That LGBT people are different than heterosexuals was used by religious leaders as a tool for unifying their followers, presumably to maintain heterosexist family values and to gather financial and bureaucratic resources to support that cause (Victor, 1994; Witten, 2004). Even though vilified by church leaders as sinners, the social view was one of quiet tolerance, and therefore, LGBT people were basically left alone until the end of the second decade of the 20th century (Diamond, 1989; Victor, 1994).

Throughout early American history, criminal laws related to homosexual activity blended Biblical prohibitions with secular legal practice. Katz (2001) records 105 legal cases involving "sodomy," "buggery," or "crime against nature" during the 19th century; although these terms applied to specific behaviors (specifically, anal intercourse involving men with men, men with women, men with children, or men with animals), the inclusion of homosexual activity between men explicitly signified both a legal and societal view that consensual sex between males was behaviorally on par with acts that included bestiality, pedophilia, rape, and murder. Moreover, as American law developed during the 19th and early 20th centuries, gradually the act of fellatio became incorporated into legal definitions of sodomy as well (Hunter et al., 1998; Katz, 2001).

Meanwhile, within the societal context, lesbians endured oppression through both homophobia and gender. For lesbians of color, there exist three marginalizing factors: race, gender, and sexual orientation. Although the extent of marginalized experiences may vary with time and region, the levels of oppression and discrimination have not been markedly reduced for any lesbians in our society. The evidence of this is in the lack of passage of any noteworthy legislation that would protect lesbians from discrimination based on sexual orientation, which leaves open many opportunities to subtly or overtly discriminate against them. Despite these obstacles, lesbians have been able to build positive and full lives, with educational, community, social, and political opportunities for many (Hunter et al., 1998).

Before the early 1900s, women who were in long-term relationships with other women were referred to as having "special friendships" or, sometimes, "Boston marriages." During this time, women enjoyed few rights, particularly when it involved the ability to live independently. For example, there was no right to vote, to hold property, or to hold a job other than teaching or nursing. Even with these restrictions, however, those in "special friendships" were often able to achieve more independence and control over their lives. In addition, a growing number of young upper- and middle-class women were attending women's colleges and socializing among themselves, thus offering a view into the world at large (Hunter et al., 1998).

At the beginning of the 20th century, the studies of Freud, Ellis, and others produced a keen interest in what was considered "deviant," a medical term that included anyone whose behaviors were different from the dominant culture. Within this new field of the study of behaviors emerged a medically based view of homosexuality that conveniently reinforced existing religious and moral views. The focus on behavior enabled the likes of Freud, Krafft-Ebing, and Ellis to classify and label gays and lesbians as "deviant," and to create an environment of fear and distrust by the dominant society. With the label of "deviant," new laws and policies emerged that pathologized the lives and behaviors of gays and lesbians (Hunter et al., 1998; Whitam, 1991).

Often, however, one's likelihood of being prosecuted under such laws depended on one's place within American socioeconomic levels (Kaiser, 1997; Witten, 2004). After World War I, the population shifted to larger cities because of increased and more varied opportunities. LGBT people who could afford mobility moved to the larger cities to meet others like themselves or simply to blend into the larger population. For example, in describing the early 20th century climate for gay men in New York City, Kaiser (1997) notes significantly different experiences for wealthy gay men, compared with their lower-class counterparts. When detailing gay life in the 1930s and 1940s, one interviewee comments, "Homosexuality was an upscale thing to be. It was defined by class. There wasn't dark cruising." At the same time, however, Kaiser notes that in less upscale locations such as Times Square, "Soldiers and sailors swarmed through this teeming crossroads, and gay men pursued them with abandon" (1997, p. 13).

New York, San Francisco, Chicago, and Los Angeles became the centers for LGBT people to gather. The growth of speakeasies during Prohibition helped foster the growth of gay bar scenes in American cities, where cruising for sex in dark, anonymous venues protected men who would not or could not risk being known as "gay" or "homosexual" (Kaiser, 1997). With the population migration to larger metropolitan areas, reformers raised alarms about the tolerant atmosphere of the larger cities, using religious reasons to object to the changes occurring (Hunter et al., 1998).

These right-wing conservative groups used intimidation to promote white power through the control of education, business, and the public at large. Membership in supremacist groups such as the Ku Klux Klan grew rapidly, as did cross burnings, beatings, and lynchings (Hunter et al., 1998; Katz, 2001). Faced with this increasing hostility, and as local and state governments continued to pass laws criminalizing homosexuals (Katz, 1997), most LGBT people experienced a growing sense of necessity to live their lives in hiding.

An example illustrating how changing views become institutionalized can be found in the collaboration of medicine and law into an influential force and power structure in society referred to as "medicalization." During the 1930s, medicalization began to change the societal view so that LGBT people were viewed increasingly as "deviants" rather than as sinners, and the practitioners of psychology and related professions began to develop modes of treatment for this newly defined deviance (Hutter, 1993; Simon, 1994). This shift in the common perception of LGBT people resulted in a harsh climate of oppression in which policies were developed to exclude or eliminate LGBT people from society (Cruikshank, 1992; Hutter, 1993).

In the years leading up to World War II, the United States military sought to screen out soldiers who might pose a high risk for long-term, postwar "psychiatric casualties"; included in this category were homosexuals. This, according to Bérubé (1991), came about despite long-standing disagreements between many top psychiatrists, who believed that gay people were "abnormal" but not unfit to serve, and military leaders, who believed that such a "disorder" should disqualify an individual from service. The pressing need for able bodies during wartime, however, led to the enlistment of hundreds of thousands of young gay men, many of whom had never before met others who shared their sexual orientation. Despite anti-gay military policy, then, military life during World War II "relaxed the social constraints of peacetime that had kept gay men and women unaware of themselves and each other" (Bérubé, 1991).

Shilts (1982) notes that the massive social shifts created by World War II brought together thousands of men who had never before known words to describe their sexual identity; San Francisco in particular grew more influential among gay men because it served as a port city during the war and as a point of discharge for those in the Pacific Theater. Because of military blacklisting and the widespread search for "subversives" conducted following the war, many of these men, according to Shilts, stayed in San Francisco, and fostered among them a new political identity. Because they had already been identified by the military as gay, they had little to hide. Their willingness to publicly confront social, political, and legal institutions through public demonstrations, political campaigns, and community organizing led to San Francisco's rapid emergence as a center of gay community growth in the 1960s and 1970s (Shilts, 1982).

Meanwhile, women went to work in the factories, taking the place of the men who went off to war. Women joined the military too, becoming a major part of the support structure for those fighting at the front lines. These two new opportunities offered women experiences of a new independence, an independence they were not prepared to give up when the war ended (Hunter et al., 1998).

After World War II, the fear of the spread of communism gave rise to an increasingly conservative American society within which distrust and fear grew against anyone considered different, including lesbians and gay men (Hunter et al., 1998). The emerging fields of mental health, in seeking to increase their postwar status and influence, offered cures for homosexuality through various treatments, including involuntary commitments to mental health hospitals, lobotomies, shock treatment, and permanent classification as "deviant." These "treatments" drove most gays and lesbians deeper underground and led to the creation of new methods by which they could communicate and socialize safely. Even with the publication of the Kinsey report of 1948, few attitudes changed, and the quest by the larger society for conformity and normalcy continued. By 1950, with the formation of the House Un-American Activities Committee (HUAC) in the United States Senate, the association of perversity, communism, and homosexuals was well established in the minds of many (Hunter et al., 1998). When the chair of the HUAC, Joseph McCarthy, charged that the federal government workforce, Hollywood, unions, and other progressive groups were being controlled or infiltrated by communists and homosexuals, the intimidation became overt, with lesbians and gay men becoming the primary targets. Men and women were fired from their jobs and evicted from their apartments if there was any suspicion they were homosexual. The military began a sweep of its ranks, dishonorably discharging anyone named as gay or lesbian, and police raided homes if they received a report that indicated the possibility of a gay or lesbian in the home (Hunter et al., 1998).

Thus, the McCarthyite 1950s brought an odd mixture of social and political setbacks and advances for gay people. The exclusionary policies and treatments that were accelerated at the end of World War II through the McCarthy era had far-reaching ramifications on LGBT people as both individuals and members of communities that were increasingly stigmatized and ostracized. The previous tolerance of lesbians and gay men in society changed to one of "blame and shame," and a formal attitude and policy in most U.S. institutions of "search out and destroy" became commonplace (Hutter, 1993). At the same time, within only a few years of President Eisenhower's executive order discharging homosexuals from federal employment (*New York Times,* 2003), poet Allen Ginsberg won a heated court battle to publish *Howl,* a collection of works (including the title poem) that, among its other challenges to American society, openly celebrated the joys of gay sex, and the Mattachine Society, a gay rights organization founded in the early 1950s, won a legal battle that ensured gay publications the right to be sent via postal mail (Kaiser, 1997). The lesbian organization, the Daughters of Bilitis was formed and began publishing *The Ladder,* a newsletter directed to lesbians. In 1956, psychologist Evelyn Hooker challenged the notion that homosexuality was a mental disorder, as did the Wolfenden Report in England in 1957 (Hunter et al., 1998).

The 1960s and 1970s were turbulent times for the country and would prove to be a cornerstone of change for LGBT people. The civil rights movement, the women's movement, the anti-poverty movement, and the anti-war movement marked the beginning of a populist movement based on social justice. Young people, many of whom were gay and lesbian became active in those movements, and, in the process became more open about their own lives as LGBT people. The historical base of hiding and fear was shifting to one of personal acceptance and a growing pride, and a growing sense of bewilderment and frustration with the ongoing oppression of people based on their sexual orientation (Hunter et al., 1998; Witten, 2004).

The police protection payoff system became the focus of attention as the first step in what is now recognized as the civil rights movement for LGBT people (Kaiser, 1997). In Greenwich Village, the simmering anger and resentment toward law enforcement boiled over in June 1969, when New York City police attempted to raid the Stonewall Inn, a Village bar frequented by regular customers from the neighborhood. Kaiser (1997) described the events: "After checking for attire 'appropriate' to gender—a requirement of New York state law—the police released most of the 200 patrons. Only a couple of the employees and some of the most outrageous drag queens were arrested" (p. 198). Kaiser notes that several spectators agreed "pandemonium started" after a cross-dressing lesbian struck back at a police officer who had hit her:

> The police were pelted with pennies, dimes, and insults, as shouts of "Pigs," "Faggot cops," and "This is your payoff!" filled the night. Morty Manford remembered a rock shattering a second-floor window above the bar's entrance, which produced a collective "Ooh!" from the crowd. The raiders quickly retreated inside and bolted the heavy door behind them. But one of the demonstrators had pulled a loose parking meter out of the ground and started to use it as a battering ram. (1997, pp. 198–199)

The Stonewall Rebellion still serves as a powerful rallying point in the gay community, with most major Pride celebrations occurring within the month of June (Hunter et al., 1998; Kaiser, 1997).

The political momentum generated by the Stonewall Rebellion led gay communities across the United States to pursue more public, sustained campaigns for inclusion in mainstream America. In 1973, homosexuality was removed from the list of mental disorders in the *Diagnostic and Statistical Manual of Mental Disorders,* a move that marked the evolution of a significant change (van Wormer et al., 2000). No longer would gay and lesbian people be subjected to draconian treatments based solely on their sexual orientation. This change offered those seeking mental health services the opportunity to obtain help in dealing with presenting issues rather than continually defending themselves because of their sexual orientation.

Activism by lesbians and gay men increased both politically and socially. Gay men and lesbians have been elected to public office, appointed to leadership positions in both public and private endeavors, and are beginning to receive recognition for their community work (Hunter et al., 1998). San Francisco specifically became a center for organizing; in *The Mayor of Castro Street: The Life & Times of Harvey Milk,* Shilts (1982) chronicles the years of conflict, struggle, triumph, and tragedy of San Francisco's gay community. The Castro District in the 1970s, Shilts notes, became a nationally recognized weather vane for gay-related issues. For example, when the Anita Bryant–led 1977 campaign succeeded in repealing the Dade County, Florida, anti-discrimination law protecting sexual orientation, Castro residents took to the streets in a crowd of roughly 3,000, shouting "We are your children" and "Two, four, six, eight, separate the church and state" (Shilts, 1982).

Harvey Milk, a camera shop owner in the Castro, emerged as the city's most visible community leader. His 1977 election to the San Francisco Board of Supervisors marked the first time an openly gay politician was elected to public office in the United States (Shilts, 1982). When, in 1978, Milk and Mayor George Moscone were shot to death by Supervisor Dan White, an estimated 40,000 marchers participated in a subdued candlelight procession from the Castro to City Hall; several months later, when a jury found White guilty of manslaughter based on the now-infamous "Twinkie defense," the city's LGBT communities erupted into massive riots, bringing further national attention not only to LGBT communities, but also the cumulative impact of years of violence, repression, and exclusion lesbians, gay men, bisexuals, and transgenders have experienced in American life (Shilts, 1982).

Shilts' 1987 bestseller *And the Band Played On* provides in-depth detail of the negative impact of homophobia on the LGBT communities, as accepted policies, practices, and beliefs throughout the human services were challenged by the onset of the AIDS pandemic. HIV/AIDS continues to be an issue of importance for gay and bisexual men in the United States. As of 2001, 46% of all reported AIDS cases in the United States were men who have sex with men, and 6% of all cases were men who have sex with men and use injection drugs (CDC, 2001a). Approximately 70% of new HIV infections occur among men, and 60% of those infections occur among men who have sex with other men (CDC, 2001).

The ordeal endured by hundreds of thousands of gay and bisexual men revealed to American society the severe degree of pain and hardship endured by individuals who were coping with both a devastating illness and the suspicion and paranoia of a homophobic culture. Yet, the LGBT communities also demonstrated leadership in the fight against HIV through education, support for safer sex practices, and targeting interventions toward areas at high risk for infection, such as bars and bathhouses (Shilts, 1988). The NAMES Project, in which quilt squares were made to memorialize those who had died from AIDS, struck an emotional chord with many American people. They had gradually come to see that people living with AIDS, and especially gay men, were human beings with lives and relationships that were much larger than, but not exclusive from, their health status or sexual practices (Hunter et al., 1998).

According to the Centers for Disease Control (2001a), "During the mid-to-late 1990s, advances in HIV treatments led to dramatic declines in AIDS deaths and slowed the progression from HIV to AIDS . . . Better treatments have also led to an increasing number of people living with AIDS in this country." Thus, in the 1990s, HIV/AIDS came to be known less as a "gay disease," but it still remained a serious issue within the gay and bisexual male communities. Approximately 42% of all new HIV infections occur in men who have sex with men. This is still the largest proportion of new infections in the United States (CDC, 2001b).

The late 1990s brought to light other serious issues regarding the oppression of gay, lesbian, bisexual, and transgender people. When University of Wyoming student Matthew Shepard was found hanging from a fencepost, beaten beyond recognition and left to die, the reality of the dangers faced by gay and bisexual men within their own communities gained national attention and discussion (Herek, 1992; Hunter et al., 1998; Witten, 2004). Similarly, when the brutal murder of Brandon Teena, a young transgender person, captured audiences' emotions in the 1999 film *Boys Don't Cry*, mainstream Americans began to learn of the unique dangers faced by those who transgress Western gender norms (Herek, 1992; Hunter et al., 1998; Witten, 2004). For her portrayal of Teena, Hilary Swank won an Oscar award for Best Actress, bringing previously unheard of attention to transgender lives and experiences. In 2000, Moises Kauffman's play *The Laramie Project* exploded onto New York's theater scene, stunning audiences nationwide with an overwhelmingly emotional chronicle of Shepard's killing in a town that many perceived as typically American. The play went on to be performed in towns across the United States, and later was adapted to television by HBO. Still, reports of anti-LGBT attacks continue to pepper headlines in queer community newspapers. For all the attention garnered by the brutal murders of Shepard and Teena, anti–hate crime laws remain largely absent from state, local, and federal law.

Even with gains in public support for gays, lesbians, bisexuals, and transgender people, homophobia and heterosexism are still major societal problems. Still, with the entry of queer-related issues into mainstream discourse, and with the recognition recently bestowed by the U.S. Supreme Court in *Lawrence v. Texas* (2003) on the legal validity of same-sex relationships, today LGBT liberation continues to evolve. Visibility continues to grow as more continue stepping forward and coming out. More lesbians, gay men, bisexuals, and transgenders have moved into the mainstream, some with children and homes in the suburbs. Understanding the history of oppression that shapes the lives and history of lesbians, gay men, bisexuals, and transgenders in the United States does not, however, completely equip social service practitioners with culturally competent skills and knowledge. To more fully understand LGBT oppression in history, culturally competent practitioners should also know how this oppression has manifested itself in practice (Ritter & Terndrup, 2002).

History clearly demonstrates that since the latter half of the 20th century, discrimination against LGBT people has escalated in the United States. Men and women have been fired from jobs and evicted from housing with discovery of their sexual orientation, or in many cases even if their sexual orientation has been only suspected (Herek, 1992; Witten, 2004). It had been common for police to raid private homes in the hopes of finding a gay or lesbian household and subsequently arrest the residents, although during the last 10 years fewer states have routinely practiced this policy (Herek, 1992). Children have been, and continue to be, routinely removed from the custody of a caregiving parent if the parent is accused of being, or found to be, gay or lesbian. Similarly, in addition to lack of custodial rights where children are concerned, LGBT couples have no legal standing relating to caregiver rights, hospital visitation, or property rights (Cruikshank, 1992; Herek, 1992; Silverstein, 1991; Witten, 2004). Violence against LGBT people has continued to escalate as LGBT civil rights activists demand recognition of their rights (Herek, 1991; Witten, 2004; Young, 1990).

The consequences of these patterns of oppression of lesbian and gay populations are numerous and affect virtually every aspect of their lives (Warner, 1993; Witten, 2004). Although some may become angry at discriminatory practices and become activists in the quest for the rights accorded everyone else, many others live a life of fear and hiding, denying themselves the freedom to be themselves to be safe (Herek, 1991; Weston, 1991; Witten, 2004).

Because of these oppressive conditions, LGBT people maintain a significant level of mistrust toward social institutions in general, and the mental health system in this country in particular. The mistrust of the mental health system is a direct result of the field's active complicity in the construction of oppressive definitions of deviance and the negative labeling of LGBT people, which has greatly enhanced the institutionalized oppression which LGBT people experience (Herek, 1992; Ritter & Terndrup, 2002; Silverstein, 1991; Witten, 2004). This mistrust constitutes a critical social issue because the public and private mental health care systems are major parts of the social and health service infrastructure in the United States.

The fields within social science (e.g., social work, psychology, and sociology) have done much to lead the way in areas of diversity and cultural awareness dealing with ethnic, race, and gender equality (Pinderhughes, 1989). In the social science literature, however, there is a noticeable silence about equality based on sexual orientation (Whitam, 1991; Witten, 2004). Although much is written about the pathology, or lack thereof, attached to LGBT life, the social services systems in this society have not yet substantially addressed the issue of whether or not there is a problem in the delivery of services to LGBT populations (Ball, 1994; D'Augelli, 1993; Dunkle, 1994; Foster, Stevens, & Hall, 1994; Greene, 1994; Hall, 1994a; Hunter et al., 1998; McHenry & Johnson, 1994; Perkins, 1991; Ritter & Terndrup, 2002; Wisniewski & Toomey, 1987; Witten, 2004).

There is some question about whether LGBT people even need to see mental health therapists. Instead, some have argued that LGBT people have been convinced they need mental health services because of the constructed view of deviance rampant in society and the resulting internalized oppression (Warner, 1993).

Historically, the treatment of LGBT people has been determined by collective views created by the confluence of religion, politics, and law in societies (Hutter, 1993). For example, homosexuality was not viewed as a pathology until 1850, with the emergence of formal theories of sexual functioning and behaviors (Friend, 1991; Hutter, 1993; Silverstein, 1991; Smith, 1988; Vance, 1991).

Within the prevailing classification of deviance, LGBT people have been constructed as being a danger to society. LGBT people have been labeled as perverts, predators upon children, practitioners of bestiality, and people incapable of moral or sexual self-control (Silverstein, 1991). Although research has found that these labels are invalid, LGBT people have, to varying degrees, assimilated these messages and labels in a process called internalized homophobia (Gonsiorek, 1991; Ritter & Terndrup, 2002; Silverstein, 1991).

Mental health researchers have not questioned their interest in studying LGBT people from a perspective of deviancy. They have focused on behaviors suggested by labeling and internalized homophobia, with the assumption that the stereotypes asserted about LGBT people are factual. They do not consider whether some behaviors might be normative within LGBT cultures, and, thus, they perpetuate stereotypes and myths (Gonsiorek, 1991).

Collective patterns of interpretation regarding human sexuality are produced and reinforced by medical science. The medicalization of homosexuality gave power to those in mental health and in law to remove from the society those whom they classified as deviant and to determine "appropriate" treatment for these individuals (Ross, Paulsen, & Stalstrom, 1988; Scull, 1977; Witten, 2004). Yet, medicalization in the mental health field is based on social construction, founded on societal pressures, where agents of law and medicine are jointly used to enforce norms, while subject to the prevailing prejudices and politics of the time (Victor, 1994). Because of the constructed societal view, LGBT people have been treated both as criminals and as mentally ill (Hutter, 1993). From the outset, then, mental health practice with LGBT people could not be a neutral practice; instead, it has been informed and driven by those in society with an agenda of oppression against those who are different from those in the dominant group (Scull, 1977; Silverstein, 1991; Witten, 2004).

For LGBT people, the institutionalization of beliefs, values, and norms by a society in which they are a minority and not given voice has been crucial in the perpetuation of destructive stereotypes, oppression, and blatant discrimination. Attempts to change societal views have been met with resistance by the majority population and met with silence by those in the mental health fields (McHenry & Johnson, 1994).

Discrimination is often tied to status characteristics (Ridgeway & Walker, 1995). Characteristics such as age, gender, sexual orientation, race, ethnicity, income, education level, and professional status symbolize, affect, and signal social power, or the lack thereof, and may result in different treatment in social and institutional settings (Ridgeway & Walker, 1995). It would be expected that respondents who are women, lesbians, people of color, and older and have less education or professional status will have had previous experiences in which they have been discriminated against, for any one or a combination of these characteristics. This negative experience in turn causes them to have higher expectations of discriminatory treatment from mental health therapists (Davison, 1991; Silverstein, 1991; Witten, 2004).

Few people even realize that the word *homosexuality* is only a recent addition to the English lexicon. Coined in 1869 by a Hungarian physician, it has become the term of choice for categorizing LGBT people in strictly behavioral language (van Wormer et al., 2000). Effectively, this allows the dominant culture to formulate long-standing attitudes about sinfulness, criminality, and sickness into supposedly value-neutral, pseudoscientific positions that claim to merely reflect objective truth. The ongoing struggle by activists to be recognized as gay or lesbian, and to reclaim derogatory terms such as "queer" or "dyke," reflects more than a simple debate about semantics. The battle over language symbolizes a much deeper struggle for power and control of history, identity, and community. The emphasis of the terms "gay" and "lesbian" is a purposeful step to instill pride in each individual, rather than to accept the medicalized term of "homosexual" with its attending meanings of disorder or pathology as ascribed in history (Hunter et al., 1998; Kochman, 1997).

Seidman (1993) cites Katz's work that describes how, before the 20th century, depictions of same-sex relationships bore little resemblance to what today is categorized as "gay" or "homosexual." Moreover, he points out that the notion of *heterosexuality* was also absent from popular discourse. This dualistic, oppositional view generates false notions of a polarized "gay versus straight" and ignores the multitude of differences that exist within these categories. Thus, as the struggle for liberation continues, it reveals countless oppositions throughout people's identities and further complicates the notion of a simple "hetero versus homo" debate (Hunter et al., 1998). We should expect that, just as the past century has recorded a significant shift in the visibility of nonmajority sexual identities, we will continue to see changes in language as LGBT communities grow and change (Hunter et al., 1998).

In addition to the struggle to overcome oppression in language and discourse, LGBT people have used a diverse range of skills to cope and survive in a sexist and homophobic culture. Some of the earliest research with gay men detailed the significance of bar life in many social and support networks (Christian & Keefe, 1997). Community support groups, ranging from coming out issues to couples groups, substance abuse, grief, and more have arisen to help LGBT people find assistance among their peers and cohorts (Cruikshank, 1992).

Across the globe in June, annual Pride celebrations mark the anniversary of the Stonewall Rebellion. The vivid, diverse displays of affirmation and affection both show the world that LGBT people are proud of who they are and that they will fight if necessary to protect themselves and their communities from violence and repression. Often, along with concerts, parades, and rallies, community members may dress as drag queens and kings for show or celebration, as a playful way of publicly defying fixed gender roles and of commemorating the role that people in drag played during the Stonewall battles.

As the visibility of LGBT people has grown, neighborhoods such as San Francisco's Castro, Greenwich Village in New York, and Chicago's Boystown have become centers of thriving communities that offer bars, shops, community centers, parks, and more. Although understanding that an LGBT individual cannot find everything she or he is seeking in one distinct area, the presence of these districts has offered sanctuary, acceptance, and connection to people who otherwise have felt isolated, vulnerable, and frightened (Hunter et al., 1998). Moreover, awareness of these districts in major urban places has served as a beacon to bring individuals living in rural, isolated areas closer to other LGBT people (Hunter et al., 1998).

To have reached the point of disclosing one's identity as a gay man or lesbian, a person has already endured a number of challenges from the micro, meso, and macro systems in which she or he operates. Even the presence of supportive, accepting loved ones at the interpersonal level does not negate the levels of discrimination, violence, hatred, and shaming that occur in the larger systems of American life (Ritter & Terndrup, 2002). Old LGBT people especially have witnessed a tremendous change in the visibility of their communities during their life spans, across culture, religions, careers, families, and interpersonal relationships (Jones & Nystrom, 2002).

For openly identified LGBT people, coming out is a key issue that defines all relevant survival values. Simply reflecting back to a client her or his own views, or awkwardly offering one's "tolerance" or "acceptance," does not indicate that a practitioner understands the sincere contemplation and emotional work that the client has put into establishing sufficient trust to share this knowledge (Ritter & Terndrup, 2002). A culturally competent practitioner working with LGBT people, while acknowledging the larger problems facing gay-identified people, will recognize the achievement an individual has made when, despite overwhelming pressures to survive by "passing" as heterosexual, she or he asserts, "I am gay." Doing so, whether in an intimate practice setting or a larger community, makes a whole range of personal, private thought and effort public and, in many ways, more meaningful for the person claiming a gay identity for her- or himself (Ritter & Terndrup, 2002).

CULTURALLY COMPETENT KNOWLEDGE THEORY AND PRACTICE SKILLS FOR LGBT PEOPLE

The first barrier any social service provider will need to address with LGBT people is the long-standing, institutional oppression of their communities by the helping professions. We are only 30 years removed from the American Psychiatric Association's declassification of homosexuality as a mental illness and sexual deviation, and the *DSM-IV* still lists gender identity disorder as a condition manifested in children (van Wormer et al., 2000). Lindhorst (1997) cites DeCrescenzo's 1984 study showing that social workers may be more homophobic than either psychiatrists or psychologists. As a result of the medicalization of LGBT life, both the feminist movement and the gay liberation movement have focused their politics against those institutions that have used the medical model to create homophobic norms that have lead to oppression of LGBT people (Seidman, 1993; Smith, 1997).

To even categorize lesbian, gay, bisexual, and transgender persons as a single community overlooks the reality that they are actually four distinct groups (Hunter et al., 1998). Culturally competent practice, then, is more than simply acknowledging and tolerating a service recipient with an LGBT orientation. The practitioner must also demonstrate knowledge of issues unique to each community, with the understanding that individuals may or may not relate to such a categorization (Hunter et al., 1998).

For lesbians, ongoing issues of importance include social networks/social isolation, relationship stability, financial stability, health care, discrimination and violence, community, and alcohol and substance abuse (Hunter et al., 1998; Jones & Nystrom, 2002).

For gay men, relevant issues include HIV/AIDS, medical care, grief and loss, alcohol and substance abuse, social isolation and social networks, and discrimination and violence (van Wormer et al., 2000).

For bisexual people, issues of concern may include identity issues within heterosexual and gay communities, discrimination, HIV/AIDS, social networks, and relationship stability (Hunter et al., 1998).

For transgender people, important issues include employment and financial stability; social isolation; safety and violence; health care; access to insurance, Medicaid, or Medicare; competent mental health service; and living environments (Witten, 2004).

Because anti-LGBT prejudice still often leads to violence, a real fear of disclosure may exist in settings where a person is uncertain about what information will or will not be shared by the practitioner with others. This is particularly true for work with LGBT people in rural settings, where everyone is part of a much smaller community and the actions of everyone are more apparent. The need to conform to the community's social values is critical, which influences both the client and the practitioner. Boulden (2001) describes how for many gay men outside of urban centers, "don't ask, don't tell" is often the prevalent cultural expectation. As such, then, it becomes very difficult for a practitioner to remain bias free without being noticed within the community (Foster, 1997).

LGBT people have been "multicultural people, having to learn to exist in at least two cultures simultaneously" (Jones & Nystrom, 2002; Metz, 1997). LGBT people are socialized within the dominant culture, and only later begin to identify with their lesbian, gay, bisexual, or transgender culture, in contrast with members of other minority groups who are socialized first by their own groups, then later by the dominant group (Ritter & Terndrup, 2002; van Wormer et al., 2000). Thus, social workers will encounter LGBT people at many different stages of identity formation. It is not the job of the practitioner to determine the trajectory of the client's coming-out process. For many, this process is an ongoing, lifelong event, given that in a heterosexist society, one must continue to combat the assumption that heterosexuality is a superior, more ideal identity (Metz, 1997). By first acknowledging the achievement of coming out, and then focusing on strengths or assets within the client, a practitioner moves the helping relationship to a level where self-actualization and growth are more likely to occur (Ritter & Terndrup, 2002).

CONTACT SKILLS WITH LGBT PEOPLE

Recently, research has begun to document the problematic history of the mental health system with respect to the LGBT communities (Herek, 1992; Silverstein, 1991). Most research has focused on the concerns LGBT people have when receiving treatment, highlighting the mistrust many experience in seeking help (Hall, 1994b; Trippett, 1994). This is a major problem because a significant body of research in counseling and psychotherapy has identified trust as a key element in successful treatment outcomes. Client trust of the counselor is, thus, crucial to the successful achievement of the counseling goals set forth by the client and counselor (Ritter & Terndrup, 2002; Watkins & Terrell, 1988). The client's perception of the quality of mental health services received seems to be related to the client's trust in the therapist (Silverstein, 1991).

Social workers will better serve their lesbian and gay male clients by working diligently throughout the process to more fully know themselves and their own feelings regarding homosexuality. Because coming out itself requires LGBT people to establish trust in a relationship, the practitioner affirms this work by offering back to the client her or his most authentic self. If a practitioner is tolerant of LGBT people but is personally repulsed by the idea of LGBT public displays of identity or affection, she or he needs to seriously consider whether or not she or he can effectively work with members of these communities (Ritter & Terndrup, 2002). Practitioners must guard against the more subtle forms of homophobia, such as lack of acknowledgement of the special stresses faced by LGBT people, drifting from the presenting issues, or refocusing on the person's sexual orientation rather than the issues brought forth by the client (Friedman, 1997).

Van Wormer and colleagues (2000) and Bricker-Jenkins (1991) propose the following guidelines for strengths-based practice with LGBT people:

> *Seek the positive* in terms of people's coping skills and you will find it; look beyond presenting symptoms and setbacks; and encourage clients to identify their talents, dreams, insights, and courage.
>
> *Listen to the personal narrative,* the telling of one's own story in one's own voice, a story that ultimately may be reframed in light of new awareness of unrealized personal strength.
>
> *Validate the pain* where pain exists; reinforce persistent efforts to alleviate the pain (of themselves and others) and help people recover from the specific injuries of oppression, neglect, and domination.
>
> *Don't dictate: collaborate* through an agreed upon, mutual discovery of solutions among helpers, families, and support networks. Validation and collaboration are integral steps in a consciousness-raising process that can lead to healing and empowerment. (Bricker-Jenkins, 1991)
>
> *Move from self-actualization to transformation of oppressive structure,* from individual strength to a higher connectedness. (van Wormer et al., 2000, pp. 20–21)

Effective referrals with LGBT communities require that the practitioner take the time to know what is available in her or his area for LGBT people. Large urban areas are likely to have more easily identifiable gay communities and resources (Smith, 1997), but for individuals in rural areas, access to basic mental health services may be limited already, let alone access to LGBT-affirming professionals (Lindhorst, 1997). Moreover, an LGBT person may be less likely to encounter others through formal organizations than through chance encounters (Boulden, 2001). Knowing which resources exist and where they are located, their purpose, and whether or not they will be helpful to gay male and lesbian clients becomes even more critical the further one is removed from large cities. Also, different resources and needs occur along the spectrum of age, where different social groups exist to provide community members access to activities, support, and fellowship among peers (Jones & Nystrom, 2002).

To truly put her- or himself in the client's shoes, the practitioner will search, ask questions, and seek out those who know the appropriate answers. Understand that the LGBT communities themselves are assets to individuals, *and* that LGBT colleagues can assist in the search for resources as well. Appropriately, to effectively assist LGBT service recipients, a conscientious practitioner will go through a coming-out process of her or his own, as an ally to the community. Taking this step empowers the social worker to understand more fully the spectrum of identities, sexual or otherwise, within which she or he operates on a daily basis (Ritter & Terndrup, 2002; van Wormer et al., 2000).

Problem Identification Skills with LGBT People

Christian and Keefe (1997) note the existence of heterosexist bias in the research of gay male populations when life satisfaction in older men was correlated with being part of a long-term relationship. This is a telling example of how easily professionals will ascribe their own norms and values to those of different populations. Because government institutions still fail to recognize the validity of LGBT relationships, many LGBT people have used this lack of sanction to explore different dynamics of intimacy, long-term partnership, and affiliation. What a practitioner may perceive as problematic may in fact be viewed by the service recipient, and her or his social group, as an asset (Ritter & Terndrup, 2002).

Practitioners and clients must also work through the prevalence of anti-gay stereotypes and mischaracterizations. The generalization that gay men are likely to have had more sexual encounters than average and that the rise of HIV/AIDS led them to pursue long-term relationships, ignores evidence that many men chose long-term relationships for years before the emergence of AIDS in the gay community. Also, the notion that gay teachers might "entice" students into homosexuality by being open ignores not only existing data but also the possibility that gay youth themselves are actively seeking information, resources, and positive role models. This stereotype is particularly damaging given growing evidence of a high suicide rate among LGBT adolescents (Kulkin, Chauvin, & Percle, 2000). Also, the assumption that gay culture focuses exclusively on youth inhibits any recognition of the ways in which LGBT people have successfully handled the challenges of living past age 40 (Kochman, 1997).

Research dating back to Evelyn Hooker's historic studies of gay men in the 1950s and 1960s has shown that for mental health issues, gay-identified people are indistinguishable from non–gay-identified people (Cruikshank, 1992).

At the macro level, however, structures of oppression including racism, sexism, homophobia, and heterosexism produce cultural conditions that inhibit the lives and well-being of LGBT people across race, ethnicity, religious affiliation, income level, gender, age, social class, and location (Hunter et al., 1998).

For most, sexism is defined as a belief that gender or sexual orientation gives rights, privileges, and power to some while denying such rights, privileges, and power to those who do not conform to the identity norms that maintain power for heterosexual men (Seidman, 1993). Further, Cruikshank (1992) argues that attacks on LGBT people are punishment for not reproducing, a racist fear of loss of power or domination by white men.

These observations became more readily apparent, Seidman (1993) observes, as gay liberation movements themselves grew and became more conscious of the diverse issues within its communities. By having to confront and work through racism within LGBT communities, and understanding how white LGBT men and women may, knowingly or unknowingly, operate to oppress LGBT people of color, activists have challenged the notion of a unitary gay identity. Recognizing the multitude of identities, oppressions, conflicts, and struggles that are encompassed within LGBT cultures, we move closer to recognizing the harmful, and inherently false representation of a simple "gay versus straight" dichotomy perpetuated by mainstream institutions, including the social sciences and helping professions (Hunter et al., 1998).

Problem identification with LGBT people should include an honest assessment of the cultural barriers still working against their communities. However, there must also be an honest attempt to inventory the work that has been done to confront these oppressive structures and create positive change (Ritter & Terndrup, 2002). For example, at an interpersonal level, a client who is beginning the coming-out process may only have a nominal sense of the history related to the community with which she or he is beginning to find an identity. Or, a social group that is working to organize its members to take action may seek out information on what has or has not worked in other settings. Reframing perceived problems, using a structural analysis and historical insights, encourages service recipients to see themselves in the context of larger issues and communities. Moreover, these steps proactively move an individual away from the emotional pain of isolation and loneliness by stimulating their awareness of others who have shared and confronted similar challenges (Ritter & Terndrup, 2002).

Assessment Skills with LGBT People

As we would expect in any assessment, a practitioner is obligated to focus first and foremost on the client's presenting issues. Although there is little or no difference between biopsychosocial assessment applications for LGBT people and other populations, practitioners need to be even more strongly aware of the history of terms, movements, barriers, and beliefs related to sexual orientation. Moreover, in a culture in which, at the macro level, homophobia and

<table>
<tr><td>**CASE**</td><td></td></tr>
</table>

Case Study Integration Exercise on Contact, Problem Identification, and Assessment Skills

Annie, age 68, and Sue, age 72, live in Boston and have been together for 26 years. Annie is white and Irish-Catholic; Sue is African American. A retired middle-school teacher and professional cellist, respectively, they have led an active life together, frequently traveling and taking great interest in cultural events and the arts. Sue is a very active gardener; she loves doing yard work, while Annie enjoys maintaining their house and cooking. Although both are "out" about their identities and their long-term relationship, neither is active in the Boston lesbian scene, which they consider to be oriented too much to youth and politics for their participation.

Last year, Sue broke her hip, and has undergone a slow, somewhat painful recovery process. The injury and subsequent recovery have forced her to give up most of her favorite activities; she cannot spend time working in the yard, nor can she maintain the posture or technique necessary to play the cello. Moreover, she still needs to use a walker to move about the house, and driving herself is out of the question. Although she sees her physician regularly and attends physical therapy, the recovery is taking longer than expected. Although she claims she is not depressed, Sue frequently feels tired and spends much more time watching television than she ever did before. She has withdrawn from contact with most of her friends, especially those with whom she performed as a musician. She declines to attend when invited to social functions, and when visitors come to see her and Annie, she usually withdraws early, citing her need to rest.

Annie has assumed sole responsibility of caring for Sue. She feeds, bathes, dresses, and transports Sue to her appointments, picks up prescriptions, and tries to arrange activities to cheer Sue up. Also, in addition to the housework that she has always done, Annie has made efforts to maintain the yard and garden, so that Sue will not see them fall into disrepair. Annie misses their artistic and cultural outings, especially those to area museums, galleries, and concerts. When she urges Sue to go, Sue typically tells her to just go on ahead, or "Find someone else to go with you." Like Sue, Annie is also tired and frustrated. She has tried to support and encourage Sue, but after being rebuffed a number of times, she has grown weary.

Because of the stagnant recovery process, and the noticeable shift in Annie and Sue's interactions, Sue's physician referred them to Joan, a geriatric social worker. Age 44, white, and Jewish, Joan has worked for 15 years with old adults. Although she is not lesbian, she has worked with several clients who are older LGBT people, and she feels comfortable interacting with their communities. After initial resistance, Sue agreed to accompany Annie to meet Joan at her office. As they shared the story of the past year, Joan listened sympathetically, asked a few brief questions, and expressed admiration for the ways in which both Annie and Sue have coped with the situation in which they have found themselves. She also asked a few leading,

---

heterosexism abound, the need for an asset-based focus is even more apparent (Nystrom & Jones, 2003). LGBT people already hear from a number of different sources that they are, or that they have, problems. To hear it again from a social worker does little to help them empower themselves and does a

open-ended questions to determine how long they had been together, and to learn of the ways in which they have built a life together across a number of challenges.

Joan's empathic, open approach gave Sue and Annie space to feel comfortable sharing their experiences with her. She did not hasten to inform them of her different sexual orientation, but did share details about her own experiences, and those of friends and loved ones who were gay or lesbian-identified. This also gave Joan an opportunity to ask a few questions about family backgrounds and about the challenges of maintaining a racially mixed lesbian relationship for nearly three decades. Sue especially grew more visibly relaxed, and soon Joan was able to direct the conversation toward identifying the challenges facing the couple.

Sue began by saying that she knew she had become more of a bother to Annie, that she hates not being able to do things for herself, and that she is frequently angry with herself both for breaking her hip and for not recovering more rapidly. It has been particularly heartbreaking for her to not play the cello, she said, and listening to old concerts or seeing her musician friends does little to comfort her because it reminds her of what she can no longer do. Annie spoke up, saying that she absolutely does not consider Sue a burden, that she would do whatever was necessary to help the recovery along. However, she said, she was worried; Sue's appetite had decreased, she slept more frequently, and Annie was less sure of how she could perk Sue up.

Joan carefully shifted the conversation toward the recovery process, asking Sue to take her through the steps she had taken to get well, and where she had seen unexpected barriers arise. Sue spoke well of her doctor, but said she had difficulty relating to her physical therapist, "A skinny little kid right out of college who comes at me like I'm in a cheerleading camp." She felt that not only could the younger woman not relate to her age difference, but also that she could not personally connect in any way other than her therapy regimen.

Annie spoke up then, suggesting that Sue would have more energy for her physical therapy if she would just eat more, to which Sue answered, "I'm not gonna eat if I don't feel hungry!" Joan, then, noted that typically older adults do lose some appetite, and that, as long as Sue was eating, they should expect this as a part of the normal aging process. She used this as an opportunity, then, to discuss how there may be two distinct sets of challenges occurring for Sue and Annie: one related to Sue's hip injury, and the other to the adjustments people are forced to make as they grow old.

Joan noted that overall, Sue likes her primary physician, but feels frustrated working with her physical therapist. Also, because so many of her favorite activities involved physical mobility, Sue is grieving her perceived loss of efficacy. Moreover, she feels that she has lost a vital connection to many of her peers. Annie, meanwhile, is deeply invested in helping Sue recover, but is overwhelmed from having to do it alone. Moreover, both women are moving into later years in which their capacities are changing; how do they know what is normal, and what is related to the stresses of the recovery process?

great deal to continue enforcing the negative consequences of their ascribed identity (Nystrom & Jones, 2003).

As the LGBT communities grew in public visibility, so also came the emergence of subcultures within. In other words, once the larger heterosexist culture was challenged, subgroups within gay culture felt more emboldened to make similar strides in their own communities. Liberation, in effect, spread through the movement as people grew into their voices and assumed a stance of self-determined resistance to the threat of shame and retribution, even if it meant challenging the assumed leaders of the LGBT movements (Seidman, 1993).

Although offered in the context of work with gay and lesbian elders, Metz's (1997) guidelines for staff development hold true across a spectrum of diverse groups: (1) to listen to each other with respect and sensitivity; (2) to work hard at understanding racism, classism, ageism, sexism, and heterosexism in ourselves and in our institutions; (3) to become aware of words or phrases in our language that dehumanize people whose racial, ethnic, or class background and sexual orientation differ from our own. This work is critical to establishing a safe space in which gay male and lesbian service recipients feel safe, free of discrimination, and above all else, welcome in the helping relationship (Metz, 1997).

To an extent, one's membership in the lesbian, gay male, bisexual, and transgender communities is chosen by the personal and, therefore, political forces that shape each individual's experiences. Certainly this is defined largely by the opposition of other cultural institutions, but LGBT cultures have generated a substantial amount of artistic, literary, and social movement. Also, the development of electronic networking has offered opportunities for individuals to overcome isolation to seek out resources and support, such as electronic bulletin boards and chat rooms with more anonymity (Haag & Chang, 1997). Understanding these as assets in social service practice, professionals equip themselves with a more fully prepared knowledge of assets for individuals and communities with whom they work.

Intervention Skills with LGBT People

We have already noted the need for social workers to focus on the strengths or assets of clients and their communities. To most effectively assist their clients, however, social workers must strive to enact change at micro, meso, and macro levels of influence. By working to stay fully aware of larger changes in communities of LGBT people, a practitioner will possess a broad range of ideas and resources to offer clients when engaging in goal and role formation. Moreover, the practitioner aids clients by working within her or his own agency to establish a more LGBT-affirming practice environment. And, by recognizing the value of structures within clients' own social groups, we validate their abilities to make positive life choices and grant them the possibility of being the expert on their own experiences (Ritter & Terndrup, 2002).

For someone who is lesbian, gay, bisexual, or transgender, attempts to assimilate into the mainstream do not negate the fact that he or she will always be perceived as different, a minority. This perception can be internal or external and may only change when society works to eliminate all symbols of homophobia (Cruikshank, 1992). Recognizing the truth in this statement, social workers must strive to be congruent in both their private dealings with clients and their public beliefs and. attitudes. To offer effective services to LGBT clients, social workers must offer effective advocacy as well. By coming out, an individual already engages in emotional work beyond what is typical for many people during identity formation. LGBT people who move into more publicly active spheres take on additional emotional work by exposing themselves to potential backlash, violence, discrimination, and isolation. The social worker who commits to publicly supporting LGBT community issues honors the efforts of her or his clients and affirms the integrity of their intervention strategies (Ritter & Terndrup, 2002).

At the agency level, Metz (1997) proposes a seven-step process, known as R-E-S-P-E-C-T, for bridging gaps between LGBT people and social service providers:

> *Review* existing practices and policies in the agency. How are lesbian/gay residents, clients, consumers and staff treated at the present time?
>
> *Education* of administration, staff and residents about a range of taboo topics such as human sexualities, gender differences, and the many kinds of human relationships.
>
> *Sharing* ideas and experiences for the unlearning of homophobia and heterosexism. Some staff members may reveal that they have a lesbian or gay relative or friend; they may themselves be gay or lesbian, and by revealing this in a safe environment, become a force of agent for change within the agency.
>
> *Promotion* of diversity and the *prevention* of homophobic practices. A comparison of heterosexism with the other "isms" of racism, sexism, classism, and ageism is a helpful way to alert staff to this form of discrimination of non-heterosexual people.
>
> *Exploration and evaluation* of areas for continued learning and teaching. The bridging process is an ongoing one that needs to be informed by the changing climate in society, policy development and increased knowledge on the part of social service providers.
>
> *Change* can be one of the most difficult steps of the seven step process. Human beings and the systems they create tend to be resistant to the change process. Persons tend to change when they see valued others changing and when they are actively involved in the planning and implementation of change.
>
> *Transition* to a diversity-friendly facility and practice . . . requires continued support and attention by administrators. Teaming people who have greater levels of comfort with others who are resistant or uncomfortable is one way of supporting the transition. Providing a safe place where specific questions can be asked about gay and lesbian relationships and discussion of myths and stereotypes encourages people to examine their knowledge and experience base with the opportunity to modify and change their perceptions. (Metz, 1997, pp. 39–41)

When embracing oneself as different from the perceived sexual majority has been a life-taking risk, LGBT people have found ways to build movements that simultaneously challenged the status quo and themselves to grow, change,

| CASE | **Case Study Integration Exercise on Intervention and Termination Skills** |

Joan presented a detailed care plan to Sue and Annie that used a variety of intervention strategies. First, she offered to work with Sue's physician to find a physical therapist more competent in geriatric practice, so that Sue might feel more comfortable doing her exercises and discussing any problems arising during the process. Second, Joan would arrange for a respite care worker to come twice a week to help with Sue's meals, transportation, and hygiene, thus allowing Annie a chance to rest and take care of her own needs. Third, Joan, added, she knew of a community center near Sue and Annie's neighborhood where older adults had opportunities to interact, to take or even teach art and music classes, and to go on regular group outings to cultural events in the Boston area. Finally, she asked if either Sue or Annie had heard of a group called "Women Out for Weekends." They answered that they had not. Joan then described WOW, a Boston-area group for lesbian women age 60 and above that, once a month, holds a weekend series of events that range from potlucks to guest speakers to concerts and film screenings. The purpose, she said, was to give older lesbians a chance to meet, socialize, and enjoy themselves in the company of their peers.

Joan's plan, she hoped, would help improve the progress of Sue's recovery process by putting her in touch with professionals who were better suited to her age-related needs and challenges. Second, by giving Annie a break from her caretaking roles, Joan hoped to alleviate some of the stress that both women were feeling toward each other. Next, she hoped to reconnect them, especially Annie, with communities who appreciated the same interests and activities, and who also knew firsthand the challenges of having to change roles and responsibilities because of shifts in individual capacities. Finally, Joan hoped to connect them

---

and take care of their own needs. In the 1980s, Cruikshank (1992) notes, the rise of women-centered spirituality among lesbian feminists led to the formation of a number of recovery groups such as AA, Al Anon, and Adult Children of Alcoholics within lesbian communities. Tailored more directly to the images and affinities of their communities, the groups empowered women to take care of themselves and each other. Meanwhile, although gay men had no movement comparable to women's liberation, their involvement in the hippie and anti-war movements constituted a strong reaction to ultra-masculine expectations among the dominant culture, and reorientation to a more peace-centered, gender-neutral ideal. Gay and lesbian elders in the Minnesota-based organization GLEAM (Gay and Lesbian Elders Active in Minnesota) formed a speaker's bureau to educate professionals who work with older populations (Yoakam, 1997). Understanding and conveying the accomplishments of groups across a spectrum of LGBT identities, a practitioner offers hope to her or his clients that they also can effect meaningful change in their own lives (Ritter & Terndrup, 2002).

with parts of the gay community that could be assets for their social and personal adjustments, so that Sue and Annie would feel accepted as a couple with a rich and colorful history.

When asked for their feelings about this plan, Sue and Annie immediately felt that finding a new physical therapist and arranging for respite care would be most helpful in the short term. They could see that, if conditions improved from here, they might feel more comfortable socializing through the community center. Annie, although sorely missing these activities, expressed hesitation at going without Sue. "Once she feels okay to go, I'd like to give it a shot." If they made progress from here, they told Joan, they would give some thought to trying WOW, but at least in the short term they were not ready to go yet. They agreed, however, to meet regularly with Joan, and then in six months they would evaluate the care plan together to assess their progress toward completing their goals, and to record any new challenges that had arisen. Joan stressed that Sue and Annie could, at any time, terminate their relationship, but that for now, as long as they wanted to work with her, she would be happy to work with them. Before leaving, Sue and Annie scheduled their next appointment with Joan and authorized her to make contact with Sue's physician for follow-up contact when needed.

Application Exercises

1. What different kinds of knowledge (e.g., life history, community resources, relationship status) did Joan need to use to be culturally competent? Which levels of service were used (e.g., micro, meso, macro)?
2. What steps did Joan have to take to ensure that she was providing bias-free services? What other interventions might be used?
3. How will Joan, Annie, and Sue know when they are ready to terminate their service plan? Who decides when it is time to terminate services?

Termination Skills with LGBT People

In terminating with any client regardless of sexual orientation or gender identity, certain skills and competencies are requisite. Understanding this, the practitioner must be aware of specific skills needed in the termination process with LGBT clients. At the community level, a practitioner who also identifies as LGBT may struggle to let go of a program or movement, given that she or he is also a part of the community being served by the program. Still, the protocols for reviewing client progress, evaluating the present and future, and outlining follow-up strategies remain the same. At the same time, the practitioner must be able to offer resources and referrals appropriate for the LGBT clients' assets, needs, relationships, comfort level, and desired future outcomes. This requires the practitioner to remain fully aware, competent, and comfortable with LGBT community venues and services. At all times, practitioners need to be rigorously attentive to their own language, comfort level, and beliefs, so that they will convey the most authentic professional self to their clients and community groups. Diligently working to maintain a trusting relationship will better ensure social workers' abilities to practice effectively with LGBT people (Jones & Nystrom, 2002; Ritter & Terndrup, 2002).

CLOSING THOUGHTS

As we have already noted, social service providers have a great deal of work to do to overcome their profession's history of supporting a sexist, homophobic status quo. LGBT people who interact with social workers as clients, colleagues, consumers, and administrators are still very much aware of the past stigmatization, shaming, and repression enforced on their communities by the pathological and medical models of assessment. Any effort to confront this past, educate others about the harm already done to LGBT people, and proactively move to a space of affirming, accepting practice holds social work accountable to its commitment for social justice.

Because, as Cruikshank (1992) noted, LGBT people maintain a minority status as long as all societal sanctions remain in place. A lesbian, gay, bisexual, or transgender identity does retain a political aspect, even for the most apolitical lesbian, gay man, bisexual, or transgender. Thus, social workers must be vigorous allies to the LGBT communities beyond simply providing LGBT-friendly therapy. Members of the profession should challenge each other to look beyond their own comfort zones, ask questions of themselves, their loved ones, and their colleagues, and seek to better understand the connections between larger injustices and micro-level, interpersonal challenges. Moreover, practitioners gain countless insights by seeking out supervision and counsel from those who know, firsthand, about LGBT relationships and experiences. Let those who are experts share their expertise.

Finally, we must note that any movement toward change at the micro level changes the complexion of issues at the macro perspective. Conversely, movements in the macro level undeniably affect the interpersonal work of LGBT individuals. Audre Lorde's statement, "The personal *is* political," rings true for LGBT people across the globe, given the battles they have had to wage throughout history to pursue safety, dignity, and self-actualization. Having visible LGBT movements to cite, vivid histories to share, and a growing number of resources to consult means that LGBT people have worked tirelessly to show social service providers how to meaningfully interact with members of their communities. It is, then, ultimately up to the social service providers to acknowledge, honor, and affirm these efforts by reflecting respectful, competent, and committed efforts to assisting their clients and client groups in whatever way they are needed (Ritter & Terndrup, 2002).

References

Ball, S. (1994). A group model for gay and lesbian clients with chronic mental illness. *Social Work, 39*(1), 109–115.

Bérubé, A. (1991). *Coming out under fire: The history of gay men and women in World War Two*. New York: Plume.

Boulden, W. (2001). Gay men living in a rural environment. *Journal of Gay & Lesbian Social Services, 12*(3/4), 63–76.

Bricker-Jenkins, M. & Hooyman, N. (1986). *Not for women only: Social work practice for a feminist future.* Silver Springs, MD: NASW.

Centers for Disease Control. (2001a). *HIV/AIDS surveillance report.* Rockville, MD.

Centers for Disease Control. (2001b). *A glance at the HIV epidemic.* Rockville, MD.

Christian, D., & Keefe, D. (1997). Maturing gay men: A framework for social service assessment and intervention. In J. Quam (Ed.), *Social services for senior LGBT people* (pp. 47–78). New York: Haworth Press.

Cruikshank, M. (1992). *The gay and lesbian liberation movement.* New York: Routledge.

D'Augelli, A. (1993). Preventing mental health problems among lesbian and gay college students. *Journal of Primary Prevention, 13*(4), 245–261.

Davison, G. (1991). Constructionism and morality in therapy for homosexuality. In J. Gonsiorek & J. Weinrich (Eds.), *Homosexuality: Research implications for public policy* (pp. 136–148). Newbury Park, CA: Sage.

Diamond, S. (1989). *Spiritual warfare: The politics of the religious right.* Boston: South End Press.

Dunkle, J. (1994). Counseling gay male clients: A review of treatment efficacy research, 1975 to present. *Journal of Gay and Lesbian Psychotherapy, 2*(2, Winter), 19.

Foster, S. (1997). Rural lesbians and gays: Public perceptions, worker perceptions, and service delivery. In J. Smith & R. Mancoske (Eds.), *Rural gays and lesbians: Building on the strengths of communities* (pp. 23–55). New York: Haworth Press.

Foster, S., Stevens, P., & Hall, J. (1994). Offering support group services for lesbians living with HIV. *Women and Therapy, 15*(2), 69–83.

Friedman, L. (1997). Rural lesbian mothers and their families. In J. Smith & R. Mancoske (Eds.), *Rural gays and lesbians: Building on the strengths of communities* (pp. 73–82). New York: Haworth Press.

Friend, R. (1991). Older lesbian and gay people: A theory of successful aging. *Journal of Homosexuality, 2*(3–4), 99–118.

Gonsiorek, J. C. (1991). The empirical basis for the demise of the illness model of homosexuality. In J. Gonsiorek & J. Weinrich (Eds.), *Homosexuality: Research implications for public policy* (pp. 115–136). Newbury Park, CA: Sage.

Greene, B. (1994). Ethnic-minority lesbians and gay men: Mental health and treatment issues. *Journal of Consulting and Clinical Psychology, 28*(1), 137–141.

Haag, A., & Chang, F. (1997). The impact of electronic networking on the lesbian and gay community. In J. Smith & R. Mancoske (Eds.), *Rural gays and lesbians: Building on the strengths of communities* (pp. 83–94). New York: Haworth Press.

Hall, J. (1994a). How lesbians recognize and respond to alcohol problems: A theoretical model of problematization. *Advances in Nursing Science, 16*(3), 46–63.

Hall, J. (1994b). Lesbians recovering from alcohol problems: An ethnographic study of health care experiences. *Nursing Research, 43*(4), 238–243.

Herek, G. (1991). Stigma, prejudice, and violence against lesbians and gay men. In J. Gonsiorek & J. Weinrich (Eds.), *Homosexuality: Research implications for public policy* (pp. 60–80). Newbury Park, CA: Sage.

Herek, G. (1992). *Hate crimes: Confronting violence against lesbians and gay men*. Newbury Park, CA: Sage.

Hunter, S., Shannon, C., Knox, J., & Martin, J. (1998). *Lesbian, gay, and bisexual youths and adults: Knowledge for human services practice*. Thousand Oaks, CA: Sage.

Hutter, J. (1993). The social construction of homosexuals in the nineteenth century: The shift from sin to the influence of medicine on criminalizing sodomy in Germany. *Journal of Homosexuality, 24*(34), 73–93.

Jones, T., & Nystrom, N. (2002). Looking back, looking forward: Addressing the lives of lesbians 55 and over. *Journal of Women and Aging, 14,* 3–4.

Kaiser, C. (1997). *The gay metropolis: The landmark history of gay life in America since World War II*. New York: Harvest Press.

Katz, J. (2001). *Love stories: Sex between men before homosexuality*. Chicago: University of Chicago Press.

Kochman, A. (1997). Gay and lesbian elderly: Historical overview and implications for social work practice. In J. Quam (Ed.), *Social services for senior LGBT people* (pp. 1–10). New York: Haworth Press.

Kulkin, H., Chauvin, E., & Percle, G. (2000). Suicide among gay and lesbian adolescents and young adults: A review of the literature. *Journal of Homosexuality, 40*(1), 1–30.

Lindhorst, T. (1997). Lesbians and gay men in the country: Practice implications for rural social workers. In J. Smith & R. Mancoske (Eds.), *Rural gays and lesbians: Building on the strengths of communities* (pp. 1–11). New York: Haworth Press.

McHenry, S., & Johnson, J. (1994). Homophobia in the therapist and gay or lesbian client: Conscious and unconscious collusions in self-hate. *Psychotherapy, 30*(1, Spring), 141–151.

Metz, P. (1997) Staff development for working with lesbian and gay elders. In J. Quam (Ed.), *Social services for senior LGBT people* (pp. 35–45). New York: Haworth Press.

Nystrom, N., & Jones, T. (2003). Community building with aging lesbians. *American Journal of Community Psychology, 31*–3.

Perkins, R. (1991). Therapy for lesbians? The case against. *Feminism & Psychology, 1*(3), 325–338.

Pinderhughes, E. (1989). *Understanding race, ethnicity, and power*. New York: Free Press.

Ridgeway, C., & Walker, H. (1995). Status structures. In K. Cook, G. Fine, & J. House (Eds), *Sociological perspectives on social psychology* (pp. 281–310). Boston: Allyn & Bacon.

Ritter, K., & Terndrup, A. (2002). *Handbook of affirmative psychotherapy with lesbians and gay men*. New York: Guilford Press.

Ross, M., Paulsen, J., & Stalstrom, O. (1988). Homosexuality and mental health: A cross-cultural review. *Journal of Homosexuality, 15*(1/2), 131–152.

Scull, A. T. (1977). *Decarceration: Community treatment and the deviant: A radical view*. Englewood Cliffs, NJ: Prentice-Hall.

Seidman, S. (1993). Identity and politics in a "postmodern" gay culture. In M. Warner (Ed.), *Fear of a queer planet: Queer politics and social theory* (pp. 105–142). Minneapolis: University of Minnesota Press.

Shilts, R. (1982). *The mayor of Castro Street: The life and times of Harvey Milk*. New York: St. Martin's Press.

Shilts, R. (1987). *And the band played on*. New York: Penguin Books.

Silverstein, C. (1991). Psychological and medical treatments of homosexuality. In J. Gonsiorek & J. Weinrich (Eds.), *Homosexuality: Research implications for public policy* (pp. 101–114). Newbury Park, CA: Sage.

Simon, W. (1994). Deviance as history: The future of perversion. *Archives of Sexual Behavior, 23*(1), 1–20.

Smith, J. (1988). Psychopathology, homosexuality, and homophobia. *Journal of Homosexuality, 15*(1/2), 59–73.

Smith, J. (1997). Working with larger systems: Rural lesbians and gays. In J. Smith & R. Mancoske (Eds.), *Rural gays and lesbians: Building on the strengths of communities* (pp. 13–21). New York: Haworth Press.

Trippett, S. E. (1994). Lesbians' mental health concerns. *Health Care for Women International, 15,* 317–323.

Vance, C. (1991). Anthropology rediscovers sexuality: A theoretical comment. *Social Sciences & Medicine, 33*(8), 875–884.

van Wormer, K., Wells, J., & Boes, M. (2000). *Social work with lesbians, gays, and bisexuals.* Needham Heights, MA: Allyn & Bacon.

Victor, J. (1994). Fundamentalist religion and the moral crusade against Satanism: The social construction of deviant behavior. *Deviant Behavior, 15*(3), 305–344.

Warner, M. (Ed.). (1993). *Fear of a queer planet: Queer politics and social theory.* Minneapolis: University of Minnesota Press.

Watkins, C. E., Jr., & Terrell, F. (1988). Mistrust level and its effects on counseling expectations in black client–white counselor relationships: An analogue study. *Journal of Counseling Psychology, 33*(2), 194–197.

Weston, K. (1991). *Families we choose.* New York: Columbia University Press.

Whitam, F. (1991). From sociology: Homophobia and heterosexism in sociology. *Journal of Gay & Lesbian Psychotherapy, 1*(4), 31–44.

Wisniewski, J., & Toomey, B. (1987). Are social workers homophobic? *Social Work, 32*(5), 454–455.

Witten, T. (2004). Life course analysis: The courage to search for something more: Middle adulthood issues in the transgender and intersex community. *Journal of Human Behavior in a Social Environment, 8*(3–4).

Yoakam, J. (1997). Playing bingo with the best of them: Community initiated programs for older gay and lesbian adults. In J. Quam (Ed.), *Social services for senior LGBT people* (pp. 27–34). New York: Haworth Press.

Young, I. M. (1990). *Justice and the politics of difference.* Princeton, NJ: Princeton University Press.

CHAPTER

Social Work Practice with Immigrants and Refugees

Uma A. Segal

Individuals and families from around the globe form a continuous stream of immigrants to the United States. The backlog of visa applications and waiting lists to enter the United States stretches to several years. Undocumented immigrants, both those who enter without legal papers and those who overstay their visits, abound. Refugees and asylees continue to enter in record numbers from countries in political turmoil. Disproportionately large numbers of entrants into the United States in recent years have been people of color from Asia, Africa, and South America, and despite encountering a series of barriers, an overwhelming majority remains, making this nation its permanent residence. Reasons for this ongoing influx are readily apparent, for despite the problems prevalent in the United States, it continues to be the most attractive country on earth.

There is much in the United States that Americans take for granted and that is not available in many other countries, and several amenities, opportunities, possibilities, and lifestyles in the United States are not found together in any other nation. In theory, and often in reality, this is a land of freedom, of equality, of opportunity, of a superior quality of life, of easy access to education, and of few human rights violations. It is a land that, in the 21st century, is struggling toward multiculturalism and pluralism in its institutions and social outlook. It is a land that, compared with others, offers newcomers a relatively easy path through which to become integrated into its largesse. The debate over the value of immigration persists, but it is a debate, and even though immigration policies are not without discrimination and selectivity, they are more open than they have ever been and are also more open than those of other nations. Thus, despite both political and social perceptions of foreigners following the terror attacks on September 11, 2001, on the Pentagon and the World Trade Center, despite increased security measures and scrutiny of individuals, and despite some highly disturbing xenophobic backlash, new immigrants continue to arrive in the United States in droves. And most, if not all, of the vast numbers that entered years before, whether or not they have become naturalized citizens, value the lifestyle this nation continues to allow them, because frequently for many, even when life here is difficult, it is less so than it would have been in their countries of origin.

The phenomenon of immigration is neither novel nor recent but has been part of the human experience since time immemorial with movements resulting from such causes as economics, politics, and religion in addition to a desire for exploration and adventure. Migration may occur as a response to crises, but it is also a concomitant search for opportunity, and the immigration experience to the United States begins not when immigrants arrive at its borders but long before, while they are still in their home countries. The impetus for emigrating arises there, and immigrants draw their resources—economic, social, and emotional—from there to undertake the greatest challenge of their lives. The process, starting with emigration from the home country through adjustment to life in the United States, is lengthy and complex, with the success of the immigrant dependent on the interplay of personal resources and environmental factors.

Figure 9.1 identifies the salient factors in the immigration process, regardless of country of origin or of destination, and provides a framework of the variety of dimensions involved. As practitioners work with new arrivals, it is imperative that they focus not only on the experience of the latter once they arrive in this country but also on the reasons people leave their homelands, their experience of migration, the resources they bring with them to function in unfamiliar environments, and the effects of the receptiveness of the host country (both politically and socially) to their presence. Furthermore, it is necessary that practitioners be cognizant that immigrants, regardless of the length of time they are in the United States, are constantly faced with a duality of cultures and must learn to function within norms and expectations that are frequently in conflict.

An overarching question in immigration literature is why people choose to leave one country for another. Moving to another country is arduous, even under optimum circumstances. Immigration requires elaborate preparation, great financial costs, loss of social and family ties, acquisition of a new language, and learning an alien culture. Even though the configuration of events leading to migration may differ among individuals and groups, there appears to be an interplay of two phenomena that is the catalyst for migration: (1) a

Figure 9.1 | Framework for the Immigrant Experience*

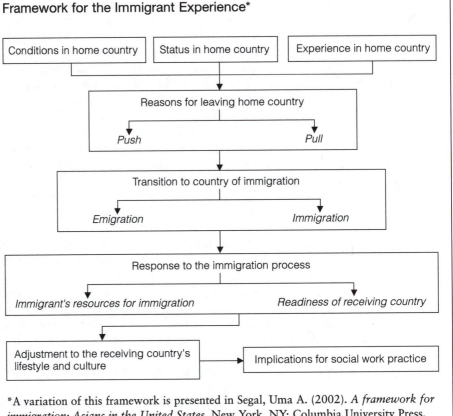

*A variation of this framework is presented in Segal, Uma A. (2002). *A framework for immigration: Asians in the United States.* New York, NY: Columbia University Press, p. 4.

push from the country of origin, or emigration, fueled by the lack of economic opportunity, by persecution from the majority or a powerful minority, or by difficulties caused by natural disasters, and (2) a pull to the country of immigration, particularly the opportunity of achieving or acquiring something that is unavailable in the homeland.

Furthermore, even though people may be interested in emigrating from their homelands to a particular country, the move is highly contingent on the receptiveness of that nation to immigrants in general, and immigrants from specific countries in particular. Most governments now have strict laws regarding immigration, but this was not always the case, and people were relatively free to live where they chose. U.S. immigration history, since the mid-18th century, has been significantly affected by legislation that has substantially colored the face of immigration during the last two and a half centuries.

HISTORY OF IMMIGRATION TO THE UNITED STATES

Little is known about immigration to the United States before 1600, and it is estimated that before Christopher Columbus arrived in the New World, the indigenous population, the Native Americans, numbered almost 12 million (Karger & Stoesz, 1998). Some believe that the first immigrants to this nation came from Northeast Asia several centuries ago, but others suggest that the population that was here before the 17th century was a mix of peoples from Polynesia, South Asia, and Europe. Early U.S. immigration history provides a profile of voluntary immigration to the United States, but little information in the mainstream literature focuses on the large numbers of involuntary immigrants, those who were brought as forced laborers (slaves) against their will from Africa and the Caribbean, as early as 1619.

Documentation of immigration appears to begin with the arrival of 102 colonists who left England in 1620 and arrived in Plymouth, Massachusetts, and marks the "start" of European migration. These colonists were followed by the Swedes, who began their migration to the United States in 1638, and soon after, the Dutch entered in 1655. From the 1600s until the mid-1770s, the immigrants were primarily colonizers from northern Europe; however, from then until the mid-1800s, immigration slowed because of local anti-immigration feelings. Governmental action and legislation of immigration began in 1790 with the passage of the first Naturalization Act that regulated the granting of citizenship to "free, white" people, barring citizenship to people of color and whites who entered the United States as indentured laborers. Since then, a number of laws have sought to legislate not only access to naturalization but also the entry of different peoples.

Thus, countries from which immigrants have entered the United States have varied during several periods in U.S. history, among other things because of immigrants' personal reasons for moving and because of legal barriers to entry. In a democratic society, such as this, it is believed that national policies reflect the opinion of the majority. Kim (1994) proposes that congressional legislative action regarding immigration revolves around issues of superiority/inferiority and inclusion/exclusion. These, in turn, translate into the quantity and quality of people allowed to enter the country. U.S. immigration history may be divided into seven periods during which legal measures formally allowed or controlled the categories of people allowed to immigrate (Kim, 1994, pp. 8–9):

1. *The colonial period (1609–1775),* during which most immigrants were from the British Isles and the colonies had little effective control.
2. *The American Revolutionary period (1776–1840),* when European immigration slowed because of war and there were general anti-foreign feelings.
3. *The "old" immigration period (1841–1882),* during which local governments recruited people from Northern Europe. Chinese were also able to immigrate without much difficulty.

4. *The regulation period (1882–1920),* when the Chinese were excluded from immigrating. However, large numbers of immigrants were admitted from Central, Eastern, and Southern Europe.

5. *The restriction and exclusion period (1921–1952),* when a quota system restricted immigration from Central, Eastern, and Southern Europe, and when all Asians were excluded from admission because of their ineligibility for U.S. citizenship.

6. *The partial liberalization period (1952–1965),* when Asians were assigned the same quota as those from Central, Eastern, and Southern Europe, and were also allowed naturalization.

7. *The liberalized policy period (1965–present),* when the quota policy was repealed to allow entry to immigrants from Third World countries.

Legislative History and Its Impact

Following are brief sketches of immigration-related legislation or action[1] that has affected diverse populations in a variety of ways from entry into the United States itself to access to fundamental rights:

1790:   *The Naturalization Act of 1790* stipulated that "any alien, being a free white person, may be admitted to become a citizen of the United States," thus disqualifying African slaves and indentured whites who entered the United States. In addition, the act established a residency requirement and renunciation of allegiance to immigrants' former countries.

1798:   The *Alien and Sedition Acts* permit the president to deport any foreigner deemed to be dangerous.

1808:   Congress banned the importation of additional slaves, but it was still legal to enslave free Africans in the United States and their children.

1819:   The *Steerage Act of 1819* was the first significant federal legislation relating specifically to immigration. Congress required ship captains to keep detailed passenger records to be reported to the United States government and set specific sustenance rules for the humane treatment of those on board.

1875:   Direct federal regulation of immigration was established by laws prohibiting the entry of prostitutes and convicts. Particularly affected by this were women from Asia, many who traveled to the United States alone as picture brides (were married in absentia), who were subjected to humiliating questioning by immigration officials.

1882:   The *Chinese Exclusion Act* was the first of many significant laws that targeted specific groups, barring them entry into the United States. This act prevented any Chinese without family members already in

---

[1]These and additional laws relevant to immigration and immigrants are available through the Web site of the Bureau of Citizenship and Immigration Services (http://www.immigration.gov /graphics/lawsregs/amendina.htm) Accessed August 14, 2003.

the United States from immigrating and created the phenomenon of "paper sons" (individuals who presented fraudulent papers indicating they were sons of immigrant Chinese people).

1885:   *Alien Contract Labor* laws prohibited certain laborers from entering the country, depriving many potential immigrants a means of earning their livelihood.

1892:   On January 2nd, a new federal immigration station was opened on Ellis Island in New York Harbor, and through it federal government officials began discharging their responsibility, which they had assumed in 1891, of inspecting, admitting, rejecting, and processing all immigrants seeking admission to the United States. During the next 30 years, more than 12 million immigrants, mainly Europeans, were processed through Ellis Island.

1907:   The *Immigration Act of 1907* reorganized the states bordering Mexico into the Mexican Border District to stem the flow of immigrants.

1907:   The *Gentlemen's Agreement* was negotiated with Japan through which no further Japanese laborers were permitted into the United States; however, it did not limit the entry of Japanese women who came in large numbers to join their husbands (and as picture brides), allowing the establishment of Japanese families.

1917:   The *Immigration Act of February 5, 1917* enumerated the categories of people who were ineligible to enter the United States. This included those who were illiterate or those who were natives of a zone defined by latitude and longitude. The geographic area identified became known as the Asiatic Barred Zone, and the act became the Asiatic Barred Zone Act. Only the Philippines, which at the time were a United States territory, and Japan, which was a U.S. ally, were permitted to send immigrants.

1924:   The *Immigration Act of 1924,* also known as the Quota Immigration Law, or the Nationality Origins Act, was a response to growing anti-immigration sentiments in the country. This act established annual immigration quotas to 2 percent of the number of a nationality group already living in the United States as of 1890. Almost no Southern or Eastern Europeans were allowed in because of this quota. In addition, the 1882 Chinese Exclusion Act had been made "permanent" in 1902, and Japanese immigration was also curtailed through the 1924 Act because significant Japanese immigration did not begin until well after 1890. The act placed no limit on immigration within the hemisphere, so there was an influx of immigrants from Mexico as employers looked south of the border for cheap labor.

1930s: During the Great Depression, immigrants were often blamed, and the large number of Mexican immigrants was identified as being culpable. Through this period, the number of deportees approximated half a million and included those whose families had been in the United States for several generations.

1940:   The *Alien Registration Act* required all aliens (non–U.S. citizens) in the United States to register with the government and receive an Alien Registration Card (now known as the "green card").

1948:   The *Displaced Persons Act* permitted entry to refugees, specifically Europeans, displaced by war. These individuals fell outside the immigration quotas.

1950:   All aliens were required to report their addresses annually.

1952:   The *1952 Immigration Act* is the true forerunner of present-day immigration. It consolidated the various immigration laws, but most specifically, it reaffirmed the per country quota, limited immigration from the Eastern Hemisphere while leaving immigration from the Western hemisphere unrestricted, established the preference system that gave priority to relatives of U.S. citizens and to those with special skills needed in the United States, and tightened screening procedures.

1965:   The *Immigration and Nationality Act* finally liberalized immigration and repealed legal discrimination because of race, gender, nationality, place of birth, or place of residence; it benefited many, especially those from the Asia-Pacific triangle. Rescinding the national origins system, it replaced it with annual quotas of the Eastern (170,000) and Western (120,000) hemispheres, with as many as 20,000 individuals being permitted entry from any one nation. This quota did not include spouses and unmarried minor children of U.S. citizens and, thus, permitted the annual number of immigrants to be substantially larger than specified. Although legislators assumed that this would redress injustices against Southern and Eastern Europeans, in actuality it resulted in such a dramatic increase in Asian immigration that it took the United States by surprise.

1978:   Separate ceilings for the two hemispheres were abolished, and a worldwide ceiling of 290,000 annually was established.

1980:   The *Refugee Act,* enacted primarily in response to refugees from Southeast Asia following the Vietnam War, removed refugees as a preference category. Under this act, the president, in conjunction with Congress, and based on the political climate of the world, determines the annual ceiling and the distribution of that ceiling among identified countries for that year (ceilings have ranged from 50,000 to 90,000). The worldwide ceiling for immigrants was dropped from 290,000 to 270,000 but does not include refugee numbers.

1986:   The *Immigration Reform and Control Act (IRCA)* was a comprehensive reform effort that legalized undocumented immigrants who had been in the country since January 1, 1982, but made it unlawful to hire undocumented workers. The majority of the 3 million undocumented immigrants that came forward for amnesty were from Mexico and Central America.

1990:   The *Immigration Act of 1990* increased the annual ceiling for immigrants to 700,000, while establishing an annual limit for certain categories of immigrants. The aim was to attract skilled workers to favor those who could make a substantial contribution to the United States. It also established the Immigrant Investor Program, under which as many as 10,000 permanent resident visas are offered to those immigrants agreeing to invest at least $1 million in U.S. urban areas or $500,000 in U.S. rural areas.

1996:   *Welfare Reform* ends many cash and medical assistance programs for most legal immigrants (and other low-income individuals).

1996:   The *Illegal Immigration Reform and Immigrant Responsibility Act (IIRIRA)* expanded enforcement operations of the Immigration and Naturalization Service, particularly at the border, and reorganized the procedures for removal of inadmissible entrants.

2001:   The *USA Patriot Act* was passed by Congress in response to the September 11, 2001, terrorist attacks on New York and Washington. This act gives federal officials greater power to track and intercept national and international communications and to prevent the entry of foreign terrorists and detain and remove those who may be within the United States.

2003:   The *Land Border Security and Immigration Improvement Act* was introduced in July 2003 for discussion to legalize the stay of hard-working, tax-paying undocumented immigrants, to expand worker and family visas, and to improve measures that target smugglers and unscrupulous employers.

Reflected in the series of legislative actions taken since 1970 are clear indicators of the major sociopolitical leanings of the U.S. population and its attitude toward immigrants. Fears of cultural differences limited Eastern and Southern European immigration. This was replaced by xenophobic reactions to racial and cultural differences as Asians began entering the United States. African immigration, other than a recognition that many were brought in as slaves, received little attention, and legal actions did not directly address African immigration. In fact, in 1939, Reid found there was little information on the 100,000 foreign-born Blacks, and there continues to be a paucity of information regarding the profound implications of slavery and legislative action on black immigration (Francis, 2000).

Implications of the Immigration and Nationality Act of 1965

The 1965 Immigration and Nationality Act had a major and permanent effect on U.S. immigration, dramatically altering the traditional origins and numbers of immigrants to the United States. Prior to the amendments to the Immigration Act of 1924 and the Immigration and Nationality Act of 1952 on October 3, 1965, which resulted in the liberalization of immigration laws, most entrants into the United States were from European countries. When the 1965 amendments (1) abolished the national origins quota system, (2) established a preference system for relatives of U.S. citizens and permanent residents, (3) exempted immediate relatives of citizens and some special groups (certain ministers of religion, former employees of U.S. government abroad, etc.), and (4) expanded the limits of world coverage to a 20,000-per-country limit, the influx of new immigrants from non-European countries was unprecedented and continues into the present.

Although minor modifications are frequently made to the Immigration Act of October 1, 1965, it remains the primary directing force of the U.S. Immigration and Naturalization Service (INS). It set the annual immigrant quota at 290,000, dividing 170,000 for the Eastern Hemisphere and 120,000 for the Western Hemisphere. INS specifications of the worldwide level of immigration and the selection procedures are detailed in Title II of the Immigration Act (INA: ACT 201), as is the preference in allocation of immigrant visas (INA: ACT 203). Even more significantly, although INA: ACT 202 identifies the numerical limitation to any foreign state, it includes a nondiscrimination clause, which states, "No person shall receive any preference or priority or be discriminated against in the issuance of an immigrant visa because of the person's race, sex, nationality, place of birth, or place of residence."

The Immigration Act specified spouses and unmarried adult children of U.S. citizens as exempt from the numerical quota and established a preferential system for the allocation of entry visas. Some modifications have occurred since the original 1965 Act, through the Immigration Act of 1990, which restructured the immigrant categories of admission. However, in many important ways, it has remained substantively the same, and it is clear that system allocations are not based on the prevention of entry of any particular group. The 1998 fiscal year limit was 675,000, and the following categories are currently identified:

Family-sponsored immigrants (480,000 annually)[2]
(1) Unmarried sons and daughters of citizens (23,400 annually)
(2) Spouses and unmarried sons and unmarried daughters of permanent resident aliens (114,200)
(3) Married sons and married daughters of citizens (23,400)
(4) Adult brothers and sisters of citizens (65,000)

Employment-based immigrants (140,000 annually)
(1) Priority workers (40,040)
    a. Aliens with extraordinary ability
    b. Professors and researchers
    c. Certain multinational executives and managers
(2) Members of the professions holding advanced degrees (40,040)
(3) Skilled workers, professionals, and other workers (40,040)
(4) Special immigrants, usually refugees adjusting their status (9,940)
(5) Employment creators, "investors" (9,940)

Diversity (55,000 annually, effective 1995)
    Nonpreferential immigrants ineligible under the other categories

---

[2]This number is in addition to the 290,000 annual limit (exempt from the 290,000 numerical cap).

IMMIGRANT CATEGORIES: DEFINITIONS AND DESCRIPTIONS

Newcomers to the United States enter under a variety of conditions. Early migrants came as volunteer immigrants, indentured laborers, or as slaves. Most however, were considered "legal immigrants," particularly in the absence of any legislation. Present-day immigrants may be categorized as voluntary immigrants (illegal or undocumented) or as refugees (and asylees). There is a general tendency to group immigrants and refugees together and to perceive them as a homogenous group. Both are foreign-born and share several similarities in that they are in a new and unfamiliar environment, so there is a tendency to regard them through the same lens. In general, however, the majority of immigrants are in the United States because of the "pull" of opportunity, whereas refugees are in this country because they have been "pushed" out of their own. As such, the personal, social, psychological, and material resources they bring with them often differ substantially and have implications for their adjustment, for the services they may require of the United States, and for what they can offer this country, particularly in the first years of their residence here. Definitions of the general category of immigrant follow, along with historical and recent data of documented immigrants, estimates of undocumented entrants, and information on refugee origins.

Voluntary Immigrants[3]

As defined by the Immigration and Nationality Act, an immigrant is "an alien admitted to the United States for lawful permanent residence . . . an illegal alien who entered the United States without inspection . . . would be strictly defined as an immigrant under the INA but is not a permanent resident alien. Lawful permanent residents are legally accorded the privilege of residing permanently in the United States.

Legal Immigrants   There is little information regarding the profile of the U.S. population before the 1820 Census; however, the Census did begin to trace the origins of the immigrant flows in that year. These are presented as aggregate data during 10-year periods by region in Table 9.1. Table 9.2 reflects the flow between the years 1991 and 2000, and Table 9.3 indicates the number of people residing in the United States between 1965 and 2000 who were foreign-born.[4] The tables clearly indicate that after 1965, entry from the Americas (North, Central, and South and the Caribbean) surpassed that from Europe,

---

[3]Appendix A, Table 9.A1 lists the number of immigrants to the United States by decade from 1820 to 2000. Table 9.A2 provides a summary of immigrants admitted by type and selected class of admission from 1986–2000. Information is provided through the Web site of the Immigration and Naturalization Service (http://www.ins.gov).

[4]The term *foreign-born* is inclusive, encompassing diverse populations that were not born in the United States. Thus, it includes naturalized U.S. citizens, permanent residents who are not U.S. citizens, legal non-immigrants (persons on student or work visas), refugees, and undocumented immigrants. Only those on visitors' visas are not included in this count.

Table 9.1 | Immigration by Region of Last Residence: Fiscal Years 1820–2000*

Region of Last Residence	1820	1821–30	1831–40	1841–50	1851–60	1861–70	1871–80	1881–90	1891–1900
Europe	7,690	98,797	469,681	1,597,442	2,451,577	2,065,141	2,271,925	4,735,484	3,555,352
Asia	6	30	55	141	41,538	64,759	124,160	69,942	74,862
Americas	387	11,564	33,424	62,469	74,720	166,607	404,044	426,967	38,972
Africa	1	16	54	55	210	312	358	857	350
Oceania	1	2	9	29	158	214	10,914	12,574	3,965
Not Specified	300	33,030	69,902	53,115	29,011	17,791	790	789	14,063

Region of Last Residence	1901–10	1911–20	1921–30	1931–40	1941–50	1951–60	1961–70	1971–80	1981–90	1991–2000
Europe	8,056,040	4,321,887	2,463,194	347,566	621,147	1,325,727	1,123,492	800,368	761,550	1,359,737
Asia	323,543	247,236	112,059	16,595	37,028	153,249	427,642	1,588,178	2,738,157	2,795,672
Americas	361,888	1,143,671	1,516,716	160,037	354,804	996,944	1,716,374	1,982,735	3,615,225	4,486,806
Africa	7,368	8,443	6,286	1,750	7,367	14,092	28,954	80,779	176,893	354,939
Oceania	13,024	13,427	8,726	2,483	14,551	12,976	25,122	41,242	45,205	55,845
Not Specified	33,523	1,147	228		142	12,491	93	12	1,032	42,418

*U.S. Bureau of the Census Internet release date February 2002.

Table 9.2 | Immigrants Admitted by Region of Birth Fiscal Years 1991–2000*

Region of Birth	1991	1992	1993	1994	1995	1996	1997	1998	1999	2000	Total
Europe	135,234	145,392	158,254	160,916	128,185	147,581	119,871	90,793	92,672	132,480	1,311,378
Asia	358,533	356,955	358,047	292,589	267,931	307,807	265,810	219,696	199,411	265,400	2,892,179
Africa	36,179	27,086	27,783	26,712	42,456	52,889	47,791	40,660	36,700	44,731	382,987
Oceania	6,236	5,169	4,902	4,592	4,695	5,309	4,344	3,935	3,676	5,136	47,994
North America	1,210,981	384,047	301,380	272,226	231,526	40,540	307,488	252,996	271,365	344,805	3,917,354
South America	79,934	55,308	53,921	47,377	45,666	61,769	52,877	45,394	41,585	56,074	539,905
Born on ship/plane	—	2	—	—	—	—	—	—	—	—	2
Unknown or not reported	70	18	5	4	2	5	197	977	1,159	1,181	3,618
Totals	1,827,167	973,977	904,292	804,416	720,461	915,900	798,378	654,451	646,568	849,807	9,095,417

*U.S. Bureau of the Census Internet release date February 2002.

Table 9.3 | Year of Entry and Region of Birth of the Foreign-Born Population (Numbers in thousands. Data are *for civilian noninstitutional population plus Armed Forces living off post or with their families on post.*)

Region	Total Foreign-Born Population	1995–2000	1990–1994	1985–1989	1980–1984	1975–1979	1970–1974	1965–1969	Before 1965
Number									
Total	28,379	6,248	4,958	4,523	3,499	2,655	1,950	1,418	3,129
Europe	4,355	733	544	416	243	277	263	320	1,557
Asia	7,246	1,556	1,295	1,243	1,203	897	492	271	289
Africa	701	260	118	100	80	67	35	21	19
Oceania	147	62	31	6	15	6	11	4	13
Latin America	14,477	3,259	2,780	2,571	1,822	1,299	1,084	705	957
Caribbean	2,813	476	455	404	391	247	248	280	311
Central America	9,789	2,289	1,980	1,871	1,193	907	696	332	520
Mexico	7,841	1,872	1,628	1,435	836	784	604	267	414
Other	1,948	417	352	436	357	122	92	65	106
South America	1,876	494	345	296	238	145	140	93	126
Northern America	698	147	56	44	47	57	28	68	250
Region not reported	755	230	133	144	88	51	37	28	43

Percent Distribution

Total	100.0	22.0	17.5	15.9	12.3	9.4	6.9	5.0	11.0
Europe	100.0	16.8	12.5	9.6	5.6	6.4	6.0	7.3	35.8
Asia	100.0	21.5	17.9	17.2	16.6	12.4	6.8	3.7	4.0
Africa	100.0	37.1	16.9	14.2	11.5	9.6	5.0	3.1	2.7
Oceania	100.0	42.4	20.9	3.8	10.0	4.4	7.3	2.8	8.5
Latin America	100.0	22.5	19.2	17.8	12.6	9.0	7.5	4.9	6.6
Caribbean	100.0	16.9	16.2	14.4	13.9	8.8	8.8	10.0	11.1
Central America	100.0	23.4	20.2	19.1	12.2	9.3	7.1	3.4	5.3
Mexico	100.0	23.9	20.8	18.3	10.7	10.0	7.7	3.4	5.3
Other	100.0	21.4	18.1	22.4	18.3	6.3	4.7	3.3	5.5
South America	100.0	26.3	18.4	15.8	12.7	7.7	7.4	4.9	6.7
Northern America	100.0	21.1	8.1	6.3	6.8	8.2	4.0	9.7	35.8
Region not reported	100.0	30.5	17.7	19.0	11.6	6.8	4.9	3.8	5.8

Source: U.S. Bureau of the Census, March 2000 Current Population Survey.

U.S. Census Bureau. (2001). Profile of the Foreign-Born Population in the United States: 2000. Washington, D.C.: U.S. Department of Commerce.

and by the next decade, immigration from Asia was the second largest. This pattern persists into the early years of the 21st century.

Undocumented Immigrants   Although there is no valid method of counting undocumented immigrants, their numbers are undoubtedly high. These are individuals who are in the United States without governmental approval and are often described as economic refugees and who flee their countries to escape economic oppression, famine, and drought, but do not fulfill the definitions set by the United Nations High Commission for Refugees as a group that is persecuted. Although undocumented immigrants lack the legal documentation to be residing in the United States, they may have entered the country legally or illegally.

Despite perceptions of undocumented immigrants being those who slip across borders without appropriate documentation, the INS (1999) states that a large proportion of all undocumented immigrants, particularly from Asian countries, are "overstays" who fail to return to their homelands when the period of their visas expires. Unlike undocumented immigrants who have few resources and cross the borders illegally in the hopes of improving their economic opportunities, the "overstays" are often skilled individuals who are unable to find jobs commensurate with their expertise. In recognition that the undocumented immigrant population is substantial and that, in many respects, it is an integral part of the U.S. society and economy, in addition to seeking to discourage illegal immigration, in 1986, Congress enacted the Immigration Reform and Control Act (IRCA). Unprecedented, this act provided opportunities for amnesty and legal settlement for those who presented themselves to the INS and could prove that they had been living continuously in the United States since 1982. However, the act also called for increased border patrols and sanctions against those who knowingly employed undocumented aliens.

Although initially the IRCA was successful in reducing the number of immigrants settling in the United States illegally, the stream of entry has once again increased. A major contributor to these continuing increases may be the difficulty in enforcing employer sanctions (Fix & Passel, 1994). The INS estimated that in 1996, approximately 5.0 million (1.9% of the total population) undocumented immigrants resided in the United States, and this number was estimated to be growing by about 275,000 annually. Table 9.4 reports the top 20 countries of origin of the undocumented population.

Refugees and Asylees

Refugees and asylees, unlike immigrants, are usually involuntary migrants. The United States has always been a refuge for those fleeing from persecution and, traditionally, has the largest number of the world's refugees (Mayadas & Segal, 2000). According to the definition presented in the 1951 convention and the 1967 protocol setting forth the mandate of the United Nations High Commissioner for Refugees, a refugee is

Table 9.4 | 1996 Estimates of Undocumented Population

Country of Origin	Population	Country of Origin	Population
All countries	5,000,000		
1. Mexico	2,700,000	11. Colombia	65,000
2. El Salvador	335,000	12. Ecuador	55,000
3. Guatemala	165,000	13. Trinidad and Tobago	50,000
4. Canada	120,000	14. Jamaica	50,000
5. Haiti	105,000	15. Pakistan	41,000
6. Philippines	95,000	16. India	33,000
7. Honduras	90,000	17. Ireland	30,000
8. Dominican Republic	75,000	18. Korea	30,000
9. Nicaragua	70,000	19. Peru	30,000
10. Poland	70,000	20. Portugal	27,000
Other	764,000		

Any person who, owing to a well-founded fear of being persecuted for reasons of race, religion, nationality, or political opinion is outside the country of his/her nationality and is unable or, owing to such fear or for reasons other than personal convenience, is unwilling to avail himself/herself of the protection of that country. (UNHCR, 1995)

This definition is accepted by the U.S. Immigration and Naturalization Service as stated in the amended Refugee Act of 1980, which governs the present policy admitting refugees into the United States (U.S. Department of Justice, 1999). This legislation established the first permanent and systematic set of procedures for the admission and resettlement of refugees, laying the foundation for a mechanism through which the president, in consultation with Congress, can establish annual numbers and allocations of refugees based on the current political climate of the world. In addition, it provides refugees the right to adjust their status to that of permanent resident after one year in the United States. A major influx of refugees was seen after 1975 and the end of the Vietnam War and the fall of Saigon, as citizens fled from Vietnam, Laos, and Cambodia to escape atrocities of the Communist regime of North Vietnam.[5] Although entries from Southeast Asia began to decline in the late 1990s, refugee movement to the United States from Europe was high. Table 9.5 presents refugee approvals and arrivals by geographic area.

[5]Appendix A, Table 9.A3 provides a summary of refugees and asylees granted lawful permanent resident status 1946–2000. Table 9.A4 reports refugee status applications from 1980–2000.

Table 9.5 | Refugee Approvals and Arrivals by Geographic Area (1990–2000)

Geographic area	1990	1991	1992	1993	1994	1995	1996	1997	1998	1999	2000
Authorized admissions[1]	110,000	116,000	123,500	116,000	117,500	111,000	90,000	78,000	83,000	91,000	90,000
Africa	3,500	4,900	6,000	7,000	7,000	7,000	7,700	7,000	7,000	13,000	18,000
East Asia	36,800	38,500	33,350	35,000	41,500	39,000	25,000	10,000	14,000	10,500	8,000
Europe	58,300	53,500	64,300	52,500	53,000	48,000	45,000	52,500	54,000	61,000[2]	44,500
Latin America/Caribbean	2,400	3,100	3,000	4,500	9,000	8,000	6,000	4,000	4,000	2,250	3,500
Near East/South Asia	5,000	6,000	6,850	7,000	6,000	5,000	4,300	4,500	4,000	4,250	10,000
Unallocated Reserve	4,000	10,000	10,000	10,000	1,000	4,000	2,000	—	6,000		
Approvals	99,697	107,962	115,330	106,026	105,137	78,936	74,491	77,600	73,198	85,592	66,546
Africa	3,318	4,430	5,667	6,813	5,748	4,895	9,681	7,854	8,443	15,581	20,084
East Asia	30,613	33,560	31,751	38,314	40,639	23,023	11,891	6,810	12,881	6,728	944
Europe	58,951	62,582	68,131	52,090	48,963	45,900	47,611	56,379	46,671	55,666[2]	32,355
Latin America/Caribbean	1,863	2,263	4,121	3,991	2,513	1,933	982	1,860	1,208	2,796	2,896
Near East/South Asia	4,952	5,127	5,660	4,818	7,229	3,068	4,246	4,539	3,931	4,725	10,193
Not reported	—	—	—	—	45	117	80	158	64	96	74

Arrivals [3]										
109,078	96,589	114,498	107,926	109,593	98,520	74,791	69,276	76,181	85,076	72,143
Africa										
3,493	4,424	5,491	6,969	5,861	4,779	7,502	6,069	6,665	13,036	17,560
East Asia										
38,370	37,264	34,202	38,302	40,601	35,956	18,343	7,781	10,475	9,963	3,557
Europe										
56,912	45,516	64,184	51,278	50,838	45,703	41,617	48,450	54,260	55,877[2]	37,664
Latin America/Caribbean										
5,312	4,026	3,777	4,377	6,437	7,618	3,541	2,986	1,587	2,110	3,233
Near East/South Asia										
4,991	5,359	6,844	7,000	5,856	4,464	3,788	3,990	3,194	4,090	10,129

— Represents zero.

[1]Data are for authorized final ceiling admissions.

[2]For 1999, includes 13,000 Kosovar refugee authorized admissions, 17,831 approvals, and 14,161 arrivals; for 2000, includes 10,000 Kosovar refugee authorized admissions.

[3]Prior to 1996, refugee arrival data were derived from the Nonimmigrant Information System of the Immigration and Naturalization Service. Beginning in fiscal year 1996, arrival data are from the Bureau for Refugee Programs, Department of State. Any comparison of refugee arrival data prior to 1996 must be made with caution. Arrivals may be higher than approvals because of the arrival of persons approved in previous years.

Note: The authorized admission levels for 1990, 1991, 1992, 1993, 1994, and 1995 were 125,000, 131,000, 142,000, 132,000, 121,000, and 112,000, respectively, including 12,000 Amerasians in 1989, 15,000 in both 1990 and 1991, 18,500 in 1992, 16,000 in 1993, 3,500 in 1994, and 1,000 in 1995. Since Amerasians enter the United States on immigrant visas, they are not included as refugee admissions. As a result, the authorized admission levels for 1990 through 1995 for East Asia have been reduced accordingly. Beginning in fiscal year 1996, there is no specific allocation for Amerasians in authorized admissions.

The category identified as "authorized admissions" indicates the ceilings set by the president for a particular year for a particular region. Arrivals may be higher than approvals because some persons who enter in a particular year were approved in previous years.

Asylees differ from refugees in that they usually enter the United States on their own volition, entering this, or other resettlement country without prior approval. Thus,

> A potential asylee is any person who is in the United States or applying for admission at a port of entry and is unable or unwilling to return to his or her country of nationality because of persecution or a well-founded fear of persecution. (U.S. Department of Justice, 1999)

Once within the United States, they apply for asylum, which may or may not result in an admission under refugee status. They are detained until a determination is made, at which time, they are either legally admitted into the country as refugees or are repatriated.

THE HISTORICAL OPPRESSION
AND SURVIVAL VALUES OF IMMIGRANTS

Xenophobia, or fear of the different, appears to be endemic in human beings. Once the earliest European settlers, who were Anglo-Saxon and Protestant, established themselves in the land of the indigenous peoples of the Americas, they systematically annihilated large segments of the original populations—both through genocide and war as well as by the introduction of contagious disease, displacement, and starvation. These early Anglo-Saxon, Protestant immigrants even frowned on European immigrants who came from Ireland and Germany after the Civil War, for they were Catholic. After 1865, the cultural background of white immigration changed again, as most came from Eastern Europe. Africans, brought forcibly to the United States to work on plantations and in mansions as slaves, merited no rights and were frequently denied even basic human dignity. Africans were brought into the country in large numbers as slaves, but voluntary immigration to the United States of black Africans was minuscule, and never higher than 0.71% between 1901 and 1965 (Dinnerstein & Reimers, 1975). Laborers were recruited from Latin America, particularly Mexico, Chile, and Peru, as long ago as in the 1860s to work in the mines and the railroads. Early Asian immigration began from China, and despite the marginalization of this population once it arrived in the United States, was open to all who were able to make the arduous journey from other lands. However, in 1882, the first discriminatory and restrictive immigration act began the regulation of individuals entering the United States. This act, the Chinese Exclusion Act, prevented Chinese workers from entering the United States for 10 years; this was subsequently extended several times and then "indefinitely." This was the beginning of regulations that severely limited the number of immigrants from Asian nations and ultimately practically curtailed it through the Asiatic Barred Zone Act, although the national quota system of the 1920s limited the numbers of people who could enter from various nations to 2% of the population currently residing in the United States from those nations.

In 1965, President Lyndon Johnson signed an amendment to the 1952 Immigration and Nationality Act, liberalizing that law, effectively ending the quota system based on national origin, race, or ethnicity, and introducing the category system mentioned earlier that favored relatives of U.S. citizens or permanent residents and those with the professional or occupational skills and training needed in the United States. Although this leveled the playing field for immigrants from all nations, it also required that most entrants who entered under categories other than through family sponsorship had high professional qualifications. Thus, the population that migrated from the mid-1960s to the early 1980s constituted a very well educated and professional group that had relatively little difficulty adapting to life in the United States.

Patterns of migration have changed in the 21st century, for although the professional stream to the United States continues, so does the stream that is family-sponsored that may not have the caliber of education and skills found among the sponsoring population. In addition, refugee groups and undocumented immigrants, respectively, frequently have few of the resources or the requisite papers to participate in the mainstream U.S. community. Regardless of changes in immigration laws, however, most immigrants and refugees have experienced discrimination and oppression at some time. They have been denied opportunities because of the color of their skin, the accent with which they speak, or the clothing that they wear. Stereotypes abound and are frequently used against particular groups. Most recently, the 2001 USA Patriot Act, which was passed in response to the terrorist attacks of September 11, 2001, may have in a number of ways, reinstitutionalized discrimination against individuals of Middle Eastern origin because they are increasingly targeted for scrutiny. Discrimination, in application, may result in oppression. Lum (2003) lists mechanisms of oppression as (a) exploitation, (b) marginalization, (c) powerlessness, (d) cultural imperialism, and (e) violence.

Despite difficulties, overt and institutionalized discrimination, and sometimes few apparent resources, most migrants to the United States stay, establish a living, and raise children in this country. Despite cultural conflicts, language barriers, and other forms of distance from the majority community, most immigrants find, and have found since the time that they began immigrating, the United States is still the land of opportunity and the land of freedom, and they draw on all their tangible and intangible resources that will permit them to survive here. Despite marginalization, often opportunity is greater for many immigrants in the United States than it was or is in the homeland. And, on balance, for almost all immigrants, there is a net gain in remaining in the United States.

CULTURALLY COMPETENT KNOWLEDGE THEORY
AND PRACTICE SKILLS FOR IMMIGRANTS AND REFUGEES

The pervasive tendency is to group immigrants and refugees together, as in this chapter. Although refugees are immigrants, and although after a year of residence in the United States, they have the option of adjusting their status to that of immigrant, the psychosocial profile of a large proportion of the refugee population has little in common with that of most immigrants. Regardless of the visa under which they come, and regardless of whether they have a visa to come at all, immigrants to the United States are in the country of their own volition. The *pull* factor of the United States attracted them, and, in all likelihood, they planned their entry carefully, bringing with them what they thought they might need in this new land and relinquishing, by choice, much at home. Regardless of how dangerous or traumatic the move, as it is for many undocumented immigrants, it is still undertaken at one's own wishes (or those of the family). Refugees, on the other hand, are *pushed* out of their homelands. Most did not leave their homes by choice, and many would probably prefer to return to their native lands if safety were not a concern. However, this is not the only difference. They leave their homes with little or no planning; they flee with few, if any, tangible belongings; they suffer inconceivable atrocities in the form of persecution, degradation, and violation; and they are witness to the destruction of their fundamental rights and lifestyles.

What refugees and immigrants share, however, is that regardless of the circumstances in their home countries, their reasons and experience of leaving there, and the process of entering the host country, most individuals of both groups arrive at their destinations with a number of assets. Those who leave their homelands, even under the most deplorable circumstances, are not the most needy, weak, and oppressed. Those who are able to access the host country have, at the very least, physical, emotional, and psychological fortitude. The weakest and the most downtrodden of the refugees, for example, are the least likely to risk fleeing their homelands, because being caught may result in a fate worse than death. In addition to personal resources, most refugees and immigrants have some support networks that allow them to become linked with resources and contacts that enable their transitions. Rarely do refugees leave alone; they are usually accompanied by family or other community members as they join their respective tangible and intangible resources to overcome difficulties they encounter.

In working with immigrants and refugees, then, practitioners may first need to identify the circumstances under which the group left its homeland and what resources it brought with it. Second, practitioners must recognize that all who come to the United States, either willingly or not, leave in their homelands much that is familiar and that ranges from the tangible to the intangible—a familiar culture, language, environment, climate, family, friends, social system, norms of behavior, and so on. And, third, practitioners must acknowledge that, regardless of how willing the United States is to accept these new arrivals in their country, all that the nation has to offer them is strange and bewildering. Through it all, the support systems on which these immigrants have relied all their lives are no longer accessible.

Thus, the stresses of immigrants and refugees in translocation are enormous. Although many are associated with the traumas of dramatic emigration-immigration processes, numerous others result from culture shock in an alien environment, where language, social structures, norms, expectations, and values substantially differ from those that have been elemental to the immigrants' understanding of themselves. In the United States, well-understood role relationships change and established patterns of interaction are questioned. When immigrants have the psychological capability of coping with these and other stresses of relocating to an unfamiliar culture, they are more likely to adjust and control the direction of their lives. On the other hand, they may experience posttraumatic stress disorder, as do many refugees. Without sufficient and appropriate social and emotional support, and perhaps therapy, they may fail to find the immigration experience satisfactory, remaining unhappy, resenting their lives in the new land, and pining for their homelands and all that is familiar. Competence, then, for the practitioner working with the immigrant or the refugee involves competence not only in social work skills and cultural competence, but understanding about the breadth and the depth of the immigration experience for each newcomer to the United States.

Lum (2003) proposes a framework for cultural competence that identifies four components: (1) cultural awareness, (2) knowledge acquisition, (3) skill development, and (4) inductive learning. He suggests that *cultural awareness* is awareness of one's own life experiences related to culture and contact with other cultures, with a conscious assessment of these experiences in forming personal prejudices and discrimination. *Knowledge acquisition,* on the other hand, involves learning about other diverse groups, focusing on their demographic characteristics, their culture and experience of oppression, their unique strengths, and critically evaluating that knowledge. *Skill development* requires tempering social work patterns of intervention with the knowledge acquired regarding cultural diversity and through self-assessment. This may include learning skills of developing relationships with clients that necessitates approaches other than the most obvious, but that are couched in an understanding of a client's culture. Finally, *inductive learning* requires that, based on the new knowledge and experience born of the preceding three components, practitioners take their discussions and understandings beyond the level of individual clients to informing others of the insights related to becoming culturally competent.

CONTACT SKILLS WITH IMMIGRANT AND REFUGEE CLIENTS

In practice with individuals not of the dominant society, several practice issues confound effective service provision and intervention related to the client system. Resistance, communication barriers, personal and family background, and ethnic community identity (Lum, 1992) are exacerbated by the experience of many immigrants and refugees, who closely guard information because of fear (perhaps unfounded) of exposure, past experience with oppression, and mistrust of authority. A number of immigrants and most refugees arrive from nations in which they do not have the freedom of speech or of choice. The mistrust of authority, including the possibility of deportation from the United States, can often erect formidable barriers as service providers probe into the lives, experiences, and feelings of new immigrants and refugees. In addition to alleviating these by establishing a good rapport and relationship, service providers must establish credibility and expert authority, including the use of directiveness and appropriate self-disclosure to provide the foundation of role relationships with clients.

Service providers, whether they are health care professionals, social service workers, or those in the world of law and finance must become aware of conditions that can hinder the development of an adequate working relationship with many immigrants and refugees. To develop rapport based on understanding and trust, service providers must educate themselves about both general and specific immigrant experiences, adjustment in the United States, and the community culture. Interventions, services, and resources must be applied with an awareness of their implications for other cultures. To the extent possible, practitioners should explain these services in understandable terms, within the context of the client's cultural norms. Only when service provider credibility, rapport, and sensitivity are established will a large segment of the immigrants or refugee population provide sufficient information or comply with the guidelines of intervention. Self-disclosure must be used to increase credibility and authority, and *understanding* must be used to develop the relationship. Although many immigrants and refugees may fear authority and avoid it, individuals from many nondemocratic, non-Occidental cultures are socialized to respect (and obey) it. Despite American emphasis on allowing people to make their own decisions, in several other cultures, once rapport and trust have been established between practitioners and clients, a clear directive is the most effective in helping in the resolution of problems. Many non-Occidental immigrant groups traditionally use personal networks to resolve issues, only seeking outside help when they have exhausted their own resources. Contact with a social worker is made when they do not know where else to turn, and they desperately need help. The relationship between the social worker and the immigrant is not perceived as an equal partnership by the latter, who regard the social worker as the one with authority, status, and knowledge and as someone who can help provide answers. Giving instructions can be most appropriate (Allen & Nimmagadda, 1999). For example, Asian clients often expect advice, which is in direct contradiction to the U.S. social work value of self-determination (Nimmagadda & Balgopal, 2000), but the use of directiveness, or providing clear advice regarding the optimal option from among a series of possibilities, can be most effective.

The barriers that can confront those working with immigrants and refugees are substantially greater with newer arrivals to the United States; however, barriers may persist through the lives of the first-generation immigrant. The culture of privacy and silence is pervasive among most immigrants, as is the tendency to avoid sharing information of a personal nature with outsiders. Furthermore, barring perhaps those influenced by the Western European tradition, most individuals and families that seek assistance from outside the boundaries of their own personal resources do so because they seek an authority with the knowledge and skills to guide them in the appropriate course of action. As such, a nondirective approach may not be the most effective. Sharing of personal experiences similar to those of the clients, likewise, should be done prudently. It may be more important to use self-disclosure (focusing on the practitioner's credentials and work with similar clients) to help establish credibility. Service providers must be culturally sensitive and must work to establish rapport and trust with immigrants and refugees before they will contemplate accepting any assistance that is offered.

There has long been discussion about the need to link theory and practice. Educators and theoreticians have written much about cultural diversity, the need to be ethnically sensitive, and the need to provide services consistent with the sociocultural framework of clients. When practitioners recognize cultural variations, draw on client resources, attempt to present options in a manner that is consistent with client norms, cultural dissonance can be reduced, and there may be a greater likelihood of service utilization. Practice models must be developed that provide guidelines for integrating cultural awareness with Western interventions to synthesize approaches that are of the greatest relevance for the client yet consistent with the guidelines of the practitioner's profession.

PROBLEM IDENTIFICATION SKILLS WITH IMMIGRANT AND REFUGEE CLIENTS

Fundamental to understanding and identifying problems with the immigrant and refugee populations, as with any other community, is establishing rapport and trust. Social workers must also present themselves as compassionate experts. Clients come to the social worker for answers, and to find the answers acceptable, they must perceive the social worker as having the resources and skills to help solve the problem for them (not provide them with the guidance to solve their own problems). Hence, in establishing rapport, the primary function is to subtly or openly negotiate respective responsibilities (Karger & Levine, 2000; Longres & Patterson, 2000). This, itself, requires a substantial change in the thinking of both the social worker and the client, who may be coming from diametrically opposed perspectives and expectations. Furthermore, clients are less likely to openly discuss the major problem and might hide behind a more superficial presenting problem, until the social workers' competence and sensitivity have been evidenced. In the view of most immigrants and refugees, social workers are always in positions of authority (see Balgopal, 2000)—they can never be "friends." Nevertheless, the social worker, as in any relationship, must listen closely to clients to understand their perceptions of the problems, always bearing in mind that intervention and services must be client driven. In addition, language is often a barrier because even if clients speak English, understandings are colored by cultural norms. Hence, when clients respond with a "yes," it might not mean that they agree and will follow through, but that they have heard what the social worker said.

In evaluating problems, social workers must explore them to understand whether the problems emanate from individuals' issues or if they are the residual effects of organizational or societal problems. Furthermore, social workers must also explore the clients' perceptions and interpretations of problems, including the most pressing or presenting ones.

Even though a social worker may have established a rapport with the client, identified the problem clearly, and worked toward an effective intervention, the process may still be aborted. The presence of a culturally competent practitioner may not reflect a culturally sensitive organization. It may be the responsibility of the practitioner to mediate between the client and the organization to modify approaches to intervention or services to meet the unique needs of immigrant clients. Likewise, it may be the responsibility of the social worker to lobby and advocate on behalf of the immigrant and refugee populations in society to ensure that their specific needs, English language education, for example, are met by the community's social service provider or that either organizations or society engage in outreach efforts to intervene in problems (such as domestic violence) that may not be brought to the attention of the larger society. Responsibilities of the social worker may also be to alert both organizations and society for the need for particular services that may not exist.

Refugees, because of the screening they receive and the process by which they enter the United States, including the initial orientation and supervision they receive through resettlement agencies, have a higher likelihood of being linked to the services they need. Often the resettlement agency will serve as an advocate in helping to develop programs when a gap is identified. On the other hand, immigrants rarely come to the attention of the social services, most do not participate in the social welfare system, and the only major service systems they use are the educational and health care systems. The social service providers must work with the medical and educational professions to identify psychosocial issues that immigrant families may be experiencing and engage in outreach efforts and appropriate interventions.

The readiness of a receiving country to accept immigrants in general or an immigrant group in particular is, itself, a complex matter and will affect the skills that social workers must mobilize in identifying problems. When immigration is viewed as inextricably bound to a nation's political, economic, and social well-being as well as its future security interests, it is more likely to be welcomed than if it is not. In general, public immigration policy is closely tied to the economy and national needs. Opportunities may be available to immigrants, yet they may be rife with obstacles, mirroring the nation's ambivalence toward a particular people. In addition to the level of economic opportunities available to a group, the country's receptiveness to it is reflected in the programs and services accessible to it. These include the basic health, education, and welfare needs of the immigrant community, but may also include programs that can provide psychosocial and emotional support.

National public policy and public perceptions may differ on receptivity to immigrant flow based on the economic needs of particular indigenous groups. The extant literature is variable regarding the effect of immigration on employment opportunities for indigenous people.[6] Some suggests that immigrants displace few native residents but secure those positions that are unfilled or that the natives are unwilling to accept (Sum et al., 2002). Employers often turn to foreign labor to meet the less stable portions of economic demands that remain unfilled by local workers. Some researchers contend that the effects of immigrants on the wages and earnings of natives are nonexistent or small, and can be positive (Sum et al., 2002). Other literature, conversely, indicates that increases in immigration can significantly hurt employment levels of some groups (Cobb-Clark & Kossoudji, 1994; Kposowa, 1995)—because it increases the supply of U.S. labor, it reduces or makes jobs more scarce for natives. Job competition is especially great between immigrants and natives at the lower end of the labor market (Center for Immigration Studies, 2001). The impact of immigrants on natives' economic options is not unitary. Much depends on the current business needs in the country and whether natives have the skills and interest to fill them. Furthermore, some immigrant groups, with a predominance of particular skills, may be considered more attractive to employers than indigenous people for other reasons. These may include the willingness to work for lower wages, cultural and social characteristics, and a strong work ethic (perhaps because of fewer social and family ties in the host country). These factors affect the integration of immigrants into the country and may result in institutionalized problems, rather than problems associated with the immigrants themselves or with their experience of migration.

ASSESSMENT SKILLS WITH IMMIGRANT AND REFUGEE CLIENTS

After problem identification, all pertinent information should be collected and processed through a culturally sensitive lens to chart the most appropriate course of intervention. It becomes essential to identify the factors contributing to the development and maintenance of the problem(s) identified, and although these may be biosocial or psychosocial, they may be influenced by individual-level variables and by meso- and macro-level factors.

---

[6]See publications of the National Immigration Forum (www.immigrationforum.org, accessed August 13, 2003) and the Center for Immigration Studies (www.cis.org, accessed August 13, 2003), both of which have studied these phenomena extensively. Literature of the former tends to identify immigrants as beneficial for the labor force whereas that of the latter suggests that it is detrimental.

If one uses Lazarus's model of conceptualization (Lazarus, 1976, 1989) for problem assessment, one would explore at least the seven dimensions he specifies:

1. Behavior—observable actions, whether they appear voluntary or not
2. Affect—felt or reported feelings and emotions
3. Sensation—feelings associated with the five senses as well as other physical sensations (possibly related to health)
4. Imagery—fantasies or imagined experiences
5. Cognition—thoughts and beliefs that often guide behavior and feelings
6. Interpersonal relationships—that may be reported or observable
7. Drugs—looks at the biochemical dimension of the individual in addition to the use or misuse of psychotropic substances

Any assessment must consider the context of individuals' behaviors and difficulties. Thus, although Lazarus's model may be an effective tool for dissecting and understanding the individual at one level, an ecological perspective, taking into account individuals' social environment, is also necessary to provide a more complete picture of clients' experiences. Significant individuals, family members, the community, social and formal organizations, and the society-at-large at different stages affect the development of individuals in a variety of ways, some of which may be effective whereas others may be less so (Zastrow & Kirst-Ashman, 2004).

In working with the immigrant or refugee, each dimension as well as the social environment should be explored within the American context as well as within the context of the immigration/cultural/cross-cultural experience. Hence, although behaviors that are exhibited should be assessed for appropriateness, the service provider should also determine whether "appropriateness" is culturally bound. Level of involvement of the family, the community, or both may also differ based on cultural background, and high levels of involvement may either represent healthy interdependence or dysfunction (or something in between).

Certainly some behaviors are universally unacceptable (e.g., stealing another person's property); however, others are idiosyncratic to the United States. A common point of divergence in behavior between U.S.–born individuals and immigrants, for example, is the use of eye contact. In many nations, those who are younger, subordinate, or female are not permitted to make, or sustain, eye contact with those who are older, superior, or male. In the United States, lack of eye contact is associated with being "shifty" or engaging in avoidance behaviors. It is then the responsibility of the worker to (1) observe the behavior, (2) understand it in light of the client's cultural norms, (3) determine if it is necessary that the client changes the behavior because it is essential for survival in this society, (4) work with the client in understanding why it is essential that this pattern of behavior be changed, and (5) help the client deal with the dissonance associated with changing patterns of behavior, including the meaning these changes may have for others in the client's community.

Thus, each of the seven factors must be so addressed. Once the worker has collected information about a factor (either reported or observed), the worker and client together must try to understand it within the framework of the immigrant or refugee experience and the unique culture to identify and develop a bicultural pattern acceptable to environments in which the client must function. It is essential to identify whether the problem facing the client is a universal human problem (such as depression, ill-health, poverty), one emanating from the immigration experience, or a cross-cultural dilemma. Intervention will have to be designed based on such an assessment.

As is stressed in all intervention exercises, assessment is an ongoing process and as information increases, there may be changes in the understanding of problems, leading to a change in goals and interventions. A holistic view of the client and the context will focus on biological (physiological) health as well as psychological health and environmental factors in understanding social functioning. This is particularly important in non-European traditions, as mental health issues are neither recognized nor acceptable in a number of societies. Mental illness merits labels of disgrace, evidence of weakness, and failure, and there is a tendency among many immigrants and refugees (even in their countries of origin) to somatize their psychosocial difficulties. Hence, service providers, particularly in the health care field, must be particularly vigilant in the process of diagnosing chronic ailments, especially among those in their young and middle adult years.

Despite a "person-in-the-environment" perspective, there can be a tendency to address immigrant and refugee issues from a micro perspective, reinforcing an Ameri-centric focus. It behooves service providers to also assess whether changes are needed (1) within organizations that provide services to these populations (or do not provide services to these "invisible" populations) by increasing outreach efforts and (2) within the ethnic community, which may have the willingness but not the ability to help individuals and families in their midst. Organizations may not only need to become culturally sensitive and make their services more accessible and attractive to refugee and immigrants, but may also need to mobilize a particular immigrant community itself to address its members' concerns by developing community service programs at the grass roots level. Furthermore, at the macro level, public policies (other than immigrant and refugee policies) may need to be so implemented that they address the needs of these populations.

Some public policies particularly affect immigrants and refugees because of their immigrant status, because of sociocultural differences that influence styles of behavior, or because of a combination of these factors. Clearly, the primary ones with continuing implications for a number of immigrants and refugees are the immigration and refugee policies. In addition to affecting immigrants (or potential immigrants) themselves, they also affect immigrants with family members or other contacts who are allowed, or disallowed, entry into the United States. Also, among the national public policies that are of major concern to the largest number of immigrants are (1) social and family

Case Study Integration Exercise on Contact, Problem Identification, and Assessment Skills

Extant literature suggests that immigrants underuse social services (Bemak, Chung, & Bornemann, 1996), and most refugees, once they have become "self-sufficient" and can support themselves, move away from public assistance (Balgopal, 2000). After initial struggles in adjustment, many immigrants and refugees establish for themselves an acceptable pattern and quality of life. Real crises begin occurring when issues of family expectations and intercultural and intergenerational differences challenge long-established traditions and norms. Frequent areas of sociocultural change (particularly gender role relationships) begin emerging early in the immigrant experience, but families attempt to address these by themselves as best they can, keeping problems within their own boundaries. Social service providers have tended to perceive this lack of service use as indicative of personal strengths and high levels of adjustment, although this may merely reflect cultural taboos toward discussing family issues outside the family (Segal, 2002).

Immigrants usually come to the attention of the social services when problems are seen with the youth in the second generation and school officials (most often) or health care practitioners (less frequently) make referrals to the social services. Most often, it is not until difficulties are significant and someone outside the family indicates concern that immigrant and refugee parents seek help for their children. Then, when the family becomes involved in services for the child, other familial problems become evident (Ahern & Athey, 1991; de Leon Siantz, 1997). As such, many social workers will find that immigrant families that seek services do so with presenting problems revolving around their children, but may be willing to utilize services for themselves once contact has been made and rapport has been established.

Major dilemmas, unrelated to the second generation, that almost all immigrants must face after they have been in the United States for several years (or even decades), revolve around the care of aging parents, most of whom remain in the homeland, and decisions regarding their own retirement (whether in the United States or their countries of origin). Thus, immigrants and refugees must deal with their own immigration and adjustment, the development of their children in a bicultural context, and the aging of their parents, yet presenting problems, most frequently, revolve around the academic and social performance of their children in the school system.

The following case may be a very typical one, regardless of the socioeconomic level of the immigrant family or the country of origin. Most immigrants and refugees, regardless of their own levels of education, have great hopes and expectations for their children in the United States and see education as the route to success (Booth & Crouter, 1997).

Case Brought to a School Social Worker

John Wong, a second-generation Chinese American 17-year-old, began showing increasing restlessness in school during the second semester of his junior year in high school. His grade point average, which until this point, had been a 3.5, appeared to be slipping as his performance in most of his classes, particularly in calculus and chemistry became increasingly erratic. On two occasions, his chemistry teacher sent notes home saying that John had lost interest in the class and this was evidenced both in his decreased level of participation and the grades of C– and D in the last two unit tests. Her concern became greater as she received no contact from the parents and suggested that the school social worker, Janice, speak to the child, because she felt the underlying problem was not academic.

After speaking with John a few times, Janice learned that he had recently begun dating and fallen in love with Susie, a non-Asian girl. In addition, it became clear that John's family did not know about his deteriorating performance in school as he had intercepted the notes the teacher had sent his parents because he usually arrives home several hours before his parents. John also provided Janice the following information regarding his family.

John's parents, George and Anita Wong, ages 53 and 48 respectively, who had both immigrated to the United States from Taiwan in 1974 as students had met in the United States and married in 1978. Both successful physicians, they have two older daughters, ages 21 and 19 who are away at college. Although Anita's older sister is in the United States in another city, her aging parents are still in Taiwan, but George's widowed mother, aged 81 now lives with them. The family is active with the local Chinese community, and socializes almost exclusively with other Chinese families that migrated from Taiwan. John says he feels more American than Chinese.

Application Exercises*

1. What problem behaviors does John evidence?
2. Is each problem behavior listed self-evident?
3. Identify possible causes for these behaviors.
4. List possible consequences of these behaviors.
5. How may the possible consequences affect the occurrence of these behaviors?
6. Do other behaviors that John is exhibiting pose potential problems for this family?
7. List reasons these may cause conflict for this family.

Meeting with the Parents

Janice scheduled a meeting with John and his parents, indicating that John's science teacher was concerned about changes in his performance. The parents were distraught that they had not been informed that John's school work was not up to par and were very anxious to meet with Janice. During this meeting, which Janice saw as an information-gathering meeting, she did not inform the parents that John had intercepted the notes; she also believed it was John's responsibility to let his parents know that he had done so and advised him that if he wished, she would assist him to do so.

The Wongs were clearly concerned about their son's success in school, stressing that education was highly important to them as a family, and as with their daughters, they expected John to attend Ivy League universities. Their expectation was, that like them, he would seek to be a physician. They believed he had the ability and it is a noble calling that would also allow him to provide his future family with a comfortable lifestyle.

---

*Possible responses found in chapter endnotes.

(continued)

CASE | *continued*

The Wongs indicated that although they understood that he was also an American, they expected that he would adhere to Chinese values. They stated they were somewhat concerned about the loss of Chinese culture and tradition in the United States, and they already saw it happening with their older daughter who, much to their dismay, was involved with a Euro-American man.

Other immediate concerns voiced by John's parents were not directly related to him. George's mother, who now lives with them, is frail and demanding. She speaks no English and there are few other Chinese in the neighborhood with whom she can socialize. She is isolated all day and needs constant attention when her son and daughter-in-law return home. They were also concerned that she may fall and hurt herself or experience some other difficulty while they were away. George withdraws into his study when the couple returns in the evening, but Anita, who is also tired after a day with patients, must entertain her mother-in-law. She sees no change in this pattern, but realistically notes that the situation will worsen as the latter becomes more frail and dependent. George and Anita argue a great deal more than they did previously.

Anita also mentioned that she was particularly concerned about her own parents who are still in Taiwan. Both she and her sister are in the United States, so there is no one to care for them. She had asked them several times to come to live with her family; however, they do not wish to leave Taiwan, and they also believe it is inappropriate for them to live with a daughter.

Application Exercises

(These additional questions should also be explored by the family.)

8. Identify areas of conflict between John and his parents.
9. Are these areas overt or covert?
10. Are these generational issues, cultural, or both?
11. What are other areas of stress for the family?
12. To what extent are these cultural?
13. To what extent are they influenced by immigration and responsibilities to those in the homeland?
14. How may these other areas of stress in the family affect John and his behavior?

welfare policies, (2) housing policies, (3) educational policies, (4) health and mental health policies, and (5) criminal justice policies. Although not designed particularly for immigrants or refugees, these policies substantially color the daily lives of immigrants, as they do for all Americans. When policies do not effectively address the problems of a particular population, an exploration of reasons is warranted. Furthermore, when policies do meet needs, policy makers would be wise to understand the ingredients for success so that it may be replicated. Policy analysis has a number of facets, not the least of which are the value-laden underpinnings and historical context of the development of a particular policy. The goals of particular policies and eligibility requirements may have implications for immigrants and refugees such that these goals may preclude immigrants and refugees from participation, as recent changes to Social Security benefits have indicated. Or these changes may be so complex that the less educated and affluent in these groups who are more likely to need them, fail to use the services for which they are eligible. This has been found to be especially true for health care benefits.

However, as in all assessments, the worker must keep sight of the strengths of clients and draw on those resources in the amelioration of the problem. When working with immigrants, furthermore, these strengths may lie in the individuals themselves, but also in the cultures from which they come as well as in the experience of immigration itself. For most to survive in an alien environment, they must have already evidenced flexibility and adaptation.

INTERVENTION SKILLS WITH IMMIGRANT AND REFUGEE CLIENTS

Problem exploration and assessment aim to design an intervention by establishing goals. As with clients of any background, unless and until there is agreement between client and worker about the direction intervention should take, progress is unlikely. Despite social work values that stress non-direction and self-determination, many newer immigrants from other cultures come for assistance to a person of authority with the belief that they will be guided, or directed, to do what is in their best interest. However, a number of mediating factors may interfere with cooperation. For example, although the social worker is in a relative position of authority, there may be no clear benefit for compliance or punishment for noncompliance. In addition, even if social workers appear empathic, but lack knowledge of clients' cultures or experiences, clients may be skeptical about options presented; if there is significant dissonance between what is proposed and their traditional norms, clients may appear to cooperate, but will not follow through in taking action. Thus, workers must educate themselves about the particular immigrant/refugee culture, understand areas of conflict, and have the empathy and interpersonal skills to work with clients to minimize barriers to achieving goals. This, itself, may be a tall order. It is particularly important for workers to bear in mind, when communication and compromise become difficult, that fundamental needs are shared by all human beings. It is merely the binding and interpretation that culture imposes that confounds the issue. The basic skills of honesty and openness, and encouraging clients to educate the worker, can go a long way in solidifying the working relationship between worker and client of different backgrounds.

Elemental in the helping process, regardless of the population served, is a commitment to the value base of social work and the profession's stress on the importance of recognizing the worth and dignity of every human being. Placing the client in the center of the helping relationship and valuing client input are essential ingredients in establishing the relationship. Particularly with new immigrants and refugees, however, workers may be placed in a position to educate these newcomers about norms and patterns of behavior that may be necessary for effective functioning in the United States, and social workers must be comfortable in providing guidance and concrete suggestions of appropriate actions. With a solid foundation, built on positive regard and mutual respect, intervention can be provided in such a way that workers remain sensitive to client culture, but clients also become aware that as residents of the United States, some cultural patterns may not be acceptable in this society, others may need to be consciously modified, yet others may naturally evolve through the bicultural experience, and some may be maintained intact.

In looking at the person-in-the-environment, as with the problem identification and assessment, the social worker will need to work with the client to identify goals as well as the targets of change. These should be the direct outgrowth of the assessment of the problems identified; thus, it is essential that the assessment be undertaken with care and cultural sensitivity to ensure its accuracy. The target for change may be the individual and family, it may be the service delivery system, it may be the society (at one or all levels of the socio-politico-economic structure), or it may involve a combination of all. Furthermore, insightful workers will identify potential barriers early and determine how best to address them.

Working with immigrant families may differ from working with other minority groups in that social workers must have an appreciation, and be able to convey an understanding, of cultural, immigration, and bicultural issues. These must include sensitivity to concerns of first-generation immigrants regarding their offspring as well as their ongoing commitments to their lands of origin and the relatives remaining there. The concerns of second-generation children are vastly different from those of their parents as they work to balance what often appear to be conflicting lifestyles. However, it is important to bear in mind that immigrants, in some ways, are no different from other minorities who must learn to navigate two systems—that of the majority culture and that of their own.

Part of the process of providing intervention to immigrant and refugee families is removing barriers between the family and the social workers. A number of barriers prevent the use of both mainstream services as well as the services of anyone outside the immediate or extended family. The more significant among the barriers may be the following:

1. A cultural unacceptability of the use of strangers' assistance. Help from someone outside the family unit can be a source of shame and guilt and can result in significant resistance to help provided by social workers.
2. A number of communication differences may exist between the social worker and the client. Even though language itself may be a major barrier, other more subtle differences may be in the use of nonverbal cues and in an understanding of topics of taboo. These can work in concert to erect significant barriers in communication and interpretation.

3. A tremendous value is placed on the privacy of the family, and regardless of the pressures experienced by the family, the family colludes in silence to prevent outsiders from both inspecting and intervening in its matters.
4. A general mistrust of authority is felt by many immigrants and refugees who enter the United States from nations where freedom is limited and oppression is prevalent. Because of fears of exposure and the ramifications of expressing need or weakness, including a fear of deportation, many immigrants and refugees do not disclose the depth or range of adjustment problems they may experience.

These barriers must be addressed by the social worker through sensitivity, insight, and a communication of an understanding of, and respect for, the immigrant's culture and experience. Only then will rapport be satisfactorily established to allow intervention to progress.

In addition to traditional intervention methods, including individual, group, and family therapies, along with advocacy and education of significant constituencies outside the client group boundaries, social workers practicing with immigrant and refugee populations may seek to use indigenous methods and resources for intervention. Although mainstream social service and mental health communities may provide significant assistance to immigrant and refugee clients, their assistance may not be as readily welcomed as it would perhaps be from natural helpers in the immigrant community. The social worker may wish to partner with an elder in the immigrant or refugee community in working with a particular client or family or may solicit the help of the extended family system to assist (both practical and intangible) of the client.

Practice in the human services is, intrinsically, fraught with a variety of difficulties. As clients and subjects in the United States become increasingly ethnically and culturally diverse, it becomes important to recognize that a variety of additional factors can complicate service provision. Although focus on providing services to ethnic minorities is increasing, focus on immigrants and refugees continues to be relatively limited, and extant knowledge about them is scattered. Despite disagreements about the transferability of interventions and research methods, some experience shows that even cross-culturally validated methods and instruments are not readily applicable across cultures and communities (Segal, 2000a, 2000b).

In practice with minorities, several practice issues confound effective service provision and intervention related to the client system. The resistance, communication barriers, personal and family background, and ethnic community identity (Lum, 1992) already identified are especially significant for first generation immigrants and refugees, many of whom arrive from nations in which they do not have the freedom of speech or of choice.

On the other hand, there is a tendency to treat descendents of immigrants of color across generations as being similar to their immigrant parents. The second (and subsequent) generation offspring of immigrants and refugees, if they are white, often comfortably blend with the majority population and self-identify with an ethnic group at will. Children of immigrants of color from Asia, Africa, and South America may continue to look foreign, but in the 21st century, are more similar to their Euro-American counterparts than is any second-generation group before. In earlier years, despite desires to become integrated into the American community, most second-generation immigrants of color were kept segregated and isolated. The most cited examples were of the *Nisei,* who caused their parents much distress as they rejected all that was Japanese, yet they were not allowed by the Euro-Americans to become a part of their society. The society in the United States has changed. Despite continuing prejudice and discrimination against people of color, the opportunity to be an integral part of the U.S. society is not only possible, it is a reality. In large segments of the country, there exists a commitment to cultural pluralism and the recognition that differences need not only be tolerated, but celebrated. There is less need for second-generation immigrants and refugees to behave in a manner that reflects only the heritage that is obvious by their physical characteristics and deny the bicultural one they inherit with their birth into the American society. It is no longer necessary to hide themselves and their feelings from those who can assist them, and the shroud of secrecy that keeps immigrants and refugees from discussing their feelings, attitudes, and experiences is lifted for this group of U.S.–born individuals. Most in this group feel American and believe they are entitled to the rights and privileges of the nation, as is any other citizen. The fears resulting from experience or from cultural taboos that encapsulate many first-generation immigrants and refugees are less apparent among the second generation of the 21st century. The resis-tance encountered in providing services to this population may be similar to that found within any U.S. group.

Service providers must still be culturally sensitive in delivering services, but the sensitivity must be directed to understanding the experience of being bicultural and any related difficulties. Often these difficulties sprout from looking "foreign" and like their parents but feeling American and similar to their peers. It is more likely that the second generation will respond well to services and interventions from mainstream human service professions. Practitioners will find that the second generation is substantially more knowledgeable than is the immigrant generation about Western medicine, financial management, business opportunities, legal matters, the U.S. political system, social services, and citizens' rights and privileges. Barriers that are erected by the individual will more often reflect personal characteristics and history than an immigrant/refugee culture or experience. Although service providers must also establish a rapport and develop a relationship of trust with second-generation clients, they may find that this group is more open about its needs, expects to have greater input into decisions about itself, and shies away from undue directiveness.

Beyond the micro level, practitioners at the meso level must also be alert to potential issues and concerns facing immigrants and refugees and their offspring. More often than not, these groups do not voluntarily seek assistance. Although medical services may be used fairly frequently by some immigrant and refugee groups, most will shy away from the social services and will come to their attention only indirectly. The most frequent source of referral appears to be the educational system. When the offspring of immigrants and refugees begin evidencing difficulties in school, either academically or behaviorally, and referrals are made to school social workers or counselors, other issues confronting the family become evident. It is especially important that social workers encourage teachers and school personnel to be particularly alert to concerns facing immigrant and refugee children as well as second-generation children. Adjustment of immigrant and refugee children, itself, may be problematic and attract the attention of personnel in the school system; however, issues facing the second generation may be less evident.

Even if the school system offers them, it does not ensure that families will pursue social service options. Nevertheless, they may become more aware of their existence and also begin to toy with the idea that using these services is not disgraceful. This is especially important since for many immigrants and refugees, their natural support systems, such as the extended family of grandparents, aunts, uncles, cousins, and siblings, are often still in the homeland and not available to them in this country.

Mainstream social service providers, furthermore, may need to recognize that the absence of immigrants and refugees among their caseloads does not necessarily mean the lack of need in these populations. These providers may need to be educated regarding immigrants and refugees, and they must, in turn, engage in outreach efforts to attract these groups to use the services from which they could benefit. In the long run, it behooves the social services and the society, in general, to extend its assistance to these new immigrants whose numbers continue to grow and who compose such a large segment of the population. As micro and meso social work services begin addressing immigrant and refugee concerns, it becomes important to focus also on macrolevel social policies that may influence and affect immigrants and refugees. Immigrant and refugee policies have significant implications for who enters the nation and under what conditions, but all social policies affect these groups as much as they affect the native U.S. population. Service providers must ensure that immigrants and refugees are aware of the rights and opportunities provided by the range of public policies and that they avail themselves of the resources that they may need to function adequately in this society. Furthermore, service providers at the micro and macro levels may need to include an awareness of immigrants and refugee needs in their advocacy and lobbying efforts as they seek to influence legislators and policy makers.

TERMINATION SKILLS WITH IMMIGRANT AND REFUGEE CLIENTS

As with any population, if goals have been achieved, clients must be prepared for the end of the intervention relationship. Although the relationship must begin with termination in view, only when goals are close to being attained does it becomes a particularly significant issue. The worker, with clients, reviews the intervention process, beginning with the presenting problem, the

| CASE | **Case Study Integration Exercise on Intervention and Termination** |

1. On what problems should the family focus?
2. What goals should be established?
3. What needs to be changed?
4. How should it be changed?

Intervention Plans with the Wong Family

During the first few sessions of intervention with the Wong family, the social worker, Janice, met individually with John, then with each of his parents, then with the parents together, and finally with the family as a whole. Through this, she assessed that John was very afraid of his parents, but more so of his father. He expressed a generalized fear of being shouted at and of being made to feel a failure and a disappointment to the family. George was a traditional Chinese father and husband, and although Anita worked, she was expected to fulfill all household responsibilities, including caring for George's mother. In addition, he expected Anita to support him in his attitudes and disciplinary position toward John, even if she disagreed. Anita appeared to be more liberal and bicultural than George. She believed that John ought not to be pushed into a field that did not interest him, and she also believed that he was bright, but was not succeeding academically because he either did not have the aptitude or the interest in science. She felt there were several alternative career paths John could take, but she observed that George was becoming increasingly conservative as he was getting older, more like his own father, and less open to input from others, particularly from her.

- The family members decided that since they had come to see Janice about John's deteriorating academic performance, this should be the primary focus.
- It also became clear that communication between the parents and John needed to be addressed.
- Although Janice believed the relationship between George and Anita was rather tense, she felt that this might not be the ideal time to address it.
- The parental generation was clearly a source of concern for the family, and Janice felt that supportive community services for George's mother would meet some of her social needs as well as ensure her safety while the family was away during the day.
- George and Anita had left Taiwan almost 30 years ago, so they were not familiar with the services that are now available for the elderly in that country.

Much of Janice's early interaction with the family involved establishing a rapport and listening to George and Anita's views on the conflicts they saw between the American and Chinese cultures, particularly in relationship to rearing children in this country. As the relationship progressed, Anita helped John voice the difficulties he experienced living up to parental expectations and excelling in both the Chinese and American cultures. For example, his parents expected him not only to be an academic success, but also to participate in leadership positions in several extra-curricular activities. In order to be a leader, he was expected to be independent, assertive, argue his position, and direct others. To be successful in the American world, he had to be American. On the other hand, when he was at home, he was expected to do as he was told, not disagree, not voice his preferences, and allow his parents to dictate his career, his life partner, and his future. In John's opinion, both these sets of behaviors require different dispositions, and it is usually not possible for one individual to be both assertive and submissive.

The focus then, was to work with John and his parents to negotiate what would be acceptable to each, and to establish when and how to communicate when there was a disagreement. Even though George appeared to be very autocratic, he stated he wanted to know how his son was feeling, and he wanted him to take charge of his life. However, he felt that John was not doing it, so he had to take control for him. John felt he could not assume responsibility for directing his life because George was dictating everything.

Although both George and Anita stated that their only area of concern was John's academic performance, when Janice suggested that there could be some options to ensure George's mother's safety and provide social support for her, George and Anita both showed substantial interest. The local area agency on aging was contacted to do a complete assessment of George's mother's needs. The family agreed to explore the local senior centers as well as to work with other Taiwanese families with older adults in the home to find a core of elders who could meet at a local center a few times a week. In addition, Janice spoke to them about looking into adult day-care facilities and home health care, so that if the time came that George's mother needed more assistance, they would know what is available in the community.

Finally, Janice suggested that there might be supportive services in Taiwan that could be of help to Anita's family. Both George and Anita indicated that they had not even considered that, assuming that, besides domestic help, there would be no social services available that Anita's parents could use. However, after discussing the possibilities for George's mother in this country, Anita felt that there must be similar programs in Taiwan, and decided that the next time she visited her parents, she would use her time there to mobilize her resources (including her cousins and other relatives) to explore and assess available options. She stated that although the guilt would always be with her because she was not close enough to take care of her parents, at least she would feel that she had put into place a set of resources that they could use as necessary.

Although none of the problems was resolved, each of the major ones was addressed, with an understanding between George, Anita, and John that the process was ongoing—whether it was in dealing with the relationship among them, with John's academic performance and career plans, or support of aging parents.

- The family recognized that the communication that existed between John and his parents was less than effective.
- The family came to the realization that it is not shameful to seek assistance from sources outside the family boundaries. Thus, community services (even mainstream ones) for the elderly may be viable in providing both the physical care and the social and emotional support isolated aging immigrants may be experiencing.
- With the realization that extra-familial supports are acceptable came a recognition that these are alternatives also for a family left behind in Taiwan, and although not the best of alternatives, under the circumstances may allow Anita to be reassured that her parents are not isolated and at risk while she is here in the United States.

(continued)

CASE | *continued*

Through this process of intervention, Janice guided the discussion and the direction. Although the parents are educated and part of the "model minority," they were struggling with personal and cultural conflicts. As Janice evidenced cultural sensitivity by ensuring that she understood the concerns of the parents, particularly as they were couched in Chinese norms and expectations, and worked within the parameters while helping bridge the gap between them and their U.S.–born child, she had to carefully balance issues of directiveness. She found that she was giving more suggestions, particularly for options for aging parents as George and Anita asked, "What should we do? What would you do?" However, as she gave these suggestions, she also had to explain that these alternatives helped fulfill filial responsibilities, not abdicate them, because social and emotional needs must be met in addition to the physical ones.

Janice met with the Wong family approximately 12 times. On the last day, she recapped that they had opened discussions between John and his parents and that they had agreed to continue exploring where John would like to go with his career. They had begun to establish contacts in the community (both the Taiwanese and the mainstream) for the support of George's mother, and they had agreed to explore available services in Taiwan for Anita's parents. She then talked about strengths, particularly those requiring being successful in another culture, the strong bond and affection among members of the family, and the commitment John had to doing well (particularly after he felt his family had begun listening to him). Finally, she indicated that she would be available in the future to discuss anything further or to explore additional resources related to current or unforeseen concerns. She also indicated that she would contact the family within a couple of weeks to see how things were progressing and would keep in touch with John through the school year.

associated problems, their antecedents and consequences, and their social constructs. Following this, together they review the route taken and the progress made and evaluate its significance for client functioning without the supportive services provided by the social worker. This evaluation explores and reinforces client strengths and alternative, nonprofessional, sources of support as well as professional resources that may be accessed if, and when, they are needed in the future, including services provided by the social worker. The social worker also presents follow-up strategies, which may include a few follow-up visits three to six months later with some telephone contacts a couple of months later to ensure that client progress has been maintained and that the client is functioning adequately. Clients must always be reassured that while it is anticipated that they will not need the services of the social worker again because they have tapped their own strengths and developed their personal resources and support system, if the need does arise, the social worker will be willing to reopen the case or be available for periodic contact.

In any intervention, most essential is to bear in mind that despite cultural differences, all peoples have the same basic needs and desires. Safety, food, and shelter for the family, health, success, friendship, recognition, and support are fundamental to all people. Certainly norms, patterns of behavior, methods of interaction, and other cultural trappings affect how, and to what extent, these needs are expressed. The social worker who begins with the professional understanding and belief in the intrinsic worth and dignity of the individual and is open to being educated and seeking knowledge regarding peoples of different backgrounds and experiences is likely to move naturally toward cultural sensitivity and will tailor basic intervention skills to become culturally competent.

SERVICES FOR THE IMMIGRANT AND REFUGEE COMMUNITIES

There exists a tendency among several immigrant and refugee groups to rely only on themselves and minimize the use of the supportive services that are available in the U.S. society. When they do, in fact, have the resources to cope with their difficulties, minimization of professional support services is a strength. On the other hand, because of the tendency to privacy and the tremendous sense of family loyalty, group sense, and issues of shame, there is an aversion to reach out even to the immigrant and refugee communities themselves for assistance. Social services workers are guilty of failing to reach out and educate these populations regarding support options that are available to them because the problems are not visible to them.

Needs are not met by the mainstream society's social services because many immigrants and refugees do not believe that the mainstream culture understands them, nor are they sure that they can trust the larger society because of the history of discrimination and the proclivity toward paternalism. They will not go to their own community members either, because it is often considered shameful to reveal that there are problems within the family, and the family must be protected at all costs. Hence, individuals within the family, and the family itself, may be extremely needy, unhealthy, or dysfunctional, yet seek little external support. The social services, in turn, may feel that there is no need because these groups do not express it.

Outreach and educational efforts must encourage the use of services that serve as surrogates to the extended family in providing support and guidance to individuals and families when their own resources (physical, financial, social, and emotional) are insufficient. Ongoing debates continue about who should be the service providers for ethnic minorities. There is disagreement about whether ethnic services best meet the needs of their own community or if services provided by more inclusive organizations are more effective. Furthermore, there is discussion about whether programs and services should be culture specific. A relatively recent publication raised a number of controversial issues in multiculturalism (de Anda, 1997), with disagreements about whether similarities or differences should establish the foundation in the delivery of services. Authors opposed each other on whether theory that drives intervention, the intervention itself, methods of evaluation of effectiveness, and research methods should be adapted and modified based on the culture of the target population.

In particularly large urban areas with substantial immigrant and refugee populations, a number of services, from health care and social services to financial planning and legal assistance have sprouted that specifically address the needs of these communities. Not always managed by immigrants, they are heavily staffed by both immigrants and refugees, a large percentage of whom are responsible for consumer contact. In large metropolitan areas such as San Francisco, Chicago, New York, and Houston, where immigrant and refugee groups are more visible, immigrants and refugees use these services heavily, whereas there is a disproportionately lower representation of immigrants and refugees in organizations that do not target these groups. It may be argued that the lower representation occurs because services that particularly target these groups divert them from mainstream services. However, it is also clear that in geographical areas where there are sufficiently large numbers of immigrants and refugees but no services specifically for them, several needs in the community remain unmet. In the absence of perceived cultural awareness by service providers, especially in sensitive areas such as money management, family discord, or limited English proficiency, immigrants and refugees are more likely to forego accessing existing services. Thus, whether or not there is a qualitative difference between immigrant and refugee service organizations and organizations that provide services to immigrants and refugees, perceptions of them differ in the community. Although immigrants and refugees may even agree that both types of organizations may be equally competent, the level of comfort they report is higher for organizations that target these groups.

Society and Immigrants in the Adjustment Process

In many respects, the United States provides a series of dichotomies. Many embrace the diversity brought by immigrant peoples, but as many abhor it. This is evident at the informal and personal levels as well as at the formal and institutional levels. Several individuals and groups of different backgrounds are integrated in the work force, yet social integration at the personal level in friendships and residential communities is still less common. Although selective integration may be a preference of minority community members as in the segmented assimilation process, it may also be the choice of the dominant society, as those who are similar still feel more comfortable with each other. The U.S. society of the 21st century, based on the civil rights legislation of the 1960s and 1970s, mandates equal opportunity for all and prohibits discrimination; nevertheless, it is difficult to enforce and most subtle forms of discrimination are often impossible to prove.

What, then, is the responsibility of the immigrant individual and the U.S. society in the process of adjustment to the United States? Much depends on the resources immigrants bring with them as well as the readiness of the receiving country to accept them. Most immigrants and refugees to the United States have brought with them a tremendous range of psychological strengths. However, they have varied greatly in their language competence, their professional and vocational skills, their economic resources, and their social supports. These are all necessary for adjustment and success in a new environment. Assimilation may no longer be the preferred goal for immigrants, but they must, as any other member of the society, have the competencies that will allow them to work and support themselves in the country.

A nation that has immigration policies that allow the entry of people who do not have the necessary survival tools must then take responsibility for providing the services, training, financial assistance, and other supportive programs to ensure that the opportunities are available through the adjustment process. In addition, these programs must be sensitive to the realization that adjustment occurs over a period of time, often taking several years. Needs, issues, and problems may emerge at different points in an individual's life and may be related to their physical and psychological health, to their financial and business security, to their bicultural experience and the raising of children, or a variety of other areas. Hence, while federal and private sector programs such as the Refugee Resettlement Program must be lauded for their aims in assisting refugees, they also provide too little for too short a time. These must be supplemented on a consistent basis, and immigrants must be made aware of their existence through ongoing outreach endeavors.

Although opportunities must be made available to immigrants and they must be also made aware of the resources and services available to all residents of the nation, it is also their responsibility to avail themselves of the opportunities. The nation must be welcoming and try to increase opportunities and minimize obstacles to a successful adjustment to the United States, regardless of whether the immigrants' goals of adjustment are acculturation and assimilation, segmented assimilation, integration, or accommodation, yet it is also necessary for immigrants to learn the society, its functioning, and its culture, because responsibility for adjustment necessitates a certain level of acceptance by the immigrant and a willingness to adapt to a new environment. Some may find it easier than may others because of the resources they bring with them and because of their perception of U.S. society based on the apparent resources they have, but they must share in the responsibility for easing their own adjustment and that of their family members. Most must have or develop the resources to function in both their own ethnic communities and in the dominant society. Social workers and others in the human services may actively reach out to immigrants and refugees to provide educational opportunities that enhance understanding of the bicultural experience, but to do this effectively, immigrants and refugees must be willing to learn about this experience. Such efforts can enhance adjustment and prevent some intercultural difficulties.

Most first-generation immigrants and refugees come from cultures where their options are limited, their socioeconomic status in life is permanent, or where personal freedom is controlled either politically or socially. Besides language, cultural, and social differences many experience in the United States, they encounter variations in social group interaction patterns. Among many immigrant groups, relationships are closely regulated by age, gender, and

generational status. These are not the predominant criteria that define relationships in the United States. Social status in the United States is highly
related to education, occupation, and income level. Many immigrants' spiritual beliefs and practices greatly influence an understanding of the world, and
a frequently found fatalistic worldview tends to permit these groups to accept
their circumstances, and therefore, sometimes be more able to adjust than
Americans, but it also makes them passive and allows them to be victimized
by circumstances that they may be able to control. Their beliefs and attitudes
toward health and healing also influence the measures they may or may not
take to use available assistance. If they believe that illness is punishment for
some behavior by the gods, either in this life or a previous one, there is less
likelihood that they will either access or comply with Western medical interventions, particularly if they are inconsistent with indigenous methods.

Bicultural services that truly understand not only the language but also the
experience of both cultures can be the most effective in helping in the adjustment of first-generation immigrants and refugees, both early in their entry into
the United States, but also later as they begin to deal with issues of managing
businesses, raising families, or coping with old age. In the process of translation, these bicultural services can interpret the U.S. culture for immigrants but
also ensure that the continuing prejudice and discrimination in the U.S. society are identified, and that, through advocacy, policies and programs are developed to address them.

CLOSING THOUGHTS

This chapter has tried to discuss issues in working with refugees and immigrants. Although they share being newcomers to this land of opportunity and
that they have left behind much, both tangible and intangible, in their homelands, that is only a portion of what they share. The 2000 Census data show
the numbers of immigrants that enter the country on an annual basis. A close
inspection of the data, available on the governmental Web site www.census
.gov should be made by any social worker interested in this population. It is
abundantly clear that there is no single profile of an immigrant or a refugee.
They range in age from infancy to well into old age. They may be single, married, divorced, or widowed; they may come with families, without families, or
as part of an extended family. They may be white, black, brown, yellow, red,
or any other color under which the human species is categorized. They may be
living in the United States legally or illegally. They may be highly professional
and skilled, or they may be unprofessional with skills that cannot be trans-
ferred to the U.S. economy. They may be extremely wealthy or very poor. They
may be fluent in the English language and speak several in addition, or they
may speak only their mother tongue, which may not be English, and they may
be illiterate even in their own language. They may be from cultures that are
highly hierarchical and autocratic, or they may be from cultures where there
is greater equality. Immigrants and refugees constitute a population that is so

diverse that to attempt to provide guidelines for working with them is highly presumptuous. However, if we do not so attempt, most social welfare services will continue to skirt this group. Underlying difficulties in working with immigrants and refugees is a far-reaching xenophobia—both of the immigrants and by them. It is difficult to assess who should be responsible for crossing this bridge—is it the host or is it the self-invited newcomer? Should the host country accommodate immigrants and refugees or should immigrants and refugees adapt to the host country? The United States has policies to allow 290,000 immigrants annually and, often, almost as many refugees and twice as many "exempt" family members for a total yearly entry rate of over one million. Therefore, should the country not attempt to accommodate them? Immigrants (and even refugees who come to the United States as a third nation of resettlement) must make application to enter the United States. Hence, they are here voluntarily. Should they not make attempts to adjust? Where does the responsibility lie?

For any immigrant community, it is a long road from its country of origin. The physical distance may be great, but the social, psychological, and emotional distance is always greater. Nevertheless, the human condition and its similarities bind people together to a much greater extent than one tends to accept. Regardless of social norms, culture, religion, or language, all people, at the very least, have the same desires for health and the ability to provide for their families. All people experience joy, fear, pain, hope, despair, and the entire range of emotions. All are vulnerable, need other human beings, and are influenced by environmental factors.

For immigrants, as for all people, much depends on the personal resources they possess. Even more than this, however, is the readiness of the receiving country to accept immigrants and their American-born descendents. Immigration policies may reflect the interests of the nation in allowing entry to certain groups of people; however, it is the opportunities and obstacles that immigrants and their offspring, particularly those of color, encounter on a daily basis that affect the ease of adjustment and mutual acceptance. Immigrants and the host nation must make a conscious level to adapt to each other—it is neither the exclusive responsibility of the host nation or of the immigrant. Furthermore, if the nation is to be truly multicultural, it must also be pluralistic and recognize, accept, and laud the differences in peoples, celebrating this as a national asset.

Endnotes

Consider the following possible responses to questions for problem identification and assessment

1. *What problem behaviors does John evidence?*

John's grades have fallen. He is restless in class and pays little attention. He is dishonest with his parents, having not only kept his deteriorating academic performance from them, he has hidden the note provided by the teacher.

2. *Is each problem behavior listed self-evident?*

Yes, each behavior is self-evident.

3. *Identify possible causes for these behaviors.*

John's grades may have fallen because he has become involved with a girl and has less time to focus on his studies. His restlessness in class may be a reflection of this distraction. However, he may also be concerned about the reaction of his parents to his girlfriend (about whom they apparently know nothing) as the parents adhere strongly to Chinese values and culture, and who are already distressed by the precedent set by his sister who is dating a non-Asian. John's interception of the notes reflects his concern in disappointing his parents and attracting their wrath for having performed poorly in school. For most Asians, education is paramount, and entry into an Ivy League university is preferred. A 3.5 grade point average is hardly sufficient to enter such a school, and John probably already feels unable to meet the expectations placed on him. On the other hand, he, himself, may not aspire to go to such a competitive school and may be either consciously, or subconsciously, sabotaging his junior year's academic standing.

4. *List possible consequences of these behaviors.*

The most immediate consequence will be the anger and disappointment of the parents. However, long-term, if John precludes his admission into an Ivy League school, he will have indirectly challenged parental authority and broken some of the strong traditional values, which include filial piety and obedience and respect, without directly confronting his parents. In addition, involvement with a non-Asian girl will allow him to further distance himself from parental expectation and Chinese norms, further lowering the control his parents have over him. On the other hand, his parents may forbid him to date the girl, causing him more distress.

5. *How may the possible consequences affect the occurrence of these behaviors?*

The challenge to the parents may cause the parents to recognize that their expectations may not be met, thus reinforcing the behaviors. But if the parents cease to emphasize entry into an Ivy League school, John may feel less burdened and inadequate and be able to excel in those areas that most interest him. However, fear of the parents may continue to ensure that John is secretive, because although he may have been caught in one instance, he may not be caught in the future.

6. *Do other behaviors that John is exhibiting pose potential problems for this family?*

Dating the non-Asian girl poses problems for the family. Although she may not be the girl that John marries, she already challenges parental expectations of the type of girl they would prefer for John.

7. *List reasons these may cause conflict for the family.*

Most groups prefer that their offspring marry within their culture because of beliefs that out-marriage dilutes the bloodline and the culture. Immigrants are particularly concerned about this because they see their culture disappearing within their own generation as they modify and abbreviate their traditions to accommodate U.S. calendars, patterns, and other factors.

8. *Identify areas of conflict between John and his parents.*

The major areas of conflict between John and his parents involve charting his future and the extent to which he is expected to adhere to Chinese norms, particularly when he appears to feel that he is more American than Chinese.

9. *Are these areas overt or covert?*

Although the grades, selection of school, and choice of marriage partner cause conflict and may be overt, the tug between American and Chinese cultures and norms underlie them and are covert.

10. *Are these generational issues, cultural issues, or both?*

These are primarily cultural issues; however, parents of all groups attempt to control the direction of their children's future, so to that extent, the intergenerational conflict is fairly universal.

11. *What are other areas of stress for this family?*

Other areas of stress for the family are the presence of George's mother in the house and her relative isolation. In addition, Anita's aging parents who wish to remain in Taiwan may cause tremendous cognitive and emotional conflict for her as well as strong feelings of guilt and helplessness.

12. *To what extent are these cultural?*

These other areas of stress are largely cultural because of the parent-child, superior-subordinate relationship defined by Confucian dictates, which require that respect for the elder and care are of the essence. To place the mother in a nursing home would be abhorrent and to send her to a senior center or an adult day care would be considered an abdication of filial responsibility, and George would never permit it.

13. *To what extent are these related to the immigration experience?*

All people are concerned about aging parents, but immigrants often have to deal with a more complex problem. When aging parents come to reside with their adult children in the United States, they are completely dependent on their children, socially, financially, and emotionally. The parents leave behind all resources, as well as their contemporaries (both relatives and friends). Usually they do not have the language to develop relationships with neighbors, and American television holds little relevance for them. The alternative is to leave parents in the homeland, but when the dictates of the culture require adult children to care for their aging parents, the natural emotional desire to ensure that they are safe is further compounded, and strong feelings of guilt and concern often overwhelm the adult children who are in no position to do more than send money to the homeland, hope that the parents remain healthy and that someone will inform them when they are not, and visit them occasionally, once a year at the most.

14. *How may these other areas of stress in the family affect John and his behavior?*

Tensions within the family may be high, especially as is evidenced in the increasing numbers of arguments between George and Anita. Anita appears to be overworked and overwhelmed, both physically and emotionally. Neither parent may have the time or the patience to listen to and work with John. Their concern about his academic success and the resulting pressure they place on him may make him assume that successful academic performance is essential to meriting their love. Thus, when he receives grades that fall below the "A" level, he may be distressed, scared, and depressed, which may affect further performance. This, in turn, may cause him to engage in secretive and avoidance behaviors, such as intercepting notes from his teachers. Once the parents learn of the interception, they are likely to mistrust John and increase tensions further within the family and with John.

References

Ahern, F. L., Jr., & Athey, J. L. (1991). *Refugee children: Theory, research, and services.* The Johns Hopkins series in contemporary mental health. Baltimore: Johns Hopkins University Press.

Allen, R., & Nimmagadda, J. (1999). Asian Indian women and feminism: A double-edged sword? *Asian Pacific Journal of Social Work, 9*(1), 26–41.

Balgopal, P. R. (Ed.). (2000). *Social work practice with immigrants and refugees.* New York: Columbia University Press.

Bean, F. D., Lowell, B. L., & Taylor, L. J. (1987). Undocumented Mexican immigrants and the earnings of other workers in the United States. *Demography, 25*(1), 35–52.

Bemak, F., Chung, R. C-Y, & Bornemann, T. H. (1996). Counseling and psychotherapy with refugees. In P. B. Pedersen, J. G. Draguns, W. J. Lonner, & J. E. Trimble (Eds.), *Counseling across cultures* (4th ed., pp. 243–265). Thousand Oaks, CA: Sage.

Booth, A., & Crouter, A. C. (1997). *Immigration and the family: Research and policy on U.S. immigrants.* Mahwah, NJ: Erlbaum.

Center for Immigration Studies. (2001, November 30). Immigration and American labor. Panel discussion transcript. Washington, DC. Retrieved from www.cis.org/articles/2001/unionpanel .html on August 13, 2003.

Cobb-Clark, D. A., & Kossoudji, S. A. (1994). *Mobility in El Norte: Employment and occupational changes for undocumented Latina women.* Normal: Illinois State University. Unpublished manuscript.

Cormier, S., & Cormier, B. (1998). *Interviewing strategies for helpers.* Pacific Grove, CA: Brooks/Cole.

de Anda, D. (1997). *Controversial issues in multiculturalism.* Boston: Allyn & Bacon.

de Leon Siantz, M. L. (1997). Factors that impact development outcomes of immigrant children. In A. Booth & A. C. Crouter (Eds.), *Immigration and the family: Research and policy on U.S. immigrants* (pp. 149–161). Mahwah, NJ: Erlbaum.

Dinnerstein, L., & Reimers, D. (1975). *Ethnic Americans: A history of immigration and assimilation.* New York: Harper & Row.

Fix, M., & Passel, J. S. (1994). *Immigration and immigrants.* Washington, DC: Urban Institute.

Francis, E. A. (2000). Social work practice with African-descent immigrants. In Balgopal P. R. (Ed.), *Social work practice with immigrants and refugees* (pp. 127–166). New York: Columbia University Press.

Immigration and Naturalization Service (INS). (1999). Illegal alien resident population. Retrieved from http://www.ins .usdoj.gov/graphics/aboutins/statistics /illegalalien/index.htm

Karger, H. J., & Levine, J. (2000). Social work practice with European immigrants. In P. Balgopal (Ed.), *Social work practice with immigrants and refugees* (pp. 167–197). New York: Columbia University Press.

Karger, H. J., & Stoesz, D. (1998). *American social welfare policy: A pluralist approach* (3rd ed). New York: Longman.

Kim, H. C. (1994). *A legal history of Asian Americans, 1790–1990.* Westport, CT: Greenwood Press.

Kposowa, A. J. (1995). The impact of immigration on unemployment and earnings among racial minorities in the United States. *Ethnic and Racial Studies, 18*(3), 605–628.

Lazarus, A. A. (1976). *Multimodal behavior therapy.* New York: Springer.

Lazarus, A. A. (1989). *The practice of multimodal therapy.* Baltimore: Johns Hopkins University Press.

Longres, J. F., & Patterson, D. G. (2000). Social work practice with Latino American immigrants. In P. Balgopal (Ed.), *Social work practice with immigrants and refugees* (pp. 127–166). New York: Columbia University Press.

Lum, D. (1992). *Social work practice with people of color.* Pacific Grove, CA: Brooks/Cole.

Lum, D. (2003). *Culturally competent practice: A framework for understanding diverse groups and justice issues.* Pacific Grove, CA: Brooks/Cole.

Mayadas, N. S., & Segal, U. A. (2000). Refugees in the 1990s: A U.S. perspective. In P. Balgopal (Ed.), *Social work practice with immigrants and refugees* (pp. 198–228). New York: Columbia University Press.

Nimmagadda, J., & Balgopal, P. R. (2000). Social work practice with Asian immigrants. In Balgopal, P. R. (Ed), *Social work practice with immigrants and refugees* (pp. 30–64). New York: Columbia University Press.

Reid, I. D. (1939). *The Negro immigrant.* New York: Columbia University Press.

Segal, U. A. (2000a). Exploring child abuse among Vietnamese refugees. In D. de Anda & R. M. Becerra (Eds.), *Violence: Diverse populations and communities* (159–191). Binghamton: Haworth Press.

Segal, U. A. (2000b). A pilot exploration of family violence among a non-clinical Vietnamese sample. *Journal of Interpersonal Violence, 15*(5), 523–533.

Segal, U. A. (2002). *A framework for immigration: Asians in the United States.* New York: Columbia University Press.

Sum, A., Fogg, N., Harrington, P., Khatiwada, I., Trub'skky, M., & Palmer, S. (2002). *Immigrant workers and the great American job machine: The contributions of new foreign immigration to national and regional labor force growth in the 1990s.* Report prepared for the National Business Roundtable, Washington, DC. Boston, MA: Northeastern University, Center for Labor Market Studies. Retrieved from www.nupr.neu.12–02/immigration_BRT.PDF on August 13, 2003.

UN High Commissioner for Refugees. (1995). *The state of the world's refugees in search of solutions.* New York: Oxford University Press.

U.S. Department of Justice. (1999). *Refugees, fiscal year 1997,* Number 4, Washington, DC: U.S. Government Printing Office.

Zastrow, C. H., & Kirst-Ashman, K. K. (2004). *Understanding human behavior and the social environment.* Belmont, CA: Brooks/Cole.

APPENDIX

The following tables are from the U.S. Department of Homeland Security. (2003). *2002 Yearbook of Immigration Statistics*. Washington, DC: Office of Immigration Statistics, http://uscis.gov/graphics/shared/aboutus/statistics/Yearbook2002.pdf

Table 9.A1 | Immigration to the United States: Fiscal Years 1820–2000

Year	Number	Year	Number	Year	Number
1820–2000	66,089,431	1851–60	2,598,214	1881–90	5,246,613
1820	8,385	1851	379,466	1881	669,431
1821–30	143,439	1852	371,603	1882	788,992
1821	9,127	1853	368,645	1883	603,322
1822	6,911	1854	427,833	1884	518,592
1823	6,354	1855	200,877	1885	395,346
1824	7,912	1856	200,436	1886	334,203
1825	10,199	1857	251,306	1887	490,109
1826	10,837	1858	123,126	1888	546,889
1827	18,875	1859	121,282	1889	444,427
1828	27,382	1860	153,640	1890	455,302
1829	22,520	1861–70	2,314,824	1891–1900	3,687,564
1830	23,322	1861	91,918	1891	560,319
1831–40	599,125	1862	91,985	1892	579,663
1831	22,633	1863	176,282	1893	439,730
1832	60,482	1864	193,418	1894	285,631
1833	58,640	1865	248,120	1895	258,536
1834	65,365	1866	318,568	1896	343,267
1835	45,374	1867	315,722	1897	230,832
1836	76,242	1868	138,840	1898	229,299
1837	79,340	1869	352,768	1899	311,715
1838	38,914	1870	387,203	1900	448,572
1839	68,069				
1840	84,066	1871–80	2,812,191	1901–10	8,795,386
		1871	321,350	1901	487,918
1841–50	1,713,251	1872	404,806	1902	648,743
1841	80,289	1873	459,803	1903	857,046
1842	104,565	1874	313,339	1904	812,870
1843	52,496	1875	227,498	1905	1,026,499
1844	78,615	1876	169,986	1906	1,100,735
1845	114,371	1877	141,857	1907	1,285,349
1846	154,416	1878	138,469	1908	782,870
1847	234,968	1879	177,826	1909	751,786
1848	226,527	1880	457,257	1910	1,041,570
1849	297,024				
1850	369,980				

Year	Number	Year	Number	Year	Number
1911–20	**5,735,811**	**1941–50**	**1,035,039**	**1971–80**	**4,493,314**
1911	878,587	1941	51,776	1971	370,478
1912	838,172	1942	28,781	1972	384,685
1913	1,197,892	1943	23,725	1973	400,063
1914	1,218,480	1944	28,551	1974	394,861
1915	326,700	1945	38,119	1975	386,194
1916	298,826	1946	108,721	1976	398,613
1917	295,403	1947	147,292	1976,TQ[1]	103,676
1918	110,618	1948	170,570	1977	462,315
1919	141,132	1949	188,317	1978	601,442
1920	430,001	1950	249,187	1979	460,348
1921–30	**4,107,209**	**1951–60**	**2,515,479**	1980	530,639
1921	805,228	1951	205,717	**1981–90**	**7,338,062**
1922	309,556	1952	265,520	1981	596,600
1923	522,919	1953	170,434	1982	594,131
1924	706,896	1954	208,177	1983	559,763
1925	294,314	1955	237,790	1984	543,903
1926	304,488	1956	321,625	1985	570,009
1927	335,175	1957	326,867	1986	601,708
1928	307,255	1958	253,265	1987	601,516
1929	279,678	1959	260,686	1988	643,025
1930	241,700	1960	265,398	1989	1,090,924
				1990	1,536,483
1931–40	**528,431**	**1961–70**	**3,321,677**	**1991–2000**	**9,095,417**
1931	97,139	1961	271,344	1991	1,827,167
1932	35,576	1962	283,763	1992	973,977
1933	23,068	1963	306,260	1993	904,292
1934	29,470	1964	292,248	1994	804,416
1935	34,956	1965	296,697	1995	720,461
1936	36,329	1966	323,040	1996	915,900
1937	50,244	1967	361,972	1997	798,378
1938	67,895	1968	454,448	1998	654,451
1939	82,998	1969	358,579	1999	646,568
1940	70,756	1970	373,326	2000	849,807

[1]Transition quarter, July 1 through September 30, 1976.

Note: The numbers shown are as follows: from 1820–67, figures represent alien passengers arrived at seaports; from 1868–92 and 1895–97, immigrant aliens arrived; from 1892–94 and 1898–1999, immigrant aliens admitted for permanent residence. From 1892–1903, aliens entering by cabin class were not counted as immigrants. Land arrivals were not completely enumerated until 1908. See Glossary for fiscal year.

Source: Office of Immigration Statistics (2003), *2002 Yearbook of Immigration Statistics.* Washington, DC: Office of Homeland Security. Website: http://www.uscis.gov/graphics/shared/aboutus/statistics/Yearbook2002.pdf

Table 9.A2 | Immigrants Admitted by Type and Selected Class of Admission: Fiscal Years 1986–2000

Type and Class of Admission	1986	1987	1988	1989	1990	1991
Total, all immigrants	601,708	601,516	643,025	1,090,924	1,536,483	1,827,167
New arrivals	376,110	386,995	377,885	402,431	435,729	443,107
Adjustments	225,598	214,521	265,140	688,493	1,100,754	1,384,060
Total, IRCA legalization	X	X	X	478,814	880,372	1,123,162
Residents since 1982	X	X	X	478,814	823,704	214,003
Special agricultural workers	X	X	X	X	56,668	909,159
Total, non-legalization	601,708	601,516	643,025	612,110	656,111	704,005
Preference immigrants	269,556	269,328	259,499	274,833	272,742	275,613
Family-sponsored immigrants	212,939	211,809	200,772	217,092	214,550	216,088
Unmarried sons/daughters of U.S. citizens[1]	10,910	11,382	12,107	13,259	15,861	
Spouses of alien residents[1]	110,926	110,758	102,777	112,771	107,686	110,126
Married sons/daughters of U.S. citizens[2]	20,702	20,703	21,940	26,975	26,751	27,115
Siblings of U.S. citizens[2]	70,401	68,966	63,948	64,087	64,252	63,462
Employment-based immigrants[2,3]	56,617	57,519	58,727	57,741	58,192	59,525
Priority workers	X	X	X	X	X	X
Professionals with advanced degrees or aliens of exceptional ability	X	X	X	X	X	X
Skilled workers, professionals, other workers	X	X	X	X	X	X
Special immigrants	2,992	3,646	5,120	4,986	4,463	4,576
Employment creation	X	X	X	X	X	X
Pre-1992	53,625	53,873	53,607	52,755	53,729	54,949

281

Immediate relatives of U.S. citizens[4]	223,468	218,575	219,340	217,514	231,680	237,103
Spouses	137,597	132,452	130,977	125,744	125,426	125,397
Children[5]	40,639	40,940	40,863	41,276	46,065	48,130
Orphans	9,945	10,097	9,120	7,948	7,088	9,008
Parents	45,232	45,183	47,500	50,494	60,189	63,576
Refugees and asylees	104,383	91,840	81,719	84,288	97,364	139,079
Refugees adjustments	99,383	86,840	76,274	79,143	92,427	116,415
Asylee adjustments	5,000	5,000	5,445	5,145	4,937	22,664
Other immigrants	4,301	21,773	82,467	35,475	54,325	52,210
Amerasian (P.L.100-202)	X	X	319	8,589	13,059	16,010
Cancellation of removal[6]	413	2,441	3,772	3,384	889	782
Children born abroad to alien residents	3,450	3,174	2,997	2,740	2,410	2,224
Cuban/Haitian entrants (P.L.99-603)	X	4,634	29,002	2,816	710	213
Diversity	X	X	X	X	X	X
Diversity transition	X	X	X	X	X	X
Legalization dependents	X	X	X	X	X	X
Nicaraguan Adjustment and Central American Relief Act (NACARA), Sec. 202 entrants (P.L. 105-100)	X	X	X	X	X	X
Nationals of adversely affected countries (P.L.99-603)	X	3,037	6,029	7,068	20,371	12,268
Natives of underrepresented countries (P.L.100-658)	X	X	X	X	8,709	9,802
Parolees, Polish/Hungarian (P.L. 104-208)	X	X	X	X	X	X
Parolees, Soviet/Indochinese (P.L. 101-267)	X	X	X	X	X	4,998
Registered nurses and their families (P.L.101-238)	X	X	X	X	2,954	3,069
Registry, entry prior to 1/1/72	73	8,153	40,029	10,600	4,651	2,289
Other	365	334	319	278	491	555

(continued)

Table 9.A2 | *continued*

Type and Class of Admission	1992	1993	1994	1995	1996	1997	1998	1999	2000
Total, all immigrants	973,977	904,292	804,416	720,461	915,900	798,378	654,451	646,568	849,807
New arrivals	511,769	536,294	490,429	380,291	421,405	380,719	357,037	401,775	407,402
Adjustments	462,208	367,998	313,987	340,170	494,495	417,659	297,414	244,793	442,405
Total, IRCA legalization	163,342	24,278	6,022	4,267	4,635	2,548	955	8	421
Residents since 1982	46,962	18,717	4,436	3,124	3,286	1,439	954	4	413
Special agricultural workers	116,380	5,561	1,586	1,143	1,349	1,109	1	4	8
Total, non-legalization	810,635	880,014	798,394	716,194	911,265	795,830	653,496	646,560	849,386
Preference immigrants	329,321	373,788	335,252	323,458	411,673	303,938	268,997	273,700	342,304
Family-sponsored immigrants	213,123	226,776	211,961	238,122	294,174	213,331	191,480	216,883	235,280
Unmarried sons/daughters of U.S. citizens[1]	12,486	12,819	13,181	15,182	20,909	22,536	17,717	22,392	27,707
Spouses of alien residents[1]	118,247	128,308	115,000	144,535	182,834	113,681	88,488	108,007	124,595
Married sons/daughters of U.S. citizens[2]	22,195	23,385	22,191	20,876	25,452	21,943	22,257	24,040	22,833
Siblings of U.S. citizens[2]	60,195	62,264	61,589	57,529	64,979	55,171	63,018	62,444	60,145
Employment-based immigrants[2,3]	116,198	147,012	123,291	85,336	117,499	90,607	77,517	56,817	107,024
Priority workers	5,456	21,114	21,053	17,339	27,501	21,810	21,408	14,898	27,706
Professionals with advanced degrees or aliens of exceptional ability	58,401	29,468	14,432	10,475	18,462	17,059	14,384	8,581	20,304
Skilled workers, professionals, other workers	47,568	87,689	76,956	50,245	62,756	42,596	34,317	27,966	49,736
Special immigrants	59	8,158	10,406	6,737	7,844	7,781	6,584	5,086	9,052
Employment creation	651	583	444	540	936	1,361	824	286	226
Pre-1992	X	X	X	X	X	X	X	X	X

Immediate relatives of U.S. citizens[4]	347,870	258,584	283,368	321,008	300,430	220,360	249,764	255,059	235,484
Spouses[5]	197,525	127,988	151,172	170,263	169,760	123,238	145,247	145,843	128,396
Children[5]	82,726	69,113	70,472	76,631	63,971	48,740	48,147	46,788	42,324
Orphans	18,120	16,037	14,867	12,596	11,316	9,384	8,200	7,348	6,536
Parents	67,619	61,483	61,724	74,114	66,699	48,382	56,370	62,428	64,764
Refugees and asylees	65,941	42,852	52,193	112,158	128,565	114,664	121,434	127,343	117,037
Refugees adjustments	59,083	39,495	44,645	102,052	118,528	106,827	115,451	115,539	106,379
Asylee adjustments	6,858	3,357	7,548	10,106	10,037	7,837	5,983	11,804	10,658
Other immigrants	93,271	71,424	48,938	58,726	70,597	57,712	91,944	123,824	128,793
Amerasian (P.L.100-202)	943	239	346	738	956	939	2,822	11,116	17,253
Cancellation of removal[6]	12,349	9,032	428	4,628	5,812	3,168	2,220	1,468	1,013
Children born abroad to alien residents	1,009	978	902	1,432	1,660	1,894	1,883	2,030	2,116
Cuban/Haitian entrants (P.L.99-603)	2	2	2	10	29	42	47	62	99
Diversity	50,945	47,571	45,499	49,360	58,245	40,301	X	X	X
Diversity transition	X	X	X	X	X	X	41,056	33,468	33,911
Legalization dependents	55	—	21	14	64	184	34,074	55,344	52,272
Nicaraguan Adjustment and Central American Relief Act (NACARA), Sec. 202 entrants P.L. 105-100)	23,641	11,267	1	X	X	X	X	X	X
Nationals of adversely affected countries (P.L.99-603)	X	X	X	X	X	X	X	1,557	20,371
Natives of underrepresented countries (P.L.100-658)	X	X	X	X	X	X	X	10	880
Parolees, Polish/Hungarian (P.L. 104-208)	39	105	64	20	X	X	X	2	X

(continued)

Table 9.A2 | *continued*

Type and Class of Admission	1992	1993	1994	1995	1996	1997	1998	1999	2000
Parolees, Soviet/Indochinese (P.L. 101-267)	13,661	15,772	8,253	3,086	2,269	1,844	1,225	1,827	3,163
Registered nurses and their families (P.L.101-238)	3,572	2,178	304	69	16	1	1	—	1
Registry, entry prior to 1/1/72	1,304	947	671	469	362	195	176	166	269
Other	1,155	1,427	614	523	519	420	273	237	855

[1]Includes children.
[2]Includes spouses and children.
[3]Includes immigrants issued third preference, sixth preference, and special immigrant visas prior to fiscal year 1992.
[4]Effective in fiscal year 1992, under the Immigration Act of 1990, children born abroad to alien residents are included with immediate relatives of U.S. citizens for calculating the annual limit of family-sponsored preference immigrants.
[5]Includes orphans.
[6]Was suspension of deportation prior to April 1, 1997; changed by the implementation of the Illegal Immigration Reform and Immigrant Responsibility Act (IIRIRA) of 1996.
— Represents zero.
X Not applicable.

Source: Office of Immigration Statistics (2003). *2002 Yearbook of Immigration Statistics*. Washington, DC: Office of Homeland Security. Website: http://www .uscis.gov/graphics/shared /aboutus/statistics/Yearbook2002.pdf

Table 9.A3 | Refugees and Asylees Granted Lawful Permanent Resident Status by Enactment, Fiscal Years 1946–2000

Enactment	1946–50	1951–1960	1961–1970	1971–1980	1981–1990	1991–2000	Total 1946–2000
Total	213,347	492,371	212,843	539,447	1,013,620	1,021,266	3,492,894
Presidential Directive of 12/22/45	40,324	X	X	X	X	X	40,324
Displaced Persons Act of 6/25/48	173,023	236,669	4	X	X	X	409,696
Orphan Act of 7/29/53	X	466	X	X	X	X	466
Refugee Relief Act of 8/7/53	X	188,993	28	2	2	X	189,025
Refugee-Escapee Act of 9/11/57	X	24,263	5,199	X	X	X	29,462
Hungarian Refugee Act of 7/25/58	X	30,491	258	2	1	X	30,752
Azores & Netherlands Refugee Act of 9/2/58	X	10,057	12,156	X	X	X	22,213
Refugee Relatives Act of 9/22/59	X	1,432	388	X	X	X	1,820
Fair Share Refugee Act of 7/14/60	X	X	19,714	82	3	1	19,800
Refugee Conditional Entrants Act of 10/3/65	X	X	39,149	102,625	329	X	142,103
Cuban Refugee Act of 11/2/66	X	X	135,947	252,119	105,898	116,604	610,568
Indochinese Refugee Act of 10/28/77	X	X	X	137,309	37,752	107	175,168
Refugee Parolee Act of 10/5/78	X	X	X	46,058	92,971	265	139,294
Refugee Act of 1980, 3/17/80	X	X	X	1,250	776,664	904,289	1,682,203
Refugee	X	X	X	X	734,259	807,437	1,541,696
Asylee	X	X	X	1,250	42,405	96,994	140,507

X Not applicable

Source: Office of Immigration Statistics (2003), 2002 *Yearbook of Immigration Statistics.* Washington, DC: Office of Homeland Security. Website: http://www .uscis.gov/graphics/shared/aboutus/statistics/Yearbook2002.pdf

Table 9.A4 | Refugees-Status Applications: Fiscal Years 1980–2000

Year	Applications pending beginning of year	Applications filed during year	Applications approved during year	Applications denied during year	Applications otherwise closed during year	Applications pending end of year
1980 (April–Sept.)	16,642	95,241	89,580	6,149	1,197	14,957
1981	14,957	178,273	155,291	15,322	3,998	18,619
1982	18,619	76,150	61,527	14,943	6,631	11,668
1983	11,668	92,522	73,645	20,255	2,489	7,801
1984	7,801	99,636	77,932	16,220	604	12,681
1985	12,681	80,734	59,436	18,430	1,842	13,707
1986	13,707	67,310	52,081	9,679	3,362	15,895
1987	15,895	85,823	61,529	13,911	6,126	20,152
1988	20,152	105,024	80,282	11,821	5,632	27,441
1989	27,441	190,597	95,505	33,179	4,005	85,349
1990	39,524	135,251	99,697	29,805	24,904	20,369
1991	20,369	123,492	107,962	12,644	5,700	17,555
1992	18,238	133,786	115,330	14,886	6,780	15,028
1993	15,028	127,676	106,026	20,280	5,107	11,291
1994	15,582	142,068	105,137	20,557	19,485	12,471
1995	12,471	143,223	78,936	32,412	34,251	10,095
1996	10,095	155,868	74,491	26,317	59,589	5,566
1997	5,566	122,741	77,600	22,725	17,270	10,712
1998	10,712	124,777	73,198	31,001	6,768	24,522
1999	24,522	111,576	85,592	19,094	6,358	25,054
2000	25,042	91,854	66,546	21,010	10,482	18,858

NOTE: The Refugee Act of 1980 went into effect April 1, 1980. The pending beginning of fiscal year 1990 figure does not match the pending end of fiscal year 1989 figure due to changes in the processing of Soviet refugees residing in the republics of the former Soviet Union. The beginning fiscal year 1990 figure excludes the initial questionnaires submitted by refugee applicants residing in the republics of the former Soviet Union. Changes in the number of applications pending from 1991 to 1992, 1993 to 1994, and 1999 to 2000 are due to revisions in the data from reporting offices.

Source: Office of Immigration Statistics (2003), *2002 Yearbook of Immigration Statistics*. Washington, DC: Office of Homeland Security. Website: http://www .uscis.gov/graphics/shared/aboutus/statistics/Yearbook2002.pdf

Social Work Practice with Persons with Disabilities

CHAPTER 10

Ruth I. Freedman

People with disabilities are part of the broad spectrum of culturally diverse social work practice. It is essential to recognize and value the diversity within and among this group of individuals and the varied effects of disability on their lives. They are young and old, rich and poor, urban and rural, and from varied ethnic and cultural backgrounds. They may also be women of color, gays and lesbians, immigrants or refugees, or elders. People with disabilities are often viewed as a minority group. Similar to other cultural minorities, they share a history of stigma and discrimination and have organized politically and legally to address the forces of oppression they have encountered.

There is wide variation in the nature, extent, and experience of disability. People with a disability have either a permanent physical or mental impairment or a chronic health or mental health condition that may vary widely in specific type of impairment or condition, types of functional impairment or activity limitations, level of severity of impairment, degree of visibility of the disability to others, age at onset of the condition, and course or progression of the condition (Asch & Mudrick, 1995). These factors and many other variables provide a context for understanding the "origin, experience, and effects of disability" (p. 202). Interestingly, disability is "the one minority that anyone can join at any time, as a result of a sudden automobile accident, a fall down a flight of stairs, cancer, or disease . . . And since disability catches up with most of us in old age, it is a minority that we all, if we live long enough, join" (Shapiro, 1993, pp. 7–8). Similarly, Zola suggests that disability not be viewed as a fixed status (that is, either you have it or you don't) but, rather, as a "continuously changing and evolving set of characteristics" (1993, p. 10). People without disabilities are in a sense, "temporarily able-bodied . . . the issue of disability for individuals . . . is not *whether* but *when,* not so much *which one,* but *how many* and *in what combination*" (Zola, 1993, p. 18).

DISABILITY CONCEPTS

There have been various approaches both historically and currently to conceptualizing, defining, and measuring disability. Disability is a social construct, reflecting varied societal views and cultural values. Broadly speaking, there are two prevailing conceptual models of disability (Hahn, 1999): (1) the functional limitations paradigm reflecting medical and economic understandings of disability, and (2) the minority group paradigm reflecting sociopolitical interpretations of disability.

The medical view of disability, underlying the functional limitation paradigm, is based on notions of biomedical impairment and pathology. The assumption is that the disabling condition is a "trait lodged within a person, rather than a construct of external surroundings" (Hahn, 1999, p. 5). In addition, the functional limitation paradigm may reflect an economic definition of disability. People are considered disabled if they are limited in the roles and tasks they can perform, particularly for vocational functioning. For example, disability as defined by the federal Social Security program refers to "inability to engage in any substantial gainful activity by reason of any medically determinable physical or mental impairment which can be expected to result in death or has lasted or can be expected to last for a continuous period of not less than 12 months." (Social Security Act, Sections 223(d), 1614(a)(3)(B), 42 U.S.C. Sections 416(i), 423(d), and 20 C.F.R. Sections 404.1505, 416.905(a)).

In contrast to the functional limitations model, the minority group model is based on a sociopolitical definition of disability that concentrates on interactions between the individual and environment (Hahn, 1999). Disabilities are viewed through the environmental constraints (social, political, attitudinal) imposed on people with impairments. The actual impairments of individuals may be "less handicapping than the barriers of stereotyped attitudes and architectural constraints" (Scotch, 1988, p. 164). This focus shifts from viewing and treating disability as an impairment or deficit of the individual to modifying disabling environments in which the individual with disabilities functions.

THE DEMOGRAPHICS OF PERSONS WITH DISABILITIES

Prevalence

Estimates of the extent of disability in the United States vary, depending on how disability is defined, by whom, and for what purposes. Various governmental agencies, programs, legislative statutes, and national surveys use different definitions of disability. The American with Disabilities Act of

1990 defines disability as (1) a physical or mental impairment that substantially limits one or more of the major life activities of such individual, (2) a record of such an impairment, or (3) being regarded as having such an impairment. This definition is quite broad, including persons who currently have significant limitations in major life activities, but also "people who have had an activity limiting impairment in the past but are now recovered, and people regarded by others as having an impairment that limits their activities" (LaPlante, 1992). The ADA definition covers disabilities that are "visible" (e.g., blindness, orthopedic impairments, cerebral palsy) as well as many "hidden" conditions (e.g., epilepsy, cancer, HIV/AIDS, arthritis, heart disease).

According to the U.S. Census 2000, about one in five Americans (49.7 million) has some type of long-lasting condition or disability (U.S. Census Bureau, 2003). Census 2000 asked for disability information from all people aged 5 and older in the civilian non-institutionalized population. Two questions about disability were included in the Census 2000, on which the Census disability definition is based: (1) long-lasting impairments or conditions (sensory or physical), and (2) difficulties performing certain activities because of physical, mental, or emotional conditions. It is important to note that the Census 2000 does not include information about persons under age 5 or persons living in institutions (e.g., nursing homes, mental hospitals, institutions for persons with mental retardation and developmental disabilities). Census data therefore provide a likely conservative estimate of prevalence of disability, given the exclusion of these groups of people.

Disability rates vary across the life span, and by gender. The likelihood of having a disability increases with age. According to Census 2000 data, people 65 and older were much more likely than were people of working age (16 to 64) to report a sensory, physical, mental, or self-care disability, or a disability causing difficulty going outside the home (U.S. Census Bureau, 2003). Among people 65 and older, the rate of disability is 43.0% for women and 40.4% for men (U.S. Census Bureau, 2003). In addition, comorbidity (the incidence of multiple conditions) increases with age, particularly among older women (Jans & Stoddard, 1999).

Among children and adolescents under 5 to 15 years old, an estimated 2.6 million have disabilities (U.S. Census Bureau, 2003). The prevalence rate is higher for boys (7.2%) than for girls (4.3%) (U.S. Census Bureau, 2003). Boys are also more likely to receive special education services than are girls, composing about two-thirds of the students in special education (Wenger, Kaye, & LaPlante, 1996). It is not known whether this discrepancy is because of differences in prevalence rates or other eligibility factors (Jans & Stoddard, 1999, p. 51).

Disability also varies by race and ethnicity. According to Census 2000 data, the highest overall estimated disability rate (24.3%) was shared by two groups—respondents who reported *black* and respondents who reported *American Indian* and *Alaska Native*. Asians had the lowest disability rate (16.6%) of any of the racial and ethnic groups examined in the

Census 2000. Hispanic respondents reported higher overall disability rates (20.9%) than did non-Hispanic whites (18.3%) (U.S. Census Bureau, 2003).

The increased rate of disability among minorities is likely related to various socioeconomic conditions including low income and poverty, employment in physically dangerous jobs, lack of insurance coverage, low educational attainment, and faulty testing and assessment (Smart & Smart, 1997, p. 9). In addition, there may be cultural differences in how disability is experienced and reported (Jans & Stoddard, 1999). Overall, the cumulative effects of poor socioeconomic status and poor health place minorities at greater risk of disability and at greater risk of not receiving services if they have a disability (National Council on Disability, 1993).

There is a significant employment gap between working-age persons with disabilities and without disabilities. In a national survey of persons with disabilities (National Organization on Disability, 2000) only 32% of working-age people with disabilities were employed full or part-time, compared with 81% of those without disabilities. Working men with disabilities earned on average only 72.1% of the amount nondisabled men earned annually, whereas working women with disabilities made 72.6% as much as those without disabilities (Kaye, 1998). Women with disabilities may face "double jeopardy" in the workplace because of both their gender and their disability status: "As women, they are less likely to participate in the workforce, and they earn less than men. As people with disabilities, women face a lack of jobs, inaccessible work environments, and much lower wages than those with no disability" (Jans & Stoddard, 1999, p. 17). Similarly, many persons with disabilities from racial/ethnic minorities face discrimination because of both their minority status and disability. People with disabilities who are African American, American Indian, or Asian Pacific American do not have the same opportunities for assistance, employment, or income as their white counterparts do (National Center for the Dissemination of Disability Research, 1999).

Not surprisingly, people with disabilities are also more likely than people without disabilities (29% versus 10%) to live in poverty with household incomes of $15,000 or less (National Organization on Disability, 2000). Women with a work disability are more likely to live in poverty than are men with a work disability (33.8% and 24.2% respectively). There is a high prevalence of disabilities among low-income families receiving welfare benefits under the Temporary Assistance to Needy Families (TANF) program. Families receiving TANF welfare benefits are nearly twice as likely as higher-income families are to have a child with a disability or with a severe disability (Lee, Sills, & Oh, 2002). "In particular, single-mother families are more likely than two-parent families or single-father families to have a child with a disability or a severe disability, regardless of income level" (Lee, Sills, & Oh, 2002, p. 3). Moreover, 38% of the single mothers receiving TANF have disabilities themselves, and 25% have severe disabilities.

Future Demographic Trends

Some disability researchers have noted an increase in overall disability rates in the United States because of many demographic, medical, social, and economic factors (Fujiura, 2001; Seelman & Sweeney, 1995; Zola, 1993). Fujiura notes the following trends that may influence the rising rate of disability: (1) aging of the population has resulted in increased functional activity limitations; (2) poverty is associated with an increase in rate of childhood disability; (3) medical advances have increased survival rates of low birth-weight infants and persons with severe injuries; (4) emerging conditions have been recently recognized as disabilities, such as multiple chemical sensitivity or chronic fatigue syndrome; and, (5) the American Disabilities Act (ADA) incorporates a broad civil rights–oriented definition of disability (2001, pp. 9–10).

According to Seelman and Sweeney, an "expanding or new universe of disability" has emerged, resulting from changing social and environmental conditions (1995, p. 2). These factors include but are not limited to the following: "violence and abuse; aging; substance abuse and stress; inadequate prenatal care; low birth weight; adolescent pregnancy and childbearing; poor nutrition; environmental/toxic exposures, such as alcohol, smoking, drug abuse, and lead; sexually transmitted diseases, including pediatric HIV and AIDS; injuries; and, child abuse and neglect" (p. 2). These trends point to a growing relationship between conditions for poverty and risk for disability, although it is unclear to what extent these conditions are causes or consequences of disability.

THE HISTORICAL OPPRESSION AND SURVIVAL VALUES OF PERSONS WITH DISABILITIES

People with disabilities are often considered a "minority" group or culture because they share a history of oppression, discrimination, and stigma with other minority ethnic or cultural groups. They are "bicultural, living in both a disability minority world and an 'able-ist' majority world" (Olkin, 1999, p. 297). In a survey of people with disabilities conducted by the National Organization on Disability (2000), 47% of respondents say that they share a sense of common identity with people with disabilities. However, many people with disabilities may be reluctant to focus on that aspect of their identity, given their past experiences with stigmatization. Moreover, "disability as a unifying concept is by no means an obvious category" (Scotch, 1988, p. 163). People with a wide range of physical and mental impairments may or may not perceive common needs and concerns, or choose to organize by this experience. Many people acquire their disabilities later in life and may not readily share a disability minority group consciousness. Also, people with disabilities frequently share "membership" in multiple minority cultures and may choose to self-identify primarily by their gender, sexual orientation, ethnicity, national origin, or other cultural characteristics.

People with disabilities have a shared history that has often been oppressive and included abuse, neglect, sterilization, stigma, euthanasia, segregation, and institutionalization (Braddock & Parish, 2000). Society has tended to isolate and segregate individuals with disabilities, and, despite some improvements, such forms of discrimination against individuals with disabilities continue to be a serious and pervasive social problem (Americans with Disabilities Act, 1990). People with disabilities face discrimination in various aspects of their lives, including employment, housing, education, and transportation. They encounter multiple barriers (architectural, transportation, communication and attitudinal) that prevent them from full community participation, independent living, and economic self-sufficiency. Like many other minorities, "people with disabilities are disadvantaged as much or more by discrimination as by their physical limitations" (Asch & Mudrick, 1995). Pervasive negative attitudes about people with disabilities (e.g., as dependent, abnormal, incompetent, childlike, or dangerous) are among the most disabling obstacles they face.

Disability Rights Activism

Since the late 1960s, many individuals and groups have engaged in civil rights advocacy and political action to address forces of oppression. Some disabled people "came to see their disability in the same political sense as blacks viewed their race or women their gender" (Scotch, 1988, p. 165). A southern black woman with disabilities reflected on her involvement in the civil rights and disability rights movements and the commonality of these struggles: "I am very proud to say that I was born colored and crippled. Now I am black and disabled" (Gainer, 1992, p. 31).

Political advocacy by disability rights activists and grassroots cross-disability organizations have helped change society's perception of disability, expand civil rights protection, and increase architectural and transportation accessibility. The disability rights social movement played a vital role in the passage of the Americans with Disabilities Act (ADA) of 1990, which gives civil rights protections to individuals with disabilities similar to those provided to individuals on the basis of race, color, sex, national origin, age, and religion. This legislation prohibits discrimination on the basis of disability in public accommodations, employment, transportation, state and local government services, and telecommunications.

The Independent Living model grew out of the disability activism and minority perspective of the 1960s and 1970s. This model is based on the premise that the biggest obstacles faced by persons with disabilities are political, social, and economic and that consumers must advocate for civil rights, accessible environments, and full community integration. Consumer independence and self-determination are key cornerstones of the Independent Living model. Consumers are responsible for their own decisions about their lives, including deciding on the services and supports they need and the hiring of staff or caregivers. The first Center for Independent Living was established in Berkeley, California, in the 1970s by Ed Roberts, a University of California, Berkeley, student and disability activist. Centers for Independent living spread rapidly both nationally and internationally. "As of 1997, the twenty-fifth anniversary of the Center for Independent living, the 175,000 mark had been passed in terms of number of people served, and hundreds of CILs were in operation" (Rothman, 2003, p. 38).

The coming together of people with disabilities to organize around common social needs and social change efforts has helped reduce the isolation experienced by many individuals and families and has promoted positive coping and reframing of disability issues (Kirshbaum, 1994). A disability "culture" has emerged based on contextual, environmental, or social dimensions of disability. Key themes embedded in the disability culture perspective include the following: an emphasis on universal design and access, respect for expertise and adaptations derived from personal disability experience, power differential issues and empowerment, and interdependence (Kirshbaum, 2000, pp. 11–13).

Although persons with disabilities share a common history of oppression, disability culture is "not simply the shared experience of oppression" (Gill, 1995). "The elements of our culture include, certainly, our long-standing social oppression, but also our emerging art and humor, our piecing together of our history, our evolving language and symbols, our remarkable unified worldview, beliefs, and values, and our strategies for surviving and thriving" (Gill, 1995, p. 3). Similarly, Steven Brown, co-founder of the Institute on Disability Culture, describes disability culture as a "set of artifacts, beliefs, and expressions created by disabled people to describe our own life experiences" (Brown, 2001, p. 2). Brown notes that disability culture is not the only culture that most persons with disabilities belong to—they are also members of different nationalities, religions, colors, and so on. "If we consider all the possibilities of all disabilities and all cultures, it's probably more accurate to say that there are 'cultures of disabilities'" (Brown, 2001, p. 2).

CULTURALLY COMPETENT KNOWLEDGE THEORY AND PRACTICE SKILLS FOR PERSONS WITH DISABILITIES

Cultural Perceptions of Disability

There are wide variations across ethnic and cultural groups in beliefs, attitudes, and interpretations of disability. Many persons from minority cultures do not define or interpret disability in the same way as the "mainstream" dominant American culture does. Prevailing beliefs about disability in the United States are based heavily on Western cultural values of individualism, independence, and productivity, and on concepts of pathology, rationality, and science. The medical model of disability exists largely in isolation of other aspects of an individual's life, such as family, community, and culture. It is important to recognize that "our own traditional 'American' way of addressing issues of chronic illness and disability is, in itself, not culture-free, but a unique product of our nation's history, legal system, and social structure" (Groce & Zola, 1993).

Persons from ethnic and minority cultures have their own unique and long-standing cultural beliefs, practices, and support systems that may influence their attitudes toward persons with disability and their interactions with the disability service system. "Culture influences beliefs about causation of disability, conditions that qualify as disability, behavioral expectations concerning people with disabilities, and expected actions of others in response to an individual with a disability (Arnold, 1987, as cited in Schaller, Parker, & Garcia, 1998, p. 41). For example, some cultures interpret disability as an act of God that one must accept rather than attempt to change, but other cultures see the presence of a whole and healthy spirit housed within an impaired body (Harry et al, 1995). Some families may have feelings of guilt, responsibility or shame associated with having a family member with a disability, based on their religious and cultural beliefs (National Center for the Dissemination of Disability Research, 1999). Some people believe that a disability represents retribution for the sins of previous generations (Harry et al., 1995).

Varying cultural interpretations of disability may result in different coping strategies and approaches to treatment by individuals with disabilities and their families. Minority families may seek help from folk healers, tribal elders, or spiritual leaders, in addition to or instead of medical or rehabilitation professionals. They may rely heavily on community supports, particularly the church. Among Southeast Asian groups, there may be a reluctance to use mental health services, given the cultural values of saving face and stoicism (Harry et al., 1995). Cultural mistrust may be apparent among some African Americans with disabilities, based on their prior negative experiences in seeking assistance from the rehabilitation or service systems and on misdiagnosis and inappropriate treatment by mental health services (National Center for the Dissemination of Disability Research, 1999). Many people from minority cultures have language and communication barriers that may complicate their ability to obtain helpful information about disabilities and resources.

People from diverse cultures may interpret and experience disability differently, so it is erroneous to assume that all people within a particular culture share identical perspectives. There is diversity, change, and adaptation within minority cultures, as well as within mainstream cultures, in individuals' and families' attitudes and responses to disability. Many social and contextual variables relate to cultural background and may shape or influence people's perceptions. "Cultures are fluid and are greatly influenced by acculturation, generational status, gender, social class, education, occupation, and numerous other variables" (Harry et al., 1995, p. 106). It is important to recognize the heterogeneity within specific cultures and to avoid making broad generalizations about any group that may lead to stereotyping and false assumptions.

Common Assumptions about Disability

Fine and Asch (1988) put forth and then challenge some common assumptions about disability that have guided theory and research in the field of social psychology during the past decades. These assumptions (which are applicable in the field of social work) have influenced social interactions and professional relationships with people with disabilities and their families. Fine and Asch identified the following assumptions:

1. Disability is located solely in biology, and thus disability is accepted uncritically as an independent variable.
2. When a disabled person faces problems, it is assumed that the impairment causes them.
3. The disabled person is a "victim."
4. Disability is central to the disabled person's self-concept, self-definition, social comparisons, and reference groups.
5. Having a disability is synonymous with needing help and support. (1988, pp. 8–12)

These assumptions about disability are in a sense "disabling" because they cast people with disabilities in powerless and "not quite human" roles and reinforce the divide between disabled and nondisabled people. Fine and Asch speculate on how these assumptions evolved and why they continue to persist. They suggest that "attributing neediness and lack of control to people with disabilities permits those who are not disabled to view themselves as having more control and more strength in their lives than may be the case" (1988, p. 16). Moreover, these assumptions put the blame on the individual with the disability for adaptation and change and neglect the need for environmental changes (institutional, physical, or attitudinal).

Professional Values and Service System Trends

Many of these common assumptions are also reflected in professional attitudes and interactions with people with disabilities and their families. Some professionals have tended to focus exclusively on the deficits of people with disabilities, to view them as helpless victims, or to pathologize these individuals and their families. Professionals have often focused on biomedical aspects of the individual's impairment and neglected to consider the role of the sociocultural context of the individual's environment. Many social workers and other clinicians view disability as negative values such as tragedy, stress, and caregiver burden. These people often fail to examine the strengths of the individual or the environment or to help families develop effective coping strategies.

During the past several decades, however, there have been dramatic shifts in how professionals view and treat persons with disabilities and their families, and how services are delivered. The disability service system (particularly for people with mental retardation and mental illness) has moved from a primarily segregated institution-based model of care (before the late 1960s), to community-based services in the 1970s and 1980s, to consumer-driven individualized supports in the 1990s. There has been a shift from facility-based and professionally directed continuum of services to development of person-centered flexible community supports for consumers and families. Some of the key values and principles underlying the supports model are empowerment of consumers of services, opportunities for full inclusion in the community, and enhanced quality of life. The goal is to enable people with disabilities to have real opportunities and exercise real choices regarding their life decisions, such as where to live, work, and socialize.

These changes in service delivery models have necessitated changes in relationships between professionals (including social workers) and individuals with disabilities and their families. Professionals need to rethink their roles in this new individual supports paradigm and develop news ways of collaboration—shifting emphasis from planning, providing, and managing services for consumers to brokering, enabling, and facilitating supports that are determined by consumers with disabilities and their families. Redefining professional roles in the disabilities field is a work in progress. French and Swain state, "Central to a changing relationship is the changing paradigm from a medical to a social model of disability and, with this, possibilities for professionals to work for and with disabled people in confronting the barriers of institutional discrimination" (2001, p. 751). There is some debate regarding the extent to which this shift in power from professionals to consumers has actually occurred. French and Swain note that despite the potential for a changing relationship, there is "little evidence of any shift in relationships between professionals and disabled people . . . power relations and structures are, by their nature, deeply ingrained, and cosmetic changes mask lack of fundamental change . . ." (2001, p. 751).

CONTACT SKILLS WITH CLIENTS WHO HAVE DISABILITIES

Overcoming Resistance and Communication Barriers

Some people with disabilities may be reluctant or resistant to seek professional help because of prior negative experiences with the service system (e.g., misdiagnosis or inappropriate treatment). Many individuals have found the service system unresponsive to their needs (Balcazar, 2001; Beaulaurier & Taylor, 2001; Mackelprang & Salsgiver, 1999). They often feel that they are not listened to or respected regarding their perceived needs and preferences. The process of seeking help from the formal service system may make them feel passive, needy, or helpless. Some people feel that that they have been paternalized, pathologized, or blamed for their conditions when they have sought help. Other individuals may be reluctant to seek services because of shame or embarrassment about their conditions.

Inaccessibility of services is a major barrier for many people with disabilities. Although accessibility has significantly improved during the past decade because of the passage of ADA and increased activism, transportation and architectural barriers are still commonplace. For some people with physical disabilities, the act of physically getting to appointments at a clinic or agency is difficult (e.g., inaccessible public transportation, no elevators, inaccessible bathrooms). In addition, communication barriers may make it difficult for persons with disabilities to interact with the service system. For example, people who are deaf or who have other auditory or communication impairments may be unable to communicate with professionals who do not offer alternative communication methods such as interpreters, signers, and listening devices. Similarly, people with visual impairments may need to have written agency materials (applications, brochures, contracts) available in Braille or large print. People with cognitive disabilities such as mental retardation or severe learning disabilities may face obstacles in understanding complex information provided by agencies, such as program eligibility criteria or applications for public entitlements.

In addition, people from minority cultures with disabilities may resist or be reluctant to seek help because of cultural or language barriers. Persons whose primary language is not English face significant obstacles in obtaining assistance from agencies in which staff do not speak their native language or do not have translators available. People may find it difficult to confide in and trust professionals who are not from their own culture or familiar with its values. Immigrant status adds to and may intensify these concerns. "For those immigrants who are here illegally, the fear of being sent back makes many reluctant—or extremely fearful—to come forward to request services for disabled family members. The fear of being sent back to chaotic economic or political situations can only be compounded by the fact that their native countries may well have not services available for their disabled family members" (Groce & Zola, 1993, p. 1052). Also, some immigrant parents are afraid that their children will be taken away from them and institutionalized if they are located by authorities (Groce & Zola, 1993).

During the contact phase of the social work process, social workers should consider the following guidelines to help overcome client resistance to seeking services and to minimize the multiple barriers faced by people with disabilities:

Understand and Respect the Cultural Context of the Individual   Social workers must recognize and value the diverse cultural contexts of individuals with disabilities to understand their experiences, identify problems or needs, and help mobilize resources to address their concerns. Social workers must be cognizant of how cultural background influences individuals' and families' interpretation of disability, expectations and goals, coping strategies, and help-seeking behaviors.

Ideally, professional staff in agencies should reflect the cultural makeup and diversity of consumer populations, but often this is not the case (Schaller, Parker, & Garcia, 1998). Social workers should make every effort to become familiar with the cultures of the clients they serve. One helpful strategy is to get to know gatekeepers or leaders of the community to develop a better understanding of their culture and values, and to seek their input about community needs (Balcazar, 2001). For example, school teachers, religious leaders, elders, and traditional healers can provide valuable information about cultural and community attitudes and responses (Groce & Zola, 1993). In some cases, agencies have hired members of the community as paraprofessionals to assist with client outreach and contact.

In a similar vein, some people with disabilities may prefer to work with professionals who themselves have disabilities, so they can build on a shared cultural experience and foster greater understanding and sensitivity. Kirshbaum (1994) points to the value and benefit of using staff "peer clinicians" (psychotherapists with personal disability experience) in clinical interventions with families with disability issues. The peer clinicians "frequently function as cultural intermediaries and reframing agents," counteracting some of the negative connotations typically associated with disability (1994, p. 11).

Social workers who do not have disabilities must gain knowledge about and appreciate the "disability culture" to help bridge cultural gaps experienced by their clients with disabilities. Olkin (1999) suggests that clinicians immerse themselves in the culture of disability—by reading about the personal experiences of people with disabilities and by obtaining specific information about disabilities and disability culture. Social workers should also make efforts to meet informally with members of disability advocacy groups or independent living centers to hear the stories and concerns of consumers and their families. Personal relationships with peers or family members with disabilities go a long way toward demystifying disability.

Don't Trade One Set of Stereotypes for Another   There is clearly danger in making broad-based stereotypic assumptions that all persons with a particular type of disability think or behave a certain way, or that all persons with disabilities from particular ethnic cultures have similar attitudes or experiences. Social workers must recognize the enormous diversity within these groups and understand how various background and contextual variables help shape each person's unique experiences. "Social class, generational status, religion, gender, geographic location, ability, and personality are all aspects of diversity that will influence and interact with an individual's level of acculturation to the ways of the dominant society" (Harry et al., 1995, p. 101). Groce & Zola note that although it is not practical to learn the infinite details of specific cultures in detail, it is "important for practitioners to be sensitive to the patient's heritage, to their own heritage, and to what happens when different heritages and belief systems come together" (1993, p. 1054).

Be Aware of One's Values and Attitudes toward Disability   Because stereotypes of people with disability are so pervasive and deeply ingrained in our society, social workers and other professionals may internalize negative feelings and fears. Research on attitudes of nondisabled people toward people with disabilities has shown that "the fear of and aversion to disability and illness often leads to fear and rejection of people who have disability and illness. Social workers need to be self-aware of their own personal values and cultural heritage and how their beliefs and experiences may influence their relationships with clients with disabilities and their families. They may have to "recognize their own apprehensions of impairment to become effective change agents of the attitudes of people with and without disabilities" (Asch & Mudrick, 1995, p. 753). Olkin (1999) notes that it is important for therapists to understand and manage negative countertransference, to become comfortable with the topic of disability, and to develop skills in incorporating disability issues in treatment.

Recognize and Value the Role of the Family   Social workers need to be aware of families' beliefs, values, and attitudes about disability. To build relationships with families, it is important to identify which members of the family should be approached or are viewed as head of household (Robinson & Rathbone, 1999). Most services and supports are typically geared to individuals within nuclear family units, so professionals need to be responsive to the needs of extended families and alternative family systems that play a vital role in many minority cultures. "The extended family is able to offer members emotional, economic, and enculturation support. Therefore, family should be defined by a consumer and his/her family in a way that makes sense for them. Acknowledging the importance of family may be key for developing appropriate and effective interventions" (Schaller, Parker, & Garcia, 1998, p. 44).

Establishing a Responsive Service Delivery System

Harry and colleagues (1995) discuss the importance of culturally inclusive services for students with severe disabilities and their families. This culturally inclusive approach has relevance for establishing a responsive service delivery system with individuals with disabilities of all ages and their families. Building personal relationships and finding common ground with individuals with disabilities and their families is of primary importance for professionals. Harry et al. note that brief formalized assessment tools are generally ineffective and may alienate families who are more comfortable with a personal approach. Professionals should consider multiple aspects when building respectful and trusting relationships with individuals and families (Harry et al., 1995):

1. *Home language:* Professionals should ask, rather than make assumptions about what language is spoken in the home and by which members (p. 102).
2. *Culturally appropriate developmental norms:* Goal setting for students with severe disabilities must take into account that norms for personal and social development differ across cultures (p. 102).
3. *Residential and work-related goals:* The meanings of work and independent living are culturally based—professional emphasis on the value of work and residential options may not be shared by all families (p. 102).

4. *Interpretation of disabilities:* Differing cultural interpretations of disability may lead to different views about treatment and kinds of coping strategies used by families (p. 103).
5. *Concepts of the family:* Different concepts of family (e.g., nuclear family vs. extended family, individual health vs. collective health) have important implications regarding people's attitudes toward disabilities (p. 103).
6. *Alternative and communication modes:* Parents of students with severe communication difficulties may vary in their comfort with and preference for technological augmentative communication systems (p. 103).
7. *Child-rearing practices:* Professionals should respect the family's cultural values underlying traditional child-rearing practices, which may differ from mainstream American values regarding issues such as equity and personal choice (p. 103).
8. *Parental advocacy:* Professionals must recognize that some parents may find it difficult to challenge or collaborate with professionals, given their cultural views and history regarding hierarchical professional relationships (pp. 103–104).

These issues are important for social workers to consider in developing culturally inclusive services for children, adults, and families. Along the same lines, Schaller, Parker, and Garcia (1998) discuss the need for rehabilitation counselors to make adaptations in the provision of services based on cultural values and beliefs of consumers. First, Schaller and colleagues suggest the importance of recognizing and valuing the bicultural/bilingual status of individuals and families. Second, cultural knowledge must be incorporated into service provision—through location of services in ethnic communities, language accessibility through interpretation and translation, communication that conveys both information and meaning, acknowledgement of the importance of families, and the use of culturally sensitive assessments. A third strategy identified by Schaller et al. (1998) for providing culturally responsive services is incorporating informal supports and natural helping networks such as extended family members, elders, community centers, and churches.

Cultural brokering is an approach to providing culturally competent services to persons with disabilities. Jezewski and Sotnik define cultural brokering as the process of "bridging, linking, or mediating between groups or persons of differing cultural backgrounds for the purpose of reducing conflict or producing change" (2001, p. 21). Cultural brokering involves mediating, negotiating, advocating, networking, and other strategies to prevent or reduce conflicts that may arise from differing beliefs and values of the consumer and the service system. Assessment, problem solving, and communication are important skills for cultural brokers (Jezewski & Sotnik, 2001).

Practicing Relationship Protocols

Individuals with disabilities and family members are more likely to feel at ease and develop a trusting relationship with the social worker if their initial meetings have a personal and respectful tone (Harry et al., 1995; Schaller, Parker,

& Garcia, 1998). For many clients, interpersonal interactions are more effective than relying on written communications. In face-to-face meetings, social workers should allow time for informal introductions and conversation and avoid going straight to asking questions about the "problem." In a way that conveys respect and interest, ask about the person's interests, family, and community. This will help to set a personal tone and may provide helpful information about the person's background and values. People are more likely to share their "stories" informally through open-ended discussion, rather than in response to formal questioning. If specific forms or assessments do need to be filled out, conduct this business toward the latter part of the meeting or at a later meeting.

Social workers should ensure that their relationship protocols respect the client's cultural background: preferred ways of addressing the client and family members, knowing who is perceived in the family as the head of household, who should be invited to attend the initial meetings, who should be asked to be involved in decision making. "An awareness of, and sensitivity to, a family's view of proper social behavior, purpose of the interview, preferred language, issues of time and pace, and information-sharing styles needs to be incorporated into interviewing practices" (Schaller, Parker, & Garcia, 1998, p. 44). If a social worker is unfamiliar with the cultural norms of a particular individual or family, he or she should find out this information beforehand—by asking knowledgeable staff, community members, or the client or family directly.

Developing mutual trust and respect is a critical aspect of the relationship-building process. Social workers must communicate respect and empathy in their interactions with clients and their families to make clients feel valued and at ease. Reassuring clients about the confidentiality of information sharing is also essential in this trust-building process. Rothman describes three components that are necessary for effective helping relationships: "A belief in the competence of the worker, a belief in the essential worth of the client as a person who deserves dignity and respect, and a belief that together, worker and client can create a change and an improvement in the client's problem" (2003, pp. 182–183). Showing interest in the client as a whole person rather than just focusing on the person's disability are important ways to communicate belief in the essential worth of the person and that person's capacity for change.

Using Professional Self-Disclosure

Some clients may assume that professionals with disabilities are more likely to understand their situations and share common experiences of their personal and societal struggles. Peer counseling is an important and valued component of many independent living and self-help programs for persons with disabilities. However, there is limited research on the issue of whether similarity in disability status between counselor and client affects treatment, and those research findings are unclear (Olkin, 1999).

Rothman warns that workers who share a client's disabling condition "must be careful not to assume that the clients have the same issues about their disability as the worker does. Especially if the a client has come for help about something not immediately related to the disability, it is important for the worker to self-monitor and stay where the client is rather than grounding the relationship-building process on the shared disability . . ." (2003, p. 181). Although a shared disability may be helpful in establishing a bond between client and worker, ultimately the relationship must focus on the specific needs and circumstances of the individual, whose disability may or may not play a big role in his/her life.

Enhancing Listening and Communication Skills

Social workers must communicate with clients in a manner that "conveys both information and meaning" (Schaller, Parker, & Garcia, 1998). Individuals with disabilities and their families have significant need for honest, accurate information about the nature of their disabilities and available resources. This information needs to be communicated in a nonthreatening style, using lay terms wherever possible and avoiding technical and professional jargon. Social workers need to allow adequate time in their meetings to carefully explain and clarify information and to elicit and address client's questions.

The meaning and context of information is equally important to communicate. Many individuals and families may have difficulty understanding the meaning of the information conveyed, particularly with printed information. "Low context communication" that emphasizes objective information devoid of interpersonal sensitivity may create barriers for people from culturally diverse backgrounds (Schaller, Parker, & Garcia, 1998). For example, Harry (1992) describes how differences in language, experience, and expectations set the stage for a tremendous gap in communication between culturally different parents and special education school personnel. "The district's extensive use of written communication in English compounded problems (of mistrust and confusion). Even when most letters and reports were sent in Spanish, their meaning was still not clear because of the use of educational jargon, the inadequate information and experiential base from which the parents operated, and because of the need for a more personalized style of communication" (Harry, 1992, p. 183). Social workers and other professionals need to be aware of and sensitive to the individual's and families' information-sharing styles and needs to be better able to communicate both information and meaning.

The communication process may pose particular challenges when a client has communication, sensory, or cognitive impairments. For example, a person who is deaf may use sign language, lip-read, or require the use of an interpreter in meetings. It is important that social workers find out in advance from clients or staff what specific communication methods and supports are preferred and would be helpful during meetings (e.g., interpreters, communication boards, other assistive devices). In addition, the lighting, noise level, and potential distractions in the meeting room may pose challenges for clients with sensory or attention disorders. Attending to these environmental aspects facilitates the communication process. For persons with cognitive limitations, the social worker will need to communicate information in clear and concrete terms, break information into smaller segments if possible, and allow time for questions and repetition of information as needed. Sensitivity and responsiveness to clients' specific communication needs require the social worker's time and perseverance. Attention to these important factors is a critical step in the trust-building process, signaling to clients that they are valued and that their opinions matter.

PROBLEM IDENTIFICATION SKILLS WITH CLIENTS WITH DISABILITIES

Gaining Problem Understanding

Too often, professionals who work with people with disabilities view the disability as the focus of the person, ignoring other equally important or more important characteristics of the individual or the individual's situation (e.g., person's gender, social class, family structure, occupation, etc.). In the problem identification stage of social work practice, social workers must "strive to see the disability as one aspect, but not necessarily the defining aspect, of a human being who comprises many facets" (Olkin, 1999, p. 302). Although social workers may work with some people whose main problems do relate to their disabling conditions (e.g., adjusting to the recent onset of a disability, experiencing disability-related job discrimination, seeking information about sexuality and disability), other clients may have issues that do not relate directly to their disabilities (e.g., grief over loss of partner, obtaining welfare assistance, coping with sexual abuse). "Social workers must learn to distinguish between situations in which disability is and is not a client's or family's principal concern. Because people with disabilities seek social services for situations not specific to issues presented by their impairments, a generalist approach to social work practice is most applicable" (Asch & Mudrick, 1995, p. 755).

It is also important to recognize the valuable roles of family members and address the problems and needs of the family unit as well as the individual, particularly during life cycle transitions that may "exert a centripetal pull on the family system" (Rolland, 1989, as described in Kirshbaum, 1994, p. 10). There is emerging interest in the changing needs of people with disabilities and their families across the life span (Seltzer, Krauss, & Heller, 1990). The increased longevity of persons with disability, the increased likelihood of acquiring a disability in later years, and the large number of families providing care to family members with disabilities across the life span have all probably contributed to this recent interest. Life-span developmental theory looks at changes in the family life cycle, experienced either by the family as a whole or by individual family members. "The onset of disability, whether the birth of a baby with a disability, a disabling event in a parent, or a significant exacerbation of a disability—usually is experienced as a traumatic change. Even in families with stable and long-term disabilities, developmental transitions or

life cycle points (such as childbearing) can trigger earlier trauma and also create family disequilibrium and vulnerability" (Kirshbaum, 1994, p. 9).

Wikler (1981) described various family stresses that emerge and reemerge
over time because of the discrepancies between expectations and performance
of the child with developmental disabilities. These stresses include stigmatized
social interactions, the prolonged burden of care, the lack of information
about the disability and behavioral management issues, and grieving.
Clinicians who understand these chronic stresses can serve these families better and can anticipate periods of difficulty and thus perhaps ameliorate some
of those stresses. The extent to which families experience crisis is mediated by
the family's interpretation of the stressor event and the familial resources available for managing the stressor (Wikler, 1981). For example, a strong extended
family network, a supportive marital partner, contact with another parent
with a disabled child, nonjudgmental professionals, and a tolerant community
are potential mediators or buffers of the family's stressful events.

Social workers should not focus exclusively on the subjective and objective burdens experienced by families of children with disabilities. They should
ask families whether they have experienced any benefits and positive impacts
in caring for family members with disabilities. Perceived benefits may include
satisfaction with the accomplishments of their family members, a strengthened
and more cohesive family system, increased tolerance and understanding,
opportunities for personal growth and fulfillment, and a greater awareness
and appreciation of life (Marsh, 1992; Seligman & Darling, 1989). Some studies have found that adult family members with mental retardation have made
positive contributions to their parents, providing help with household tasks
and companionship, particularly helpful as parents age and are themselves in
need of assistance (Blacher & Baker, 2002).

It is also important to recognize that many people with disabilities are
parents themselves. There are approximately eight million families with children under 18 years who have one or more parents with a disability—just
under 11% of all families in the United States (Olkin, 1999). In a survey of
more than 1,200 parents with disabilities (about 75% had physical disabilities), many respondents reported facing attitudinal barriers and discrimination
(Kirshbaum, 2000), including pathologizing assumptions by professionals and
society about their parenting abilities and about potential negative impacts of
their parenting on their children. Although many parents with disabilities
experienced practical obstacles (e.g., transportation, housing, recreational
access) and social obstacles (e.g., unemployment and poverty), they also
reported positive outcomes such as parental and child resilience and acquired
expertise in problem solving.

Viewing Micro, Meso, and Macro Level Problems

Fawcett and colleagues (1994) present a contextual-behavioral model of
empowerment that has much relevance for problem identification and problem solving in social work practice. These researchers discuss how the environment may be more or less facilitative of empowerment of people with

disabilities—the process by which people gain control over events, outcomes, and resources. The environment exerts control at various levels: "(1) the micro level (e.g., family, peers); (2) meso level (e.g., relationships among micro systems within neighborhood organizations and other contexts; and (3) meta or systems level (e.g., culture, economic system)" (Fawcett et al., 1994, p. 476).

These environmental factors are important for social workers to consider in the problem formulation stage of practice. Fawcett et al. (1994) identify meso level and meta or macro level environmental stressors and barriers that constrain the daily lives of individual with disabilities: lack of opportunity, discrimination, punishment and behavioral requirements, environmental barriers and hazards (e.g., lack of curb cuts, dilapidated housing); and poverty and associated deprivation. The environment also may provide positive support and resources that facilitate the empowerment of individuals with disabilities and their families: information and prompts, family and peer support, models and mentors, positive reinforcement, financial and material resources, supportive policies and laws, and culture.

Social workers need to examine the dynamic interplay of these meso and macro environmental influences along with micro level person and group factors that also exert influence on empowerment status. Fawcett et al. (1994) identify two sets of person/group factors that are important to examine: (1) the competence and experience of the individual, including the person's knowledge and critical consciousness, skills, past history, and values and beliefs; and (2) the physical and biological capacity of the individual, including the person's mental and physical health and the type and degree of existing impairment (e.g., mobility, auditory, cognitive). The influence of these individual factors at the micro level must be evaluated within the broader environmental context.

ASSESSMENT SKILLS WITH CLIENTS WITH DISABILITIES

Using a Biopsychosocial Perspective

There is a good fit between the principles of social work practice and the service needs of people with disabilities and their families. Social workers should use an ecological person-in-environment approach in which the individual and family are viewed within the context of the social system. Instead of focusing exclusively on the individual's adaptation to his or her environment, social workers need to examine how environments may constrain or facilitate the individual's functioning and quality of life. For many people with disabilities, their biggest problems relate to environmental stressors and barriers (e.g., discrimination, lack of opportunity, architectural barriers). Social workers need to work with people with disabilities and other advocates to reduce the disabling impact of social and physical environments.

At the same time, many people with disabilities may have specific biomedical needs (e.g., need for AIDS treatment, dialysis, pain management, sexual counseling) and psychological needs (psychosocial adjustment to disability, self-esteem issues, depression, anger, social isolation). Social workers can help coordinate interdisciplinary assessments that look across these biomedical and psychosocial needs of the individual and family and how environmental variables influence the person's situation. Ultimately, assessment should lead to identification and mobilizing of resources to address identified needs.

Identifying and Mobilizing Client Cultural Strengths

People with disabilities are often pathologized by professionals and by society—viewed as helpless, dependent, victims, tragic, and so forth. "Professionals often have difficulties recognizing the capacities of the individuals to help themselves. This is in part a legacy of the medical model and of the arrogance of our professional effectiveness mentality" (Balcazar, 2001). It is important that social workers incorporate a strengths perspective in the assessment process, helping individuals and families to identify strengths and competencies, to develop positive coping strategies, and to mobilize support.

Harry et al. (1995) identify several strategies to facilitate meaningful assessment of students with severe disabilities from diverse cultures. These guidelines are equally applicable to the social work assessment process with adults or children with disabilities. First, Harry et al. suggest that appropriate family members should be invited to observe or participate in all assessment procedures (1995, p. 104). Decisions about which members are most appropriate should be made in collaboration with the individual with the disability and the family because patterns of authority and responsibility may vary. Social workers should ensure that assessments are held at times and in places convenient for the family. Once the assessment has been completed, evaluators should allow extended time to explain the results in layperson's terms to the individual and family. "In cases where the parents hold very different explanations of the etiology or meaning of a severe disability, professionals should be prepared to engage in extended interactions with the family regarding this issue" (Harry et al., 1995, p. 104).

For persons from non–English-speaking cultures, or for whom English is not their primary language, assessments should be conducted in the individual's dominant language whenever possible. It may be helpful to use individuals from the community to help interpret and to serve as liaisons. Harry et al. (1995) stress the importance of using independent interpreters familiar with the culture of the individual and family (rather than a family member or staff person related to the assessment). This allows for greater possibility of accurate, unbiased interpretation. Moreover, "children should never be used as interpreters, partly because they may not have the knowledge base to transfer technical concepts adequately and partly because this places the child in a position of inappropriate power vis-à-vis the parent" (Harry et al., 1995, p. 104), particularly problematic in hierarchical cultures.

For linguistically and culturally diverse persons with disabilities, the use of formal standardized assessments (e.g., intelligence, adaptive functioning, vocational tests) may be biased and not accurately measure an individual's needs

Case Study Integration Exercise on Contact, Problem Identification, and Assessment Skills

Case Background

Evelyn Jean-Francois is a 30-year-old Haitian American woman who has been recently diagnosed with HIV/AIDS. Evelyn is a legal immigrant who came to the United States with her family 10 years ago. She lives in a subsidized apartment in Boston with her teen-age son Jean Paul and her 50-year-old mother Claire. Evelyn was divorced three years ago. Her ex-husband has a history of substance abuse and provides only sporadic child support for their son. Claire has a heart condition and is unable to work—she helps a great deal with caregiving and household tasks.

Evelyn is a nursing aide in a nursing home. She has recently missed a lot of work because of her AIDs-related symptoms. Evelyn has a chronic cough, no appetite, problems sleeping, and finds herself crying a lot. She is concerned that she may infect her patients or family. She is also fearful that the nursing home will fire her if they find out about her AIDS diagnosis or if she misses any more time from work. She does not have health insurance or disability benefits.

Evelyn has told her mother about the HIV/AIDS diagnosis, but has not discussed this with her son. She has informed her ex-husband about the diagnosis (whom she suspects infected her with the virus), but he refuses to talk with her about it. Evelyn's son Jean has been a strong junior high school student until recently. However, his teacher has informed the family that in the past few months he has skipped several classes, had some fights with other students, and is failing several courses. The teacher suggested that they meet to discuss these school issues.

Evelyn and her mother are Catholic and attend Mass regularly in a neighborhood church. She and her mother are afraid to discuss the AIDs diagnosis with their priest or fellow church members. They feel embarrassed and ashamed about their situation, and are afraid that the church will reject them.

Evelyn has just started to meet with a social worker at a neighborhood health clinic to get help "to deal with everything." However, she is somewhat unsure and mistrusting about whether the young Caucasian social worker will be able to understand her situation and help her and her family.

Application Exercises

A. Contact Stage

1. What key aspects of Evelyn's location and context are important for the social worker to consider during the contact stage? (e.g., living arrangement, family structure, children, employment, health care, church)
2. How might Evelyn's multiple identities (gender, ethnicity, age, sexual orientation, social class, religion, immigration status, native language) influence her relationship with the social worker?
3. What are potential barriers (e.g., resistance, communication) in establishing a relationship between the young Caucasian social worker and Evelyn?
4. How might the social worker and her agency help to overcome these barriers?
5. What steps can the social worker take to understand and respect the cultural context of Evelyn and her family?

(continued)

CASE | *continued*

6. What are the social worker's own values and attitudes toward HIV/AIDS and how might these attitudes influence her relationship with Evelyn?
7. How can the social worker help Evelyn feel at ease during initial meetings and develop a trusting relationship?
8. If the social worker has personal experience in dealing with AIDs (herself, close family member or friend), should this information be disclosed to Evelyn?

B. Problem Identification and Assessment Stages

1. What are ways the social worker can help Evelyn to describe her problems in her own words?
2. What are ways to assess Evelyn's biopsychosocial needs?
3. To what extent are Evelyn's problems and her family's concerns interrelated?
4. How might the social worker help Evelyn view her problems within a broader environmental context?
5. What environmental factors (meso and macro) might constrain or facilitate Evelyn's and her family's situation?
6. What strategies may help to reduce environmental barriers or constraints (e.g., stigma, job discrimination, lack of health insurance)?
7. What aspects of Evelyn's environment may provide positive supports and resources for Evelyn and her family?
8. How can the social worker help Evelyn and her family develop positive coping strategies and mobilize needed supports?

and capabilities. Social workers should be aware that standardized tests are frequently not based on the norms of minority populations and, thus, should be used and interpreted with great caution. Alternative assessment approaches should be used in these situations, such as informal procedures and observations and portfolio assessments that use anecdotal records and samples of an individual's work over time (Harry et al., 1995).

There is also concern about the impact of disabling conditions on the reliability and validity of tests (including ability, diagnostic, and neuropsychological testing). "Most tests are normed on populations that explicitly exclude persons with disabilities, and there is scant research on the impact of disability on the meaning of test items or on the process of taking the test. Not surprisingly, then, when persons with disabilities are given such tests, they tend to incur over- or underinflated scores, which is then interpreted as indicative of pathology" (Olkin, 1999, p. 211). For some persons with disabilities, it may be necessary to make modifications in testing procedures. The ADA requires that "reasonable accommodations" be made in testing individuals with disabilities. Test modifications might include changes in the test medium (e.g., from written English to Braille and using a reader or audiotape in place of written material), changes to the time limits for taking the test, and changes to the test content (Olkin, 1999, p. 216).

INTERVENTION SKILLS WITH CLIENTS WITH DISABILITIES

Establishing Goals and Agreement

Establishing goals for intervention and agreement or contracting between the social worker and client are important first steps in the intervention stage. Goals are "terminal or ultimate outcomes that the client and worker would like to have achieved upon completion of the intervention phase" (Lum, 1992, p. 97). The statement of goals should be specific, task-centered, and include measurable outcomes. Olkin (1999) emphasizes the importance of establishing positive treatment goals that go "beyond deficit reduction." Instead of focusing exclusively on the amelioration of negative symptoms (e.g., depression, anxiety, and anger), therapists working with clients with disabilities should include goals related to the optimization of functioning (e.g., health, well being and hardiness) (Olkin, 1999, p. 155).

The social worker and client should jointly develop the goals, framed from the client's perspective and stated in the client's own words whenever possible. By asking clients what they hope to accomplish and listening to their perceived needs and preferences, social workers help clients develop a plan of action that emphasizes clients' strengths and capabilities as well as identifies individual needs or problems. DeJong and Miller stress the importance of developing "well-formed goals with the client within the client's frame of reference" (1995, p. 730). The process of defining achievable goals is challenging because clients often do not have specific goals in mind when they enter helping relationships. Social workers must work with clients to help them develop well-formed goals. According to DeJong and Miller well-formed goals are important to the client; small; concrete, specific, and behavioral; seek presence rather than absence; have beginnings rather than endings; are realistic within the context of the client's life; and are perceived by the client as involving hard work (1995, p. 730).

Some goals may focus on changes required at the individual level (e.g., improve job readiness skills, increase self-esteem, enhance marital communication). However, it is also important to help clients identify environmental barriers (political, social, economic) and opportunities to affect those systems (e.g., joining a disability advocacy organization or participating in a legislative campaign for affordable housing). Stated goals may specify desired services (counseling, advocacy, referrals), and actions in which consumers may engage (Mackelprang & Salsgiver, 1999, p. 212). A plan of action may also include information on formal resources and informal supports that may exist in the clients' neighborhoods and communities and help clients access available resources.

During this goal setting process, both the social worker and the client must believe in the client's capacity to change (Rothman, 2003). Some clients with disabilities may have diminished confidence about their abilities to make changes in their lives—they may experience a sense of hopelessness about their situations or about the possibilities for change and improvement. The social worker's goal is to help the client "believe that change is possible and within the client's power to achieve" (Rothman, 2003, p. 176). Before the social worker can assist the client in this process, the worker must believe that the client has the inherent capacity to change. Rothman (2003) notes that this is sometimes a special challenge for workers who may view their client's disability as a major impediment and experience themselves a sense of hopelessness about the client's situation. "In order to believe in the client's ability to improve his or her circumstances, the worker must self-examine, self-monitor, and self-observe . . . workers must be sensitive not only to the client's perceptions of the place of disability in the overall problem, but of their own as well." (p. 176).

Using Indigenous and Social Work Intervention Strategies

Social workers have the potential to intervene at various levels of the social system (individual, family, group, and community) to promote supportive environments for individuals with disabilities and their families. Interventions based on an ecological person-in-environment approach are most appropriate and well suited to social work practice. Slater and Wikler suggest that social workers assume the roles of "systems convener, systems activator, systems trainer, and family therapist" (1986, p. 388). As a systems convener, the social worker helps individuals and families identify external sources of support. As a systems activator, the social worker mobilizes the resources of extended family members to fulfill a number of functions, including assistance with daily care, planning, and advocacy. Social workers provide systems training by providing specific information and training to consumers and families. These roles reflect a shift in emphasis from planning, providing, and managing services for consumers to brokering, enabling, and facilitating supports that are determined by individuals with disabilities and their families.

Prevention is also an essential component of social work intervention with individuals with disabilities and families. Social workers must address the problems of poverty and the sequelae of poverty—poor health care, inadequate housing, alcohol and substance abuse, child abuse and maltreatment, and violence—to prevent disabilities or to minimize their negative consequences. Social workers may find that in their work with some clients and families, it is important to address the root causes as well as consequences or effects of the disability.

Social workers are well suited to intervene in various roles and capacities, particularly regarding case management, advocacy, and family-based interventions.

Case Management

Social workers can assist clients whose disabilities may affect various aspects of their lives and who require services and supports that span various delivery systems (e.g., health, educational, vocational, social, and psychological services). Typically, a wide variety of clinical disciplines (including medicine, psychology, neurology, social work, special education, and vocational rehabilitation) are involved in the assessment, planning, and provision of services. Social workers can help coordinate the multiple services that address individual and family needs and provide linkages between the various service providers (e.g., housing, health care, mental health care, education, vocational training). Social workers can help families learn about available services and supports and ways to access needed services. Many clients, particularly from minority cultures, may choose to seek help from informal supports in their communities such as spiritual leaders, folk healers, or tribal elders. Social workers can help individuals and families identify and mobilize informal supports and formal services that address their specific needs.

Advocacy

Social workers can play a vital role in advocating for the civil rights of clients regarding education, employment, education, housing, medical care, and insurance. They can help clients understand their legal rights and obtain benefits to which they are entitled by law. Clients need specific information about eligibility for various entitlement programs and assistance in applying for these benefits. For example, social workers can assist clients in obtaining information about various income support programs such as Social Security Disability Insurance, Supplemental Security Income, and Worker's Compensation.

The ADA is a means to ensuring full participation of people with disabilities in the mainstream of American society. Social workers can help clients understand the provisions of the ADA, and the specific protection provided by this legislation from discrimination in employment, educational opportunities, public services, and telecommunications. For example, they can inform clients that employers are prohibited from inquiring about disabilities before employment and that the law requires "reasonable accommodation" by employers in making jobs and facilities readily accessible and usable. In addition, social workers can help clients seek legal advice in cases where they feel they have experienced discrimination.

According to the ADA, individuals may not, by reason of their disability, be excluded from participation in or be denied the benefits of the services, programs, or activities of public agencies. Social service agencies are among those public entities whose facilities must be accessible to people with disabilities. Orlin recommends, "health and social service agencies, with the assistance of disability community groups, audit their physical facilities and evaluate their policies, practices, and procedures to ensure that they do not discriminate against individuals with disabilities in the delivery of services either by denying them services or by failing to provide service in the most integrated setting" (1995, p. 236).

Family-Based Interventions

Current theories of practice in the disabilities field emphasize the importance of family-based interventions that incorporate the strength and coping resources of families. Although much of the professional literature regarding family-based practice deals with families of young children with disabilities, social workers and other professionals also need to develop practice models that deal with families of adults with disabilities, and families in which the person with the disability is a spouse or a parent.

Schilling (1988) identified a variety of interventions that have been used in helping families with children with disabilities, including individual and group counseling, parent training groups, parent-to-parent programs, counseling and support groups for siblings, and other supportive services such as respite care and specialized day care. Although all these services have merit, Schilling stressed that no single approach is ideally suited to the needs of this population because of variations in disabilities, families' coping patterns, and available resources.

At the other end of the age spectrum, Kropf (1997) has identified helpful clinical interventions to assist older parents of adults with developmental disabilities. Psycho-educational approaches can provide older parents "information about the changes that their son or daughter is experiencing in adulthood, and provide a forum to bring together older parents as a source of mutual aid" (1997, p. 45). Older parents may also require assistance with their own developmental tasks as aging individuals, and with futures planning, in which they develop a plan for their adult child's future living arrangements, when the parents are no longer able to provide care.

Kirshbaum (2000) discusses the need for interventions to support families in which the parent has a disability. In a national survey of more than 1,200 parents with disabilities, numerous social and environmental barriers were identified including these: discrimination, transportation, housing, recreational access, lack of access to infant care adaptations, and barriers to child care (Barker, & Maralani, 1997). Fifteen percent of respondents in this national survey reported attempts to have their children taken away from them. Through the Looking Glass (a disability culture-based organization in Berkeley, California) integrates infant mental health and family therapy approaches to respond to the needs faced by parents with disabilities and their children. This organization emphasizes the need to respect the personal experiences and expertise of parents with disabilities and to provide infant care adaptations and supports to assist parents with tasks such as feeding, diapering, and bathing babies. Overall, this program uses a "contextual view of parenting that refocuses on the elements in the social network and environment that are compensatory and nurturing versus undermining and stressful" (Kirshbaum, 2000, p. 18).

According to Dunst, Trivette, and Deal (1988), professionals need to "rethink" intervention practices with families and adopt a social system perspective of families that moves beyond the individual with disability as the sole focus of the intervention toward the family as the unit of intervention. Family-based interventions should emphasize empowerment of families, family identified needs and aspirations, family capabilities and strengths, and personal social networks as primary sources of support (Dunst et al., 1988). Turnbull and colleagues (1993) suggest that professionals help families to develop cognitive coping strategies that enhance family members' self-esteem, sense of control, personal meaning, and well-being.

Proposing an Integrative Micro, Meso, and Macro Intervention Approach

The Fawcett et al. (1994) contextual–behavioral empowerment model (described earlier in this chapter) illustrates an integrative intervention approach to empowering individuals with disability and their families. This approach uses many strategies and tactics that facilitate empowerment at different intervention levels and contexts. At the person/group (micro level), social workers can enhance individuals' experience and competence by increasing knowledge about issues and facilitating the development of skills (e.g., goal setting, problem solving, and communication). Social workers also can protect and maintain the physical and biological capacity of individuals by establishing health promotion and health prevention programs.

At the meso and macro levels of intervention, social workers can work to remove environmental stressors and barriers and to enhance the supports and resources of persons with disabilities. Fawcett et al. identify the following helpful strategies to remove stressors and barriers: develop and enhance opportunities for involvement and goal attainment, reduce discrimination and other barriers to equal opportunity, remove punishment and reduce requirements for behavior, remove or minimize environmental barriers and hazards, and provide economic supports to reduce deprivation associated with poverty (1994, p. 482). In addition, they suggest multiple tactics to enhance the supports and resources of persons with disabilities, including the following: provide information about issues and alternatives and prompts to take action, strengthen family and peer support, enhance access to positive models and mentors, increase positive reinforcement for constructive actions, enhance availability and accessibility of resources and opportunities, advocate for changes in policies and law, and strengthen or enhance positive aspects of the culture.

This model reflects the "dynamic interplay among person or group and environmental factors" (Fawcett et al., 1994, p. 475). Social workers may intervene at various levels and within various contexts (e.g., with individuals, families, small groups, neighborhoods, and organizations) to facilitate the empowerment process.

TERMINATION SKILLS WITH CLIENTS WITH DISABILITIES

Reviewing Client Progress

The termination or ending stage of the social worker's relationship with the client offers an opportunity for the worker and client to review progress, make plans for the future, and implement some follow-up strategies. Social workers must help clients with disabilities assess the progress they have made during the relationship. Has the client achieved the goals that were initially established during the intervention phase? In what areas has the client made most progress? In what areas is there still work to be done? Has the client grown in his or her capacity to change, or to effect change in his or her environment? Have these changes helped improve the client's situation or circumstances? These are questions that the social worker and client can reflect on and discuss, as they evaluate the client's present circumstances and make plans for the future.

Most clients and workers experience positive emotions regarding termination and can identify specific areas of progress, growth, and achievement. However, some clients may be unhappy or dissatisfied with the relationship with their worker and, in fact, may terminate the relationship prematurely. The termination or dropout rate is high among multicultural clients, including persons with disabilities, and therefore of great concern. Some clients may have had prior negative experiences with social service agencies or may feel that their worker or the agency does not understand or respect their cultural values or beliefs. Others may have problems getting to appointments because of child-care or transportation problems. Clients with certain disabilities may be unable to access services because of architectural barriers, lack of accessible transportation, or lack of competent interpreters. Social workers and agencies must examine the various reasons for premature termination to see if there are ways to eliminate barriers and enhance cultural responsiveness (at the worker or agency level).

In other situations, termination of the professional relationship results from the time-limited nature of the treatment or service, not necessarily because of the client's growth or progress, or the client's desire to terminate the relationship. For example, clients' health insurance typically limits the number of paid mental health visits with a social worker or other therapist. Given the short duration of these treatments, termination issues may need to be dealt with by the therapist and client from the outset. For some persons with significant disabilities and needs for ongoing supports, termination from time-limited services may be perceived by the client (or therapist) as premature and may be stressful for both the client and the social worker. Identifying ongoing supports for the client and helpful linkages to resources are important steps in the termination process, particularly when the brief treatment work appears "unfinished" or inadequate to address the clients' full range of needs.

Evaluating the Present and Future and Outlining Follow-Up Strategies

In addition to reflecting on past and current progress, the worker and client should formulate a plan for the future that may involve negotiating new goals, developing new strategies for change, or making referrals to new resources. Because many clients with disabilities have needs that may require ongoing long-term assistance and support, the termination phase should help the client in connecting with formal and informal supports and services. The focus should be on linking clients to resources within their family, neighborhood, and communities. During this stage, efforts should be made to help the client generalize and maintain the gains that they have made. For example, if treatment has focused on the acquisition of social skills for a young adult with developmental disabilities, then the social worker should work with the client

Case Study Integration Exercise on Intervention and Termination Skills

Case Background

Maria Diaz is a 45-year-old American woman with Down syndrome who lives with her 70-year-old parents, Eva and Roberto Diaz, in Brooklyn, New York. The Diaz family emigrated from Puerto Rico to the United States in 1978. Maria works part-time in an office mailroom. Her father works two janitorial jobs to support their family. Mrs. Diaz is a retired hotel worker.

Although Maria functions well on a day-to-day basis and is able to make basic decisions about her schedule, free time, or hobbies, she does not have the cognitive capacity to plan or make decisions independently about major life matters (e.g., finances, medical care, housing). She depends heavily on her parents for help with life decisions and generally complies with their advice.

Maria helps her family by doing many household chores—this has been beneficial to her mother who has medical problems that limit her physically. Maria is also very close to her three married siblings who live nearby. Outside of her close family circle, she has no friends or social life.

Maria's case manager (a social worker from the state mental retardation agency) believes that Maria has the potential to be more independent and more socially involved with peers in the community, but that she has been over-protected by her family at home. The social worker recently suggested to the Diaz parents that they begin to plan "for the future," to think about where Maria will live and who will take care of her when they are no longer able to provide care. The social worker suggested convening a family meeting with Maria, her parents, and her siblings, to discuss their hopes, expectations, and concerns about the future and to consider making some residential, financial, and legal (e.g., guardianship) plans. The social worker warned that there are waitlists for public services, so it is important for the family to get Maria's name on the list for future services.

The Diaz parents are resistant to the idea of having a planning meeting with the social worker and their family. The concepts of future plans and government responsibility for their daughter's care are foreign to them. They are uneasy about involving professionals in their private matters. They are not overly worried about Maria's limited independence—"she gets by okay" with their help. From their cultural perspective, it is the family's responsibility to take care of their own. Although they are concerned about Maria's future when they are gone, they have faith that this matter is "in God's hands." They hope and pray that Maria's siblings will care for her when they are no longer able. However, they have never discussed these issues with the siblings, nor have they have asked Maria about her own preferences.

Application Exercises

A. Intervention Stage

1. What are helpful ways for the social worker to initiate the process of goal formulation with Maria and her family? What kinds of questions might be helpful in beginning this dialogue?
2. What might be appropriate goals for intervention with Maria and her family?

(continued)

CASE | *continued*

3. Are the goals based on the client's frame of reference?
4. What specific outcomes and behavioral objectives should the social worker and family hope to achieve? Over what period of time?
5. Do the intervention goals agreed on fit the belief system and culture of the Diaz family?
6. How might the social workers' perspective on appropriate intervention goals differ from the families' views? How should these conflicting views be negotiated?
7. In what ways might Maria's preferences differ from her parents' goals?
8. What are strategies to help the family members understand and reconcile their differing perspectives?
9. To what extent do the established goals focus on change at the individual level (Maria, family) and change at the meso and macro level (e.g., formal resources, informal supports, advocacy, and legislation)?
10. To what extent do the established goals emphasize client/family strengths and capabilities as well as client/family needs and problems?
11. What are specific intervention roles that the social worker can play in this situation (e.g., information, training, advocacy, case management, family therapy)?

B. Termination Stage:

1. What are ways the social worker can review with Maria and her family the progress they have made during their relationship in terms of the established intervention goals?
2. In what areas has growth or desired change occurred? In what areas have goals not been achieved? What factors or constraints may account for lack of progress in certain areas?
3. What types of follow-up plans should the social worker suggest to ensure a positive termination?
4. Do the follow-up plans help to connect Maria and her family with ongoing formal resources and informal supports if needed?

to help him or her transfer these skills to other situations or settings, perhaps through the use of homework assignments, role plays, or exercises in the client's natural environment. The social worker should work with the client and family about how to preserve the gains made and ensure that necessary supports are available in the client's environment.

A follow-up plan should be developed to ensure a gradual and successful termination. The social worker and client may gradually reduce the frequency of their sessions, set up some follow-up appointment after termination to monitor progress, and make arrangements for telephone follow-up as needed. For clients with long-term disabilities and ongoing support needs, in-person contact and follow-up visits with the social worker may help clients maintain gains and plan for future needs.

CLOSING THOUGHTS

Social work practice with individuals with disabilities is similar to practice with other culturally diverse groups. Many persons with disabilities "are essentially bicultural, going back and forth between the disabled community and the nondisabled larger society" (Olkin, 1999, p. 155). Social workers must understand and respect the multiple cultural context(s) of persons with disabilities and incorporate cultural knowledge and sensitivity at each stage of the social work process. The challenge of social work practice is to empower persons with disabilities, reduce the disabling impacts of their social and physical environments, and promote their full inclusion in communities.

References

Americans with Disabilities Act of 1990, as amended, 42 U.S.C. Section 12102(2).

Asch, A., & Mudrick, N. R. (1995). Disability. In *Encyclopedia of social work* (19th ed., pp. 752–761). Washington, DC: National Association of Social Workers.

Balcazar, F. E. (2001). Strategies for reaching out to minority individuals with disabilities. *Research Exchange, 6*(2), 9–13.

Beaulaurier, R. L., & Taylor, S. H. (2001). Social work practice with people with disabilities in the era of disability rights. *Social Work in Health Care, 32,* 67–91.

Barker, L. T., & Maralani, V. (1997). *Challenges and strategies of disabled parents: Findings from a national survey of parents with disabilities.* Berkeley, CA: Through the Looking Glass.

Blacher, J., & Baker, B. L. (Eds.) (2002). *The best of AAMR: Families and mental retardation.* Washington DC: American Association on Mental Retardation.

Braddock, D., & Parrish, S. (2002). An institutional history of disability. In D. Braddock (Ed.), *Disability at the dawn of the 21st century and the state of the states* (pp. 1–61). Washington DC: American Association on Mental Retardation.

Brown, S. E. (2001). Editorial: What is disability culture? *Institute on Independent Living Newsletter,* Retrieved from http://www.independentliving.org/newsletter/12–01.html in December 2001.

DeJong, P., & Miller, S. D. (1995). How to interview for client strengths. *Social Work, 40,* 729–736.

Dunst, C., Trivette, C., & Deal, A. (1988). *Enabling and empowering families: Principles and guidelines for practice.* Cambridge, MA: Brookline Books.

Fawcett, S. B., White, G. W., Balcazar, F. E., Suarez-Balcazar, Y., Mathews, R. M., Paine-Andrews, A., Seekins, T., & Smith, J. F. (1994). A contextual-behavioral model of empowerment: Case studies involving people with physical disabilities. *American Journal of Community Psychology, 22,* 471–496.

Fine, M., & Asch, A. (1988). Disability beyond stigma: Social interaction, discrimination, and activism. *Journal of Social Issues, 44,* 3–21.

French, S., & Swain, J. (2001). The relationship between disabled people and health and welfare professionals. In G. L. Albrecht, K. D. Seelman, & M. Bury (Eds.) *Handbook of disability studies.* Thousand Oaks, CA: Sage.

Fujiura, G. T. (2001). Emerging trends in disability. *Population Today, August/September,* 9–10.

Gainer, K. (1992). I was born colored and crippled. Now I am disabled and black. *Mouth; the voice of disability rights, Sep/Oct,* 31.

Gill, C. J. (1995). A psychological view of disability culture. First published in *Disability Studies Quarterly,* Fall 1995.

Retrieved from http://www.independent living.org/docs3/gi111995.html

Groce, N., & Zola, I. K. (1993). Multiculturalism, chronic illness and disability. *Pediatrics, 91,* 1048–1055.

Hahn, H. (1999). The political implications of disability definitions and data. In R. P. Marinelli, & Dell Orto, A. E. (Ed.), *The psychological and social impact of disability* (pp. 3–11). New York: Springer.

Harry, B. (1992). Cultural diversity, families, and the special education system: Communication and empowerment. New York: Teachers College Press.

Harry, B., Grenot-Scheyer, M., Smith-Lewis, M., Park, H., Xin, F., & Schwartz, I. (1995). Developing culturally inclusive services for individuals with severe disabilities. *Journal of the Association for Persons with severe Handicaps, 20,* 99–109.

Jans, L., & Stoddard, S. (1999). *Chartbook on women and disability in the United States* (An InfoUse Report H133D50017-96). Washington, DC: U.S. Department of Education, National Institute on Disability and Rehabilitation Research.

Jezewski, M. A., & Sotnik, P. (2001). *Culture brokering: Providing culturally competent rehabilitation services to foreign-born persons.* Center for International Rehabilitation Research Information and Exchange (CIRRIE) Monograph Series. Buffalo: University of Buffalo, State University of New York.

Kaye, H. S. (1998). Is the status of people with disabilities improving? *Disability Statistics Abstract, May* (21), 1–4.

Kirshbaum, M. (1994). Family context and disability culture reframing: Through the looking glass. *Family Psychologist, Fall,* 8–12.

Kirshbaum, M. (2000). A disability culture perspective on early intervention with parents with physical or cognitive disabilities and their infants. *Infants and Young Children, 13,* 9–20.

Kropf, N. P. (1997). Older parents of adults with developmental disabilities: Practice issues and service needs. *Journal of Family Psychotherapy, 8,* 35–52.

LaPlante, M. P. (1992). How many Americans have a disability? *Disability statistics abstract no. 5, June 1992.* Retrieved from Disability Statistics Center Web site http://dsc.ucsf.edu/UCSF on December 16, 2002.

Lee, S., Sills, M., & Oh, G. (2002). Disabilities among children and mothers in low-income families. *Institute for Women's Policy Research. Research-in-brief, #D449,* 1–7.

Lum, D. (1992). *Social work practice & people of color.* Pacific Grove, CA: Brooks/Cole.

Mackelprang, R. W., & Salsgiver, R. O. (1999). *Disability: A diversity model approach in human service practice.* Pacific Grove, CA: Brooks/Cole.

Marsh, D. T. (1992). *Families and mental retardation: New directions in professional practice.* New York: Praeger.

National Center for the Dissemination of Disability Research. (1999). At a glance. *Research Exchange, 4*(1).

National Council on Disability (1993). *Meeting the unique needs of minorities with disabilities: Report to the President and the Congress.* Washington, DC: National Council on Disability.

National Organization on Disability (2000). *2000 N.O.D./Harris Community Participation Study.* New York: National Organization on Disability.

Olkin, R. (1999). *What psychotherapists should know about disability.* New York: Guilford Press.

Orlin, M. (1995). The Americans with Disabilities Act: Implications for social services. *Social Work, 40,* 233–239.

Robinson, E. G., & Rathbone, G. N. (1999). Impact of race, poverty, and ethnicity on services for persons with mental disabilities: Call for cultural competence. *Mental Retardation, 37,* 333–338.

Rothman, J. C. (2003). *Social work practice across disability.* Boston MA: Allyn & Bacon.

Schaller, J., Parker, R., & Garcia, S. B. (1998). Moving toward culturally competent rehabilitation counseling services: Issues and practices. *Journal of Applied Rehabilitation Counseling, 29,* 40–48.

Schilling, R. F. (1988). Helping families with developmentally disabled members. In C. S. Chilman, E. W. Nunnally, & F. M. Cox (Eds.), *Chronic illness and disability* (pp. 171–192). Newbury Park, CA: Sage.

Scotch, R. K. (1988). Disability as the basis for a social movement: Advocacy and the politics of definition. *Journal of Social Issues, 44,* 159–172.

Seelman, K., & Sweeney, S. (1995). The changing universe of disability. *American Rehabilitation, 21,* 2–13.

Seligman, M., & Darling, R. B. (1989). *Ordinary families, special children: A systems approach to childhood disability.* New York: Guildford Press.

Seltzer, M. M., Krauss, M. W., & Heller, T. (1990). *Family caregiving over the lifecourse.* Paper presented at the Roundtable on Aging and Developmental Disabilities, Boston, MA.

Shapiro, J. P. (1993). *No pity: People with disabilities forging a new civil rights movement.* New York: Times Books, Random House.

Slater, M. A., & Wikler, L. (1986). "Normalized" family resources for families with a developmentally disabled child. *Social Work, 31,* 385–390.

Smart, J. F., & Smart, D. W. (1997). The racial/ethnic demography of disability. *Journal of Rehabilitation, 63,* 9–15.

Social Security Act, Sections 223(d), 1614(a)(3)(B), 42 U.S.C. Sections 416(i), 423(d), and 20 C.F.R. Sections 404.1505, 416.905(a).

Turnbull, A. P., Patterson, J. M., Behr, S. K., Murphy, D. L., Marquis, J. G., & Blue-Banning, M. J. (1993). *Cognitive coping, families, and disability.* Baltimore: Paul H. Brookes.

U.S. Census Bureau. (2003, March). *Disability Status: 2000* (Census Brief C2KBR-17)). Washington, DC: U.S. Department of Commerce, Economics and Statistics Administration, Bureau of the Census.

Wenger, B. L., Kaye, H. S., & LaPlante, M. P. (1996). Disabilities among children. *Disability Statistics Abstract, March* (15), 1–4.

Wikler, L. (1981). Chronic stresses of families of mentally retarded children. *Family Relations, 30,* 281–288.

Zola, I. K. (1993). Disability statistics, what we count and what it tells us: A personal and political analysis. *Journal of Disability Policy Studies, 4,* 9–39.

11

Social Work Practice with Older Adults of Color

Blanca M. Ramos, Lani Jones, and Ronald Toseland

As the 21st century unfolds, the older adult population in the United States continues to increase rapidly. At the same time, the number and proportion of older adults of color is growing at an unprecedented rate (Villa & Torres-Gil, 2001). Increased international migration resulting from globalization and improved medical conditions are major contributing factors to the dramatic growth. Increasingly, older adults of color are coming to the United States accompanying younger relatives or to reunite with their first-generation immigrant children. These demographic trends coupled with a heightened awareness of the roles of race and ethnicity on the aging experience underscore the need for cultural competence in social work practice with older adult clients.

Culturally competent practice with older adults begins with the recognition that aging is a natural process but presents specific, age-related challenges. Thus, people of all ethnic backgrounds face similar biopsychosocial changes associated with aging, some of which can be difficult. For example, old age can bring the loss of a partner, older friends, and kin; declining physical health and income; and loss of social status and participation in society (Butler & Lewis, 1977). Yet, these daunting circumstances occur within an environmental-structural setting that can either enhance or limit opportunities for an optimum aging experience (Morales & Sheafor, 1995). For older adults of color, the historical period in which they have lived continues to be marked by exposure to oppressive conditions, which renders old age particularly challenging.

Cultural competency in social work practice also requires a keen recognition of the enormous diversity and heterogeneity of older adults of color.

Older adults of color can trace their roots to a number of ethnic origins including African, Latino, Asian and Pacific Islander, and First Nations Peoples. Individual factors such as gender, age, sexual orientation, and socioeconomic status each contribute to the heterogeneity of this older adult group.

In this chapter, we discuss older adults of color drawing primarily on similarities while calling attention to individual group differences. The chapter begins with a discussion of the demographics of older adults of color in the United States, followed by an illustration of historical oppression and survival values of this population. We continue with a review of culturally competent theory and practice skills for older adults of color and complete the discussion with an adaptation of culturally competent skills for practice with older adults of color. A case study is provided for illustration.

THE DEMOGRAPHICS OF OLDER ADULTS OF COLOR

According to the 2000 Census, there were nearly 35 million persons age 65 and older in the United States, representing 12.4% of the population; 16.4% of the older adult population was composed of people of color. As of 2000, African Americans made up the largest percentage of the older adults of color population (8.0%), followed by Latinos (5.6%), Asian or Pacific Islanders (2.4%), and American Indian or Native Alaskans (<1%).

Predictions for population growth in older Americans include a rise during the next 30 years from 12.4% to 20%. The number of older adults of color is expected to increase at an even faster rate to 25.4%. The growth of specific older adults of color populations is projected to be quite dramatic. For example, older adult whites are expected to increase by 81% by 2030, but older adult Latinos are expected to increase by 328%, and other racial and ethnic groups are expected to increase by 219% (Administration on Aging, 2001).

Census 2000 data clearly indicate that older adults of color are disadvantaged compared with their white counterparts. Overall, 10.2% of the older adult population live below the poverty level, but only 8.9% of the older adult whites were poor compared with 22.3% of African American older adults, and 18.8% of Latino older adults (Administration on Aging, 2001). Compared with whites, older adults of color were found to rely more heavily on Social Security and SSI payments than on private pensions or savings for income (Torres-Gil & Moga, 2001). For example, the median net worth reported by African American heads of household age 65 or older was only $13,000, compared with $18,000 for whites (Administration on Aging, 2002). Census 2000 indicates that older adult women were found to have a higher poverty rate than were older adult men (13% versus 7%). Notably, poverty among older adult women of color was more severe than among white women, and for some subgroups, it was quite high. For example, Latino women living alone or with nonrelatives had a poverty rate of 38.3%, and divorced black women between the ages of 65 and 74 had a poverty rate of 47% (Administration on Aging, 2002).

Older adults of color are similarly disadvantaged educationally. According to the 2000 United States Census, 74% of white older adults had completed high school compared with 63% of Asian and Pacific Islanders, 46% of African Americans, and 37% of Latinos. Moreover, the 1998 Current Population Survey indicates that 16% of white older adults have completed college, compared with 7% of older adult African Americans, and 5.4% of Latinos (Administration on Aging, 2002).

Ford and Hatchett (2001) cite several studies that indicate that older African American men have higher rates of many major illnesses when compared with whites. For example, prostate cancer rates in men age 65 and older are 30% higher in African Americans than in whites. The impact of disease also appears to show racial disparities. African Americans aged 65 to 74, for example, have an 80% greater risk of becoming disabled after a serious illness than do whites (Cohen, 1993). Older adults of color also fare more poorly on measures of self-reported health. Whereas 26% of the white older adults rate their health as fair or poor, 41.6% of African Americans and 35.1% of Latinos report fair or poor health status (Administration on Aging, 2002).

Access to health care is an additional concern. For example, almost twice as many African Americans as whites reported delaying receiving health care because of cost considerations (9.6% versus 5.0%), and fewer Latinos report receiving preventive care such as mammography (Administration on Aging, 2002). Life expectancy is also dramatically lower for older adults of color than for older adult whites. As of 1997, life expectancy was 77.1 years for whites and 71.1 years for African Americans (Administration on Aging, 2002). This discrepancy in life expectancy is not surprising given the limited access of older adults of color to health care. Factors associated with low levels of socioeconomic status and educational attainment may also contribute to greater disability and shorter life expectancy for some older adults of color for whom gaining necessary information about preventive health care and disease management is very difficult (Kim, Bramlett, Wright, & Poon, 1998; Kotchen et al., 1998).

Although older adults of color are disadvantaged in many respects compared with their white counterparts, several encouraging factors are worth noting. For example, although African Americans report higher levels of depression, they also appear to have higher levels of life satisfaction. This may be partly because of the more extensive social support networks found among African Americans compared with their white counterparts (Ford & Hatchett, 2001). Some evidence indicates that the familial role of older adults of color differs considerably from that of whites. The extended family is central to the emotional well-being of many Latino older adults. Older adult Latinos between the ages of 65 and 74, for example, were found to be four times more likely to live with their adult children than were white Anglos (Choi, 1999). Similarly, many older adults of color do not experience the same disadvantages in their own communities as they do in larger society. Furthermore, ethnic and cultural factors may greatly influence how older adults of color respond to the negative outcomes of living in oppressive environments. These, in turn, can differentially ameliorate or exacerbate their harmful effects on the aging process.

THE HISTORICAL OPPRESSION AND SURVIVAL VALUES OF OLDER ADULTS OF COLOR

Aging as part of the life cycle is universal. At the same time, the concept of "old age" is socially constructed and varies across cultures. In every society, old age denotes a person's chronological age and physiological condition and connotes the social attitudes about aging and the status accorded to the aged. For example, an important area where a society's attitudes about aging can be observed is its public policy. In the United States, old age is primarily defined using the chronological cutoff of 65, the referent established by the Social Security Act of 1935 to begin receiving benefits. This legislation, as well as others, reflects a general belief about society's ethical and moral obligation to assist its older adults. Additional policies intended to assist older adults include provisions to reduce discrimination and increase their access to private and public facilities, as well as entitlement programs that bestow on them a legal right to receive public assistance, and social services (DiNitto, 1999). The primary focus of the 1965 Older Americans Act (OAA), the most important law recognizing the social service needs of older adults, was to coordinate comprehensive services for people over 60, establishing the Administration on Aging (DiNitto, 1999; Suppes & Wells, 1996). Unfortunately, although these policies are intended to benefit all elders in the nation, they mostly do not reach, or adequately serve, many older adults of color.

Social security—which, for older adults in general, is usually a major source of income—is funded by employer and employee contributions and may not be available for many older adults of color, particularly immigrants. Some may have migrated late in life and might not have been able to accrue eligibility time or find employment in the United States, and others may have held jobs without retirement benefits. The latter is not uncommon, for example, among immigrant Latina women who are often employed as domestic workers for long periods. Among older adults of color who do receive social security benefits, these often do not provide adequate incomes, do reflect gender disparities, and are well below the general standard of living. In 1998, for 33% of Latino older adults receiving social security, this was their sole source of income, with men receiving an average of $804 and women $543 per month (National Council of *La Raza*, 1998).

Despite the vulnerable sociodemographic profile of older adults of color, who as a whole face a multitude of economic, health, and psychosocial adversities, entitlement programs intended to mitigate these needs, for the most part, do not reach them. This is primarily because of limited accessibility, discrimination, bureaucracy, and language and cultural barriers (Dietz, 1997; Tennstedt & Chang, 1998). Even legislation especially designed for older adults, such as the OAA, often does not translate into appropriate services for older adults of color. For example, the 1981 amendments to OAA set service priorities that include information and referral programs for non–English-speaking older adults, transportation, and nutrition programs (Suppes & Wells, 1996). Yet, some data suggest that progress implementing these mandates among Latino older adults, for instance, has been slow. Information in Spanish may not be readily available, and nutrition programs, such as Meals-on-Wheels, may not include culturally appropriate menus and their meal sites may be located far away from Latino neighborhoods (Ramos et al., 2002).

Given the relatively poor health status of older adults of color and the accompanying need for long-term care and health services, which most are not able to afford with private funds, public policy is crucial to help facilitate their access to services. However, health programs and services, such as Medicare and Medicaid, are continuously scrutinized and subject to cutbacks and changes that can negatively affect the health status of older adults of color. For example, impending reforms that decrease services and benefits and raise age eligibility and out-of-packet expenses will limit older adults' access to health care services and increase their economic vulnerability (Villa & Torres-Gil, 2001).

In the United States, the social roles and expectations for older adults are prescribed by western cultural values. Although there are increased efforts to emphasize the strengths and joys of growing old, societal attitudes that devalue old age are prevalent, and older adults are often victims of ageism. *Ageism* refers to the prejudices and negative stereotypes inflicted on older adults simply because they are old (Butler, 1989). For older adults of color, the aging experience in U.S. society goes beyond ageism and is further influenced by racial, ethnic, and cultural factors. For example, older adult women of color may find these factors intersecting with issues of gender. In addition, ageist attitudes and behaviors are compounded by the oppressive conditions they face because of their disadvantaged minority group status.

Older adults of color, like mainstream older adults, are often victimized by the exaggerated fears, myths, and misinformation about the biopsychosocial changes of aging, hindering one's ability to adjust to the normal changes associated with aging. Ageism is also used to justify its harmful effects on oppressed populations. For example, the oppressive aspects of ageism result in derogatory verbal and nonverbal behaviors, segregated housing, and discrimination in the labor market based solely on a person's characteristics, namely age (McInnis-Dittrich, 2002).

Some of the social disadvantages for older adults of color are evidenced by their precarious socioeconomic profiles and marginal living conditions. As previously noted, poverty, low educational attainment, poor health status, limited access to health care, and high rates of many major illnesses are issues of major concern. Experiences of oppression related to gender and sexual preference are not limited to mainstream society and further heighten the risk and vulnerability for some older adults of color. Older adult women of color have different experiences based on their ethnic ties. Even within their own racial and ethnic communities, older adult women of color, for whom poverty is quite high, can experience oppression and sexism (Comas-Diaz & Greene, 1994). Clearly, being female, aged, and a racial or ethnic minority can often place an older adult woman of color in "multiple" jeopardy.

Despite a myriad of social, economic, and physical needs, older adults of color have historically encountered barriers to services that could enhance the quality of their lives. Limited accessibility and availability of safe, affordable, and empathic services are compounded by the bureaucratic, rigid nature of service agencies that perpetuate long-standing prejudices, stereotypes, and discriminatory practices (Aleman, 2000).

Many older adults of color share the social disadvantages of living in oppressive conditions stemming from racism, prejudice, and discrimination. At the same time, older adults of color are ethnically and culturally diverse. Disadvantaged minority groups have varied social, cultural, and political histories that differentially affect the nature and source of their oppressive realities. Diverse ethnic groups have experienced and been affected by a unique range of structural forces that include slavery, political colonialism, migration, immigration, ethnocultural translocation, and transculturation. To illustrate, many First Nations People, such as the Cherokees in their Trail of Tears, were forcibly moved, often by foot, from one area of the United States to another (ethnocultural translocation). Similar to some Mexicans residing in the Southwest for generations, the First Nations People suddenly found themselves stigmatized, deemed inferior, and obligated to ascribe to drastically different cultural norms, beliefs, and behaviors (transculturation). For some of their older adults, the lingering effects of these traumatic events may be particularly powerful because many older adults have lived with these painful memories for long periods.

Furthermore, individual characteristics such as racial and physical features, degree of acculturation, and immigration status play an important role in shaping the aging experience among older adults of color. For example, most African American older adults have long lived in a society obsessed with skin color where their daily realities unfold within a race-conscious environment. In fact, in the United States, skin color has historically served as one of the most pervasive justifications to oppress persons of dark pigmentation. The practice of categorizing people using a black-white dichotomy translates to older adults of other disadvantaged ethnic groups, such as Latinos. Darker-skinned Latino older adults experience double discrimination from both mainstream society and other Latinos whose light skin color and physical features more closely resemble those of the arbitrary standard of whites. Data indicate that dark-skinned older adults Latinos experience racial prejudices and housing discrimination on being perceived as blacks (Ramos, 2002).

Historically, people from oppressed groups have drawn on their own cultural values and communities for survival and continuity of racial and ethnic identities. In communities of color, nonwestern and unique ethnocultural factors are both evident and have varying time depths. For some groups, such as Mexican American and First Nations People in the Southwest, cultural roots were well established before the arrival of Anglo American culture. The present cultural patterns of African Americans reflect, at least in part, some traditional practices that survived despite the dispersal of their ancestors throughout the United States on arrival from the African continent as slaves. Many Latino and Asian American families have continued to practice culturally specific norms for generations, many of which are consistently readapted and revitalized because of continual, heavy immigration.

In general, ethnic and cultural factors may be at the root of the tremendous strength and resilience found among older adults of color. For many, their racial and ethnic identities are sources of pride, support, and strength. Likewise, cultural norms and traditions offer older adults of color the means to help cope, adapt, or resist oppressive environments. Among older adults of color, the aging experience is generally shaped by collectivistic values that, in contrast to the mainstream value of individualism, emphasize an intricate, intertwined relationship with their families and communities. For example, a preference for high levels of intergenerational interdependence within the family promotes stable caregiving systems for older adults. This dynamic has been extensively documented among Latino and Asian American groups for whom familism and filial piety, the cultural values at the root of older adult caregiving, prescribe the obligation to provide material and emotional support for aging family members, particularly when they are frail and disabled (O'Leary, 2000). Cultural values promoting reciprocity and social responsibility are also present in African American families and communities, where network supports for older adults are created through mutual-aid systems that include both blood-related and fictive kin (Gonzales, 2000).

Beyond the nuclear and extended families, older adults of color generally have access to other sources of natural supports, including friends, neighbors, and religious groups. For many, the church affords social, material, and emotional supports. Among Latinos, religious beliefs and practices help older adults deal with difficult situations by providing comfort, guidance, and consolation. Participation in some religious rituals, such as prayer and private or community mass, helps them cope with illness and the loss of love ones (Falicov, 1998). Korean American older adults, particularly the most recent immigrants, often resort to the church as a unifying mechanism that provides close ties to their cultural roots and assistance in navigating in their new homeland.

For African American older adults, the black church plays a pivotal role in helping mitigate the myriad adversities they encounter in their daily lives. It provides instrumental and expressive long-term care for older adults within a family-like atmosphere where fellow church members are adopted as fictive kin (Gonzalez, 2000; Johnson, 2000). The black church offers African American older adults a coherent belief system that is sensitive to their history of oppression. This religious ideology provides an explanation and a rationale for the deleterious effects of the life-long struggles they have experienced (Johnson, 2000).

Another cultural value that plays an important role in the lives of many older adults of color is respect. Respect recognizes a person's social worthiness and prescribes older adults and ancestors are to be treated with deference. For example, among First Nations People, the word "older adult" refers to a person worthy of great respect, someone who has attained old age, and one who possesses wisdom, dignity, and valuable lifelong experience (Weibel-Orlando, 2000). Cultural traditions that place great value on older adults are also prevalent among Asian American groups. Among the Japanese, older adults have the right to be honored and treated with respect. This right, which is enjoyed as a result of both ascription and achievement, is reinforced by family structures and social attitudes about the aged who embody the most-immediate historical ties to the past (O'Leary, 2000).

Older adults of color are often regarded as vital to their communities where the cultural contexts promote a high social status and active roles for aging members. African American and Latino older adults are often viewed as role models, provide family caregiving, and frequently serve as leaders in religious, civic, and local governance organizations (Torres-Gil & Moga, 2001). First Nations older adults are considered essential and valuable members of their communities. They are the transmitters of cultural traditions across generations and serve as wise teachers and mentors providing advice to the young (Sellers, 2000; Weibel-Orlando, 2000).

CULTURALLY COMPETENT KNOWLEDGE THEORY AND PRACTICE SKILLS FOR OLDER ADULTS OF COLOR

The growing body of literature on cultural diversity includes a number of frameworks for culturally competent practice with people of color, each with its own distinct terminology, methods, and skills. Less attention has been centered on developing practice models that specifically address culture and ethnicity in work with older adults of color.

According to Lum (2000), culturally diverse knowledge refers to the information, awareness, and understanding of the multicultural experience and encompasses the histories, societal dilemmas, and cognitive-affective-behavioral characteristics of people of color. Culturally diverse knowledge provides the theoretical foundation for competent social work practice with older adult men and older adult women of color.

Cultural competence is "the ability to understand the dimensions of culture and cultural practice and apply them to the client and social environment" (Lum, 2003, p. 63). It refers to the knowledge and skills a social worker must develop to be effective with clients whose cultures are different than that of mainstream society (Lum, 1999). Several frameworks urge practitioners to build cultural competency within themselves by addressing diversity issues at the emotional, cognitive, and behavioral levels (Cross, Bazron, Dennis, & Issacs, 1989; Green, 1999; Harper & Lantz, 1996; Lum, 1999). Fundamental components of culturally competent practice are cultural awareness, knowledge acquisition, skill development, and inductive learning (Lum, 2003). This section will highlight some important aspects of these components as they relate to practice with older adults of color.

In general, cultural awareness denotes a capacity to recognize one's own cultural values and their impact on professional attitudes and behaviors. Cultural awareness entails an appreciation for cultural differences and the ability to challenge biased assumptions and stereotypes based on race and ethnicity. In practice with older adults of color, social workers must also become aware of their own value-ridden views about aging and challenge those that reflect ageist beliefs as they intersect with racial, ethnic, gender, and socioeconomic factors. Social workers must recognize how their professional values, knowledge, and skills may conflict with the values of older adults of color in a helping relationship (Applewhite, 1998).

Through knowledge acquisition, a social worker develops a set of competencies that reflect a greater understanding of the body of information pertinent to culturally diverse practice. These competencies have been discussed by Lum (2003) and apply in social work practice with older adults of color. Here, a social worker is familiar with the knowledge base and terminology essential to culturally diverse practice, and with the demographics, values, strengths, and histories of oppression of older adults of color. Competencies related to knowledge acquisition also include a practitioner's ability to think critically about issues of cultural diversity, to apply both systems and psychosocial theories to multicultural situations, and to draw from a range of theories from across the social science disciplines.

Applewhite (1998) identified specific areas of knowledge for culturally competent practice with older adult Latinos that are directly relevant to social work practice with older adults of color in general. These include a social worker's understanding of the problems and situations faced by older adults of color, particularly as they are influenced by race, ethnicity, biculturalism, and socioeconomic status. Practitioners must learn about older adult immigrants, the various cultural backgrounds found among older adults of color, and language preferences and communication styles. Familiarity with the help-seeking behaviors of older adults of color and the perceived effectiveness of social services and providers in meeting their needs is also important. Overall, cultural competence with older adults of color requires knowledge about human behavior and the roles of multicultural values around family, spirituality, and group identity in shaping this behavior (Applewhite, 1998; Lum, 2003).

To become culturally competent, one must gain a clear understanding of how the theoretical models used to explain the aging process may apply to older adults of color. Because most of these theories do not address culture and ethnicity and are based on white, middle-class older adults, their applicability to older adults of color is often limited. The field of gerontology, like other practice areas, is still trying to develop ways to best incorporate the important dimensions of culture and ethnicity (Applewhite, 1998).

Several authors have examined the cultural competence of theories that seek to explain how biological, psychological, and social factors influence aging. Applewhite (1998) notes that biological perspectives view aging as inescapable and common to all persons regardless of race or ethnicity and as is influenced by genetics, human decline, and environmental factors. Social workers need to remember that these theories do not appropriately account for individual and group variation. Such is the case, for example, with longevity where cultural and ethnic factors may differentially influence life expectancy as they concomitantly enhance or limit life choices, opportunities, and the well-being of older adults of color.

Applewhite (1998) also suggests that developmental theory, which is prevalent in the field of aging psychology, may not be culturally relevant. From this perspective, the life cycle takes place through stages that follow a universal pattern from early infancy to old age. These life stages, which are assumed to be the same for everyone, are sequential and have predetermined beginning and end points. Furthermore, expectations about successful life stages are deeply embedded in middle-class, western values. In practice with older adults of color, the principles of this theory must be applied with caution because they do not fully acknowledge the powerful influences of culture and ethnicity in the ways in which old age as a life stage takes place and is experienced (Applewhite, 1998).

Some theories that focus on the macro or societal levels of old age address race and ethnicity by emphasizing the social disadvantages of older adults of color. For example, the *double jeopardy* theory suggests that older adults of color face a double burden as a result of old age and membership in an oppressed racial or ethnic group, both of which devaluate their status in society (Aleman & Fitzpatrick, 2000). Although this theory partially explains racial and ethnic disparities and the disadvantaged social status of older adults of color, its tendency to portray these older adults as victims, ignoring the strengths they possess, is not consistent with culturally competent practice. As suggested by Fong and Furuto (2001), cultural competence needs to incorporate a strengths-based perspective that is congruent with social work values. In practice with older adults of color, social workers must go beyond the clients' problems and liabilities and recognize their strengths and positive attributes, particularly those that have been instrumental to their life satisfaction and long survival.

The theory of assimilation, which views minority status and cultural distinctiveness as temporary, has not been applied to all racial and ethnic groups. According to this theory, everyone living in the United States, regardless of race or ethnicity, gradually acquires the cultural values from the mainstream culture and ascends into the middle class. Yet, many communities of color have been in the United States for generations, but have not raised their economic level and continue practicing traditional, culture-bound values and norms. For example, younger family members are often acculturated but continue practicing traditional familial ceremonies, tribal politics, and religious rituals and customs (Aleman & Fitzpatrick, 2000). In work with older adults of color, social workers must pay close attention to the influences of the assimilation perspective on the helping process. The assumption that everyone eventually assimilates equally is deeply embedded in the fabric of U.S. society and manifests itself not only in the professional attitudes and behaviors of the practitioner but also in the policies underlying the provision of social services.

Cultural pluralism theory is one of the few that directly applies to cultural competence with people of color because it is consistent with the profession's value of understanding diversity and has an explicit focus on clients in their own contexts (Pillari, 2002). The main underlying premise is that different racial and ethnic groups can interact relatively equally within one larger society while maintaining their cultural distinctiveness and integrity (Parrillo, 2000). As Devore and Schlesinger (1987, p. 10) phrase it, this perspective recognizes the presence of "distinct, identifiable ethnic subcultures that affect how people think, feel, and act." Within this framework, cultural differences in attitudes, norms, values, and structures are viewed positively (Pillari, 2002). For older adults of color, pluralistic theory is consistent with recent efforts to acknowledge the roles of race and ethnicity in the aging experience. Proponents of critical theory stress the need to challenge older theories and assumptions in social gerontology, particularly the concept of "age as leveler," which asserts that all older adults, regardless of racial and ethnic background, have a uniform experience by virtue of their chronological age (Johnson, 2000).

The previously described theories, though not exhaustive, provide a glimpse into their use and cultural relevance to older adults of color. When examining a theory that explains aging, or any other phenomena, practitioners must ask if its implicit values fit with the values of a particular client's culture (Sharf, 2000). Understanding the cultural values underlying theories of human behavior, gerontology, and social work practice is essential in culturally competent practice with older adults of color.

Cultural competence knowledge theory is important because it allows practitioners to link their observations of an older adult client's situation with the dynamic cultural processes that explain them. This knowledge helps social workers identify and understand the overt as well as the subtle cultural meanings of an older adult client's attitudes and behaviors. At the same time, developing culturally competent practice skills is essential. Social workers must be prepared to draw from a broad range of skills that enable them to practice effectively with older adults of color in a variety of settings. These skills are derived from social work practice principles and are based on the practitioner's own cultural awareness and knowledge acquisition (Lum, 1999). Cultural competence skills relate to a social worker's ability to incorporate culture and ethnicity throughout the helping process with clients.

Consistent with the thrust of this book, the remainder of this chapter will focus on connecting culturally competent social work to the practice process stages of beginning, middle, and end. Following the culturally competent practice (CCP) framework, Lum's (2003) contact, problem identification, assessment, intervention, and termination skills for cultural competence will be discussed as they relate to older adult clients of color. Throughout the helping process, the worker should be prepared to consider culture and ethnicity as they intersect with issues of gender, level of acculturation, and socioeconomic status of older adults of color. An integrated case study will be used for illustration.

CONTACT SKILLS WITH OLDER ADULTS OF COLOR CLIENTS

Contact is perhaps the most important phase in the helping process. During the initial interaction the client-worker relationship begins to develop and the nature of this encounter can be decisive in retaining the participation of a multicultural client (Lum, 2000). At this stage of the helping process, cultural competence can enhance the development of trust and rapport, two essential requirements for building a successful client-worker relationship. For example, older adults of color tend to drop out after the first session, particularly when they perceive that the worker does not understand their social realities and cultural preferences. Similarly, language barriers between an older adult of color and the practitioner in the initial interaction may contribute strongly to a client's decision to discontinue services. Given that older adults of color rarely seek formal services, and that those who drop out seldom get services elsewhere, their continued participation in the helping process is essential (Davis & Proctor, 1989). The following skills can help practitioners increase their cultural competence during the contact phase as they address potential issues related to resistance to services, communication barriers, culturally competent service delivery, relationship protocols, and professional self-disclosure. Awareness of gender-related issues within culture groups also continues to be essential to good practice with older adults of color.

Overcoming Resistance and Communication Barriers

As with any client, an older adult of color may arrive at the initial session feeling anxious and with little control over an uncertain situation, sometimes even resentful and angry because accessing services may not be voluntary (Kirst-Ashman & Hull, 1993; Lum, 2003). Older adults of color may also be skeptical about the practitioner's ability to understand their ethnic and cultural realities and distrustful because of previous experiences of prejudice and discrimination in social service settings. Assimilation and acculturation are complex, but vital, issues to be considered during contact with older adult clients of color. The worker must keep an open mind and remain flexible throughout the sessions as more information about the older adult clients' level of acculturation and assimilation unfolds. Understanding that older adults of color exist at various levels of acculturation and assimilation further challenges the social worker to set an appropriate stage for future interactions with this population.

To minimize clients' resistance, social workers should be able to help older adults of color feel at ease, alleviate their anxiety, and work through the negative attitudes and feelings they may have about coming to the helping process. In an effort to increase comfort level, using a respectful title to address the client demonstrates the worker's efforts to better understand the client's cultural practices. Every effort should be made to build the clients' trust by conveying warmth and a genuine desire to understand their social realities. Genuineness is an essential attribute in developing trust because it involves relating to the older adults in a sincere, honest manner (Kirst-Ashman & Hull, 1993).

At times, practitioners experience negative feelings and reactions that may be triggered by an older adult of color's resistance. Practitioners working with older adults of color may benefit from cultural investigations to find the causes underlying resistance that may go beyond those typically encountered in a practice session. Awareness of the client's cultural beliefs concerning help-seeking behaviors and history of oppression are critical. For example, many older adults of color may find it difficult to ask for assistance outside their familial and other natural support systems. To some, seeking help outside the family and going to a social worker may signify a public recognition of their family's failure to meet their needs, thus resulting in feelings of guilt and shame. At the same time, the notion of asking for help outside their communities may run counter to the values of endurance, stoicism, and acceptance that have been instrumental in their long-lasting survival in oppressive environments. Cultural prescriptions about the roles of older adults as experts in life and advisors to new generations may also contribute to an older adult's reluctance, particularly if the practitioner is young and, in some cases, if the worker is a female.

Similarly, many older adults of color, by virtue of their chronological age, have lived during times when overt racism and discrimination were practiced in the United States. As a result, some may have first-hand experience of the repercussions of unfulfilled governmental promises, such as the treaty agreements signed with First Nations People, racial segregation, denial of individual rights, and unpunished ill treatment from government officials and service providers. Of utmost importance, culturally competent social workers need to remember that a certain degree of resistance in the context of the contact phase is normal. Workers should also have the ability to differentiate between an older adult client's doubts and reservations concerning professional social services and an unwillingness to change unhappy, painful situations and strive for a better quality of life.

Although overcoming resistance is an important goal during the contact phase of the helping process, minimizing communication barriers to facilitate rapport and the beginning of a client-worker relationship is equally pivotal. In practice with older adults of color, the worker should try to decrease language barriers, which involves paying special attention to the client's linguistic preferences and, at times, even familiarity with a different language. A culturally competent worker is able to determine promptly a client's English proficiency, a task that is not always simple and straightforward. In some cases, recognizing when a client has little or no knowledge of the English language can be obvious; in others, the situation may be more complex. For example, some older adults will seem to be more English proficient than they really are as they articulate some common words and phrases they know, nodding in response to the worker's questions or statements in a way that signals apparent understanding. Practitioners need to be patient and take the time to carefully ascertain whether these verbal and nonverbal cues truly reflect a client's English fluency, or are an attempt to be polite, respectful, and agreeable with the worker who, according to some cultural prescriptions, should not be contradicted. Moreover, some older adults of color are fully bilingual, but English may not always be their first choice, and at times, they may prefer to alternate between languages. Among Latino older adults, for instance, it is not uncommon to switch from English to Spanish to express feelings and emotions more intensively throughout a session (Ramos, 2002). At the same time, some clients may prefer to describe painful situations in English as a way of distancing themselves from their emotionally laden content (Altarriba & Santiago-Rivera, 1994). Practitioners should keep in mind that a client who is experiencing a crisis or powerful emotions may have difficulty communicating in a second language, which for many older adults of color is likely to be English (Castex, 1998).

Again, social workers should not automatically assume that an older adult of color is fluent in a particular language or prefers a different language solely based on physical characteristics or family names. Many older adults of color are monolingual and only speak English. Some, because of societal pressures, were forced to abandon their languages of origin, or were deprived of the opportunity to learn the languages of their ancestors. Sometimes this can be an extremely sensitive issue, one that may trigger feelings of guilt, embarrassment, and anger. Practitioners must be cautious about how they approach it and be ready to recognize and validate these feelings.

In determining language proficiency among older adults of color, it is essential to consider their educational level. Sometimes they may speak a language fluently, but are otherwise illiterate. Many older adults of color lived during times or in places where educational opportunities were denied or not readily available to them.

When a practitioner and a client cannot communicate because of language differences and a bilingual/bicultural worker is not available, a translator may be needed. Practitioners should make every effort to use trained translators who are knowledgeable about both the client's language and culture and are willing to familiarize themselves with the literature on using translators (Pine et al., 1990). Social workers must be cognizant of the difficulties inherent in using translators and prepare to address them effectively. For example, some concepts do not translate across cultures, and some translators may have difficulty with certain topics because of their own emotional issues or cultural background, or they may censor or edit the client's narrative (Root, 1998). In general, practitioners should be able to phrase questions and comments about language proficiency carefully and sensitively and recognize when an older adult client declines to use a translator primarily because of pride or a desire not to inconvenience (Root, 1998).

Enhancing Listening and Communication Skills

Competent listening, a basic interpersonal skill of an effective social worker, is vital to culturally competent practice with older adults of color. According to Cournoyer (2005), a practitioner who is skilled in listening attentively hears the clients' words and speech, encourages clients to express themselves fully, and observes their nonverbal communications. For example, a worker who follows attentively what an older adult client is saying will be more likely to hear the message, particularly when the client has low levels of English proficiency or education. It is important to focus exclusively on the older adult's words and sounds rather than letting the worker's own evaluative thoughts about them or a client's accented speech or external appearance (e.g., traditional attire, physical characteristics, etc.) distract from the focus of the meeting. An ability to restrain from making premature evaluative conclusions about what an older adult of color is communicating helps workers lessen the effect of their own cultural biases and stereotypes on their interpretation and understanding of the client's message. As Lum (2000) notes, stereotypes provide structure to an ambiguous interaction and can betray communication. When an older adult of color is of a different, unfamiliar cultural background, a worker may immediately resort to previously formed stereotypes about the client's racial or ethnic group. As a result, practitioners may hear what they expect to hear, and those stereotypes then become a reality as a self-fulfilling prophecy.

In addition to hearing and understanding accurately, practitioners should be able to observe closely a client's nonverbal communications and recognize that these may vary cross-culturally. For instance, although making eye-to-eye contact is typically expected between a client and a worker, some older adults of color may define this nonverbal behavior as intrusive or, depending on age differences, disrespectful and presumptuous. Practitioners must familiarize themselves with a client's culturally bound nonverbal patterns and be respectful of them while refraining from taking personally those cues that seem insulting (Lum, 2000).

Workers must also self-monitor their own nonverbal communications, paying special attention to those that may convey a different, sometimes offensive, message to the older adult client. For example, using eye-to-eye contact, when intense or continuous, can be perceived as challenging or a form of intimidation (Cournoyer, 2005). In general, practitioners should not stare at a client, but they must be particularly careful with older adults of color because this nonverbal behavior signals a power differential, a position of greater status or power (Cournoyer, 2005).

The worker's body position and seating arrangement in relation to the client should account for cultural preferences regarding interpersonal space. For some older adults of color, physical closeness may be acceptable and even desirable, but others may find it too intimate or disturbing. For example, in many Asian cultures it is considered disrespectful to have a barrier (e.g., a desk) between the client and the worker. Moreover, basic practice skills in competent verbal communication are of utmost importance in work with older adults of color. Practitioners must be able to express themselves clearly and to politely ask for clarification when they are not sure about what the client has said. The worker's communication style, which is essential in eliciting responses, should be simple, positive, and nonjudgmental. Sensitive, open-ended questions may help clients experience the session as an interview rather than as an interrogation. Some First Nations older adults may not be accustomed to a direct style of communication, and practitioners need to be especially attuned to disguised requests or indirect responses to questions (Brave-Heart, 2001).

Social workers must be attentive to their own verbal and nonverbal communications because these may, directly or indirectly, reflect stereotypical assumptions about people or convey a patronizing, condescending attitude toward a client (Cournoyer, 2005; Lum, 2003). For example, in many Asian cultures, escorting the client to the door when the session has ended is a way of demonstrating respect. Although these skills are important in work with any client, they are indispensable in cultural competent practice with older adults of color given their histories of racism and oppression.

Practicing Relationship Protocols

Relationship protocols, the codes of ceremonial courtesy and formality that often serve as a prelude to conducting business, are heavily influenced by cultural values and behavioral norms (Lum, 2000). To enhance effectiveness in work with older adults of color, practitioners need to be skillful in recognizing those protocols that are consistent with a client's specific culture. For example, some Latino older adults may prefer to begin a session with a friendly conversation that provides an open, free exchange of information with the worker. Rather than proceeding directly to the presenting problem, which may be viewed as rude and undermine the development of rapport, a practitioner can initiate a conversation about everyday pleasantries emphasizing mutual, reciprocal exchanges (Lum, 1999, 2000). Although this requires investing extra time at the beginning of an interaction, it is an important step that increases an older adult client's comfort level and reduces tension and anxiety in preparation to disclose private, emotionally laden issues.

Preferred cultural prescriptions about proper behavior toward an older adult must be observed throughout the session. With some older adults of color, a worker can acknowledge the special status accorded by their communities by addressing the client in a deferential, solicitous, and attentive manner. Nonverbal communications such as head nodding and silence may be intrinsic to relationship protocols. For Asian American and Latino older adults, seemingly affirmative nodding or long gaps of silence may be ways to signal respect for the worker who is perceived as an authority or expert with specific knowledge and skills. Asian American clients, for example, who nod in affirmation, smile, or utter phrases such as "yes" and "oh, I see" may not necessarily be agreeing but, rather, may be attempting to encourage the practitioner to continue sharing words of wisdom (Root, 1998). Older adults of color from various ethnic groups may not be very verbally expressive during a session or will wait quietly to be addressed by the worker before speaking. Silence may also be used to avoid confrontation or to thoughtfully consider what has been said (Root, 1998; Weaver, 2003). For instance, a First Nations older adult may choose to remain silent to avoid offending the practitioner (Brave Heart, 2001). Workers need to develop competence in interpreting the meaning of these nonverbal behaviors within the practice setting correctly and take a more active, directive approach when culturally acceptable.

Using Professional Self-Disclosure

Professional self-disclosure can help enhance the development of rapport and build trust with older adults of color. Self-disclosing on a common topic allows the worker to become a real person and to humanize the helping relationship (Lum, 1999). This is consistent with both cultural norms and the racial and ethnic realities of older adults of color. In practice with older adult Latinos, cultural norms that impinge on relationship protocols, such as the friendly exchange that takes place at the beginning of a session, require professional self-disclosure, a necessary precursor to building trust. Self-disclosure can also help older adult clients who, because of previous experiences of severe racism and oppression, may feel especially vulnerable in a practice setting. By the sharing of themselves, practitioners help set an egalitarian environment and establish a sense of connectedness that can transcend a client's view of the worker who, as a representative of mainstream society, holds greater power. Practitioners must be especially aware of their potential to replicate the dynamics of societal racist and oppressive relations within the context of the helping process (Pillari, 2002). An ability to acknowledge and demonstrate sensitivity to issues of oppression through self-disclosure may also contribute to building credibility. Topics related to the client's background such as grand-children, travel, clothes, and other areas of common interest are also appro-priate for professional self-disclosure (Lum, 1999).

Establishing a Responsive Service Delivery System

Central to cultural competence with older adults of color is a delivery system that is responsive to their specific needs. Social workers should have the abil-ity to assess and influence the cultural competence of the agency where they practice. An agency that supports culturally competent practice is more likely to attract older adults of color, who otherwise may not seek assistance, and to provide services that more effectively meet their needs. According to Chow (2001), an assessment of an agency's level of cultural competency should con-sider factors related to who uses the services, the nature of the services, and the agency context. Primarily, social workers in settings that provide services to older adults need to be sensitive to issues of racial and ethnic representation among the agency's client population. The client profile should reflect the cul-tural diversity of the overall community including differences both between and within groups. Practitioners should bring any disparities to the attention of the management and offer suggestions about how to expand participation of underrepresented older adults of color.

Next, the worker needs to ascertain which agency services, if any, reach the older adults of color population and identify gaps and potential barriers to their effective delivery. Agencies that serve older adult clients of color will want to focus on services that address issues of acculturation and language and that adhere to specific cultural values. To this end, practitioners will need to consider factors associated with the accessibility, availability, appropriate-ness, and outcome of services (Chow, 2001). For example, many older adults of color may not be able to use services because they do not have the necessary resources, including insurance, finances, or transportation (Lum, 1999). Lack of knowledge about existing programs, stigma, and language and cultural barriers can also limit the accessibility older adults of color have to services. Practitioners should advocate for the development of culturally relevant programs and mobilize resources to make agency services more accessible to older adults of color. For example, services for African American older adults could be made available at a neighborhood setting located on a bus line in a primarily African American community. Similarly, to make a Meals on Wheels program culturally relevant for Korean American older adults, it should offer dishes that reflect this particular ethnic group's dietary preferences.

Third, a social worker should be able to determine whether the agency has a commitment to cultural competence, and how it is implemented. Sometimes an agency's mission statement or philosophy may include a commitment to cultural diversity, but little is done within the agency context to ensure culturally appropriate service delivery. Workers can encourage administrators to recognize the need for services to be delivered in a culturally competent manner, put in place proactive policies and procedures, continue staff education and training, conduct aggressive community outreach efforts, and make the agency's environment more appealing and conducive to cultural competent practice (Chow, 2001; Damskey, 2000). For example, the agency setting can convey a feeling of inclusion and a welcoming atmosphere by employing bilingual-bicultural staff, displaying art, playing music, and making available written material that reflects the diversity of its older adult clients.

PROBLEM IDENTIFICATION SKILLS WITH OLDER ADULTS OF COLOR CLIENTS

Gaining Problem Understanding

As workers seek to understand problem situations that are painful, dangerous, or unbearable for older adults of color, they must be able to recognize that clients bring to the helping process their own perceptions of a problem, which are greatly influenced by race, ethnicity, and culture. The awareness and validation of such salient factors ultimately increases the usefulness of information gained, effectiveness of problem interpretation, and enhances the potential for appropriate service delivery. Gerontologists generally agree that services for older adults need to be designed to take into account inter- and intra-cultural and geographic differences within and across groups.

The building of a trusting relationship and the willingness to jointly identify client problems are clear indications that the worker and client are moving into the second stage of the helping process. At this stage, they are able to validate the problem initially identified. The problem statement, which is derived from the problem identification process, should addresses the specific circumstances, behaviors, and feelings of the client. Problems are usually indications of unfulfilled needs and unsatisfied wants (Lum, 2000). It should not be assumed that all older adults of color bring the same "stories" of problem identification into the helping process. Older adults of color will define problems in relation to their own worldviews, which consist of the values, beliefs, and attitudes underlying perceptions, expectations, and behavior (Ramos & Garvin, 2003). Culturally competent practitioners should be able to recognize cross-cultural differences in problem definitions and make every effort to minimize the influence of their own cultural biases in defining and prioritizing an older adult of color's presenting problems.

Practitioners must use culturally appropriate means to obtain information. For example, people of color, including older adults, are often reluctant to engage in early self-disclosure with social and mental health professionals because of historical experiences of exploitation and discrimination (Davis & Proctor, 1989). Culturally competent practice requires that workers be knowledgeable about the specific dynamics of giving and receiving information among the various racial and ethnic groups because these can have a bearing on an older adult of color's presenting problem.

Acculturation and resettlement are complex processes that can pose great challenges for immigrant older adults of color. These often entail learning a new language, changing social and economic conditions, and loss of status and connections to family members (Damskey, 2000). How members of mainstream society perceive older adults of color can influence the helping process and serve as a means to define their problem situations. For some older adults of color, living embedded in the realities of two worlds can be overwhelming and debilitating. Practitioners must be attentive to the cultural as well as systematic forces that may influence the problem situation. At the same time, workers can help clients "surmount even the most devastating systematic barriers" (Devore & Schlesinger, 1999, p. 206).

When working with older adults of color, practitioners must understand that for many the role of "older adult" in the life course is held with pride. This sense of pride can create protective barriers to "outsiders" who want to enter and possibly alter a system that has functioned through many historical and social changes. Workers must provide older adults of color adequate time to acknowledge changes in the problem situations and support the client in identifying strengths and resources that can be marshaled to improve their quality of life. Most important, the clients' views of the problem and their own priorities should be respected and validated. Culturally competent workers will ask, listen, and restate the problem before making judgments. Social workers must also be aware that racial and ethnic groups differ in their explanations of etiology, symptom recognition, treatment procedures, and desirable outcomes. Although members of the same culture share the ability to understand and cope with a problem based on skills learned from personal, family, and community sources, no single profile fits all members of any specific ethnic group. Generalizable data only provide a starting point for evaluation and cannot be substituted for the practitioner's actual engagement activity, which is exploring the clients' reality of the problem. Furthermore, each older adult of color must be viewed within his or her own social context.

Within a culturally competent practice framework, problem identification begins with the use of a nonpathological approach. Labeling, for example, should be avoided. Information to be gathered should be balanced between the client's personal data and relevant socioenvironmental factors influencing the problem areas (Lum, 2000). For older adults of color, race and ethnicity can define social status and shape individuals' behaviors and access to resources. Race and ethnicity may interact with personal conditions (e.g., functional impairment) and social structures (socioeconomic status) to influence help seeking, including the use of formal and informal care. Accordingly, the aging process and quality of life of older adults of color are inevitably affected by the experiences of a lifetime of racial discrimination.

Reframing the Problem Orientation

Reframing involves helping clients revisit thoughts about the problem, about themselves, or about others who are important to them or who may have contributed to their difficulty. When appropriate, workers should help clients revisit these cognitions with the goal of developing a more accurate picture. The reframing process allows an older adult of color to move beyond the problem and view it in a different way. For example, an African American older adult male who has suffered from a severe psychiatric disability since he was 20 and who has not been able to financially provide for his family may perceive himself as a failure in life. Reviewing events where he has succeeded, including those the client does not define as successes, may help enhance feelings of self worth. This strategy offers workers an opportunity to convey respect for the client's experiences and perceptions as they begin to develop a road map for change. A social worker becomes a great resource in identifying opportunities to assist clients in reframing from a negative perspective to a positive perspective of the problem situation.

Viewing Micro, Meso, and Macro Level Problems

Like other clients, older adults of color exist as part of various systems and can often trace the roots of a problem to interactions with individuals, groups, institutions, and forces beyond their control (Lum, 2004). To better understand the dynamics of a presenting problem, practitioners must consider the complex interplay of micro, meso, and macro level systems as they interact with the ethnic and cultural realities of the older adult of color. At the micro level, workers focus on the role a client's biopsychosocial characteristics may play in the problem situation. Practitioners also ascertain if members of the client's micro system, such as family, friends, and small groups, can be linked to the roots of the problem.

A culturally competent worker must go beyond a micro context, however, and view the problem from a broader perspective that considers meso level and macro level influences. Several writers underscore the need to recognize potential links between problems and environmental factors in cross-cultural practice (Browne & Mills, 2001; Devore & Schlesinger, 1999; Lum, 1996). For example, in work with older adults of color, the absence of ethnic-specific community organizations that offer culturally congruent social services and recreational activities can greatly affect problem situations because it can contribute to a client's sense of alienation and isolation, particularly among recent immigrants. Similarly, environmental pressures stemming from oppressive conditions, prejudicial attitudes, and discriminatory behaviors can greatly contribute to the presenting problems. Van Soest (2003) underscores the harmful psychosocial effects of oppression, for which economic class is considered a prime indicator. Older adults of color traditionally have been affected by unfair, racist policies and procedures that regulate the distribution of resources, even those necessary to have their more basic needs met. Thus, societal structural conditions, such as the state of the economy, can be a major source of stress for older adults of color, especially for those with limited financial means (Lum, 2004). Globalization trends affect the market economy and can be connected to some of the problems experienced by older adults of color given the inequitable nature of U.S. society. The human cost of globalization includes long-term physical, emotional, social, and economic damage to individuals, families, organizations, and communities (Ramos & Briar-Lawson, 2004).

ASSESSMENT SKILLS WITH OLDER ADULTS OF COLOR CLIENTS

Using a Biopsychosocial Perspective

Assessing the spectrum of changes associated with biological, psychological, and social developments for older adults is a critically important step in the helping process. Almost all approaches to practice view accurate and thorough assessment as central to the success of treatment. A thorough assessment should identify areas in which an older adult of color functions adequately and areas where the client faces significant challenges. A gerontological and culturally oriented assessment focuses on the evaluation of clients' assets rather than on dysfunctional elements. Such assets include coping abilities, natural support systems, problem-solving abilities, and tolerance of stress. In addition, the assessment should strive for a biopsychosocial balance between subjective internal reactions and objective external factors.

Workers must carefully consider clients' contextual ethnocultural factors that reflect the complexities of the client's biopsychosocial needs. Many of an older adult of color's psychological stresses, worries, and strained interpersonal relations result from unfavorable environmental and living conditions such as poor housing and lack of access to health and social services. The information gained through the assessment process provides an important foundation for understanding expectations of life changes and helps identify those conditions that are not part of the course of aging (McInnis-Dittrich, 2002). For older adults of color, the aging experience is greatly influenced by cultural-specific patterns of behaviors that vary across ethnic groups as well as by the environmental realities that challenge, facilitate, and undermine their ability to cope and adapt.

The assessment of persons of color has often overlooked or devalued the role of ethnocultural forces in shaping a client's presenting problems. Davis and Proctor (1989) identify areas that could potentially lead to errors in assessment. First, labeling a problem without appropriate factual information or supportive evidence. Second, failing to detect or observe problems that in fact do exist or to truly understand the client's situation. Overlooking an older adult of color's racial, ethnic, and cultural backgrounds can result in inaccurate assessments, which, in turn, may lead to inappropriate conclusions about the client's problem-in-the-situation, and, at times, misdiagnosis or underdiagnosis.

When assessing the mental health status of an older person of color, workers must recognize cross-cultural differences in how mental health is conceptualized and its symptoms can be manifested. For example, depression is a common condition among older adults in general, and older adults of color may be especially vulnerable because of the myriad stressors they encounter daily (Marwaha & Livingston, 2002). Yet, when a worker is not familiar with the clients' culturally preferred modes of expressing symptoms, depression may often go undetected or misdiagnosed. Similarly, many older adults rarely seek help from mental health professionals. Among some First Nations older adults, psychosocial complaints are usually conveyed to professionals by means of physical ailments, some of which are not commonly recognized as symptoms of mental health distress. As a result, mental health conditions may be difficult to diagnose for First Nations older adults (Neligh & Scully, 1990).

Social workers must make every effort to place the "identified problem" in their cultural contexts because these may influence how older adults of color articulate presenting problems and seek solutions. To this end, workers must ask themselves questions such as these: What are the meanings of illness and wellness for this client? How does the client cope and adapt? What are the roles of family and community in the client's life? A thorough biopsychosocial assessment that considers specific ethnic and cultural resources, strengths, and limitations can assist workers in developing safe and culturally appropriate intervention plans aimed at supporting, restoring, or replacing levels of functioning of an older adult of color.

Identifying and Mobilizing Client Cultural Strengths

Culturally competent practitioners honor the profession's commitment to respect human diversity by placing all clients in their own cultural context and then drawing on their strengths. Applying a strengths perspective to the assessment process means that the social worker will make every effort to assist clients to discover, explore, and use their own strengths and resources to achieve and maintain their goals (Saleebey, 1997). The strengths perspective in the assessment process centers on identifying the assets that older adults of color have retained or developed, which, in turn, may help them compensate for other life losses and challenges. In this sense, workers and clients assume the roles of "investigators" as they jointly discover an older adult of color's unique inner strengths and community resources, which can have a powerful effect in motivating the client to work toward growth and change (Appleby, Colon, & Hamilton, 2001; McInnis-Dittrich, 2002). This dynamic can ultimately accentuate an older adult of color's resiliency and help maintain the focus on sociopolitical rather than individual obstacles to change and self-actualization.

INTERVENTION SKILLS WITH OLDER ADULTS OF COLOR CLIENTS

In the intervention process stage, practitioners seek to effect positive change between a client and the problem situation (Lum, 1999). A culturally competent intervention is consistent with the cultural values, norms, attitudes, and behavioral preferences and expectations of the client's racial or ethnic group (Marin, 1993). This involves developing and implementing an intervention plan that meets the older adults' needs while considering individual and cultural characteristics. A social worker must be particularly skillful in establishing goals and agreement, using indigenous and social work intervention strategies, and integrating micro level, meso level, and macro level intervention (Lum, 1999).

Establishing Goals and Agreement

Establishing goals and agreement is a vital step toward change, and an important element of the intervention process stage. According to Hepworth and colleagues (2002), goals serve several valuable functions, such as providing direction to the helping process, guiding the use of appropriate intervention strategies, ensuring that clients and workers agree about outcomes, and assisting clients in monitoring their progress. In practice with older adults of color, workers must explore and set goals in the context of the client's ethnic and cultural milieu. Studies have found that people of color tend to respond positively to clear and concrete goals because they instill confidence in the client that the helping process will bring about the achievement of positive outcomes (Pillari, 2002). Goals can also help identify environmental resources, which are often crucial to the problem solution for older adults of color.

Goal setting is a joint effort between the client and the worker (Lum, 1999). Formulating goals in conjunction with a client can be especially valuable in work with older adults of color. It provides an opportunity to empower clients and enhance their self-efficacy (Harper & Lantz, 1996). Active participation in the negotiation and decision-making processes affords them a sense of control of their life situations, which is not a common experience for many older adults of color because of ageism and historical oppression. Sometimes people of color are referred under pressure or mandates to services where practitioners already have predetermined goals in mind that do not necessarily reflect the client's cultural and ethnic realities. Further, these goals are often based on stereotypical assumptions of the client's age, gender, socioeconomic, racial, and ethnic characteristics (Harper & Lantz, 1996).

Established goals are more likely to be acceptable and culturally relevant to older adults of color when these are time limited, provide specific information regarding desirable outcomes, take into account the client's significant others, and, if possible, are stated by clients in their own words (Lum, 2000). Similarly, contracting must be viewed as a partnership or common agreement where practitioners may not be as prone to impose their definitions of the problems on clients and suggestions are made in light of the client's ethnic reality (Devore & Schlesinger, 1987).

A culturally competent worker should also be able to recognize situations where an older adult of color may refuse or be reluctant to work collaboratively in establishing goals because of ethnic or cultural factors. For older adults of color from cultural backgrounds where social hierarchy is the norm, a worker's invitation to participate in an egalitarian process may be surprising, confusing, and sometimes difficult to accept. Similarly, cultural prescriptions about relationship protocols, such as deferential interaction to convey respect for the practitioner as an expert, may not deem this practice appropriate. In these instances, a worker must be able to acknowledge a client's immediate refusal or reluctance and demonstrate respect, patience, and understanding. Through an open discussion, workers may gain a better understanding of the underlying reasons, and clients may feel more comfortable identifying intervention goals.

Older adults of color can be encouraged to participate using probes and indirect, and open-ended questions and by offering options that are based on concerns and interests articulated by the client in the previous stages of the helping process. Probes that require clients to "describe specifically how they will know when a particular problem is resolved" can prove especially helpful (Cournoyer, 1996 p. 257). Research with Latino older adults found that, although initially reluctant to enter into the decision-making process, when these techniques were used, Latinas did become active participants and enthusiastically identified and provided clear descriptions of desirable goals (Ramos, 2002). Social workers should make every effort to include older adult of color clients in establishing goals and agreement. People of color who experience conflict in establishing goals tend to drop out in the early stages of the helping process (Jackson, 1995). At the same time, practitioners should observe closely the clients' reactions and never ask or expect them to give up their fundamental cultural value systems (Cournoyer, 2005).

Using Indigenous and Social Work Intervention Strategies

Once the goals and agreement have been established, the worker identifies the most appropriate intervention strategies for successful goal attainment. Effective intervention strategies in practice with older adults of color must be relevant to the client's specific problem, unique experiences, social environment, and cultural context. These ought to be consistent with the notion that culture and ethnicity influence human behavior and are valuable tools for social work intervention (Applewhite, 1998). As discussed with regard to goal setting and agreement, decisions about intervention strategies must be made in conjunction with the client. Clients who understand an intervention and its relevance to their problem situation and goals are more likely to be invested and cooperate in the change effort (Harper & Lantz, 1996). A strategy to enhance the clients' participation is to request opinions about what could be done to alleviate the problem situation. In doing this, the worker acknowledges that the client has the power to make choices and allows older adults to provide options that are in harmony with their own cultural values and life experiences (Lum, 1999).

In work with older adults of color, practitioners should be able to draw on a range of intervention strategies that are congruent with a client's ethnic reality and individual and cultural preferences. Of utmost importance is to include in this repertoire indigenous interventions, which are alternative cultural ways of helping and effecting change (Lum, 1999). Here, workers are able to identify and use the clients' "natural strengths that are inherent in their own traditions and communities" effectively (Green, 1999, p. 91). Most older adults of color have in place a primary natural support system, which may include family, friends, church, and natural healers that functions as a first-tier of coping survival network. Indigenous natural support resources may be a part of this network system. For example, indigenous healers may work collaboratively with practitioners, as is also desirable in goal setting, in selecting interventions can help clients feel a better sense of control over goal accomplishments and their role as active participants in the helping process. Similarly, teaching older adults of color how to ask questions at a physician's office could help them feel empowered to request necessary information about their health on their next doctor's visit and, thus, more in control in this area of their lives. Practitioners should encourage clients to identify situations over which they are still in charge even though their choice and power may be limited to making small decisions such as which church service to attend (McInnis-Dittrich, 2002).

An important criterion of an effective intervention is a focus on the recent history of a problem and on effecting change in the near future (Lum, 2000). In work with older adults of color, however, practitioners must be able to recognize and accommodate a client's need to talk about the distant past. Although the focus should not be on dwelling on the past, acknowledging earlier life experiences may be critical for addressing their present problem situation. The worker should listen attentively for potential client descriptions of coping strategies that were successful in the "olden days" and, perhaps, in the "old country" that could be effective in goal attainment (McInnis-Dittrich, 2002). The process of recalling prior life experiences, reminiscing, is an important intervention strategy in gerontological social work, and is particularly relevant in practice with older adults of color. Studies have found reminiscence to be an effective intervention strategy in work with some older adults of color, including Asian Americans and Latinos (Atkinson, Kim, Ruelas, & Lin, 1999; Zuniga, 1989). Similarly, the culturally competent worker should be able to recognize that among some older adults of color reminiscing may have a special meaning. In their communities, older adults are the storehouses of social memories and group lore. Reminiscence serves as a medium for passing on knowledge about a group's rituals, customs, and history, which younger members have not yet acquired and others may have forgotten (Gary Wright, personal communication with Blanca Ramos, January 2003).

Within the helping process, reminiscing validates these traditional roles and helps clients strengthen their senses of self-worth. Retrieving positive events and feelings that reinforce them are worthwhile, valued human beings makes older adults of color feel good about themselves (McInnis-Dittrich, 2002). Through reminiscence, older adults of color can also disclose relevant personal information using a familiar, culturally acceptable form of communication. The challenge for the practitioner is to be able to help a client feel comfortable sharing life experiences, make connections with their present and future situations, and, at the same time, maintain the focus of the intervention.

During the intervention process, workers articulate their professional frames of reference, that is, their feelings, beliefs, thoughts, opinions, hypotheses, and conclusions about the client's problem situation (Cournoyer, 2005). Thus, in work with older adults of color, the practitioners' continued awareness of their own cultural values and beliefs and constant attention' to client-worker cultural differences are crucial. The rationale for all intervention strategies must be clearly linked to the mutually agreed-upon goals and not be driven by practitioners' culturally biased assumptions and conclusions about what is best for the clients based on ageism and racial and ethnic group stereotypes. The social work principle of self-determination also needs to be emphasized throughout the intervention phase with older adults of color.

The worker can respect and honor what the older adults want for themselves for the direction and focus of the change effort, but applying this principle is not always simple and straightforward (McInnis-Dittrich, 2002). A case in point is family caregiving where the older adults' wishes may be at odds with those of their caregivers. Here, the worker must be skillful in balancing both requests, while upholding the principle of client self-determination. Relevant intervention strategies should take into account culturally specific patterns of older adult caregiving as well as the client's acculturation status and individual preferences. For some older adults of color, extensive family involvement in their lives and decision making, prescribed by the cultural value of familism, is acceptable and sometimes even expected. Based on a recent study (Ramos, 2002) of Latino older adults, those who have more recently arrived appear to be comfortable allowing the family to take charge and play an active role in making choices that affect them. Within this context, an older adult is knowingly following a cultural prescription, and it could be considered a form of self-determination. The worker must be sensitive and respect the older adults' cultural preference, yet still find ways to ensure opportunities for autonomy and empowerment.

Proposing an Integrative Intervention Approach

Throughout this chapter, we have discussed older adult clients of color as participants in various systems. Social workers formulate goals and develop intervention plans for change that envisions clients both as individuals and as part of the larger environment. Keeping this in mind, practitioners need to be prepared to develop integrative interventions that flow through the micro level, meso level, and macro level. By so doing, the social worker can formulate a plan that addresses the crisis or immediate problem of the individual, define and mobilize community efforts to resolve the current issue and prevent reoccurrence, and meet the challenges of larger society systems to empower and strengthen the group as a whole.

Multiple interventions can be adapted for use in working with older adult clients of color. A culturally competent worker understands that the dynamics of race and ethnicity differ among cultural groups, thus requiring knowledge of multiple interventions. The worker and client together determine the type of intervention based on a complete evaluation of the client, problem, and psychosocial elements (Lum, 2000). Focusing on three basic multicultural practice principles throughout the process can help workers engage and provide continuous and culturally appropriate interventions with older adult clients of color. Lum (2000) defines these as change the person and the environment, adapt to the language of the client, and practice culturally appropriate listening.

As an illustration, many workers focus on micro interventions that address the immediate problem of the individual client. Use of problem-solving interventions and engaging clients in support groups or neighborhood groups are important methods. However, working with older adults clients of color poses additional concerns regarding transportation, poor health, and issues of isolation that may provoke an intervention at the community level. For instance, by mobilizing community leaders, extended family, and community networks at the meso level to improve the physical conditions of a neighborhood (e.g., clear walkways and paths, consistently maintain sidewalks), older adult clients may find it less complicated to access local services and supports. Mobilizing community groups to develop plans of action that address the larger social issues affecting ethnic and racial groups (e.g., unemployment) will facilitate change on both the individual and societal levels. Developing social policy, inventing or accessing funding streams for community-based, culturally sensitive programs and services, or ensuring implementation of programs based on legislation are all modes of intervention at the macro level (Lum, 2000). The ultimate goal for workers at this stage is to alter the social, economic, and political situations of their clients within the multiple systems in which they exist.

TERMINATION SKILLS WITH OLDER ADULTS OF COLOR CLIENTS

Termination, the ending phase of the helping process, is a critical stage where clients and workers formally resolve their professional relationships. At this time, practitioners guide concluding activities that stabilize desired changes and empower clients to continue functioning competently, but now independently of the social worker (Miley, O'Melia & DuBois, 2001). In general, termination is a time to review progress, consolidate the work that has been accomplished, and resolve remaining issues. It is also a time to help clients look toward the future, anticipate and prepare for problems that may arise, and determine what personal and environmental resources they have at their disposal to resolve these challenges.

In culturally competent practice with older adults of color, termination may require more time and planning to embrace the necessary ethnic realities and cultural nuances. For example, a practitioner needs to be familiar with the client's natural support networks and prepared to address issues associated with immigration status and past experiences of loss caused by uprooting (Ramos & Swingle, 2003). Of particular relevance, endings can be instrumental in helping older adults of color recognize their own achievements and build a sense of mastery (Miley et al., 2001). Making home visits can enhance a practitioner's understanding of the client's sociocultural contexts and further the chances of successful intervention and termination processes.

Not all terminations are planned or anticipated, and they often can occur prematurely, particularly among older adults of color. According to Lum (2000), premature termination may occur because of dropout after the first session, unsuccessful intervention, or unresolved resistance. Practitioners need to be wary of the cultural norms underlying specific behaviors associated with termination. For instance, in some Asian cultures, older adults may attempt to terminate prematurely based on the belief that they should not become a burden to the worker (Ho, 1987).

The worker needs to recognize that the meaning of termination can vary for each individual client because of the interplay of personal, ethnic, and cultural variables. In social work, the word "termination" refers to "discontinuation" or "conclusion," but this term can also have negative connotations and should be used with caution in practice with older adults. For example, it can denote finality, dismissal, and being fired (Miley et al., 2001), which can potentially trigger feelings of distress among older adults of color. The notion of finality may resemble themes associated with death and dying that may be more sensitive to some older adults given their stages of development in the life cycle. Further, messages about being dismissed, terminated, or fired may be equated with the sense of rejection and alienation many older adults of color have experienced as a result of life-long adverse circumstances associated with poverty and historical oppression and discrimination. Thus, a culturally competent practitioner may opt to describe the last phase in a helping relationship to an older adult of color as one of endings and transitions (Shulman, 1999).

Reviewing Client Progress

Reviewing the progress and growth clients have attained during the helping process serves a positive function because it can solidify changes and reaffirm a client's sense of achievement (Miley et al., 2001). A worker and an older adult of color jointly can systematically review the progress that has been made, the accomplishments that have been achieved, and what work remains to be done by recalling the intervention goals initially formulated. During this review, practitioners must help clients enhance their sense of competency by giving them credit for the positive changes made and by identifying and reinforcing the clients' personal skills and strengths that contributed to progress toward the intervention goals (Miley et al., 2001). In this way, termination can be empowering to older adults of color as well as a celebration of their strengths, resiliency, and abilities to overcome adversity.

To enhance an older adult of color's sense of accomplishment, while reviewing progress, a culturally competent worker should acknowledge the roles of culture and ethnicity in the dynamics of giving and receiving praise. Practitioners need to be aware of their own cultural influences in the manner in which they convey praise for positive changes and to recognize whether this is congruent with that of the client. Further, workers should have the ability to adjust their styles in accordance with each diverse older adult's preferred pattern of communication. For example, some Latino older adults may perceive positive comments divested of visible enthusiasm as hollow and not genuine, thus, reducing their potential effectiveness. On the other hand, some Asian American older adults may prefer a less effusive style of communicating praise, which would be more consistent with cultural norms regarding the expression of emotions.

Similarly, workers should be able to understand a client's immediate reactions to praise within their ethnocultural contexts. Although the benefits of positive regard and the recognition of one's accomplishments may be universal, the ways in which these are experienced and the accompanying observable responses may be differentially influenced not only by personal characteristics but also by cultural scripts and factors associated with minority status. For example, some older adults of color may have difficulty accepting individual recognition for their accomplishments because of collectivistic values and cultural ascriptions that emphasize the virtues of modesty, humbleness, and humility.

Practitioners should also be attuned to culturally specific communication protocols used by clients to manifest this difficulty accepting praise, to more accurately gauge the true meaning underlying their verbal and nonverbal cues. Sometimes, older adults of color may respond with discomfort, appear to be uninterested, and deny and minimize their successes, which they often attribute to the worker and other members of the client's system. For example, among some older adult Latinos, it may be customary to look down, feel embarrassed, and politely refuse praise. There may also be times when older adults of color will respond to a worker's efforts to highlight their personal skills and abilities with skepticism and disbelief, a response that should not be surprising given their long histories of continuous put down, discrimination, and devaluation as a result of minority racial or ethnic group membership. It is important not to misconstrue these types of responses because they are usually not intended to negate or diminish the positive feelings and the sense of empowerment that positive regard can evoke.

A culturally competent worker should not be dissuaded by behavioral cues during the progress review from giving clients praise and credit for the positive changes made, reaffirming their sense of achievement, and highlighting strengths and resilience. Although conducting a strengths-oriented review of the client's goals is pivotal in work with all clients (Miley et al., 2001), it is particularly relevant in practice with clients from traditionally disempowered, oppressed groups. Thus, reviewing client progress provides a valuable opportunity for powerful work with older adults of color.

Evaluating the Present and the Future

Helping clients identify areas for future work is an important activity in termination because it conveys to clients that the work will continue after the ending, encouraging competent functioning beyond the relationship (Miley et al., 2001; Shulman, 1999). Here, connections are made between the progress and growth clients have attained during the helping process and how clients might approach future challenges (Miley et al., 2001). Using an empowering approach to social work practice (Miley et al., 2001), practitioners can conduct a thorough review that highlights a client's strengths, thereby facilitating these connections and empowering older adults of color to transition with confidence in their ability to resolve issues on their own.

When evaluating the present, workers should help older adults of color build on their existing coping skills and point out natural resource systems that could support and enhance their resiliency as they move forward in their lives. For example, it can be useful to review and strengthen relaxation techniques and cognitive strategies, which clients previously found to be effective in coping with difficult situations, to be used when new adverse life events are encountered. Using the family and other indigenous support systems accessed during the helping process can lessen the feelings of loss and center attention on what has been gained through the intervention. Religion is very important to many older adults of color, so reinforcing their involvement with their places of worship and fellow parishioners can be extremely helpful. Encouraging participation in local community organizations and activities that advocate for and promote a specific cultural heritage can be beneficial. Workers must be careful and suggest social activities that are financially and linguistically accessible, as well as congruent with the client's cultural preferences.

Contemplating termination can engender a variety of emotional reactions in clients, including older adults of color. Ambivalent feelings such as apprehension, sadness, loss, ambivalence, abandonment, and rejection may be present. At the same time, clients may feel good because of their success and progress and experience an increased sense of empowerment and pride in their accomplishments (Fortune, Pearlin, & Rochelle, 1992). Workers need to be especially attuned to an older adult of color's emotional reactions to termination because how these are manifested may vary cross-culturally. A culturally competent worker, should be able to recognize subtle verbal and nonverbal clues, keeping in mind the client's gender, cultural background, and language preferences. When ambivalent feelings about termination arise, the worker should acknowledge them in a gentle and culturally appropriate manner.

Culturally competent workers should consider incorporating some type of meaningful ritualized celebration to formally mark the ending phase of the helping process. Rituals can play a positive role in termination by delineating a transition point for social workers and clients, underscoring progress, celebrating strengths, and anticipating potential future successes (Gutheil, 1993; Miley et al., 2001). A ritualized celebration can also provide a structure for expressing thoughts and emotions associated with the termination experience, helping clients cope with uncertain, contradictory feelings (Miley et al., 2001). For older adults of color, a tangible recognition, such as a certificate or pin, can provide an appropriate symbol that signifies completion of the work process and a smooth transition to another phase in their lives (Ramos & Swingle, 2003). Ramos and Swingle (2003) found that for Latino older adults, receiving a certificate on completing a group work intervention had a positive effect on the termination experience and helped enhance their sense of accomplishment and self-worth.

Follow-Up Strategies

To encourage competent functioning beyond the helping process, a worker needs to develop a carefully conceived follow-up plan to be thoroughly reviewed with the client during the termination session. For older adults of color, follow-up strategies can take several forms. First, practitioners should review with clients existing community services and resources that can meet future needs, keeping on hand relevant printed material. These services should be consistent with the older adult's educational level and financial status. It is imperative that workers be especially aware of linguistically and culturally relevant resource systems. Similarly, most state and county offices for the aging offer information and referral services that should be brought to the attention of older adults of color who may be unaware of their existence. Workers should be willing to accompany clients to places of interest as a form of introduction and support. This also provides the worker with an opportunity to identify and remove potential barriers associated with accessibility, availability, and cultural congruency.

Second, workers should consider referring older adults of color to appropriate programs and services. For example, clients who have been seen individually can be referred to support groups. When making referrals, calling the contact person in the client's presence and setting a time for the older adult to visit is highly recommended. Practitioners can also work collaboratively with an indigenous organization in the client's community to organize a linguistic and culturally relevant support group.

Case Study Integration Exercise on Intervention and Termination Skills

Case Study

Mrs. Marta Alvarez is a 72-year-old Latina who was born and raised in Puerto Rico. Doña Marta lives with her husband of more than 50 years, Don José, who is 75 years old. The couple moved to the U.S. mainland about 40 years ago. Both have limited English reading and writing skills, but they can speak and understand it somewhat. Doña Marta was able to attend high school but never graduated. Don José is a retired factory worker, and the couple is economically dependent on his Social Security benefits. Doña Marta stayed home, raising their three children and performing household duties. The children are already grown and have moved to the Island and the West Coast. Mrs. Alvarez and her husband reside in a small, ethnically diverse city in New Jersey. Don José was drawn to the area from Puerto Rico because of the employment opportunities in the mills during the 1960s. Mr. and Mrs. Alvarez have witnessed many economic changes in their community, and what was once an economically thriving area is now beset with empty and abandoned factories. The memories of the past and the realities of the present in the macro environment have given community members, especially older adults, a sense of hopelessness and regret.

Doña Marta, a quiet and pleasant woman, is the primary caregiver for her husband who has Type II diabetes and heart disease. She spends a great deal of emotional energy worrying about his health, which has been rapidly deteriorating. Doña Marta is deeply committed to the care of her husband and feels an obligation to be available to meet his needs personally 24 hours a day. She believes that taking care of Don José is her sole responsibility and does not entertain the idea of having someone else provide his care. She knows there are formal services available for older adults that could assist her, particularly in her role as caregiver, and Mr. Alvarez, but has not sought any help from them. Mrs. Alvarez has been going to Dr. Martinez, a Spanish-speaking physician of Latino heritage, for health care, and feels slightly more comfortable discussing issues and concerns with him.

Doña Marta is a caring woman, always available to other members of the community who often seek her assistance, but she holds strong convictions against seeking help from formal networks and nonkin interpersonal relationships. She has difficulty sharing her own feelings and information about her personal life. During her last medical visit, Dr. Martinez expressed concern about her depressed affect and her overall health status. He estimated that exposure to the multiple stressors associated with her caregiving situation had begun to take its toll. At the physician's insistence, Doña Marta reluctantly agreed to seek help. Mrs. Alvarez came to the human services agency where you are employed as a social worker.

During the initial session, Doña Marta sat quietly, with a distressed look on her face. Occasionally, she became weepy, but was trying to control herself. At one point, Doña Marta began to weep openly and apologized profusely for being a "burden" with her problems. After some encouragement, however, she shared that she was very worried because her husband's kidneys were now functioning at such a low level that he would soon need to have dialysis once a week, or he would die. Her husband was very depressed and frightened about this change in his condition. Mrs. Alvarez was fearful about the procedure and worried about her ability to han-

(continued)

CASE | *continued*

dle the extra caregiving responsibilities resulting from her husband's overall failing health. A major concern related to the couple's financial difficulties, which have been exacerbated now that they cannot earn some extra money through her cooking for neighborhood social activities or through Mr. Alvarez' light carpentry jobs.

Mr. and Mrs. Alvarez have a limited circle of Latino friends, belong to a Hispanic senior citizens social club, and attend the local Spanish-speaking Catholic Church. However, Doña Marta noted that it was becoming more and more difficult for them to attend social activities and even to leave the house just to meet with friends. She repeatedly stated her reluctance to share her troubles with others because she did not want to "burden" anyone with them. She also did not want her husband, an "orgulloso" (proud) man to lose any "dignidad" (dignity) by having others feeling sorry for him. She believed that this would only depress him more. Mrs. Alvarez did not want her children to leave their own families to give her emotional support during this time, although she knew that if she asked they would "drop everything" to be with them. Clearly, this major change in her husband's health status has brought Doña Marta to a crisis point.

Application Exercises

Contact, Problem Identification, and Assessment Skills

Read the case study just presented. In groups of four or five students, discuss strategies for culturally competent practice using the following questions. After 30 minutes of discussion, each group reports back to the entire class.

1. What structural factors might facilitate or impede Mrs. Alvarez's ability to continue coming to your agency for services? What steps would you take to make your own work space and the agency's environment more comfortable and culturally appealing to Mrs. Alvarez?

2. What ethical and value conflicts could arise in working with this client system? Explain the differing sides of the dilemmas. How would you deal with these issues?

3. What specific cultural communication protocols must you observe to enhance the development of trust and rapport for building a successful client-worker relationship with Mrs. Alvarez?

4. What strategies would you use to minimize the influence of your own cultural biases in defining and prioritizing Mrs. Alvarez's presenting problems?

Third, in practice with older adults of color, it is particularly important to reassure a client that the worker will be available in the future if needed. For example, the worker can offer to contact clients periodically after termination to inquire whether they need any additional services. Workers can also make provisions so that clients are able to check in occasionally until they feel comfortable with ending. In this sense, it is helpful to discuss open-door policy

5. What factors in Mrs. Alvarez's environmental context (e.g., historical oppression) could have contributed to, or continued exacerbating, her presenting problem situations? How would you link some of Mrs. Alvarez's sociodemographic characteristics to the problem situations?

6. What specific needs, issues, and problem areas or client concerns would you consider addressing in your initial assessment of this client system? Why do you think these are important in your work with Mrs. Alvarez?

7. What strengths or assets in this client system would you initially emphasize to help Mrs. Alvarez compensate for her life losses and challenges?

Intervention and Termination Skills

Read the case study presented earlier. In groups of four or five students, discuss strategies for culturally competent practice using the questions listed below. After 30 minutes of discussion, each group reports back to the entire class.

1. What alternative intervention options that are consistent with Mrs. Alvarez's own cultural values and life experiences would you consider? How comfortable would you feel working with an indigenous healer as a culturally appropriate alternative for helping Mrs. Alvarez's and effecting change?

2. Do you think that reminiscing could be an effective intervention strategy in your work with Mrs. Alvarez? If so, recalling what particular types of experiences in Mrs. Alvarez's distant past could be most effective in goal attainment? Please provide the rationale for your responses.

3. What intervention strategies could help Mrs. Alvarez overcome systemic barriers and change her environmental conditions? How would you, in your role as worker, help bring about changes in Mrs. Alvarez's social environment through interventions that integrate the microlevel, mesolevel, and macrolevel?

4. What types of messages should and should not be communicated to Mrs. Alvarez in relation to termination? What meanings could Mrs. Alvarez potentially attribute to this term given the ethnic and cultural factors that characterize this client system?

5. How can engaging Mrs. Alvarez's natural support systems help her through and beyond the termination process? How would you identify and engage these natural strengths inherent to the client system?

6. Identify the factors that could potentially enhance or hinder your ability to conduct a culturally competent practice with Mrs. Alvarez and with older adults of color in general. These should include the clients' as well as your own individual, ethnic, and cultural characteristics.

guidelines. Follow-up meetings can also be beneficial. Similarly, clients can be placed on mailing lists and invited to educational seminars or workshops that are consistent with the client's linguistic and cultural preferences. Though this agenda may seem overwhelming to some social workers, effective planning and follow-up strategies that reflect cultural competence can help ensure that future challenges in the life of an older adult of color client do not turn into crisis situations.

CLOSING THOUGHTS

This chapter has discussed culturally competent practice with older adults of color. We offered guidelines to enhance practitioners' ability to understand the dimensions of culture and cultural competence and to apply them to older adult clients of diverse racial and ethnic backgrounds. It is hoped the reader will view our discussion as a first step and will be encouraged to think about aging in ways that incorporate the cultural meaning and dynamics of growing old as they differ cross-culturally. For older adults of color, this implies understanding ageing as it takes place in multiple interacting levels including poverty, racism, and other structural sources of oppression. Cultural competence with older adults of color requires continuous learning, disciplined effort, and an ability to maintain an open, nonjudgmental perspective in the face of new and sometimes unexpected, unpredictable behaviors. It also involves advocating for policies and programs that foster the empowerment of older adults of color within the larger society, and are anchored in a culturally competent practice that pays special attention to their cultural and environmental contexts. Practicing with older adults of color in this millennium presents social workers with new and exciting challenges.

References

Administration on Aging (2001). Profile of older Americans. Retrieved 9/12/02 from www.aoa.dhhs.gov/aoa/STATS/profile/2001/11.html

Administration on Aging (2002). The many faces of aging: Resources to effectively serve minority older persons. Retrieved 9/12/02 from http://www.aoa.dhhs.gov/minorityaccess/stats.html

Aleman, S. (2000). Mexican-American Elders. In S. Aleman, T. Fitzpatrick, T. Tran, & E. Gonzalez (Eds.), *Therapeutic interventions with ethnic elders: Health and social issues* (pp 5–8). New York: Hawthorne Press.

Aleman, S., & Fitzpatrick, T. (2000). Culture-specific theoretical and conceptual models of aging. In S. Aleman, T. Fitzpatrick, T. Tran, & E. Gonzalez (Eds.), *Therapeutic interventions with ethnic elders: Health and social issues* (pp. 5–8). New York: Hawthorne Press.

Altarriba, J., & Santiago-Rivera, A. (1994). Current perspectives on using linguistic and cultural factors in counseling the Hispanic client. *Professional Psychology: Research and Practice, 25,* 388–397.

Appleby, G. A., Colon, E., & Hamilton, J. (2001). Diversity, oppression, and diversity and social functioning: Person-in environment assessment and intervention. Boston: Allyn & Bacon.

Applewhite, S. L. (1998). Culturally competent practice with elderly Latinos. *Journal of Gerontological Social Work, 30*(1/2), 1–15.

Atkinson, D., Kim, A., Ruelas, S., & Lin, A. (1999). Ethnicity and attitudes toward facilitated reminiscence. *Journal of Mental Health Counseling, 21*(1), 66–81.

Brave Heart, M. Y. H. (2001). Culturally and historically congruent clinical social work assessment with Native Americans. In R. Fong & S. Furuto (Eds.), *Culturally competent practice: Skills, interventions, and evaluations* (pp. 163–177). Boston: Allyn & Bacon.

Browne, C., Fong, R., & Mokuau, N. (1994). The mental health of Asian and Pacific Island elders: Implications for research and mental health administration. *Journal of Mental Health Administration, 21*(1), 52–59.

Browne, C., & Mills, C. (2001). Theoretical frameworks: Ecological models, strengths perspective, and empowerment theory. In R. Fong & S. Furuto (Eds.), *Culturally competent practice: Skills, interventions, and evaluations* (pp. 10–32). Boston: Allyn & Bacon.

Butler, R. (1989). Dispelling ageism: The cross-cutting intervention. In M. Riley & J. Riley, Jr. (Eds.), *The quality of aging: Strategies for intervention. Annals of the American Academy of Political and Social Science, 503,* 163–175.

Butler, R., & Lewis, M. (1977). *Aging and mental health* (2nd ed.). St. Louis: Mosby.

Castex, G. (1998). Providing services to Hispanic/Latino populations: Profiles in diversity. In D. Atkinson, G. Morten, & D. Sue (Eds.), *Counseling American minorities* (pp. 255–267). Boston: McGraw-Hill.

Choi, N. G. (1999). Living arrangements and household compositions of elderly couples and singles: A comparison of Hispanics and Blacks. *Journal of Gerontological Social Work, 31*(1–2), 41–61.

Chow, J. (2001). Assessment of Asian American/Pacific Islander organizations and communities. In R. Fong, & S. Furuto (Eds.), *Culturally competent practice: Skills, interventions, and evaluations* (pp. 211–224). Boston: Allyn & Bacon.

Cohen, G. D. (1993). African American issues in geriatric psychiatry: A perspective on research opportunities. *Journal of Geriatric Psychiatry and Neurology, 6*(4), 195–199.

Comas-Diaz, L., & Greene, B. (1994). Overview: an ethnocultural mosaic. In L. Comas-Diaz & B. Greene (Eds.), *Women of color* (pp. 3–9). New York: Guilford Press.

Cournoyer, B. (1996). *The social skills workbook* (2nd ed). Pacific Grove, CA: Brooks/Cole.

Cournoyer, B. (2005). *The social skills workbook* (4th ed). Belmont, CA: Thomson Brooks/Cole.

Cross, T., Bazron, B., Dennis, K., & Issacs, M. (1989). *Toward a culturally competent system of care.* Washington, DC: Georgetown University Child Development Center.

Damskey, M. (2000). Views and visions: Moving toward culturally competent practice. In S. Aleman, T. Fitzpatrick, T. Tran, & E. Gonzalez (Eds.), *Therapeutic interventions with ethnic elders: Health and social issues* (pp 5–8). New York: Hawthorne Press.

Davis, L. E., & Proctor, E. K. (1989). *Race, gender, and class: Guidelines for practice with individuals, families and groups.* Englewood Cliffs, NJ: Prentice-Hall.

Devore, W., & Schlesinger, E. (1999). *Ethnic-sensitive social work practice* (5th ed.). Boston: Allyn & Bacon.

Dietz, T. (1997). Family and formal assistance limitations: Who helps Mexican American elderly? *Hispanic Journal of Behavioral Sciences, 19*(3), 333–352.

DiNitto, D. (1999). *Social welfare: Politics and public policy* (4th ed.). Englewood Cliffs, NJ: Prentice-Hall.

Falicov, C. J. (1998). *Latino families in therapy: A guide to multicultural therapy.* New York: Guilford Press.

Fong, R., & Furuto, S. (2001). Future directions for culturally competent social work practice. In R. Fong, & S. Furuto (Eds.), *Culturally competent practice: Skills, interventions, and evaluations* (pp. 454–458). Boston: Allyn & Bacon.

Fortune, A., Pearlin, B., & Rochelle, C. (1992). Reactions to termination of individual treatment. *Social Work, 37,* 171–178.

Ford, M. E., & Hatchett, B. (2001). Gerontological social work with older African American adults. *Journal of Gerontological Social Work, 36*(3/4), 141–155.

Gonzales, E. (2000). African-American elders. In S. Aleman, T. Fitzpatrick, T. Tran, & E. Gonzalez (Eds.), *Therapeutic interventions with ethnic elders: Health and social issues* (pp 5–8). New York: Hawthorne Press.

Green, J. W. (1999). *Cultural awareness in the human services: A multi-ethnic approach* (3rd ed.). Boston: Allyn & Bacon.

Gutheil, I. (1993). Rituals and termination procedures. *Smith College Studies in Social Work, 63*(2), 163–176.

Harper, K. V., & Lantz, J. (1996). *Cross-cultural practice: Social work with diverse populations.* Chicago: Lyceum Books.

Hepworth, D. H., Rooney, R. H., & Larsen, J. A. (2002). *Direct social work practice: Theory and skills* (6th ed.). Pacific Grove, CA: Brooks/Cole.

Ho, M. K. (1987). *Family therapy with ethnic minorities.* Newbury Park, CA: Sage.

Jackson, A. (1995). Diversity and oppression. In C. Meyer & M. Mattiani (Eds.), *The foundation of social work practice* (pp. 42–58). Washington, DC: NASW Press.

Johnson, C. (2000). Adaptation of oldest old Black Americans. In E. W. Markson & L. A. Hollis-Sawyer (Eds.), *Intersections of aging: Readings in social gerontology* (pp. 133–141). Los Angeles: Roxbury.

Kim, J. S., Bramlett, M. H., Wright, L. K., & Poon, L. W. (1998). Racial differences in health status and health behaviors of older adults. *Nursing Research, 47*(4), 243–250.

Kirst-Ashman, K. K., & Hull, G. H., Jr. (1993). *Understanding generalist practice.* Chicago: Nelson-Hall.

Kotchen, J. M., Shakoor-Abdullah, B., Walker, W. E., Chelius, T. H., Hoffman, R. G., & Kotchen, T. A. (1998). Hypertension control and access to medical care in the inner city. *American Journal of Public Health, 88*(11), 1696–1699.

Lum, D. (1996). *Social work practice and people of color: A process state approach* (3rd ed.). Pacific Grove, CA: Brooks/Cole.

Lum, D. (1999). *Culturally competent practice: A framework for growth and action.* Pacific Grove, CA: Brooks/Cole.

Lum, D. (2000). *Social work practice and people of color: A process stage approach* (4th ed). Belmont, CA: Brooks/Cole.

Lum, D. (2003). Culturally competent practice. In D. Lum (Ed.), *Culturally competent practice: A framework for understanding diverse groups and justice issues* (2nd ed., pp. 3–33). Pacific Grove, CA: Brooks/Cole.

Lum, D. (2004). *Social work practice and people of color: A process stage approach.* Belmont, CA: Brooks/Cole–Thomson Learning.

McInnis-Dittrich, K. (2002). *Social work with elders: A biopsychosocial approach to assessment and intervention.* Boston: Allyn & Boston.

Marin, G. (1993). Defining culturally appropriate community interventions: Hispanics as a case study. *Journal of Community Psychology, 24,* 149–161.

Marwaha, S., & Livingston, G. (2002). Stigma, racism or choice. Why depressed ethnic elders avoid psychiatrists. *Journal of Effective Disorders, 72*(3), 257–264.

Miley, K. O'Melia, M., & Dubois, B. (2001). *Generalist social work practice: An empowering approach.* Boston: Allyn & Bacon.

Morales, A. T., & Sheafor, B. W. (1995). *Social work: A profession of many faces* (7th ed.). Boston: Allyn & Bacon.

National Council of La Raza. (1998). *Views on the impact of the social security debate on Hispanic Americans.* Submitted to the White House Conference on Social Security, December 2, 1998.

Neligh, G., & Scully, J. (1990). Differential diagnosis of major mental disorders among American Indian elderly. In M. S. Harper (Ed.), *Minority aging: Essential curricula content for selected health and allied health professionals* (pp. 165–177). Health Resources and Services Administration, Department of Health and Human Services. DHHS Publication No. HRS (P-DV-90-4). Washington, DC: U.S. Government Printing Office.

O'Leary, J. S. (2000). Japan's honorable elders. In E. W. Markson & L. A. Hollis-Sawyer (Eds.), *Intersections of aging: Readings in social gerontology* (pp. 12–28). Los Angeles: Roxbury.

Parrillo, V. (2000). *Strangers to these shores: Race and ethnic relations in the United States* (6th ed.). Boston: Allyn & Bacon.

Pillari, V. (2002). *Social work practice: Theories and skills.* Boston: Allyn & Bacon.

Pine, J., Cervantes, J. Cheung, F., Hall, C. Holroyd, J. Ladue, R., Robinson, L., & Root, M. (1990). *Guidelines for providers of psychological services to ethnic, linguistic, and culturally diverse populations.* Washington, DC: American Psychological Association, Office of Ethnic Minority Affairs.

Ramos, B. (2002). *Culture, ethnicity, and caregiving stress among Latino family caregivers.* Manuscript submitted for publication.

Ramos, B., & Briar-Lawson, K. (2004). Globalization and international implications for social work. In A. Sallee (Ed.), *Social work and social welfare: The context of a profession.* Dubuque, Iowa: Eddie Bowers.

Ramos, B., & Garvin, C. (2003). Task-centered work with culturally diverse clients. In E. Tolson, W. Reed, & C. Garvin (Eds.), *Generalist practice: A task-centered approach* (pp. 441–463). New York: Columbia University Press.

Ramos, B., & Swingle, D. (2003). *Social work practice with Latino immigrant families.* Manuscript submitted for publication.

Ramos, B., Toseland, R., Smith, T., & McCallion, P. (2002). *Latino family caregivers of the elderly: A health education program.* Manuscript submitted for publication.

Root, M. P. P. (1998). Facilitating psychotherapy with Asian American Clients. In D. R. Atkinson, S. Morten, & D. W. Sue (Eds.), *Counseling American minorities* (5th ed., pp. 214–234). Boston: McGraw-Hill.

Saleebey, D. (1997). *The strengths perspective in social work practice.* New York: Longman.

Sellers, J. B. (2000). Rural Navajo and Anglo elders aging well. In E. W. Markson & L. A. Hollis-Sawyer (Eds.), *Intersections of aging: Readings in social gerontology* (pp. 368–374). Los Angeles: Roxbury.

Sharf, R. S. (2000). *Theories of psychotherapy and counseling: Concepts and cases* (2nd ed.). Pacific Grove, CA: Brooks/Cole.

Shulman, L. (1999). *The skills of helping individuals, families, groups, and communities* (4th ed.). Itasca, IL: Peacock.

Suppes, M., & Wells, C. (1996). *The social work experience: An introduction to the profession and its relationship to social welfare policy.* New York: McGraw-Hill.

Tennstedt, S., & Chang, B. (1998). The relative contribution of ethnicity versus socioeconomic status in explaining differences in disability and receipt of informal care. *Journal of Gerontology, 53B,* S61–S70.

Torres-Gil, F., & Moga, K. B. (2001). Multiculturalism, social policy and the new aging. *Journal of Gerontological Social Work, 36*(3/4), 13–32.

Van Soest, D. (2003). Advancing social and economic justice. In D. Lum (Ed.), *Culturally competent practice: A framework for understanding diverse groups and justice issues* (2nd ed., pp. 345–376). Pacific Grove, CA: Brooks/Cole

Villa, V. M., & Torres-Gil, F. M. (2001). The later years: The health of elderly Latinos. In M. Aguirre-Molina, C. Molina, & R. E. Zambrana (Eds.), *Health issues in the Latino community* (pp. 179–208). San Francisco: Jossey-Bass.

Weaver, H. N. (2003). Cultural competence with First Nations Peoples. In D. Lum (Ed.), *Culturally competent practice: A framework for understanding diverse groups and justice issues* (2nd ed., pp. 197–216). Pacific Grove, CA: Brooks/Cole.

Weibel-Orlando, J. (2000). You can go home again. In E. W. Markson, & L A. Hollis-Sawyer (Eds.), *Intersections of aging: Readings in social gerontology* (pp. 157–166). Los Angeles: Roxbury.

Zuniga, M. (1989). Mexican-American elderly and reminiscence: Interventions. *Journal of Gerontological Social Work, 143*(3/4), 61–73.

Epilogue

This book has brought together cultural competence and practice stages, providing the reader with some updated basic concepts and making a case for how the two entities are related to each other. Each chapter on the various ethnic, gender, sexual orientation, citizen status, physical or mental ability, and age groups has addressed their particular populations from the cultural competence and practice stages perspectives. The purpose of this epilogue is to revisit cultural competence and practice stages, to identify client intersectional systems, review case study lessons, link cultural competence and professional ethics, and reflect on the future of culturally competent practice with diverse groups.

The following sections and subsections reiterate various cultural competent themes, practice stage issues, client intersectional group systems, and case study integration individuals and families that reflect the model introduced in Chapter One.

REVISITING CULTURAL COMPETENCE AND PRACTICE STAGES

Cultural competence has made a number of inroads into social service organizational programs. The Division of Cultural Competence of the Child Welfare League of America incorporates cultural competence programs, assessment, curriculum, resources, and training for its staff and member agencies and encompasses micro, meso, and macro process, knowledge, and skill aspects

(Child Welfare League of America, 2003, pp. 2, 3), which support the themes of this book:

- Cultural competence is a continuous process of learning about the cultural strengths of others and integrating their unique abilities and perspectives into our lives.
- Cultural competence is a vehicle used to broaden our knowledge and understanding of individuals and communities.
- Cultural competence or the lack of it will be reflected in how communities relate to and interact with service providers and their representatives.
- Cultural competence is having the knowledge, ability, and skill necessary to identify and address the issues facing organizations and staff that have cultural implications and having the ability to operationalize this knowledge into the routine functioning of an agency.

The emphasis is on promoting cultural competence on the organizational and community levels. Among the helpful suggestions are the following:

- Expanding knowledge about culture, cultural competence, and dimensions of culture in social service organizations
- Understanding various cultural groups within communities served by agencies
- Including culture and cultural competence in the strategic planning, policy development, program design, and service delivery process, particularly how culture affects client families and agency staff effectiveness
- Using staff development and training, hiring, retention, career advancement, performance evaluations, and employee policies to support culturally competent and linguistically appropriate practice
- Creating a positive environment where staff can explore and develop cultural understanding and create formal partnerships with community organizations to develop culturally competent policy, program design, and service delivery models
- Recruiting culturally oriented citizens for boards of directors, advisory teams, and task forces and staff for community boards and cultural activities
- Making hiring decisions that reflect population diversity and staff understanding and respect for the richness, strength, and capacity for culture and diversity
- Developing culturally competent principles in requests for proposals criteria and other contracts, which ensure applicants, contractors, or consultants positive results that are culturally competent and linguistically appropriate and address the needs of children and families served
- Resolving conflict between differing cultures interacting and the degree of tolerance and intolerance
- Developing educational and recreational activities and programs of cultural groups, such as cultural centers and festivals (for more information, see www.cwla.org)

There has also been a recent shift from practice stages to *multilevel practice process,* which reflects the trends in our text. In a historical summary of direct social work practice knowledge base, Reid (2002) highlights changing views of clients and practitioners, multilevel intervention, family therapy, action-meaning-information, and science and social work practice. He summarizes these trends during the last 30 years:

> A fresh vision of the client-practitioner relationship unfolded, one that presents clients as self-directing collaborators with knowledge and strengths and practitioners as facilitators with new awareness of the limits of their expertise and authority. New theories and methods for helping clients appeared: multilevel interventions addressed to the interactions of persons and their environments; work with entire families using systems formulations as a basis for assessment and treatment; and a focus on action, meaning, and information as the media and goals of client change. Long-term trends toward greater influence of research on practice accelerated with the arrival of novel ways of using scientific methods in practice and a multifold increase in empirically validated interventions. (2002, pp. 27–28)

Social work educators have focused on generalist, culturally diverse, and justice knowledge theory in practice process.

For example, Ungar (2002) discusses generalist ecological social work practice and identified eight critical principles in practice, which he deems "new ecology in practice":

- *Intrinsic value* or the focus on the intrinsic worth of each individual apart from the meaning of the individual to others in his or her community
- *Diversity and diverse solutions* or the emphasis on the diversity of culture and social organization as potentials for solving shared human challenges
- *Structured alliances* or the relationship between communities and services that must act to increase resources to individuals and families as well as encourage mutual self-help
- *Management by stakeholders* or the creation of a nonbureaucratic service delivery system as the structure least likely to lead to social disintegration
- *Divestment to community* or small human service delivery systems that allow resources to be divested to the community
- *Public policy and community empowerment* or the expansion of public policy to push the capacity of communities and their members toward self-functioning through providing needed resources to sustain well-being
- *Enlightened development* or the guiding principle of "what is good" for individuals and their communities
- *Ethical obligations to foster change* or the ethical obligation to achieve the preceding goals by changing practice methods and organizational structure

The emphasis on the dynamic individual self-worth, diversity, community resource allocation and delivery orientation, and social change based on the highest good is "an attempt to celebrate diversity in constructions of health and the deconstruction of the relative power of the competing discourses . . ." (Ungar, 2002, p. 493). This emphasis offers a new direction toward incorporating themes in a discussion of ecological practice process.

Regarding culturally diverse practice, Besthorn and McMillen (2002) offer an ecological practice model, which has implications for ecofeminism. They identify the following premises:

- *Nature* is one with and beneficial for humanity
- *Social, political, economic, and environmental issues* are interrelated and associated with humanity's understanding of its relationship with nature and practices stemming from it
- Social work practice must address *powerful systemic oppressions* that maintain human alienation
- *Struggles against oppressive, systemic forces* that denigrate nature are intertwined with struggles against all forces that oppress humans
- Social work practice must be committed to *social change in the social, political, and economic structures* of modern, industrial society for progressive activism
- *Material equality* is a high social priority as a new collective vision of the good life as well as of improved quality of life
- Social work should help people to *practice activities and associations that foster happiness* such as simple conversations, spiritual rituals, neighborhood/community gatherings, and related cultural ways of expressing the joy of life
- Social workers must become *community and neighborhood organizers* to help residents construct a new conceptual vision of a revitalized and satisfying community (2002, pp. 227–229)

This action-oriented ecological social work model is committed to social justice and social change based on caring and compassion. Practice process must incorporate these themes.

Still another social work paradigm advocates just practice themes. Finn and Jacobsen (2003) discuss the limitations of systems or ecological perspectives, structural or conflict approach, and the strengths and the empowerment viewpoints. They build the just practice framework based on human action in the world as a process where we can shape social order and the interplay of culture, power, and history. Practice process involves five themes that help us understand the situation and offers possible courses of action:

- *Meaning* or how to define the purpose or significance of our experiences in the world, interpret processes, and understand the social world
- *Context* or how a set of circumstances and conditions surround and influence particular events and situations and exist in a larger framework of social, political, and economic relationships and interactions
- *Power* or how power is created, produced, legitimized, and used and how one needs to understand relations of power influence in social work practice
- *History* or how historical contexts and narratives affect the interplay of social structures and human agency and how past experiences and circumstances affect prejudgments, perceptions, and relationships

- *Possibility* or how we can act in the world as creative, meaning-making beings, shaping actions, and envisioning new possibilities for action based on what has been done, what can be done, and what can exist

This new practice foundation involves worker and client as active participants and co-learners.

Finally, going full circle, we return to culturally competent practice. Hurdle (2002) stresses the importance of culturally based interventions such as traditional healing practices and folk healing. She offers examples such as the Hawaiian family conflict resolution process called *Ho'oponopono* as well as the Hawaiian community development efforts concentrating on community-based problem identification and collective community participation called *Ho'opono Ahupua'a*. The emphasis is on relational and culturally appropriate action. As Hurdle explains, "A primary focus needs to be on empowering the client systems to determine the problems to be addressed and the solutions they envision. The intervention process then uses culturally based interventions to achieve these goals. This process requires a trusting relationship to be developed with clients, which is facilitated by the use of culturally based social work practice" (2002, p. 190). Hurdle believes culture and cultural practices are process-oriented ways of helping.

In the preceding models, content-oriented action areas have replaced traditional practice stages with dynamic themes regarding how to work with clients and their situations. They offer exciting road maps for helping.

Practice Stage Principles

The contributors uncover culturally competent *practice stages principles* of the helping process, although this editor has addressed several of these themes (Lum, 2004).

Contact   Among the *contact stage* principles are the following:

- The *availability of staff* that matches the ethnic and cultural background of clients, speaks the same language, and understands the culture. For example, Latino clients who are Spanish-speaking with limited English are assessed with higher levels of pathology when the interview is conducted in English rather than Spanish. Communicating with the client in his or her native language facilitates a freer expression of feelings and problem disclosure.
- A *responsive service delivery system* that considers agency setting and ambiance; recruitment, training, and support of staff that reflects the client constituents; and instrumental resources such as child care services, culturally appropriate and language-appropriate reading and multimedia information, outreach services, and related ancillary areas.
- The concept of *resistance as a struggle against oppression* for the client and the need for the worker to overcome his or her resistance at not being in control of the client or helping process.

- The worker and the client decide on *the language that they will use in their relationship,* for example, Spanglish, a combination of English and Spanish slang, or pidgin English, abbreviated and local Hawaiian, Asian, and English words and slang.
- The need to *acknowledge and work through historical traumatic barriers* that may exist between the client, particularly First Nations Peoples, and the European American social worker. This may be a gradual and painful process of developing respect and empathy that are the basis for rapport.
- *Understanding the cultural context,* which values human relationships, harmony and unity, and thoughtful, intuitive, and indirect communication. Nonverbal communication, particularly silence, may convey cultural ways, outlooks, and understanding.
- *Communication content* in the form of stories and metaphors (e.g., talk stories in Hawaii) with the avoidance of eye contact. There may be periods of silence, which are natural and familiar to the client or a series of dropping-in sessions for small talk, which eventually leads to significant conversation.
- *Reliance on and valuing family or extended kin networks* for help with problems, which may include natural and native healers and healing practices and may precede formal professional help from social workers and mental health workers.
- The worker *wearing the historical and cultural lenses of the client* to appreciate and anticipate indigenous and cultural perceptions and viewpoints, unique experiences and events, and ethnic community culture coming from the client, while working through your stereotypes and biases. Examples include making physical contact (a greeting hug), sharing food, and attending family celebrations.
- The use of *practical professional self-disclosure* about your previous practice with types of clients that may be relevant to the problem, your personal background (birth place, school, ethnicity), affirming similarity of oppressive experiences, and asking for help with knowledge or understanding gaps involving clients.
- The developing of *trust and credibility* based on standing by your word, consistent and reliable behavior; respect and humbleness; and sharing credentials and previous work with similar groups
- The client's expectations of the worker in terms of *being practical, structured, prescriptive, and specific versus being a facilitator, allowing client choices, and supporting growth potential.*
- A *strengths-based approach* that fosters seeking the positive; listening to the personal narrative; validating the pain; collaborating and connecting the client to helpers, families, and support networks; and transforming oppressive structures.

Problem Identification   The *problem identification stage* of the helping process covers a number of issues:

- *Problem understanding spheres* covering the medical, psychological, socioeconomic, and cultural-historical; the mental, spiritual, physical, and emotional; micro, meso, and macro environmental stressors and barriers
- *Problem responses of strength and resiliency* given displacement, oppression, and alienation
- *The problem of losing face* from a shameful disclosure, a disgrace of family honor, or a disrespectful experience and the importance of saving face by maintaining dignity, honor, and self-respect
- *Problem reframing,* which centers on the want satisfaction and need fulfillment of the client or refocusing the problem according to the client's frame of reference

Assessment   The *assessment stage* involves a psychosocial perspective, which addresses socio-environmental stress impacts, resulting in psycho-individual reactions. A number of assessment areas focus on a relevant culturally competent assessment:

- *Primary group affiliation,* which may be seen in tribal identity and cultural reference groups for First Nations clients
- *Cultural explanations of health and illness,* which underscore the need to assess balance and harmony between persons and environmental contexts
- *Constructing a history of major events,* which have a traumatic effect on individuals, families, groups, communities, and whole ethnic groups such as historical traumatic response among Natives, posttraumatic stress syndrome among Southeast Asian refugees, and Central Americans who were forced to flee their countries in the 1970s
- *Use of assessment tools* to pinpoint major connections in people's lives, such as eco-maps, individual and family network graphics, and related instruments to illustrate important or missing linkages (e.g., loyalties of women of color to children and families and their special relationships with men of color)
- *A knowledge base of the person and the environment* covering these areas and relating them to immigration status, acculturation and assimilation adjustment experiences, gender roles, education attainment, employment, language fluency, and family intergenerational dynamics
- *A strengths-based assessment perspective,* which refuses to perpetuate psychopathology and advocates mobilizing client cultural strengths, fostering resiliency, resistance to oppression and discrimination

Intervention   The *intervention stage* is at the heart of cultural competence and process stages because it seeks to resolve the person and the problem situation. Among the intervention themes presented in this book are these:

- *The life story narrative* as an important point of entry to find out about the client and to understand the deep feelings from significant relationships, which may result in powerful transference and countertransference

- *The establishment of a therapeutic alliance with a client or group,* which bonds the worker, the client, and the client's community through rituals, ceremonies, and spiritual practices
- *The discovery of helpful cultural intervention modalities* such as historical trauma interventions that may be practiced by skilled indigenous clinicians on a selective basis but understood by those who are involved in the helping process; the RESPECT model (review, education, sharing, promotion, exploration and evaluation, change, transition) on the meso-agency level; and systems, prevention, case management, and advocacy on the macro level; our task is to conceptualize and execute integrative interventions at multiple sequential or simultaneous levels
- *The strengths-based and empowerment intervention strategy,* which encompasses the needs of culturally diverse clients and is a source for culturally competent practice; strengths-based beliefs—such as "every individual, group, family, and community has strengths" and "trauma and abuse, illness and struggle are sources of challenge and opportunity"—are balanced with such empowerment themes as "collective experience," "critical thinking and action," and "personal and political change"
- *The use of interventions that involve the family and related ethnic groups* where the individual client is interwoven in the fabrics of family and community; some suggest family conferencing, circle sentencing, ho'oponopono, and spirituality

Termination Finally, the *termination stage* recalls ending, retrospective review, and future forecast. Some of the termination themes mentioned by contributors are the following:

- *Interpersonal loss and the need to connect with support networks* to strengthen relationship building
- *Review of goals and progress accomplishment,* which evaluates with the client his or her sense of development; often feelings of pride in the client's success and effectiveness emerge in this evaluation
- *Cultural competence implementation and evaluation of client progress* by asking four critical questions: How is cultural competence implemented at the systems and practitioner levels? How do data, observations, and client satisfaction reflect client progress and outcomes? How is follow-up implemented? Does the client demonstrate readiness for ending services?
- *Honest appraisal of what worked and did not work* in the helping process
- *Follow-up sessions* to evaluate the present and the future and to sustain the growth of the client
- *Use of mesocommunity supportive services* in the larger community to address acculturation issues such as language, employment, education, parent-child relationships, and religious/spiritual needs

Social work practitioners and students are encouraged to review these principles and to incorporate them as part of their culturally competent practice skill repertoire.

IDENTIFYING CLIENT INTERSECTIONAL SYSTEMS

A wealth of information and insight into diverse client groups emerges from the contributors of this book. In this section, we want to group and interconnect the various themes that cut across chapters. There are many lessons for us to learn as we develop our understanding of how client groups interact and respond to psychosocial challenges.

Cultural Strengths in the Face of Oppression

How does an individual, family, group, community, and a nation survive in the midst of continuous stress, adversity, and related forms of oppression? The history of survival and the presence of cultural strengths can be seen in the contributory chapters of this book. These contributors teach us valuable lessons as we confront terrorism at home and abroad and as we face the daily challenges of living in the 21st century.

At the core of cultural strengths are the basic survival values that we learn from our culture and our elders who have gone before us. Who knows this better than First Nations Peoples? Concerning *survival values in the face of historical oppression,* Yellow Horse Brave Heart and Chase point out a number of *First Nations Peoples* values coming from the *Woope Sakowin* (generosity, compassion, respect for all creation, developing a great mind, humility, courage, and wisdom) and the Lakota tribe (interdependence, noninterference and tolerance, the carrying of the Lakota Nation in their hearts, decisions made with the next seven generations in mind, the good of the Lakota Nation above the individual, humility, respectful listening, deliberation, silence and observation, politeness, deference, the sacredness of women and children, and reserve in front of strangers). We are reminded that we must reach and rediscover collective core values that come from our cultural communities and from character building as we watch how people before us responded to challenges.

African Americans built strong structural groups that cushioned stress. Jones reminds us of the organizations, movements, and mutual aid groups that ensured survival in the midst of slavery. Specifically, there were the helping tradition (midwives, the Underground Railroad, the Freedmen's Bureau, the NAACP), the extended family (the foundation for relationships, family rituals, and self-identity), race consciousness (awareness of history and conditions and desire to uplift their race to dignity and pride), respect (for those older, privacy of information), and spiritual life (the church as a source of guidance, inspiration, and healing). African Americans have survived slavery, lynching, and other forms of blatant and subtle societal discrimination. We are reminded that cultural strength increases when people come together to build support groups and organizations that stand the test of time.

Cultural strengths also come from strong family connections. Moreno and Guido highlight the cultural strengths of *Latino Americans* in the face of historic oppression and point to such values as familialism, personalism, trust *(confianza),* respect *(respeto), simpatia,* and fatalism as key ingredients that have carried Latino Americans through times of adversity. At the core is familialism, which underscores the importance of the family as a collective entity of interdependence and kinship network supports. The family is valued as the universal point of reference for all cultural and ethnic groups. Building strong family ties is essential for developing cultural strengths.

How do people respond to unjust laws and social injustice? Morelli traces the legislated acts of racism and discrimination experienced by *Asian Americans,* particularly Chinese Americans, with the Nationality Act of 1790 and the Chinese Exclusion Act of 1882, and Japanese Americans, with Executive Order 9066 evacuating and incarcerating this group on February 19, 1942, during World War II. Asian Americans demonstrated their perseverance and resiliency in the midst of legal restrictions. In 1988, President Ronald Reagan signed a redress bill where Congress remunerated Japanese Americans still living who were in a relocation camp. Asian Americans have exercised loyalty and character as expressions of cultural strength. A strong work ethic, individualism, group support and protection, group advocacy and persistence, and family and spiritual beliefs have kept the Asian community together. These cultural qualities are worthy of cultivation.

Multiracial/multiethnic persons are most vulnerable and are the target of hate crimes. For decades, interracial marriages were banned in many states. There is a need for more multiracial studies related to social work and the helping professions. For *multiracial persons,* Fong focuses on three facets of historical oppression that have affected multiracial people: societal attitudes about hierarchy in races, racist attitudes against people of color and interracial marriage, and hostile laws and policies. Among the legal break-throughs was the pivotal U.S. Supreme Court decision of *Loving v. Virginia,* which overturned laws against interracial marriage (anti-miscegenation laws) and began the baby boom of biracial individuals. However, Fong warns that there are ongoing societal hostilities and family ambiguities concerning interracial union. Helping multiracial individuals and couples with particular issues confronting them, developing cultural survival techniques, and coping mechanisms are important areas of concern.

Women of color face the triple jeopardy of gender, race and ethnicity, and social class. Yet, they have coped and survived for many generations throughout the world. Kanuha points out that women of color have had to cope with sexism, racism, and classism in their historical context. History is replete with examples of women who have been victimized, starting with the rape and murder of First Nations women, women of the Marshall Islands, who have 5 times the rate of cancer than white women have, and women of Micronesia, who have 75 times the rate of cervical cancer than white women have because of the Bikini Atoll atomic bomb testing in 1954. Kanuha makes similar cases for immigrant women and lesbians of color who struggle with oppression. Women's rights and gender/ethnic/cultural strengths are strong issues in this text.

Lesbian, gay, bisexual, and transgender people are the most visible groups who need civil rights, liberty, and protection. Regarding this group, Nystrom observes that their treatment has been determined by collective societal views of religion, politics, and law. Social and support networks include community support groups to discuss unique prejudice and discrimination issues, annual Pride celebrations, and neighborhoods that offer sanctuary, acceptance, and connection. The struggle for social justice with groups who have sexual orientation, political, and socioeconomic concerns continues in our courts, streets, and media.

The United States is a nation of former and current immigrants and refugees. In the last 35 years, there has been unprecedented growth in our country from people who have come to America. Their hard work, talent, and sacrifice attest to their individual and group cultural strengths. According to Segal, *immigrants and refugees* have had to cope with xenophobia, the fear of being different. The push of leaving their homelands and the pull of the United States have caused them to experience stress and culture shock as well as draw on physical, emotional, and psychological fortitude. They seek out persons with similar culture, language, social system, norms of behavior, family, and friends. They draw on their resiliency to cope with adjustment stress, commonly labeled posttraumatic stress syndrome, and reach out for social service assistance.

Persons with disabilities need to be acknowledged and included in the planning of our neighborhoods and communities. Yet they are invisible, forgotten, and ignored. Freedman focuses on disability rights activism as an expression of survival values. She credits the disability rights social movement for its role in passage of the Americans with Disabilities Act of 1990, as well as for the Independent Living model, which advocates for civil rights, accessible environments, and full community integration. We now talk about consumer-driven individualized supports and person-centered flexible community supports that empower the consumer of services and move toward the full inclusion in the community.

Finally, we must take a lesson from older persons who have paved the way before us. They are our teachers and our guides who have wisdom and survival stories to share with us. With *elderly of color*, Ramos, Jones, and Toseland point out the cultural values and communities for survival, the continuity of racial and ethnic identities, their strength and resilience, collective values that intertwine with family and community relationships expressed as intergenerational family interdependence, and natural supports of friends, neighbors, and religious groups. Religious beliefs and practices are meaningful for Latinos, African, and Asian Americans and for First Nations Peoples. Respect is at the heart of the value system for the elderly. Recognition of social worthiness (wisdom, dignity, and valuable life long experiences) promotes high social status and active roles for the aged.

For all these diverse groups, we must work for social justice and inclusion, learn about survival values and ways of coping, and become their advocate and friend.

New Dimensions for Client Understanding

The contributors of this book have generated a wealth of new multiple identity dimensions that illuminate our understanding of cultural and ethnic clients. There is a growing interest in the *psycho-historical* where history and historical events affect the psyche of individuals, families, and ethnic groups. Such is the case with the theory of historical trauma. Yellow Horse Brave Heart and Chase are particularly concerned about *historical trauma* where there is cumulative emotional and psychological injury, exhibited during the life span and across generations, resulting from massive group trauma and ongoing oppression, rooted in a series of historical events that have affected an individual or a group. Yellow Horse Brave Heart and Chase speak of *historical trauma response (HTR),* which may be characterized by depression, self-destructive behavior, substance abuse, anxiety, poor affect tolerance, and a host of related symptoms. This may take the form of historical unresolved grief, which is impaired mourning from generational trauma. To be culturally competent in working with First Nations Peoples, the worker must be able to assess HTR and must be culturally congruent, adapting one's behavior to complement the cultural behavior and beliefs of the client, having sufficient knowledge of the client's culture, practicing nonintrusive observation, and adjusting to the changing behavior of the same client in different contexts. *Cultural congruence* is connected to cultural competence. If you are interested in finding out more about historical trauma, e-mail the Takini Network Inc. at takininet @aol.com.

Indigenous healing and healers are examples of alternative treatment approaches for clients who have physical, mental, and spiritual needs. Western medicine and Eastern acupuncture and herbal medicine are standard practices in the United States. People are open and seek healing from many sources. Moreno and Guido point out the importance of integrating standard medical and mental health resources and procedures with a *nontraditional system of mental health advisors* (family members, friends, and community members) as well as *nontraditional healers* (curanderos, spiritualists, and santeros) who practice indigenous, religious, and spiritual healing techniques. A culturally competent worker must understand how the Latino client and family interweave this continuum of helpers and healers in the whole process.

Intersectionality is a recent diversity concept that opens new avenues for exploring and writing about multiple identities. Kanuha brings a fresh perspective into the discussion on intersectional systems, citing the work of Warrier (2002) who takes an *intersectional approach to culture and diversity within and between cultures.* Kanuha sets forth some interesting principles of cultural competence, among which is that women of color understand themselves and are understood through multiple representations, intersected identities, and multiple consciousness that acknowledge the complex nature of race, class, gender, sexuality, nationality, religiosity, age, and other variables. Being culturally competent is to be a world traveler who learns a new language, learns nuances of communication, and becomes a different person in another world. (Warrier, 2002, p. 28) The reader should look for a growing body of literature on intersectionality, positionality, and critical consciousness (Lum, 2003), which takes us to new theory limits.

Multidimensional contextual practice (Guadalupe & Lum, 2005) is a new development in culturally competent theory building and practice that brings together intersectional multiple identity and contextual practice. Nystrom touches on this in her multidimensional understanding of lesbians, gay men, bisexuals and transgender people. Cultural competence with this population, according to Nystrom, takes a multidimensional turn where the worker must balance thinking, skills, actions, and awareness of individuals, communities, and larger cultural structures at the same time. Inherent in this *multidimensional perspective* are assessing the context of how people, groups, and communities make critical decisions, individualizing the acute awareness of each client; and understanding one's own assumptions, blind spots, and biases. In this midst, the practitioner must strive to gain greater cultural competence through supervision, education, and community resources.

There has been a recent interest in social work with immigrants and refugees (Balgopal, 2000; Potocky-Tripodi, 2002; Segal, 2002), which offers new knowledge theory and practice skills with these groups. Segal suggests that cultural competence with immigrants and refugees means *identifying the circumstances* surrounding the leaving of the homeland and resources brought with them, the receptivity of the United States to their arrival, and the accompanying stresses, particularly cultural shock. Culturally competent skills should be geared to these issues. Social work comes from a tradition of working with immigrants and refugees in the settlement house movement in metropolitan inner cities. Jane Addams and Hull House in Chicago are prime examples of those helping newly arrived groups. It is heartening that new literature about social work and immigrant/refugee communities is again sparking interest in this population.

Freedman opens a new theory window on the relationship between cultural competence and disabilities. She makes a case for cultural competence with persons with disabilities through *cultural perceptions of disability* (cultural beliefs about the etiology of disability and the person), which may result in various cultural interpretations of how to help the person and the family involved. She reminds us that it is important not to blame the person with the disability and place the responsibility for adaptation and change on that individual. Rather, we should address the need for institutional, physical, and attitudinal changes that will facilitate the environment system for the person. Not only should the culturally competent practitioner work for this perspective but changing professional values and service systems are a part of treatment and program changes.

Ramos, Jones, and Toseland understand the rich diversity among older persons of color and the varying contextual situations that are apparent when one investigates this population. They are concerned about cultural competence knowledge theory and offer the following themes: human behavior and multicultural values addressing family, spirituality, and group identity; biological, psychological, and social factors influencing aging; development theory, which considers the powerful influences of culture and ethnicity; and cultural pluralism, which encompasses *diversity and context*.

REVIEWING CASE STUDY LESSONS

The proof of social work practice effectiveness is in the *understanding of the client's psychosocial situation* and *intervention change impact* on the person and the problem. It is important to focus on the richness and variety of the case studies presented in this book, because they are *lessons learned in the helping process*. It is important to review these cases to increase our practice knowledge and skills.

Interwoven in the practice stages have been a number of case studies that illustrate how to apply the helping principles to numerous clients from various ethnic, gender, social class, sexual orientation, citizen status, and age groups. Grandchildren are increasing being cared for by their grandparents because many parents have granted custody of their children to other family members. Nearly 2.5 million grandparents are raising more than 4.5 million grandchildren, which is a 30 percent increase since 1990 (Welch, 2003). The case of Mary, a 52-year-old Native American female, who is parenting her 16-year-old granddaughter, Tanya, illustrates how working with Mary and her problems and focusing on her strengths will help the relationship between grandmother and granddaughter. It is interesting that a positive strengths perspective rather than a pathological diagnosis of the problem was helpful in this case.

Single parents overwhelmed by multiple family members, income and housing problems, and special needs children require help with daily living. Practical task-centered problem solving along with adequate resources can work for these families. The case of the Williams family, a single-parent African American woman with her five children, emphasizes the importance of meeting the daily life problem issues that face people in practical terms. The case of Pascual Mendez and his family portrays the effect of a developmentally disabled 4-year-old on a traditional Latino family. Culture, socioeconomic status, coping with caring for children with special needs, language problems, and related life survival issues are challenges in this situation.

Social workers increasingly come in contact with individuals and families who have been the *victims of war, trauma, and posttraumatic stress syndrome*. Formerly from Southeast Asia, Central America, the Balkans, and now from Afghanistan and Iraq, these clients bring with them their emotional and social needs. Likewise, the second-generation children of first-generation immigrants and refugees are clients with intergenerational and bicultural integration issues. The case of Chanda, a 25-year-old Cambodian woman, reminds us that we may face immigrants and refugees who have experienced extreme trauma in war-torn countries (e.g., forced labor, starvation, death) and illness, suffering, and terror in the United States. Becoming aware of posttraumatic stress flash backs, Chanda needs a worker who can understand and work in her cultural belief system and geopolitical context. In contrast, the case of the Wong family depicts the high-achieving *parents from another country and their American-born children* who increasingly feel pressured to perform in academics to satisfy their parental expectations. The conflict between the traditional cultural values of origin and the dominant cultural values is apparent; the need to negotiate a common ground of understanding and accommodation is critical in this family.

Domestic violence is the number one social problem confronting American families today. Domestic violence abuse and homicides, hot lines, safe-house shelters, child protective services, and domestic violence research and literature are visible in many American communities and social services centers. The case of Maile, a 45-year-old Hawaiian and Caucasian woman, her husband, Tony, a Mexican American, and their son, Michael Alika, underscores the importance of assessing such domestic violence dynamics as displacement and adjustment, physical and emotional trauma, spousal and child abuse, and the balancing of such assets as strengths, resilience, survival skills, the need for safety and protection, and making a connection with a helper. Social workers are on the front lines as responders and caretakers of victims of domestic violence.

The *special needs of the elderly* are increasing because of increased longevity, attention to nutrition, and science and medical technology. Gerontological social work involves coordinating many aspects of care in a case management umbrella. The case of Annie, age 68, and her partner, Sue, age 72, points up the need for care giving with the elderly who require physical and medical care, proper nutrition, and age-relevant support groups in the context of understanding the community resources for older lesbian populations in the urban setting. Making and bridging these connections are important for the worker, the client, and related and invested significant others. Likewise, the case of Don Jose and Doña Marta Alvarez, a 75- and 72-year-old married Puerto Rican couple, points out the importance of a culturally oriented and integrated support group to share problems such as the deteriorating physical condition of a spouse.

Cases involving *debilitating illnesses* such as HIV/AIDS and *congenital disorders* such as Down syndrome are examples of how the social worker assists clients and their families to cope with these challenging situations. The case of Evelyn Jean-Francois, a 30-year-old Haitian American woman, who has been diagnosed with HIV/AIDS underscores the dilemma of disclosing and coping with this illness in her family living, employment, and religious context. The case of Maria Diaz, a 45-year-old American woman, with Down syndrome illustrates the tension between family care and independent living and is a point of reference in a discussion on how to intervene in this situation.

Our contributors have taken these cases and have shown how to work with a myriad of clients along a varied continuum of problems from a culturally competent, practice stage, client intersectional system and case study model. The proof of the book is how people are changed in the helping process.

LINKING CULTURAL COMPETENCE AND THE NASW CODE OF ETHICS

The contributors of this volume have addressed a number of values ascribed in the National Association of Social Workers Code of Ethics:

- The value of service, particularly helping people in need and addressing social problems
- The value of social justice and the challenge of coping with social injustice
- The value of the dignity and worth of the person and the social worker's respect for this perspective
- The value of human relationships and the social worker's cultivation of contact and relationship building
- The value of integrity and the trustworthiness of the social worker
- The value of competence and the enhancement of professional social work expertise

These values are apparent in this book because contributors have discussed their population groups in terms of historical oppression, survival values, knowledge theory, practice skills, and practice stages.

Moreover, unique to the NASW Code of Ethics has been a strong emphasis and undercurrents regarding cultural competence. The social work profession integrates competence and its cultural implications throughout its standards and beliefs. In fact, the case has been made that competent practice and culturally competent practice are so interwoven that it is impossible to be competent without being culturally competent from a social work professional sense (Coleman, 1998). The Code of Ethics (NASW, 1996) views competence as a value that develops and enhances professional expertise through knowledge and skills applied to practice and is an ethical standard for social workers to provide competent services. The profession has further defined competence as "the capacity to function effectively within the context of culturally integrated patterns of human behavior defined by the group." (NASW, 2001, p. 4)

In Chapter One, we reviewed the 10 standards of the NASW 2001 Code of Ethics for cultural competence in social work practice, which is an outgrowth of a major section on cultural competence in the NASW 1999 Code of Ethics. Starting with an understanding of culture, a knowledge base of clients' cultures, and an understanding of social diversity and oppression, the social work profession has moved toward specific culturally competent guidelines, goals, and objectives that embody ethics and values, self-awareness, cross-cultural knowledge and skills, service delivery, empowerment and advocacy, diverse workforce, professional education, language diversity, and cross-cultural leadership. These standards encompass the development and practice stances of the individual social worker and social work agencies in a multilevel approach to cultural competence.

At the same time, the present task is to turn cultural competent standards into cultural competencies or skills that can be operationalized and measured.

Recent efforts have been made to follow through on implementing these standards. Fong and Furuto (2001) have operationalized cultural competence as skills, interventions, and evaluations, and I (Lum, 2003) have measured cultural competence through two research pretest and posttest instruments for social work students and instructors. But there is a need for more ways for the social work profession (educators, scholars, and practitioners) to follow through on these matters relating to cultural competence. We hope that this book supports and illumines these trends.

REFLECTING ON THE FUTURE OF CULTURALLY COMPETENT PRACTICE WITH DIVERSE GROUPS

The future of culturally competent practice in social work is indeed bright and without limits. The basic foundation of culturally competent practice in social work has been set forth in several texts that defined the meaning (Leigh, 1998), offered a framework theme model (Lum, 1999), articulated assessment, intervention, and evaluation skills for various ethnic groups (Fong & Furuto, 2001), and applied cultural competence to ethnic, gender, and sexual orientation groups and to social and economic justice (Lum, 2003).

Recently, there have been further developments in culturally competent social practice with diverse groups. For instance, Samantrai (2004) has applied cultural competence to the area of public child welfare practice. Focusing on children and the public welfare arena, she believes that there are four ingredients for becoming culturally competent: self-awareness; basic knowledge about the client's culture; understanding the dynamics of power, authority, and difference in the helping process; and developing the ability to adapt practice skills to the client's cultural context. Using this key concept, she sets forth key principles related to child welfare:

- Culturally competent practice requires knowledge, and nonjudgmental acceptance, of the client's cultural beliefs and child-rearing practices, and with what is considered respectful (or disrespectful) behavior between parents and children, between family and nonfamily, in formal and informal relationships. (Samantrai, 2004, p. 79)
- Cultural incompetence on the part of the worker can weaken the engagement of the client in a working alliance (or worse, result in no engagement or even alienation of the client), an inaccurate understanding of the client's needs and strengths, and an inappropriate and ineffective case plan. Cultural incompetence on the part of the policy makers, planners, administrators, and organizers can lead to designing programs and services that are incongruent with the realities and needs of culturally diverse clients. (Samantrai, 2004, p. 30)

We applaud this effort to apply cultural competence to dealing with child welfare issues to prepare social workers in their public child welfare practice with diverse children.

A similar effort is Fong's (2004) *Culturally Competent Practice with Immigrant and Refugee Children and Families.* Fong speaks about culturally competent contextual practice: To understand any diverse group or population such as immigrants, one must note the contexts from a culturally competent perspective. She states, "Contextual social work practice considers immigrant backgrounds, the probability and degree of trauma, and the resources available to and within the clients" (Fong, 2004, p. 6) Furthermore, Fong touches on a related theme of multiple dimensions when she explains, "Culturally competent practice means that the social worker knows the many cultures the client brings (ethnicity, religion, political systems, etc.) and realizes how each has affected the client's social functioning and behaviors. To operationalize this knowledge, the social worker must do multiple assessments focusing on the macro-level to get a context for the client's social environment." (Fong, 2004, p. 8) In a systematic framework, context and multiple assessment become practice principles for a culturally competent contextual approach in assessment areas for immigrants and refugee populations:

- Knowledge of the context of macro level environmental factors of the home country (macro level societal value assessment)
- Cultural values and beliefs of the client in the home country (personal cultural value assessment)
- The impact of the intermediary environments (multi-environmental assessment)
- Cultural values of home and host environment (differential cultural value assessment)

Culturally competent practice principles are also related to intervention planning and implementation:

- The integration of societal and cultural values of the client through macro level societal values assessments and the personal cultural value assessments in intervention planning and implementation
- The selection of interventions based on the client's personal cultural values and by the practitioner's use of differential values assessment which do not clash with the client's values
- The biculturalization of intervention (a combination of indigenous interventions and western social work interventions), using cultural values as strengths
- The awareness of different social environments and the use of multi-environmental assessment, using a solution-focused approach to problem solving with the biculturalization of intervention perspective (Fong, 2004, p. 43)

Throughout Fong's text are illustrations of how this culturally competent contextual multiple assessment and intervention approach is applied to various diverse immigrant and refugee groups.

CONCLUSION

We are in the midst of applying cultural competence to social work practice in many ways. This book connects cultural competence and the various practice stages of helping to ethnic, gender, sexual orientation, citizen status, developmentally challenged, and age groups. We have also caught a glimpse of how other social work educators and practitioners are integrating cultural competence to areas such as child welfare and to diverse populations as immigrants and refugees.

I feel fortunate to have begun my social work education career at a time when there was so little in-depth social work practice literature on people of color and when the themes of diversity, cultural competence, and multiple identities have played a major part of the current discussion in cultural and ethnic diversity. I have been forced to think, teach, and write about my observations of people based on my finite ideas and insights about culturally diverse peoples. That was 30 years ago, and much has happened in the world to draw all people closer together. Today, there is such an abundance of social work texts, educators, courses, and programs in this field that I can confidently predict that the subject of human diversity is in the good hands of a creative and committed cadre of writers and teachers. In the years ahead, there will be many more applications of culturally competent social work practice.

References

Balgopal, P. R. (Ed.). (2000). *Social work practice with immigrants and refugees.* New York: Columbia University Press.

Besthorn, F. H., & McMillen, D. P. (2002). The oppression of women and nature: Ecofeminism as a framework for an expanded ecological social work. *Families in Society, 83*(3), 221–232.

Child Welfare League of America (2003). *Cultural competence* (pp. 1–4). New York: Author.

Finn, J. L., & Jacobson, M. (2003). Just practice: Steps toward a new social work paradigm. *Journal of Social Work Education, 39*(1), 57–78.

Coleman, H. L. K. (1998). General and multicultural counseling competency: Apples and oranges? *Journal of Multicultural Counseling and Development, 26(3),* 147–156.

Fong, R. (Ed.). (2004). Culturally competent practice with immigrant and refugee children and families. New York: Guilford Press.

Fong, R., & Furuto, S. (Eds.). (2001). Culturally competent practice: Skills, interventions, and evaluation. Boston: Allyn & Bacon. http://www.cwla.org/

Guadalupe, K., & Lum, D. (2005). *Multidimensional practice: Diversity through context.* Belmont, CA: Thomson Brooks/Cole.

Hurdle, D. E. (2002). Native Hawaiian traditional healing: Culturally based interventions for social work practice. *Social Work, 47*(2), 183–192.

Leigh, J. W. (1998). *Communicating for cultural competence.* Boston: Allyn & Bacon.

Lum, D. (1999). *Culturally competent practice: A framework for growth and action.* Pacific Grove, CA: Brooks/Cole.

Lum, D. (Ed.) (2003). *Culturally competent practice: A framework for understanding diverse groups and justice issues.* Pacific Grove, CA: Brooks/Cole–Thomson Learning.

Lum, D. (2004). *Social work practice and people of color.* Belmont, CA: Brooks/Cole–Thomson Learning.

National Association of Social Workers (NASW). (1996). *NASW code of ethics.* Washington, DC: Author.

National Association of Social Workers (NASW). (2001). *NASW Standards for Cultural Competence in Social Work Practice.* Retrieved from www.naswdc.org/pubs/standards/cultural.htm.

Potocky-Tripodi, M. (2002). *Best practices for social work with refugees and immigrants.* New York: Columbia University Press.

Reid, W. J. (2002). Knowledge for direct social work practice: An analysis of trends. *Social service review, 76*(1), 6–33.

Samantrai, K. (2004). *Culturally competent public child welfare practice.* Pacific Grove, CA: Brooks/Cole–Thomson Learning.

Segal, U. (2002). *A framework for immigration: Applications to Asians in the United States.* New York: Columbia University Press.

Ungar, M. (2002). A deeper, more social ecological social work practice. *Social Service Review, 76*(3), 480–497.

Warrier, S. (2002). *It's in their culture: Culture, competency and violence against women.* San Francisco: Asian and Pacific Island Institute on Domestic Violence, Asian Pacific Islander American Health Forum.

Welch, L. (2003). Grandparents to the rescue. *Parade,* July 20, pp. 4–5.

Index